VOICES FROM NEPAL

VOICES FROM NEPAL

UNCOVERING HUMAN TRAFFICKING THROUGH COMICS JOURNALISM

DAN ARCHER

UNIVERSITY OF TORONTO PRESS

Toronto Buffalo London

Toronto Buffalo London
utorontopress.com

ISBN 978-1-4875-5501-6 (cloth)
ISBN 978-1-4875-5502-3 (EPUB)
ISBN 978-1-4875-5505-4 (PDF)

Library and Archives Canada Cataloguing in Publication

Title: Voices from Nepal : uncovering human trafficking through comics journalism / Dan Archer.
Names: Archer, Dan, author, artist.
Series: ethnoGRAPHIC (University of Toronto Press)
Description: Series statement: ethnoGRAPHIC | Includes bibliographical references.
Identifiers: Canadiana (print) 20240359364 | Canadiana (ebook) 20240359399 | ISBN 9781487555016 (hardcover) | ISBN 9781487555054 (PDF) | ISBN 9781487555023 (EPUB)
Subjects: LCSH: Human trafficking – Nepal – Comic books, strips, etc. | LCGFT: Comics journalism. | LCGFT: Nonfiction comics. | LCGFT: Comics (Graphic works)
Classification: LCC HQ281 .A73 2024 | DDC 362.88/51095496 – dc23

Cover design: Val Cooke
Cover image: Dan Archer

We welcome comments and suggestions regarding any aspect of our publications—please feel free to contact us at news@utorontopress.com or visit us at utorontopress.com.

We wish to acknowledge the land on which the University of Toronto Press operates. This land is the traditional territory of the Wendat, the Anishnaabeg, the Haudenosaunee, the Métis, and the Mississaugas of the Credit First Nation.

University of Toronto Press acknowledges the financial support of the Government of Canada and the Ontario Arts Council, an agency of the Government of Ontario, for its publishing activities.

ONTARIO ARTS COUNCIL
CONSEIL DES ARTS DE L'ONTARIO
an Ontario government agency
un organisme du gouvernement de l'Ontario

Funded by the Government of Canada
Financé par le gouvernement du Canada
Canada

To Madhu and Jaya,
without whom this
book wouldn't have
been possible.

CONTENTS

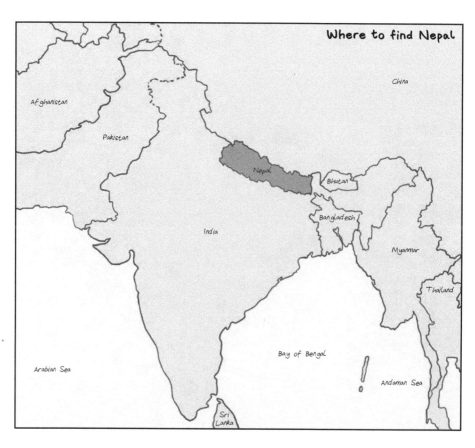

Where to find Nepal

Afghanistan

Pakistan

China

Nepal

Bhutan

India

Bangladesh

Myanmar

Thailand

Arabian Sea

Bay of Bengal

Andaman Sea

Sri Lanka

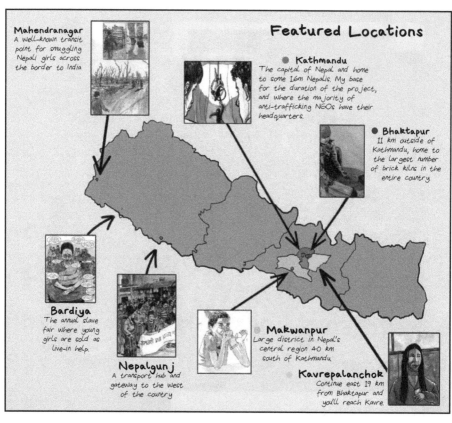

Featured Locations

Mahendranagar
A well-known transit point for smuggling Nepali girls across the border to India

● **Kathmandu**
The capital of Nepal and home to some 16m Nepalis. My base for the duration of the project, and where the majority of anti-trafficking NGOs have their headquarters.

● **Bhaktapur**
11 km outside of Kathmandu, home to the largest number of brick kilns in the entire country.

Bardiya
The annual slave fair where young girls are sold as live-in help.

Nepalgunj
A transport hub and gateway to the west of the country

Makwanpur
Large district in Nepal's central region 40 km south of Kathmandu

Kavrepalanchok
Continue east 19 km from Bhaktapur and you'll reach Kavre.

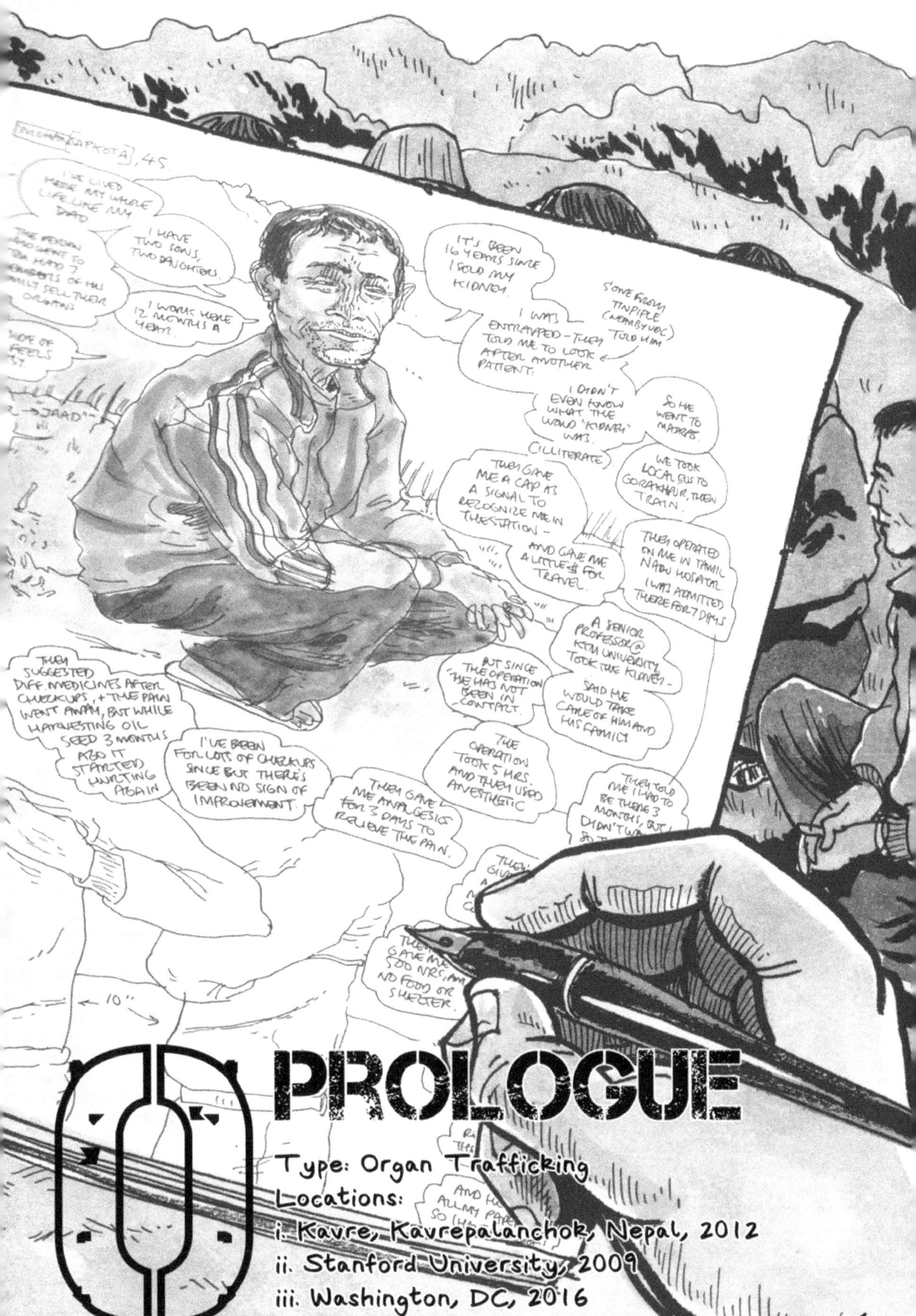

KAPKOTA, 45
I'VE LIVED HERE MY WHOLE LIFE, LIKE MY DAD
I HAVE TWO SONS, TWO DAUGHTERS.
I WORK HERE 12 MONTHS A YEAR.
IT'S BEEN 16 YEARS SINCE I SOLD MY KIDNEY.
S'ONE FROM TINPIPLE (NEARBY VDC) TOLD HIM
I WAS ENTRAPPED - THEY TOLD ME TO LOOK AFTER ANOTHER PATIENT.
I DIDN'T EVEN KNOW WHAT THE WORD "KIDNEY" WAS.
(ILLITERATE)
SO HE WENT TO MADRAS.
WE TOOK LOCAL BUS TO GORAKHPUR, THEN TRAIN.
THEY GAVE ME A CAP AS A SIGNAL TO RECOGNIZE ME IN THE STATION -
AND GAVE ME A LITTLE $ FOR TRAVEL.
THEY OPERATED ON ME IN TAMIL NADU HOSPITAL.
I WAS ADMITTED THERE FOR 7 DAYS
A SENIOR PROFESSOR @ KTM UNIVERSITY TOOK THE KIDNEY -
BUT SINCE THE OPERATION HE HAS NOT BEEN IN CONTACT.
SAID HE WOULD TAKE CARE OF HIM AND HIS FAMILY
THEY SUGGESTED DIFF. MEDICINES AFTER CHECKUPS, + THE PAIN WENT AWAY, BUT WHILE HARVESTING OIL SEED 3 MONTHS AGO IT STARTED HURTING AGAIN
I'VE BEEN FOR LOTS OF CHECKUPS SINCE BUT THERE'S BEEN NO SIGN OF IMPROVEMENT.
THE OPERATION TOOK 5 HRS. AND THEY USED ANESTHETIC
THEY GAVE ME ANALGESICS FOR 3 DAYS TO RELIEVE THE PAIN.
THEY TOLD ME I HAD TO BE THERE 3 MONTHS, BUT I DIDN'T WA...
10"

0 PROLOGUE

Type: Organ Trafficking

Locations:

i. Kavre, Kavrepalanchok, Nepal, 2012

ii. Stanford University, 2009

iii. Washington, DC, 2016

In a tiny hilltop village, 2 hours east of Kathmandu. December 16, 2012.

Mohan Sapkota, 45

I've lived here my whole life, like my father.

I have 2 sons, 2 daughters. I work here in the field all year round.

I know someone from around here who had 7 family members sell their kidneys.

It's been 16 years since I sold my kidney. I was tricked.

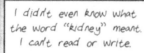

I didn't even know what the word "kidney" meant. I can't read or write.

We went to Madras, India. We took the local bus to Gorakhpur, then the train to Madras.

They gave me a cap as a signal so the people collecting me would recognize me in the station.

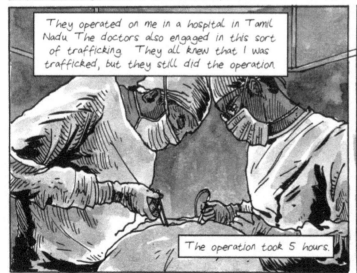

They operated on me in a hospital in Tamil Nadu. The doctors also engaged in this sort of trafficking. They all knew that I was trafficked, but they still did the operation.

The operation took 5 hours.

I was admitted there for 7 days. A senior professor at KTM* University took the kidney. He said he would take care of me and my family.

I thought that if I get this much money, I can do better in life.

*Kathmandu

2

They sent me back to Nepal with 2 Bhutanese people.

They gave me analgesics for 3 days to relieve the pain

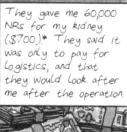

They gave me 60,000 NRs for my kidney ($700).* They said it was only to pay for logistics, and that they would look after me after the operation.

They promised me a small job, making tea, cooking for them...

...but they only gave me 500 NRs ($5) and no food or shelter.

After 2 weeks the professor's wife said I couldn't even make tea, and often insulted me.

The professor who took my kidney started a charity for those with 1 kidney...

...but he's since retired and took all the paperwork so I have no proof!

Now the lower back left side of my body feels uneasy.

I take alcohol for the pain, but not painkillers.

I have pain in the whole right side from my kidney through to my thigh down to my ankle.

The pain went away after a while, but then when I was harvesting seed oil 3 months ago it started hurting again

I've been for checkups but there's no improvement.

I wouldn't have sold it if I had known more about the risks.

*Exchange rate at the original time of writing (2012). It has since almost halved.

Mohan's story might be tragically simple, but having him tell it isn't.

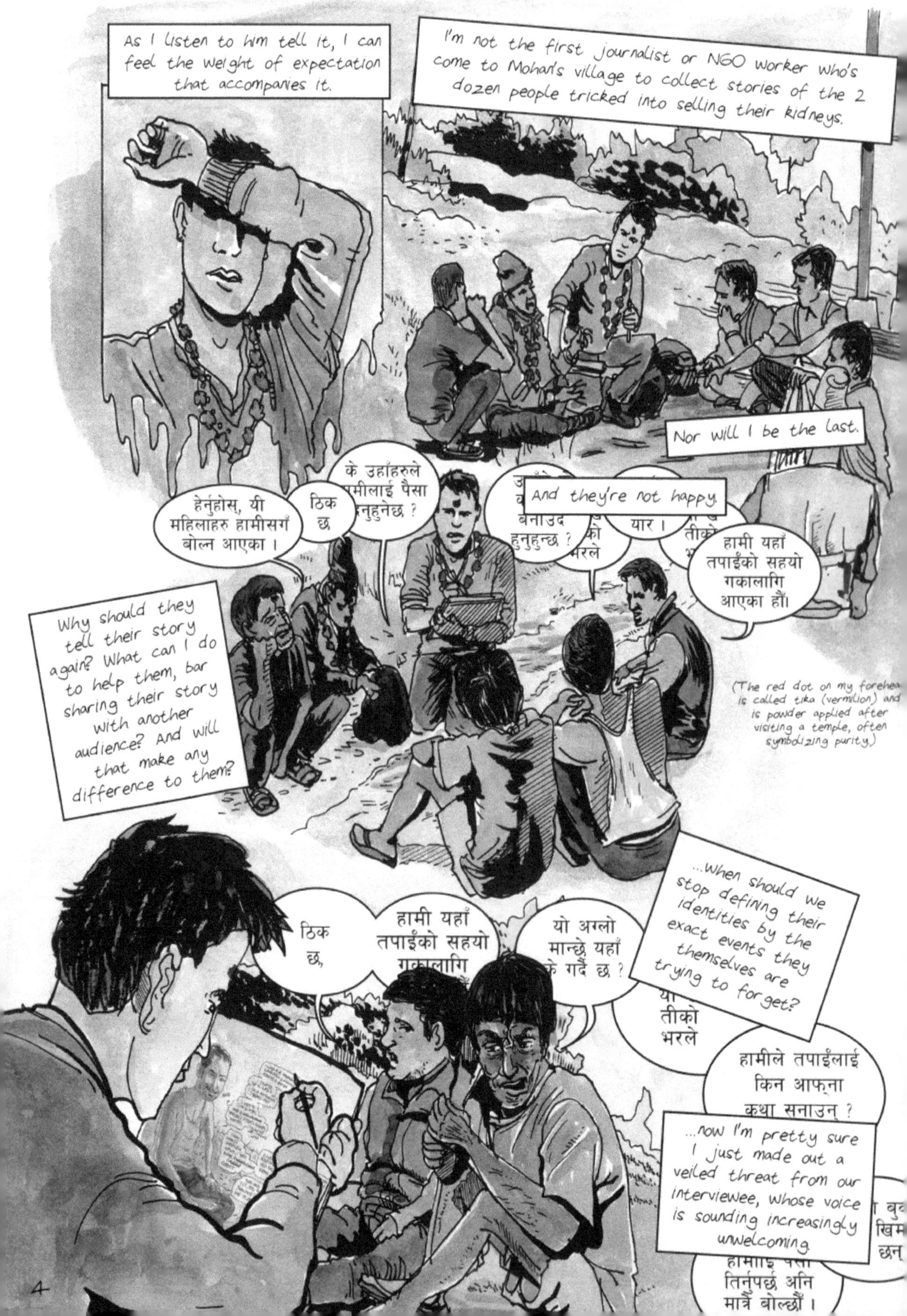
As I listen to him tell it, I can feel the weight of expectation that accompanies it.
I'm not the first journalist or NGO worker who's come to Mohan's village to collect stories of the 2 dozen people tricked into selling their kidneys.
Nor will I be the last.
हेर्नुहोस्, यी महिलाहरु हामीसगँ बोल्न आएका ।
ठिक छ
के उहाँहरुले
मीलाई पैसा
नुहुनेछ ?
And they're not happy.
बनाउद हुनुहुन्छ ?
यार ।
हामी यहाँ तपाईंको सहयो गकालागि आएका हौं।
Why should they tell their story again? What can I do to help them, bar sharing their story with another audience? And will that make any difference to them?
(The red dot on my forehea is called tika (vermilion) and is powder applied after visiting a temple, often symbolizing purity.)
ठिक छ,
हामी यहाँ तपाईंको सहयो
यो अग्लो मान्छे यहाँ के गर्दै छ ?
...When should we stop defining their identities by the exact events they themselves are trying to forget?
तीको भरले
हामीले तपाईंलाई किन आफ्ना कथा सुनाउनु ?
...now I'm pretty sure I just made out a veiled threat from our interviewee, whose voice is sounding increasingly unwelcoming
तिर्नुपर्छ अनि मात्रै बोल्छौं ।

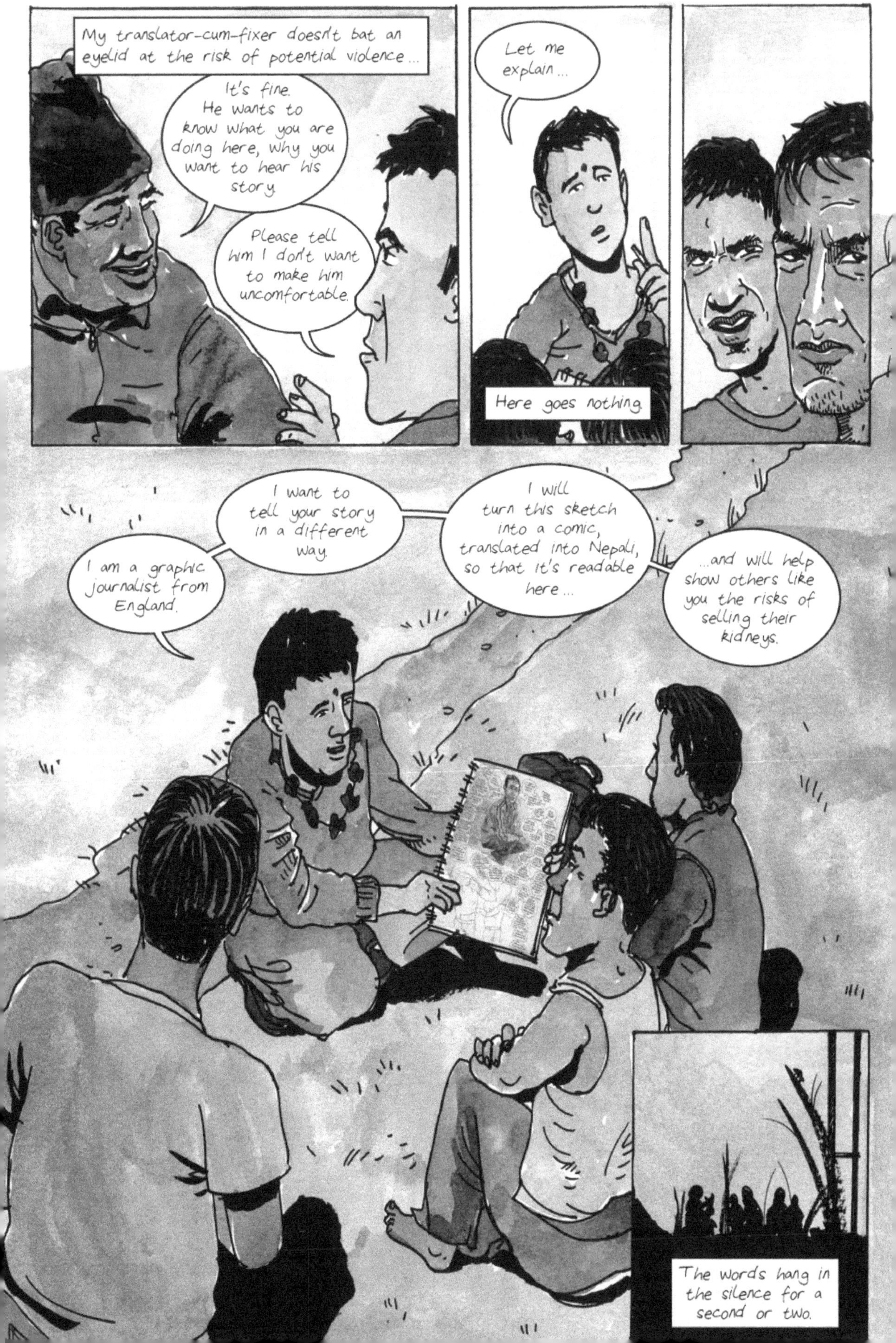
My translator-cum-fixer doesn't bat an eyelid at the risk of potential violence...
It's fine. He wants to know what you are doing here, why you want to hear his story.
Please tell him I don't want to make him uncomfortable.
Let me explain...
Here goes nothing.
I am a graphic journalist from England.
I want to tell your story in a different way.
I will turn this sketch into a comic, translated into Nepali, so that it's readable here...
...and will help show others like you the risks of selling their kidneys.
The words hang in the silence for a second or two.

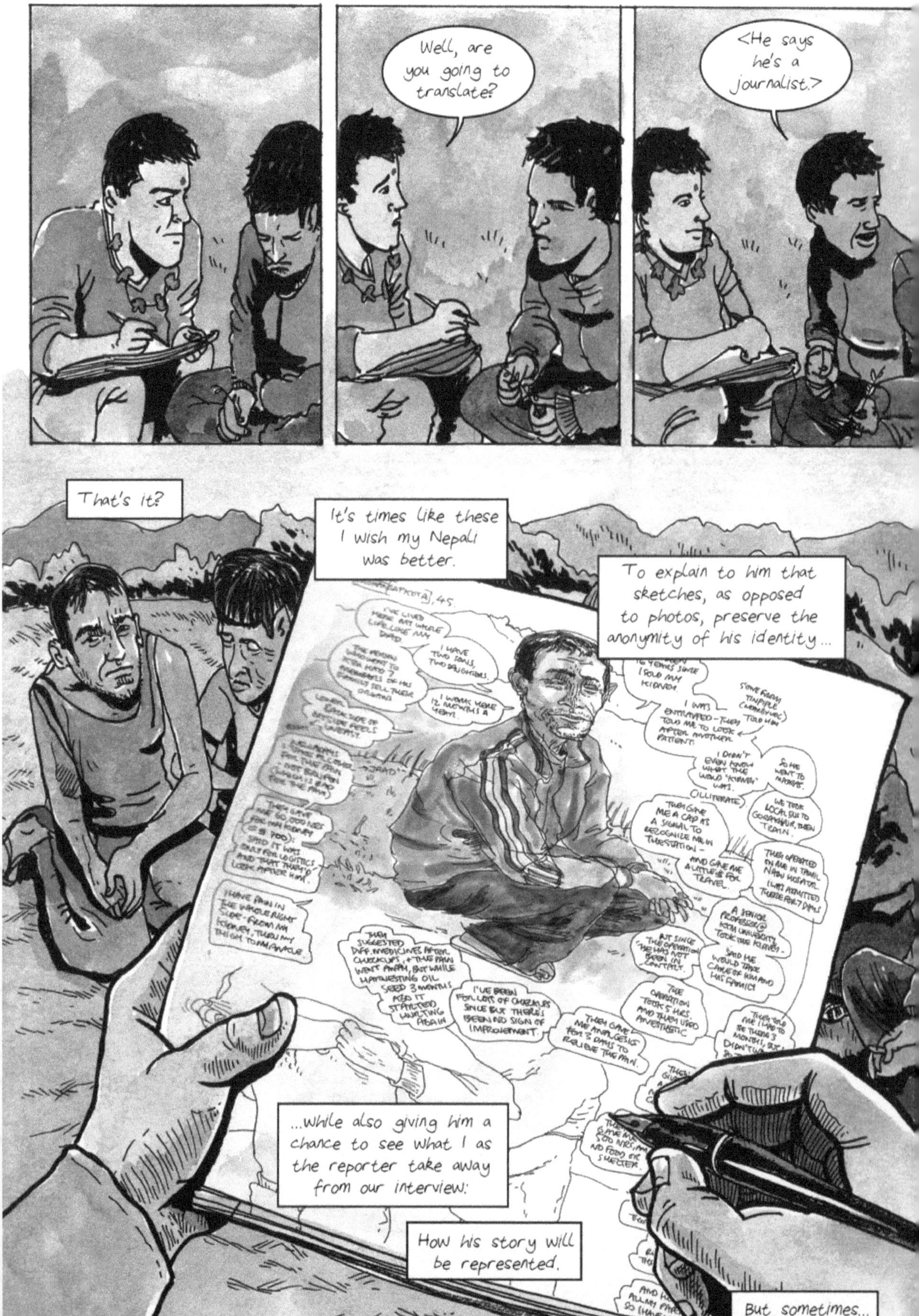
Well, are you going to translate?
<He says he's a journalist.>
That's it?
It's times like these I wish my Nepali was better.
To explain to him that sketches, as opposed to photos, preserve the anonymity of his identity...
...while also giving him a chance to see what I as the reporter take away from our interview:
How his story will be represented.
But sometimes...

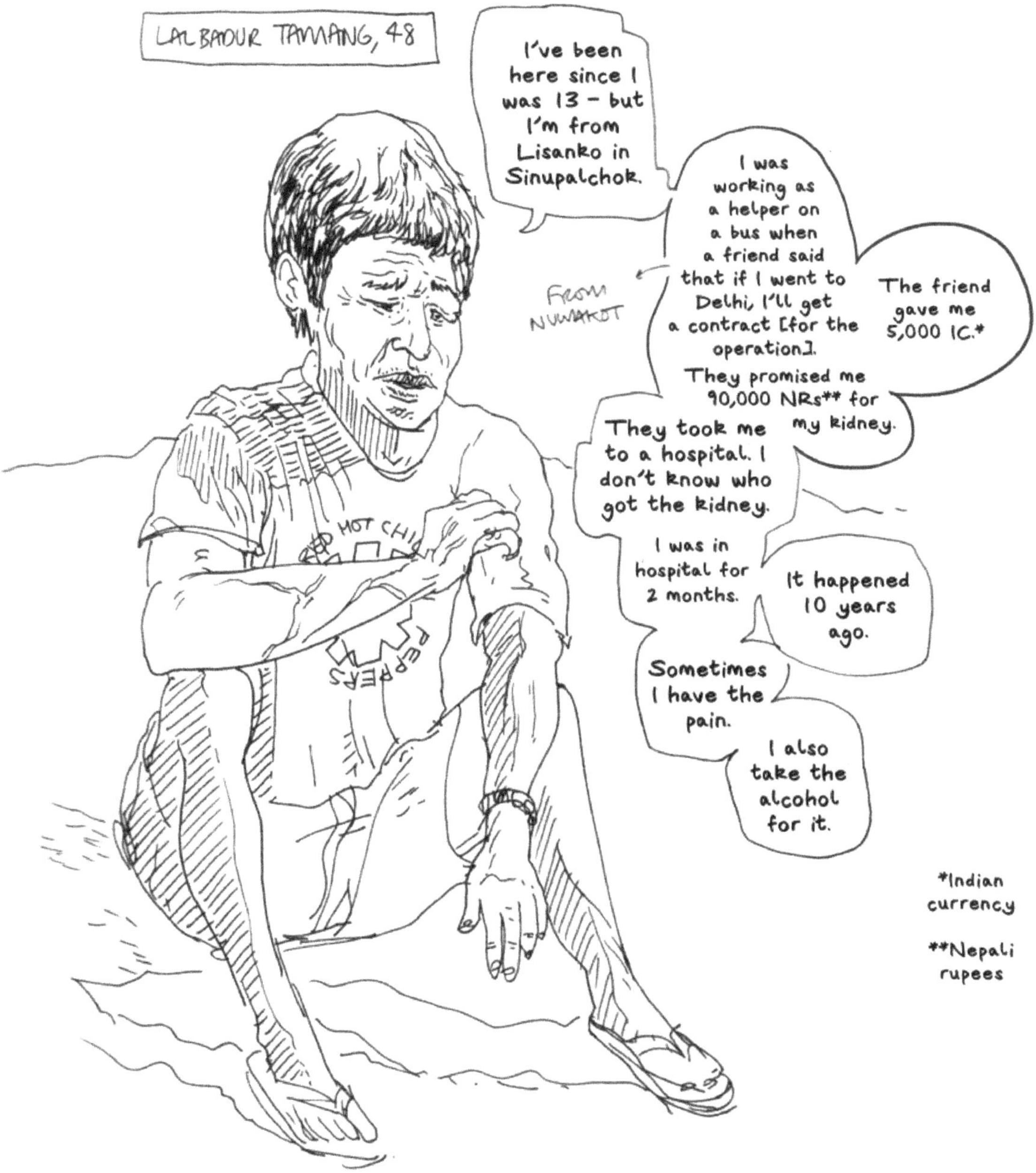
LALBADUR TAMANG, 48
I've been here since I was 13 – but I'm from Lisanko in Sinupalchok.
I was working as a helper on a bus when a friend said that if I went to Delhi, I'll get a contract [for the operation].
FROM NUWAKOT
The friend gave me 5,000 IC.*
They promised me 90,000 NRs** for my kidney.
They took me to a hospital. I don't know who got the kidney.
I was in hospital for 2 months.
It happened 10 years ago.
Sometimes I have the pain.
I also take the alcohol for it.

*Indian currency

**Nepali rupees

Kumar Buratoki Thapa, 27

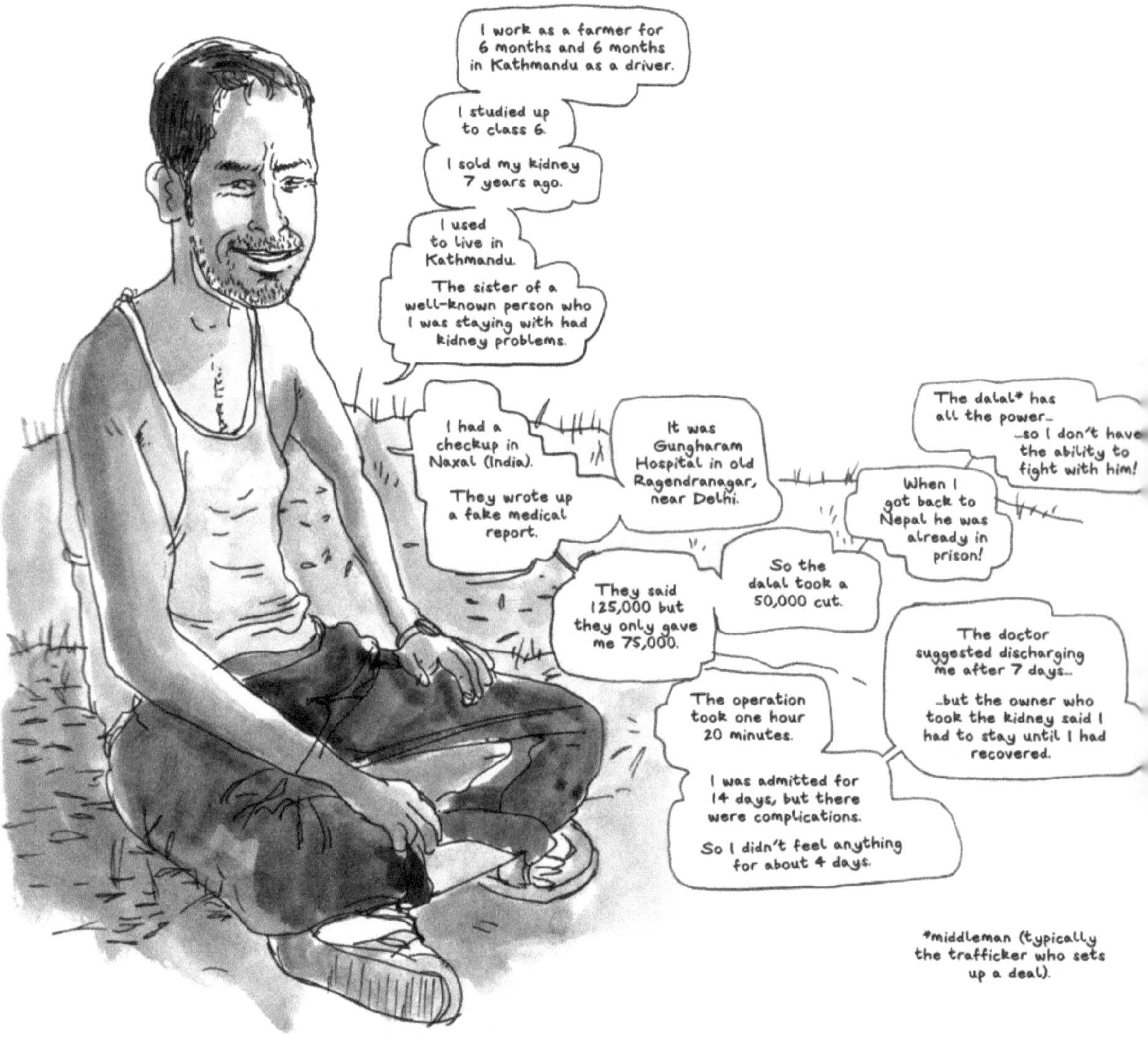
I work as a farmer for 6 months and 6 months in Kathmandu as a driver.
I studied up to class 6.
I sold my kidney 7 years ago.
I used to live in Kathmandu.
The sister of a well-known person who I was staying with had kidney problems.
I had a checkup in Naxal (India).
They wrote up a fake medical report.
It was Gungharam Hospital in old Ragendranagar, near Delhi.
They said 125,000 but they only gave me 75,000.
So the dalal took a 50,000 cut.
When I got back to Nepal he was already in prison!
The dalal* has all the power...
...so I don't have the ability to fight with him!
The operation took one hour 20 minutes.
I was admitted for 14 days, but there were complications.
So I didn't feel anything for about 4 days.
The doctor suggested discharging me after 7 days...
...but the owner who took the kidney said I had to stay until I had recovered.

*middleman (typically the trafficker who sets up a deal).

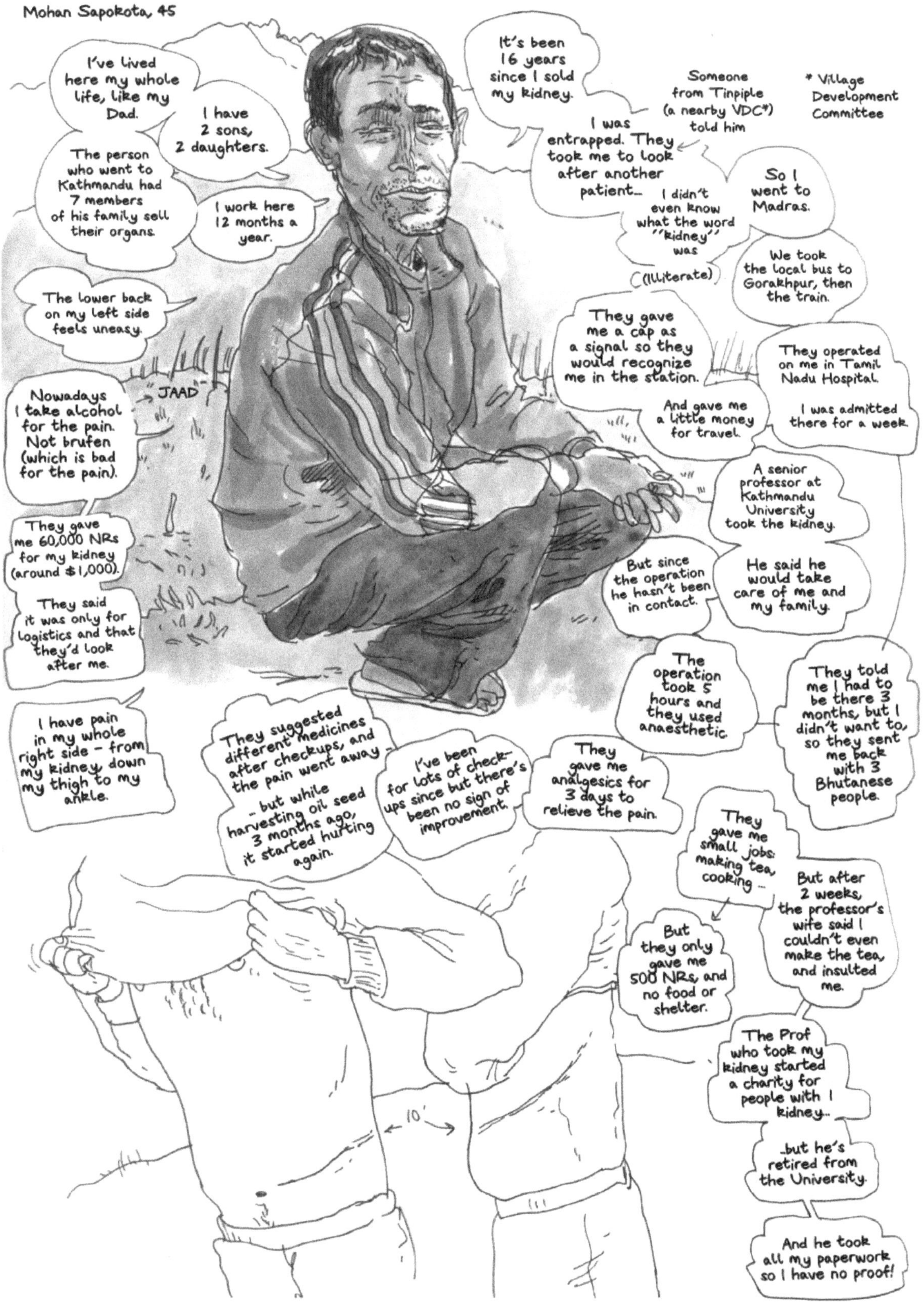
Mohan Sapokota, 45
I've lived here my whole life, like my Dad.
I have 2 sons, 2 daughters.
The person who went to Kathmandu had 7 members of his family sell their organs.
I work here 12 months a year.
The lower back on my left side feels uneasy.
Nowadays I take alcohol for the pain. Not brufen (which is bad for the pain).
JAAD
They gave me 60,000 NRs for my kidney (around $1,000).
They said it was only for logistics and that they'd look after me.
I have pain in my whole right side – from my kidney, down my thigh to my ankle.
They suggested different medicines after checkups, and the pain went away –
... but while harvesting oil seed 3 months ago, it started hurting again.
I've been for lots of check-ups since but there's been no sign of improvement.
They gave me analgesics for 3 days to relieve the pain.
It's been 16 years since I sold my kidney.
Someone from Tinpiple (a nearby VDC*) told him
* Village Development Committee
I was entrapped. They took me to look after another patient...
I didn't even know what the word "kidney" was
(Illiterate)
So I went to Madras.
We took the local bus to Gorakhpur, then the train.
They gave me a cap as a signal so they would recognize me in the station.
And gave me a little money for travel.
They operated on me in Tamil Nadu Hospital.
I was admitted there for a week.
A senior professor at Kathmandu University took the kidney.
He said he would take care of me and my family.
But since the operation he hasn't been in contact.
The operation took 5 hours and they used anaesthetic.
They told me I had to be there 3 months, but I didn't want to, so they sent me back with 3 Bhutanese people.
They gave me small jobs: making tea, cooking ...
But they only gave me 500 NRs and no food or shelter.
But after 2 weeks, the professor's wife said I couldn't even make the tea, and insulted me.
The Prof who took my kidney started a charity for people with 1 kidney...
...but he's retired from the University.
And he took all my paperwork so I have no proof!
10'

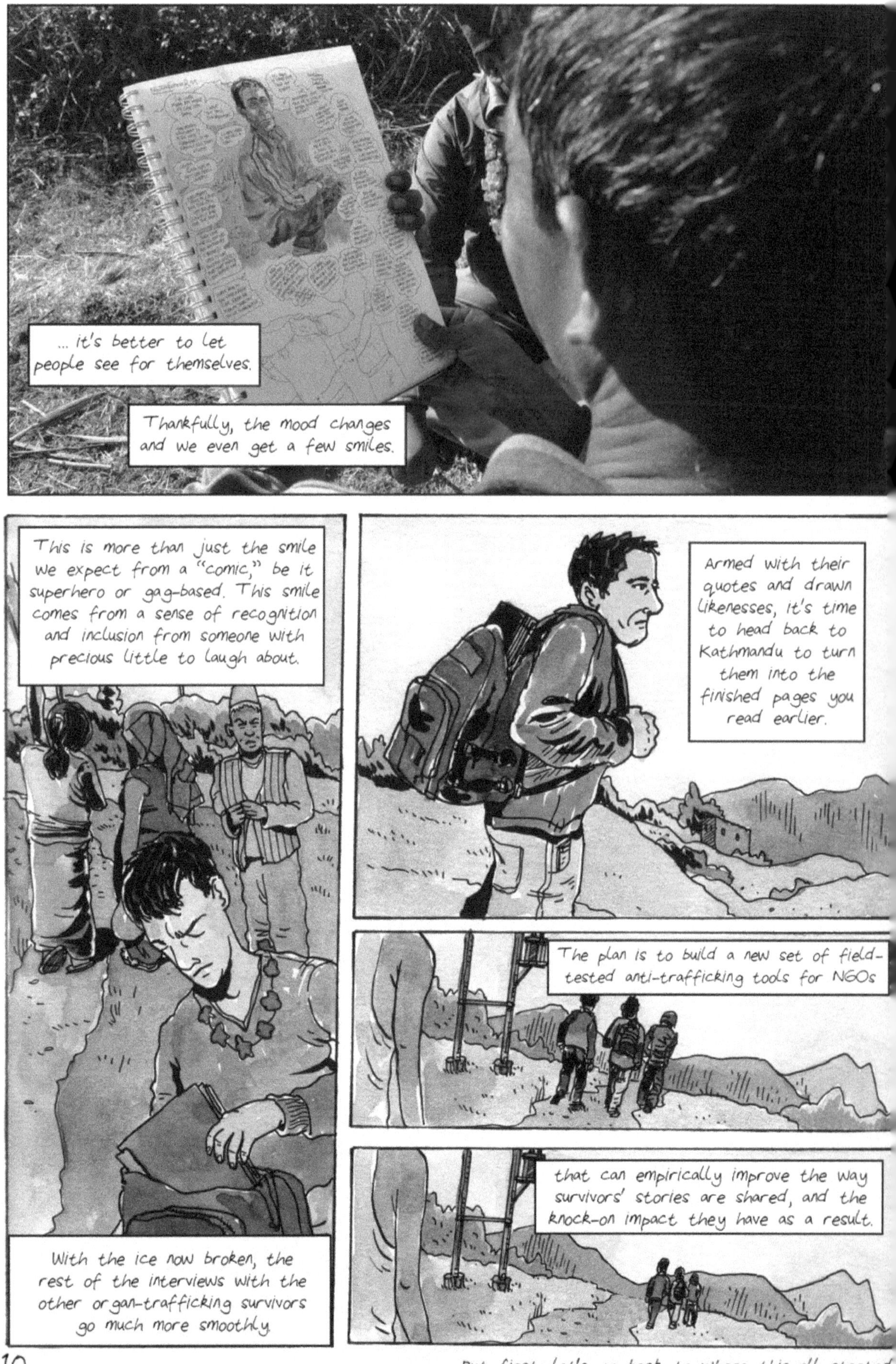
... it's better to let people see for themselves.
Thankfully, the mood changes and we even get a few smiles.
This is more than just the smile we expect from a "comic," be it superhero or gag-based. This smile comes from a sense of recognition and inclusion from someone with precious little to laugh about.
With the ice now broken, the rest of the interviews with the other organ-trafficking survivors go much more smoothly.
Armed with their quotes and drawn likenesses, it's time to head back to Kathmandu to turn them into the finished pages you read earlier.
The plan is to build a new set of field-tested anti-trafficking tools for NGOs
that can empirically improve the way survivors' stories are shared, and the knock-on impact they have as a result.
But first, let's go back to where this all started

BORDERLAND

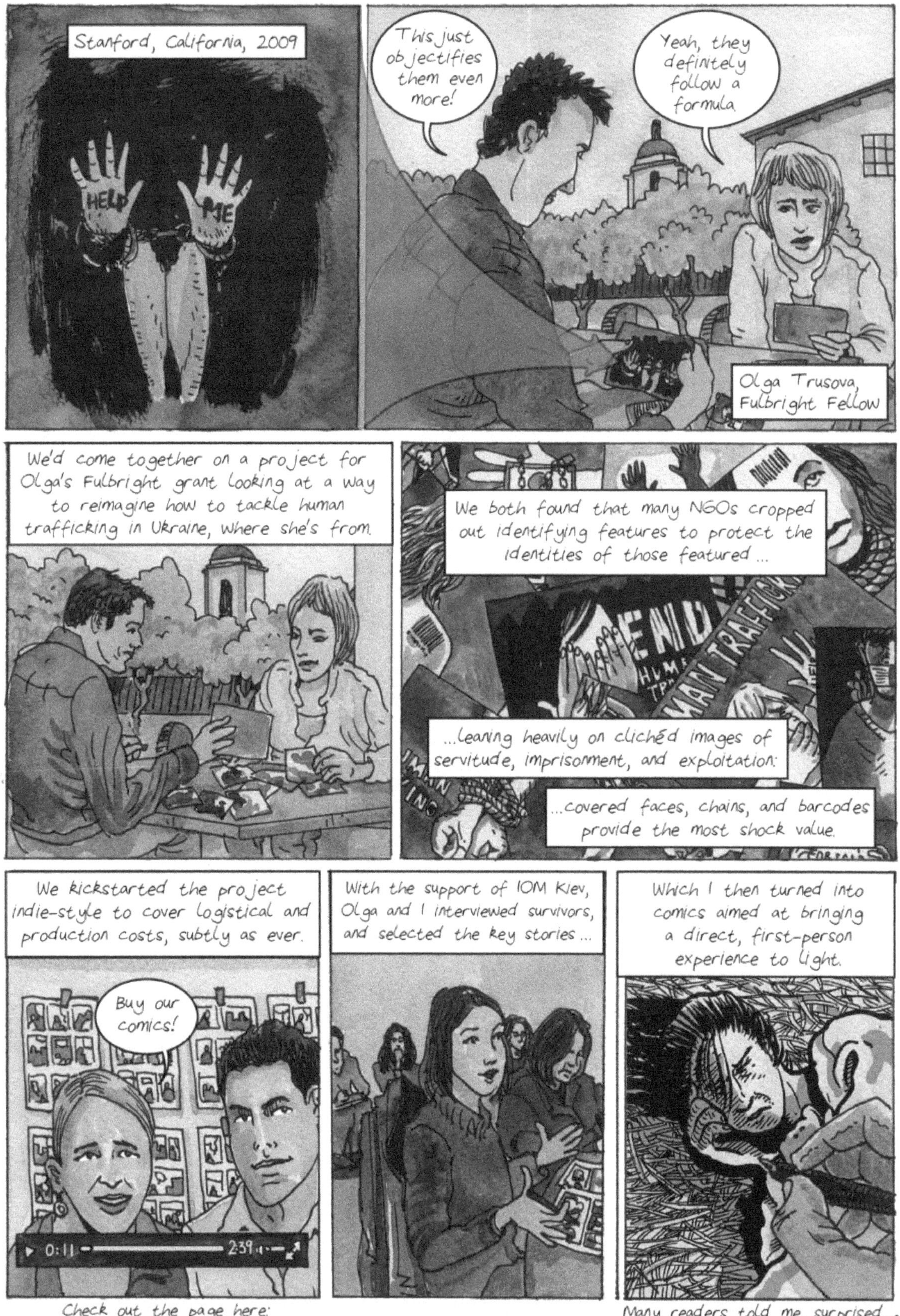
Stanford, California, 2009
HELP ME
This just objectifies them even more!
Yeah, they definitely follow a formula
Olga Trusova, Fulbright Fellow
We'd come together on a project for Olga's Fulbright grant looking at a way to reimagine how to tackle human trafficking in Ukraine, where she's from.
We both found that many NGOs cropped out identifying features to protect the identities of those featured ...
...leaning heavily on clichéd images of servitude, imprisonment, and exploitation:
...covered faces, chains, and barcodes provide the most shock value.
We kickstarted the project indie-style to cover logistical and production costs, subtly as ever.
Buy our comics!
With the support of IOM Kiev, Olga and I interviewed survivors, and selected the key stories ...
Which I then turned into comics aimed at bringing a direct, first-person experience to light.

Check out the page here: https://bit.ly/BorderlandKS

Many readers told me, surprised, that they weren't so "comic."

After a lot of back and forth, we picked 7 stories from the dozens to adapt into comics.

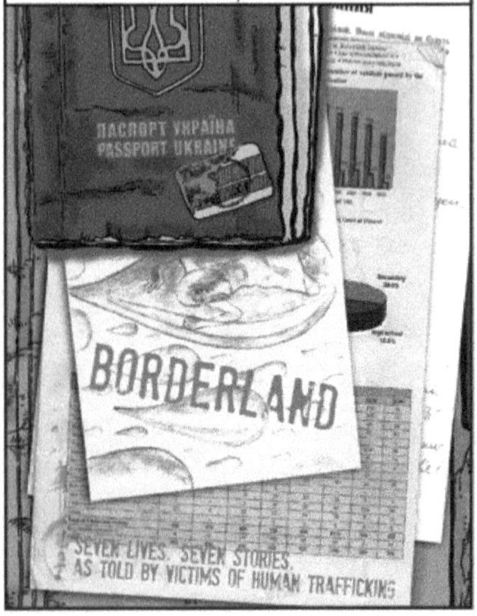
ПАСПОРТ УКРАЇНА
PASSPORT UKRAINE
BORDERLAND
SEVEN LIVES. SEVEN STORIES.
AS TOLD BY VICTIMS OF HUMAN TRAFFICKING

Each of them showed the different types of trafficking, such as male forced labor...

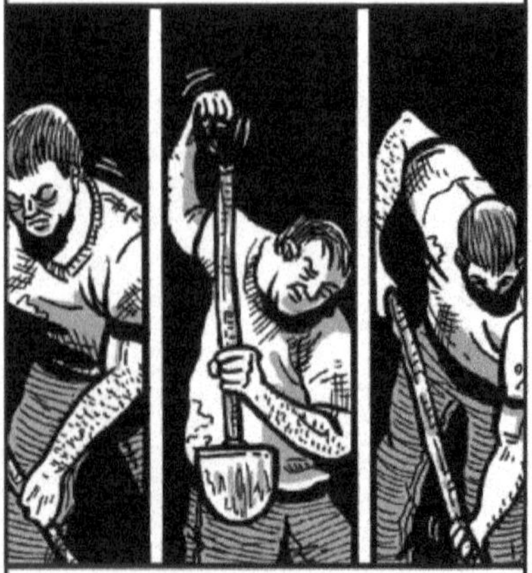

...highlighting the fact that the issue goes far beyond girls being trafficked for sex.

And that men and boys are just as prone to being trafficked too.

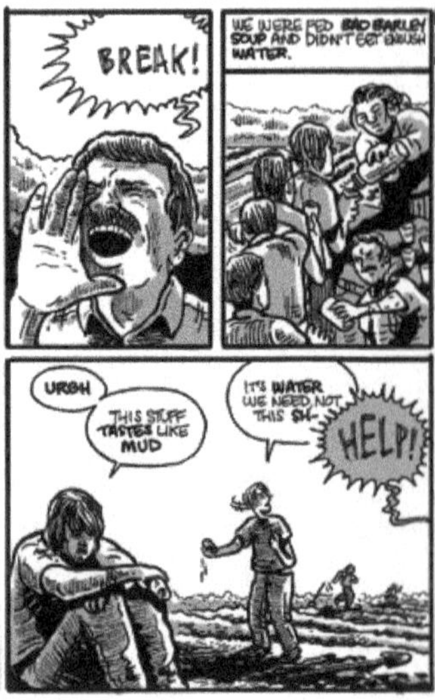
BREAK!
WE WERE FED BAD BARLEY SOUP AND DIDN'T GET ENOUGH WATER.
URGH
THIS STUFF TASTES LIKE MUD
IT'S WATER WE NEED, NOT THIS SH-
HELP!

The project was translated into Ukranian, and Russian, and distributed to at-risk schools in Eastern Europe, as well as forming part of a traveling exhibition, sponsored by USAID.

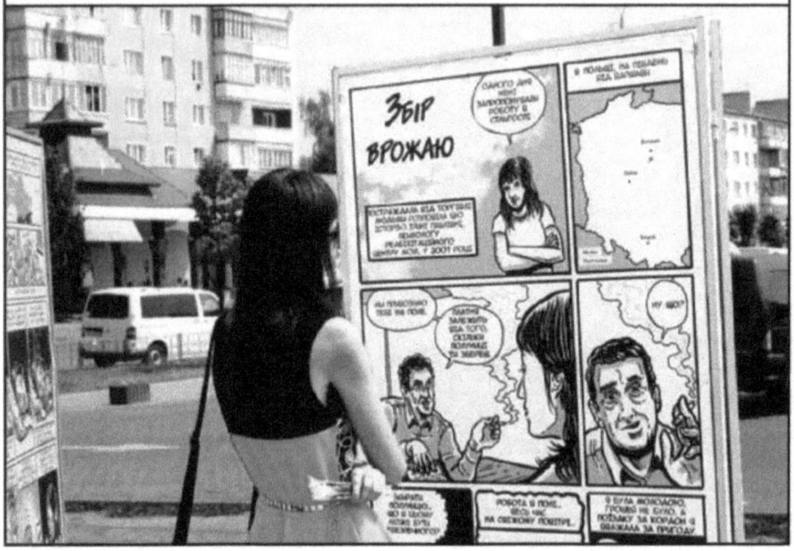
Збір врожаю

The following year, during a Knight journalism fellowship at Stanford, I met Madhu Acharya and Jaya Luintel, 2 leading journalists from Nepal.

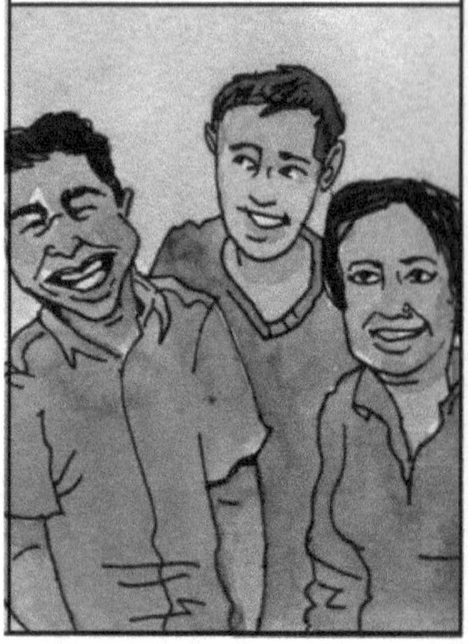

They both agreed that comics were perfect for raising awareness of human trafficking, given the low literacy rates in the worst-affected areas.

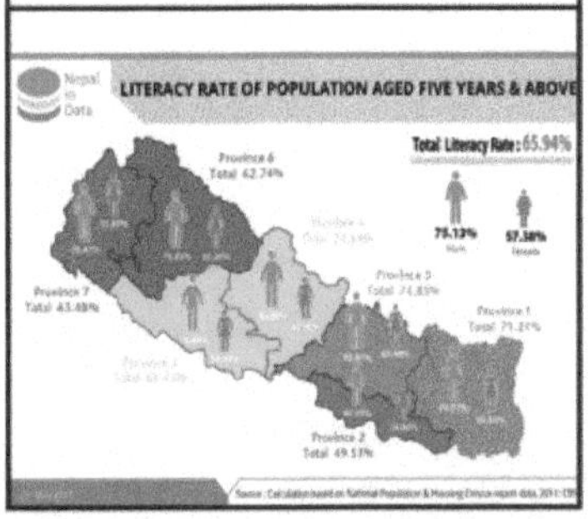
Nepal in Data
LITERACY RATE OF POPULATION AGED FIVE YEARS & ABOVE
Total Literacy Rate: 65.94%
Province 6
Total 62.74%
75.13%
57.38%
Province 7
Total 43.48%
Province 2
Total 49.53%

It was on campus that a great friend introduced me to Cecilia Mo, a rising star in the Polisci dept.

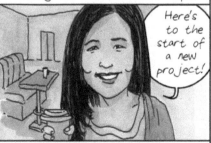

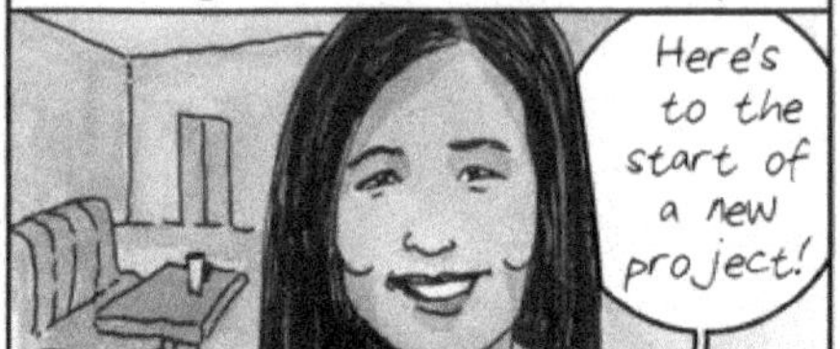
Here's to the start of a new project!

She had already run a huge survey in Nepal looking at income inequality and was interested in trafficking as her next research topic.

I had 3 main goals:

1. To produce anti-trafficking comics for NGOs in Nepal that would serve a purpose,

2. To get a better sense of how those NGOs tackle an issue as vast as trafficking,

3. To chronicle my time in Nepal through comics, somehow getting paid along the way.

WHAT IS TRAFFICKING?

The Institute of International Education, Washington D.C.

April 16, 2016

We're at a USAID (the US State Dept) meeting to present the human trafficking vulnerability study that I first started work on back in December 2012.

Me

Cecilia, my fellow investigator on the project

We took true stories of trafficking and presented them in different formats to see which had the most impact on audiences over a 6-month period.

In order to test the hypothesis that in low literacy, rural areas, the visual appeal of comics ...

...would have more impact than the dry flyers NGOs usually roll out.

Maybe we should try contacting our families?

There is no way we will be at Beatles, even if I could, waive I said I haven't seen any more heard some guy could've takel anymore and he banged himself.

almost a year. When will I get paid?

You still have debt. There is a lot more work befor you will see any money

sample story from our treatment

Our study surveyed over 3,000 respondents in rural Nepal twice, with a 6-month gap in between.

Cecilia checks the data one last time

Before we present, the group reads the most accepted definition of human trafficking, as spelled out in the 2000 Palermo protocols:

Boy this sounds dry...

I immediately think of how far removed this legalese is from the reality I've seen

"Trafficking in persons" shall mean the recruitment, transportation, transfer, harbouring or receipt of persons, by means of the threat or use of force or other forms of coercion, of abduction, of fraud, of deception, of the abuse of power or of a position of vulnerability or of the giving or receiving of payments or benefits to achieve the consent of a person having control over another person, for the purpose of exploitation.

As I read this for the hundredth time, I wish we could dispel some common misconceptions about trafficking instead.

Exploitation shall in the prostitution of others or other forms of sexual exploitation, forced labour or services, slavery or practices similar to slavery, servitude or the removal of organs. The consent of a victim of

10 Common Myths about Human Trafficking:

1. Trafficking only refers to sex trafficking.
Worldwide, many experts believe there are more instances of labor than sex trafficking.

2. It only involves young girls.
Trafficking varies from industry to industry, and also includes the forced labor of men and children. Men and boys are also vulnerable to sex trafficking, but advocates believe they are far less likely to be identified.

3. It always involves violence.
While it often does involve violent coercion, very often traffickers deploy a range of manipulative tactics such as defrauding, deceit, or blackmail to threaten their targets.

4. It involves the transport of a person across local or national borders.
Trafficking is often mistaken for people smuggling, which involves illegal border crossings. Someone can be trafficked from within their own home. "Trafficking"- and I've been asked this more than once - does not have to involve a motor vehicle.

5. If someone signed a contract or consented to their initial situation, then it doesn't constitute trafficking.
Initial consent to labor prior to acts of force, fraud, or coercion is irrelevant to the crime of trafficking. Many contracts are deliberately confusing to the signatories due to literacy or linguistic issues, or even changed after they have been signed.

6. Being trafficked means being physically held against your will.
Very often, people who have been trafficked endure their situations due to more complex reasons, such as lacking the necessities to survive outside of the current situation (familial/financial support or shelter), or they have been manipulated into feeling such shame that they feel unable to return to their communities.

7. Human trafficking is more of a problem in "developing countries."
Moving past the anachronistic label, trafficking is prevalent around the world, with very high rates in the United States and Europe.

8. Traffickers target people they don't know.
Very often survivors have reported being trafficked by trusted connections such as romantic partners or even family members. Sometimes those who have been trafficked are forced or manipulated into recruiting more of their friends.

9. Traffickers fit a common profile and are easy to identify.
The stereotypically evil portrayal of traffickers by popular media confuses the fact that many traffickers often look very respectable. Dozens of cases of trafficking have successfully been brought against a number of diplomats, for example.

10. Trafficking only occurs in underground or illegal industries.
Very often, trafficking happens in plain sight, in restaurants, construction sites, factories, or even domestic settings.

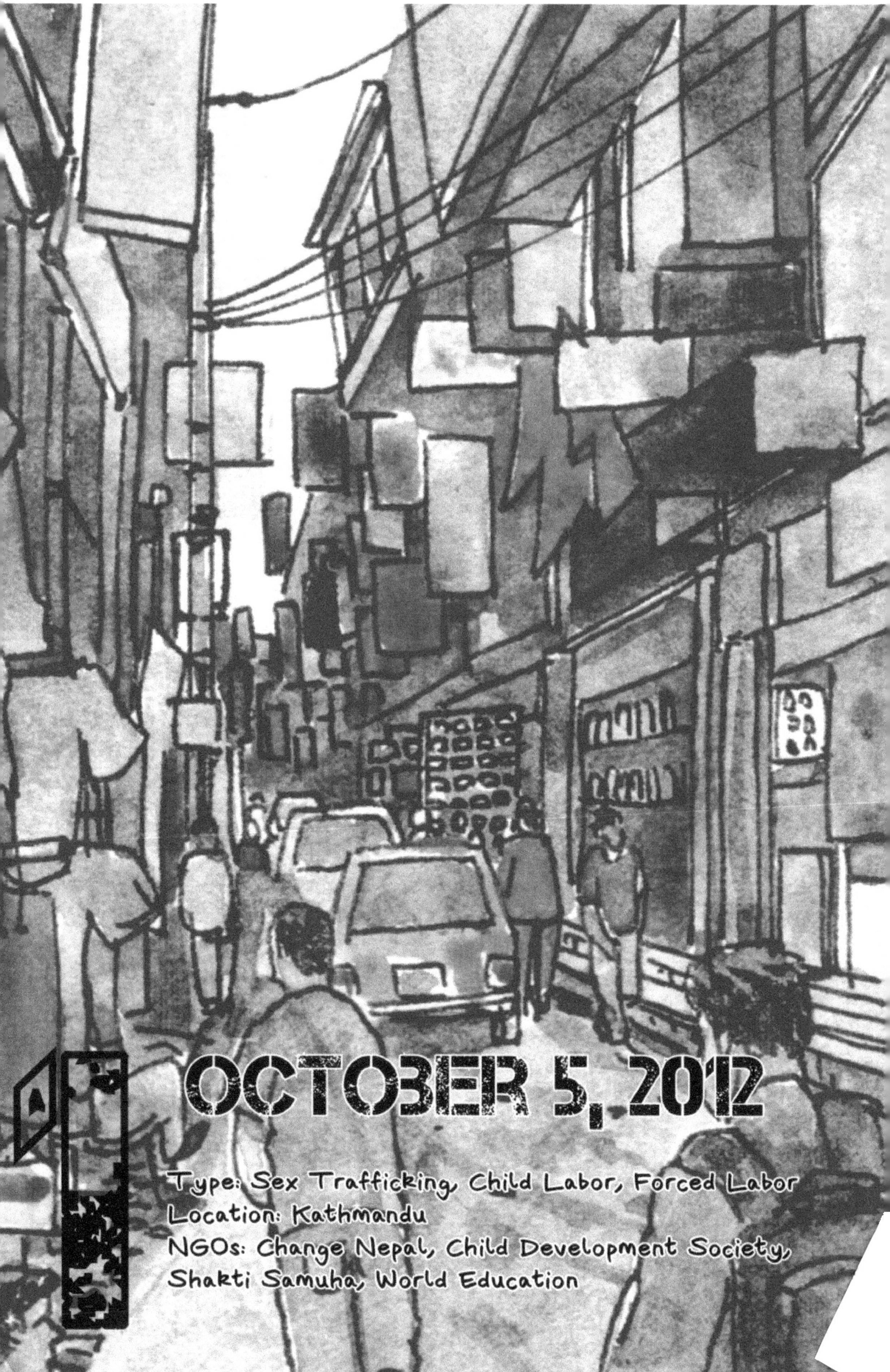

OCTOBER 5, 2012

Type: Sex Trafficking, Child Labor, Forced Labor
Location: Kathmandu
NGOs: Change Nepal, Child Development Society, Shakti Samuha, World Education

PLANNING

I finished my fellowship at Stanford in June 2011, and then returned to teaching graphic novel writing up until the summer of 2012, so I had a few months to start planning the trip. This meant cold-calling as many editors as I could to pitch them propspective stories, which I juggled alongside the inevitable barrage of pre-trip questions, to-do lists, and errands.

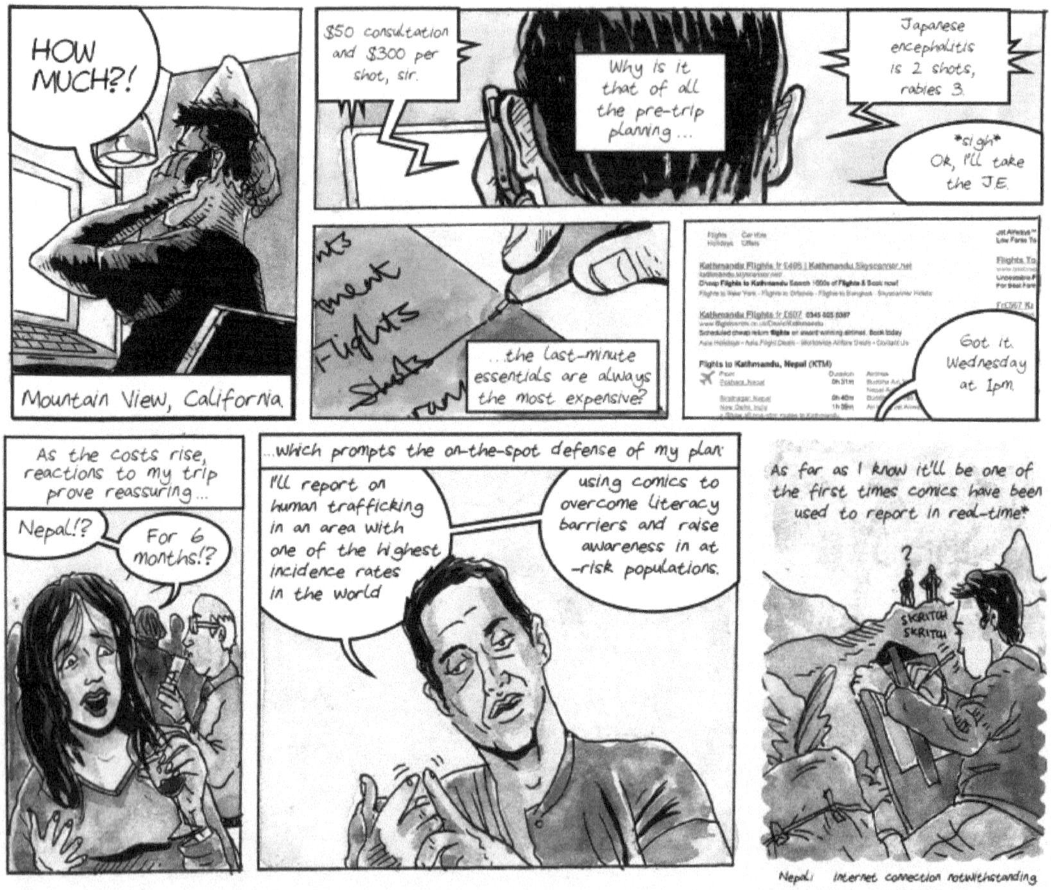
HOW MUCH?!
Mountain View, California
$50 consultation and $300 per shot, sir.
Why is it that of all the pre-trip planning...
Japanese encephalitis is 2 shots, rabies 3.
sigh Ok, I'll take the J.E.
...the last-minute essentials are always the most expensive.
Got it. Wednesday at 1pm.
As the costs rise, reactions to my trip prove reassuring...
Nepal!?
For 6 months!?
...which prompts the on-the-spot defense of my plan:
I'll report on human trafficking in an area with one of the highest incidence rates in the world
using comics to overcome literacy barriers and raise awareness in at-risk populations.
As far as I know it'll be one of the first times comics have been used to report in real-time*
SKRITCH SKRITCH

*Nepali internet connection notwithstanding.

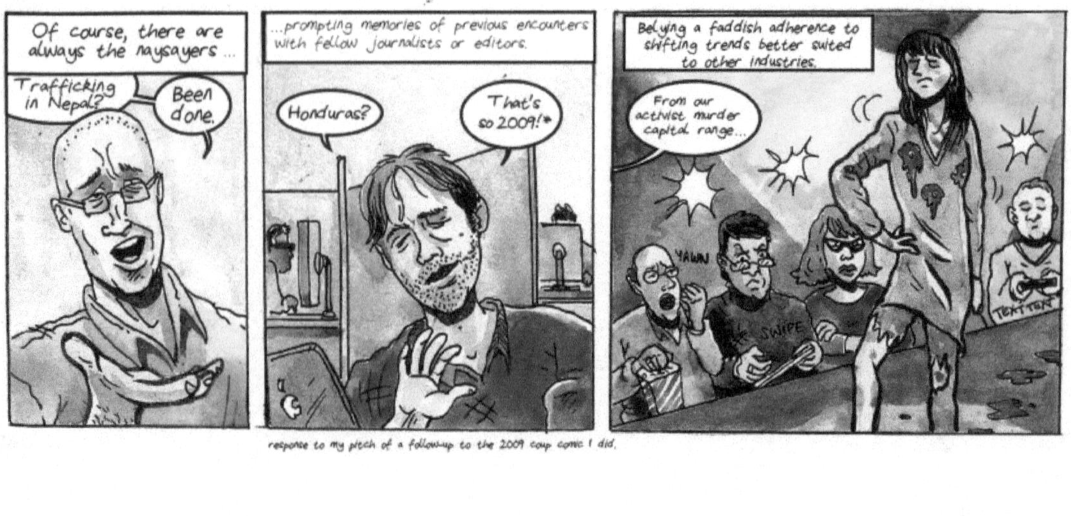
Of course, there are always the naysayers...
Trafficking in Nepal?
Been done.
...prompting memories of previous encounters with fellow journalists or editors.
Honduras?
That's so 2009!*
Belying a faddish adherence to shifting trends better suited to other industries.
From our activist murder capital range...
YAWN
SWIPE
TEXT TEXT

*response to my pitch of a follow-up to the 2009 coup comic I did.

LAST MINUTE PREP

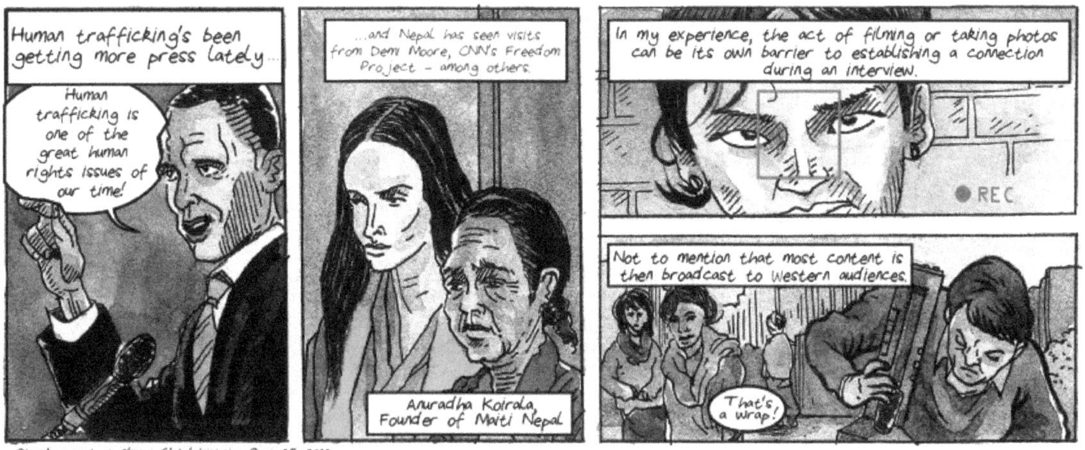

Human trafficking's been getting more press lately...
Human trafficking is one of the great human rights issues of our time!
...and Nepal has seen visits from Demi Moore, CNN's Freedom Project – among others.
Anuradha Koirala, Founder of Maiti Nepal
In my experience, the act of filming or taking photos can be its own barrier to establishing a connection during an interview.
REC
Not to mention that most content is then broadcast to Western audiences.
That's a wrap!

Obama's speech at Clinton Global Initiative, Sept 25, 2012

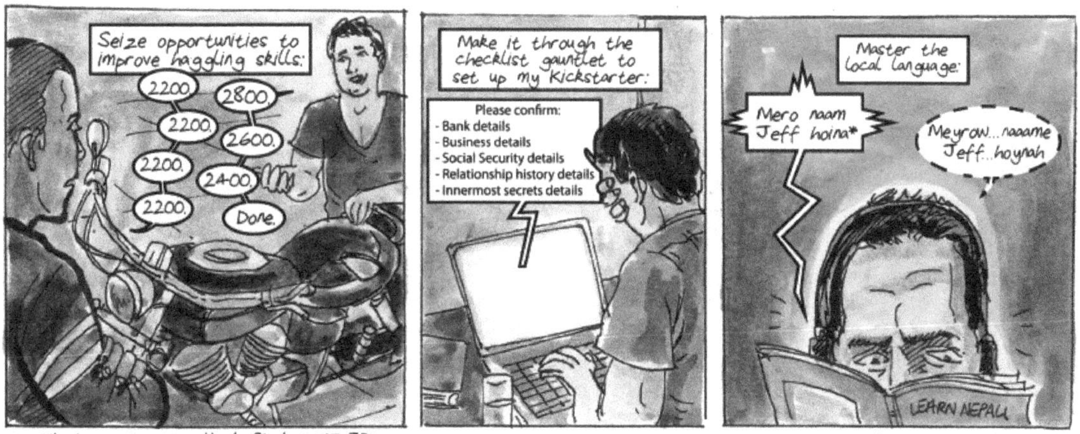

Seize opportunities to improve haggling skills:
2200.
2800.
2200.
2600.
2200.
2400.
2200.
Done.
Make it through the checklist gauntlet to set up my Kickstarter:
Please confirm:
- Bank details
- Business details
- Social Security details
- Relationship history details
- Innermost secrets details
Master the local language:
Mero naam Jeff hoina*
Meyrow...naaame Jeff...hoynah
LEARN NEPALI

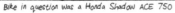

Bike in question was a Honda Shadow ACE 750

Key phrase: "My name is not Jeff"

My graphic journalism toolkit:

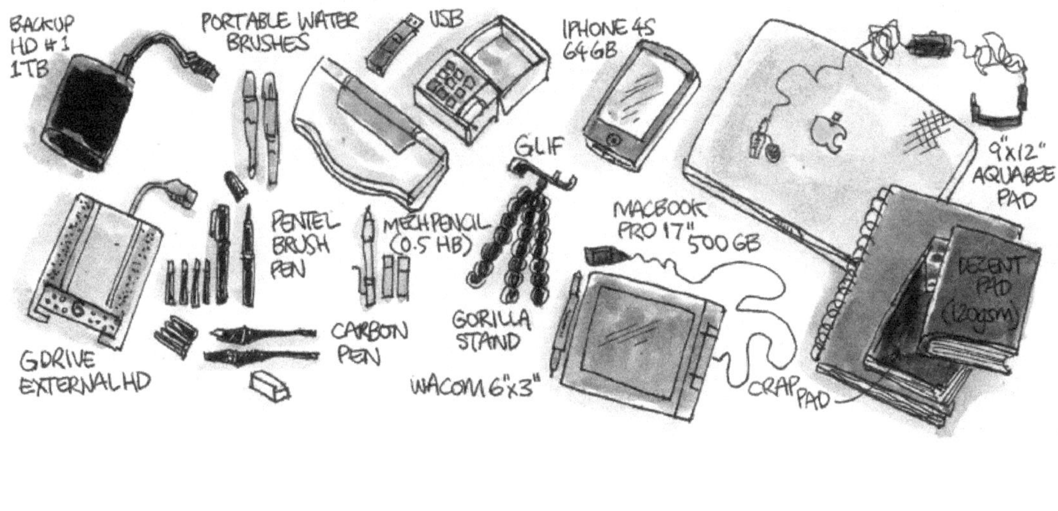

BACKUP HD #1 1TB
PORTABLE WATER BRUSHES
USB
IPHONE 4S 64GB
GLIF
9"x12" AQUABEE PAD
PENTEL BRUSH PEN
MECH PENCIL (0.5 HB)
MACBOOK PRO 17" 500 GB
DEZENT PAD (120gsm)
GDRIVE EXTERNAL HD
CARBON PEN
GORILLA STAND
WACOM 6"x3"
CRAP PAD

LONDON

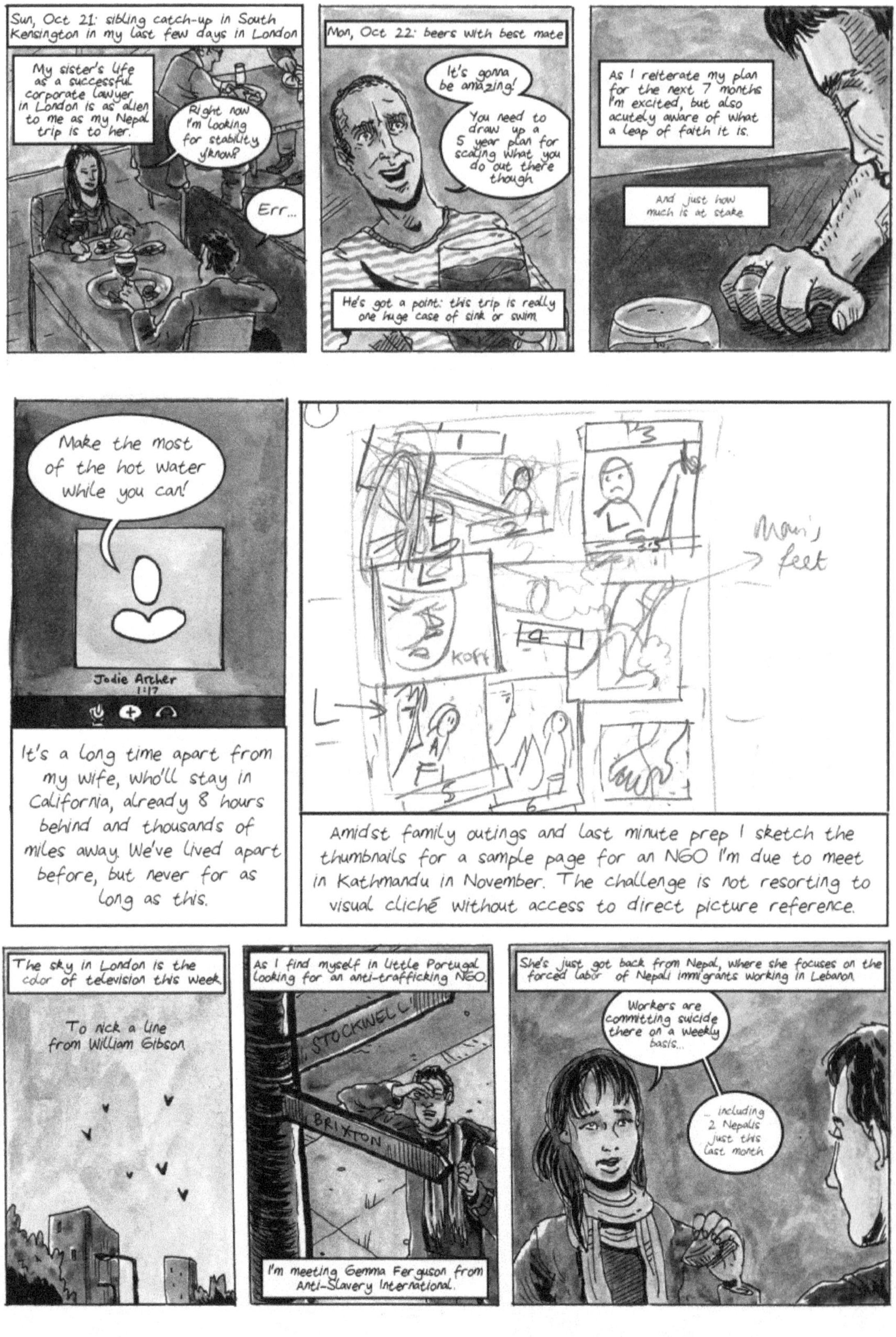

Sun, Oct 21: sibling catch-up in South Kensington in my last few days in London
My sister's life as a successful corporate lawyer in London is as alien to me as my Nepal trip is to her.
Right now I'm looking for stability y'know?
Err...
Mon, Oct 22: beers with best mate
It's gonna be amazing!
You need to draw up a 5 year plan for scaling what you do out there though
He's got a point: this trip is really one huge case of sink or swim
As I reiterate my plan for the next 7 months I'm excited, but also acutely aware of what a leap of faith it is.
And just how much is at stake.
Make the most of the hot water while you can!
Jodie Archer
1:17
It's a long time apart from my wife, who'll stay in California, already 8 hours behind and thousands of miles away. We've lived apart before, but never for as long as this.
koff
Mani's feet
Amidst family outings and last minute prep I sketch the thumbnails for a sample page for an NGO I'm due to meet in Kathmandu in November. The challenge is not resorting to visual cliché without access to direct picture reference.
The sky in London is the color of television this week
To nick a line from William Gibson
As I find myself in Little Portugal looking for an anti-trafficking NGO
STOCKWELL
BRIXTON
I'm meeting Gemma Ferguson from Anti-Slavery International.
She's just got back from Nepal, where she focuses on the forced labor of Nepali immigrants working in Lebanon
Workers are committing suicide there on a weekly basis...
... including 2 Nepalis just this last month

THE JOURNEY

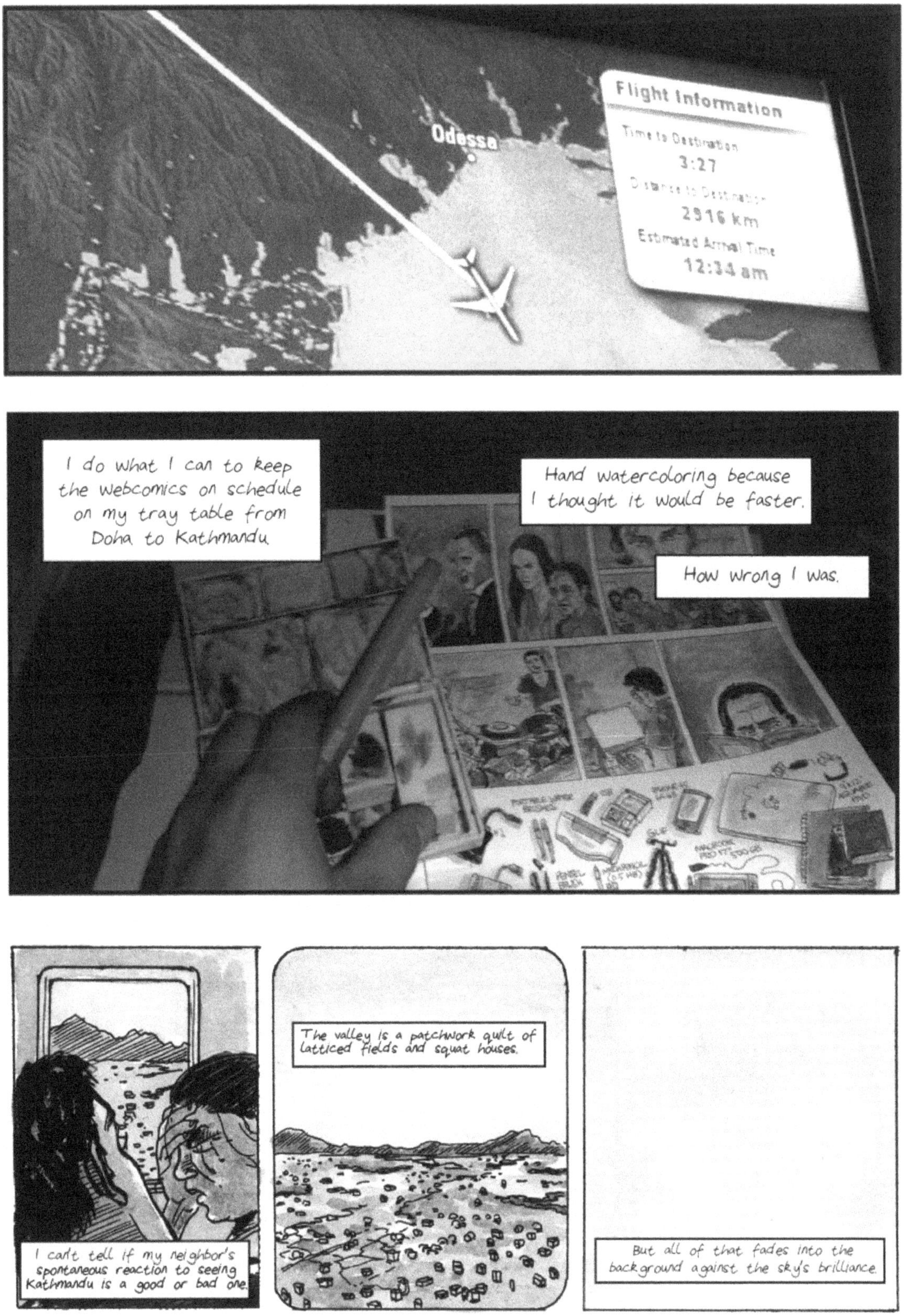
Odessa
Flight Information
Time to Destination
3:27
Distance to Destination
2916 km
Estimated Arrival Time
12:34 am
I do what I can to keep the webcomics on schedule on my tray table from Doha to Kathmandu
Hand watercoloring because I thought it would be faster.
How wrong I was.
I can't tell if my neighbor's spontaneous reaction to seeing Kathmandu is a good or bad one.
The valley is a patchwork quilt of latticed fields and squat houses.
But all of that fades into the background against the sky's brilliance.

KATHMANDU

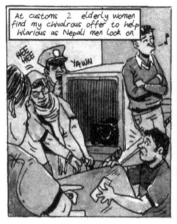

At customs 2 elderly women find my chivalrous offer to help hilarious as Nepali men look on.
HEE HEE
YAWN
It's great to see Madhu and Jaya again - especially as they save me from a horde of taxi drivers.
BEEP
BEEP
BEEP
HERO
Catching up with both of them is only complicated by the near-death experience that is driving in Kathmandu
En route to Madhu and Jaya's home we're pulled over at a police checkpoint. The officer leans in like she's gonna kiss him.
Madhu later tells me she was smelling his breath for booze.
This is spectacular!
Their 5-year-old son Aayam hasn't lost a trace of his strong American accent since the fellowship ended.
fig 1.
PUSH
fig 2.
At dinner I'm introduced to the joys of eating with my hand: fig 1: roll into ball. fig 2: push ball into gob with thumb.
On our drive back to the city, I see a few locals have taken the initiative against the cold.
... stray dogs flit in and out of view amid the piles of roadside rubble ...
... and by 9pm the pitch black is only broken up by naked bulbs hanging in concrete doorways.
I'm out like a light back at the hostel ...
... only to be woken by a soft duet from my neighbors at 5:30 the next morning

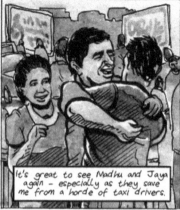

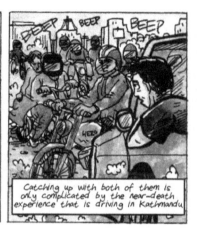

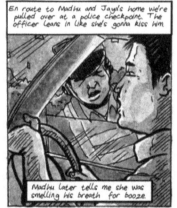

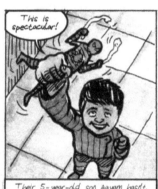

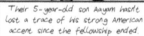

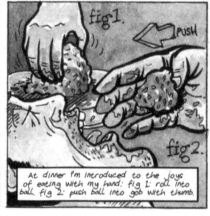

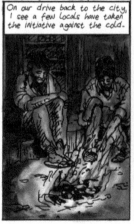

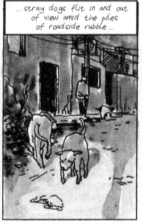

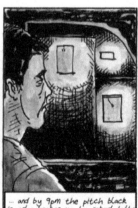

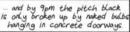

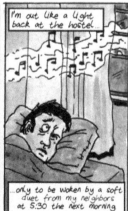

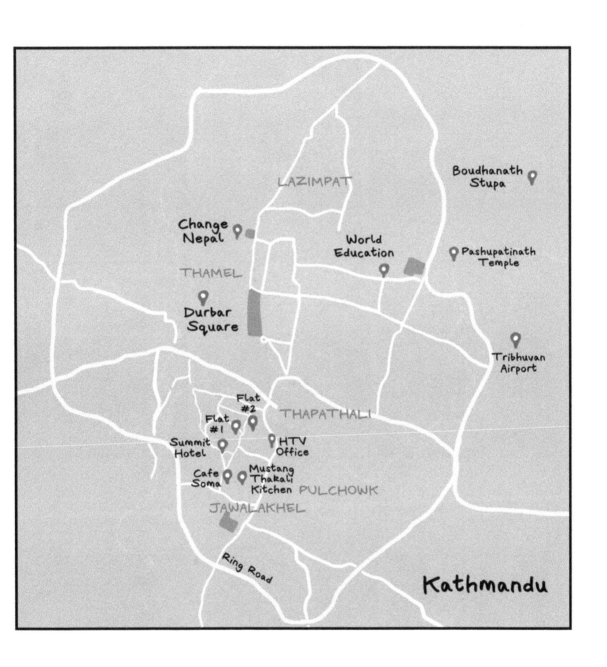

Boudhanath
Stupa

LAZIMPAT

Change
Nepal

World
Education

Pashupatinath
Temple

THAMEL

Durbar
Square

Tribhuvan
Airport

Flat
#2

Flat
#1

THAPATHALI

Summit
Hotel

HTV
Office

Cafe
Soma

Mustang
Thakali
Kitchen

PULCHOWK

JAWALAKHEL

Ring Road

Kathmandu

21

INTRODUCTIONS

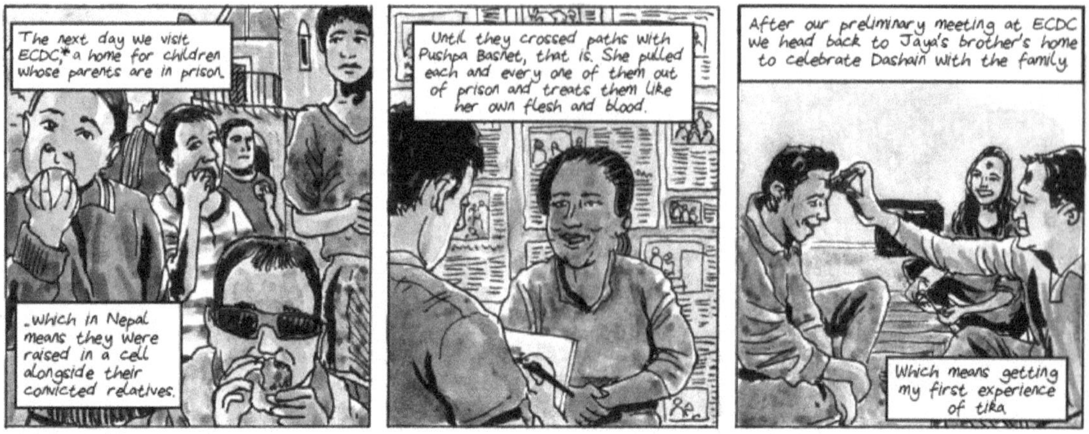
The next day we visit ECDC,* a home for children whose parents are in prison.
...which in Nepal means they were raised in a cell alongside their convicted relatives.
Until they crossed paths with Pushpa Basnet, that is. She pulled each and every one of them out of prison and treats them like her own flesh and blood.
After our preliminary meeting at ECDC we head back to Jaya's brother's home to celebrate Dashain with the family.
Which means getting my first experience of tika.

*Early Childhood Development Centre

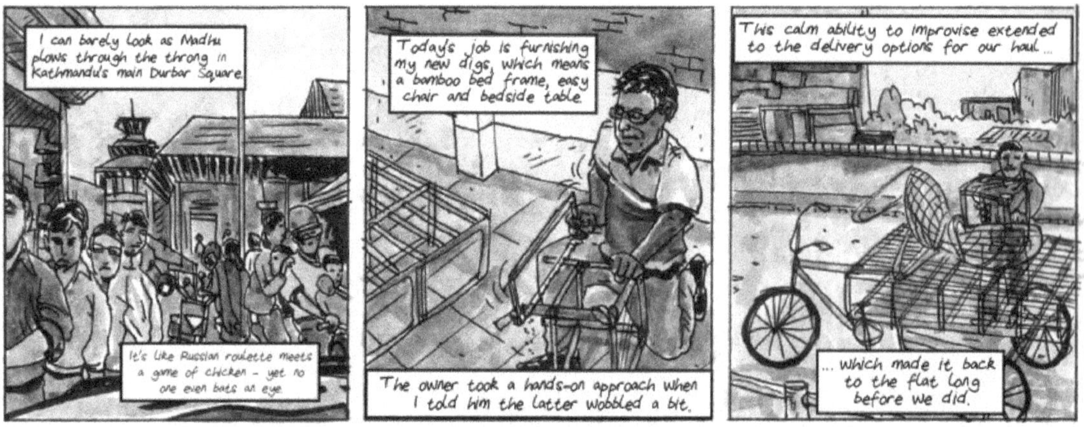
I can barely look as Madhu plows through the throng in Kathmandu's main Durbar Square.
It's like Russian roulette meets a game of chicken - yet no one even bats an eye.
Today's job is furnishing my new digs, which means a bamboo bed frame, easy chair and bedside table.
The owner took a hands-on approach when I told him the latter wobbled a bit.
This calm ability to improvise extended to the delivery options for our haul...
... which made it back to the flat long before we did.

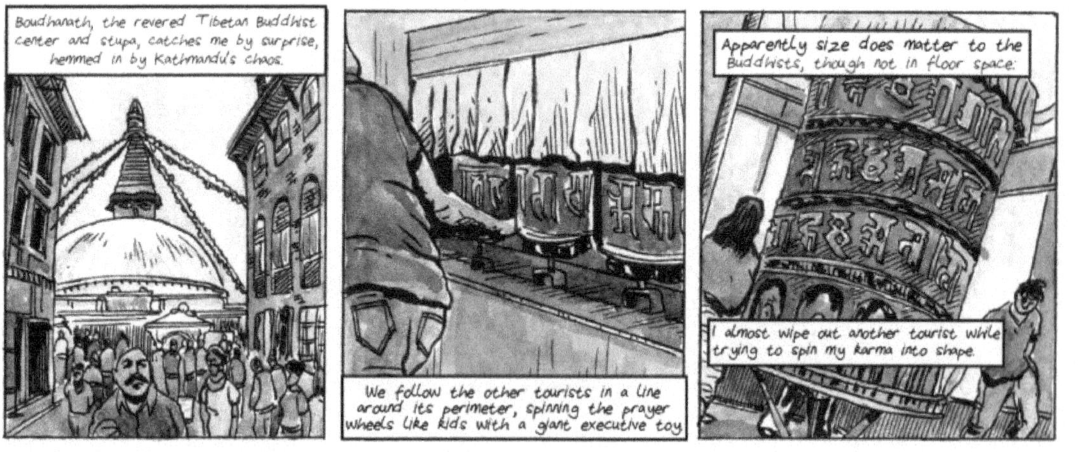
Boudhanath, the revered Tibetan Buddhist center and stupa, catches me by surprise, hemmed in by Kathmandu's chaos.
We follow the other tourists in a line around its perimeter, spinning the prayer wheels like kids with a giant executive toy.
Apparently size does matter to the Buddhists, though not in floor space.
I almost wipe out another tourist while trying to spin my karma into shape.

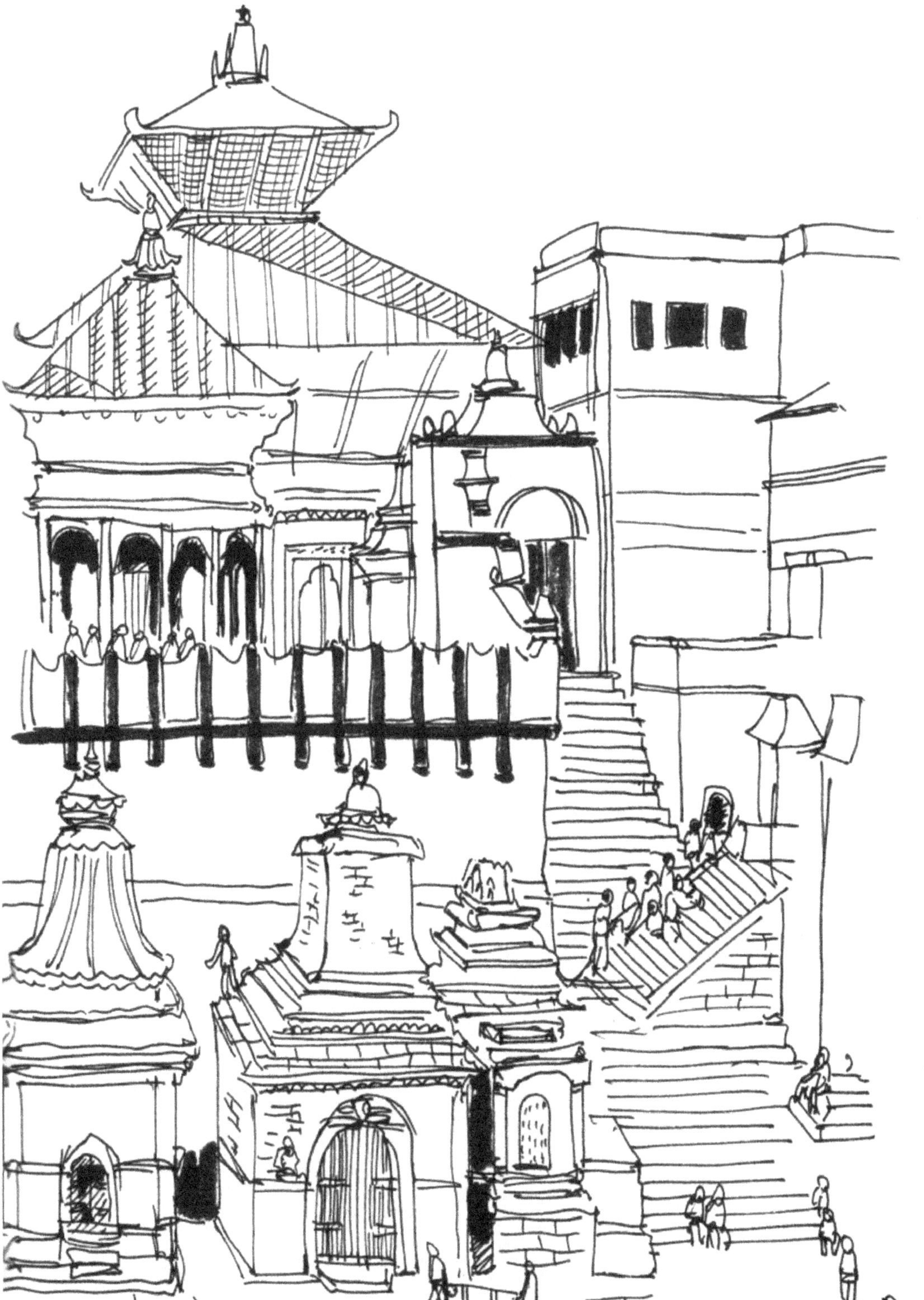

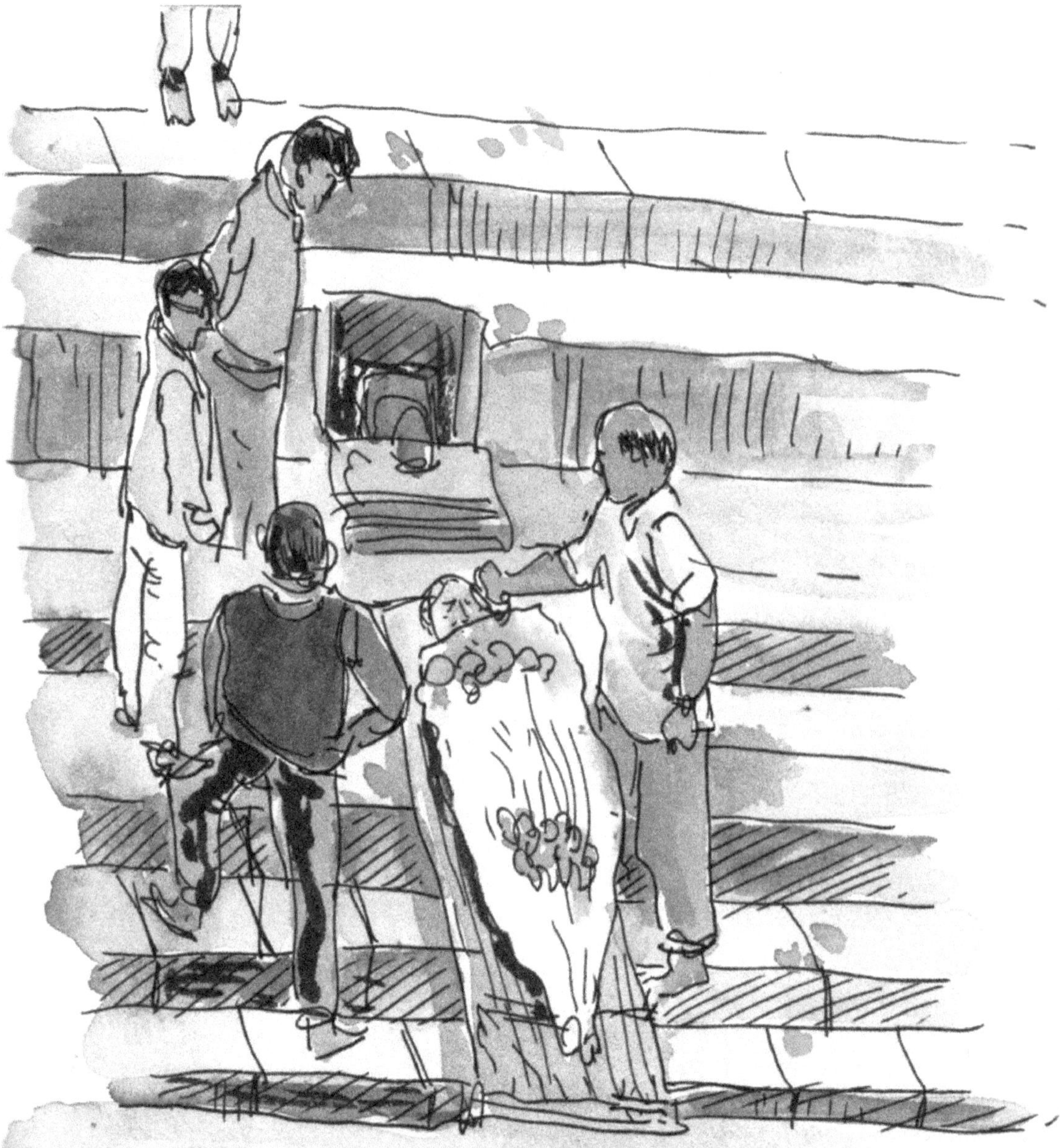

CHANGING THE NARRATIVE

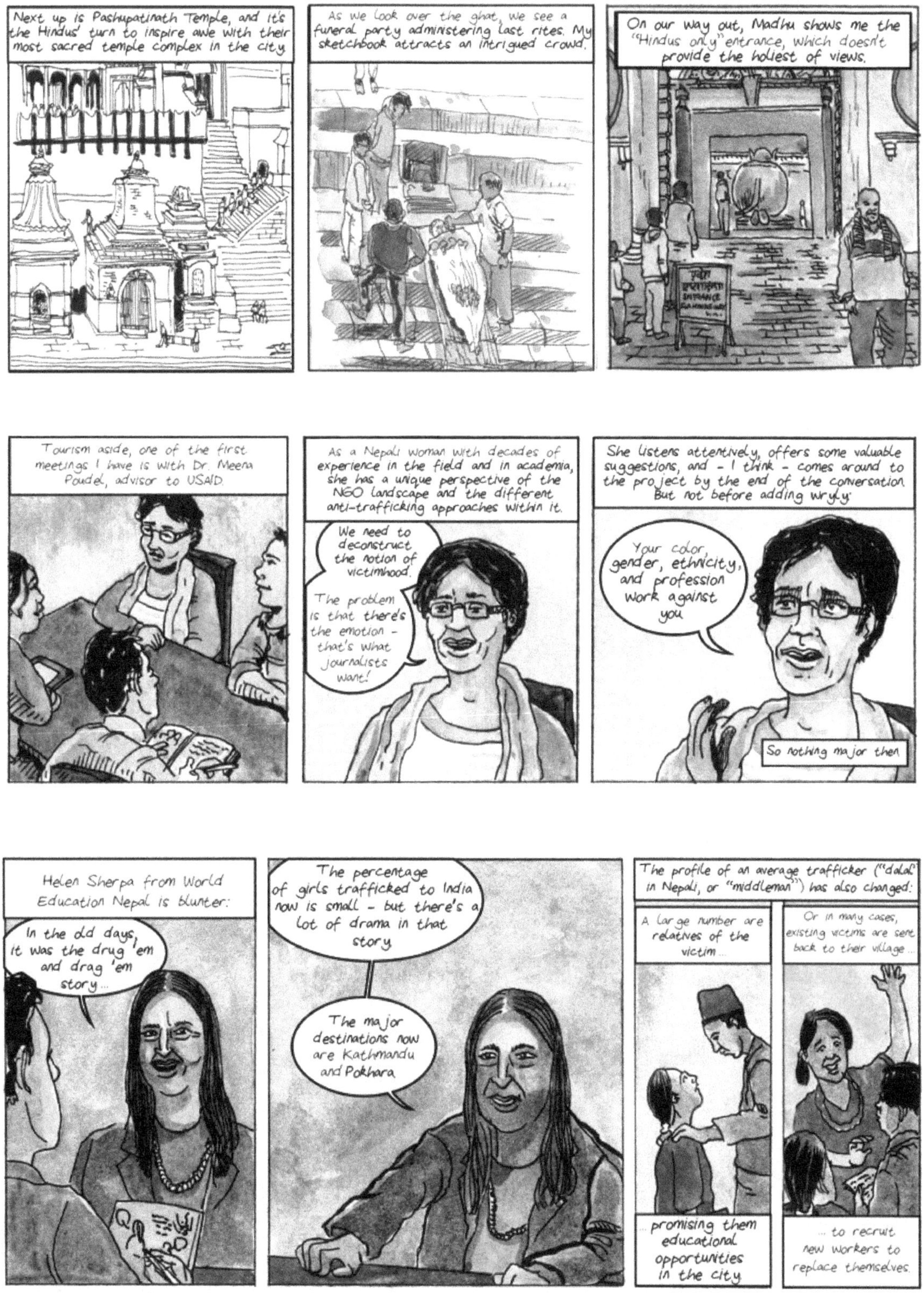
Next up is Pashupatinath Temple, and it's the Hindus' turn to inspire awe with their most sacred temple complex in the city.
As we look over the ghat, we see a funeral party adminstering last rites. My sketchbook attracts an intrigued crowd.
On our way out, Madhu shows me the "Hindus only" entrance, which doesn't provide the holiest of views.
Tourism aside, one of the first meetings I have is with Dr. Meena Poudel, advisor to USAID.
As a Nepali woman with decades of experience in the field and in academia, she has a unique perspective of the NGO landscape and the different anti-trafficking approaches within it.
We need to deconstruct the notion of victimhood.
The problem is that there's the emotion – that's what journalists want!
She listens attentively, offers some valuable suggestions, and – I think – comes around to the project by the end of the conversation. But not before adding wryly:
Your color, gender, ethnicity, and profession work against you
So nothing major then
Helen Sherpa from World Education Nepal is blunter:
In the old days, it was the drug 'em and drag 'em story...
The percentage of girls trafficked to India now is small – but there's a lot of drama in that story.
The major destinations now are Kathmandu and Pokhara.
The profile of an average trafficker ("dalal" in Nepali, or "middleman") has also changed:
A large number are relatives of the victim...
...promising them educational opportunities in the city.
Or in many cases, existing victims are sent back to their village...
... to recruit new workers to replace themselves.

THAMEL

Pramesh at Change Nepal, head-quartered in Thamel, the capital's tourist hub and unofficial red-light district, says this extends to the treatment of the girls too:

Our beneficiaries aren't locked up any more.

But they're locked up financially and socially.

The money's been invested in her clothes, her mobile.

She's already taken it.

Here they don't know about trafficking or being sold.

Compared to life back in their village, now they are in the big city! They say "We've been given a job!"

The myth of the "rescue," also typical in the trafficking narrative, is overblown, in Pramesh's opinion:

The owners know when they have a raid. So they escape.

Almost all of those arrested are beneficiaries.

They're taken to the station ...

...where they're kept in custody for a few days and not given proper food.

Then owners will come ...

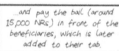

...and pay the bail (around 15,000 NRs) in front of the beneficiaries, which is later added to their tab.

To prove that they're the only ones that care about them. That they're the Godfathers.

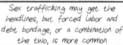

Sex trafficking may get the headlines, but forced labor and debt bondage, or a combination of the two, is more common.

Geographically, many villages can only sustain themselves for 6 months of the year ... ...so the dalals take advantage of their economic conditions with high-interest loans.

Youraj Roka from Child Development Society

Unable to pay back their loans, whole families are sent to live at the kilns or send their children to work as porters in the mines.

Which means pulling the kids out of education.

Child Workers in Nepal reports that 48% of child porter families are indebted to local money lenders.

The average age of a child porter is 13.

Average weight they carry is 37 kg.

38% of them have had accidents.

Longest journey they walk is 27 hours.

The majority of child laborers are trafficked internally.

TIBET/CHINA

Dang, Rolpa, and Pyuthan districts: child porters

NEPAL

KTM

Kavre, Ramechhap: brick kilns

INDIA

Raxaul, Sirlahi Sari factories

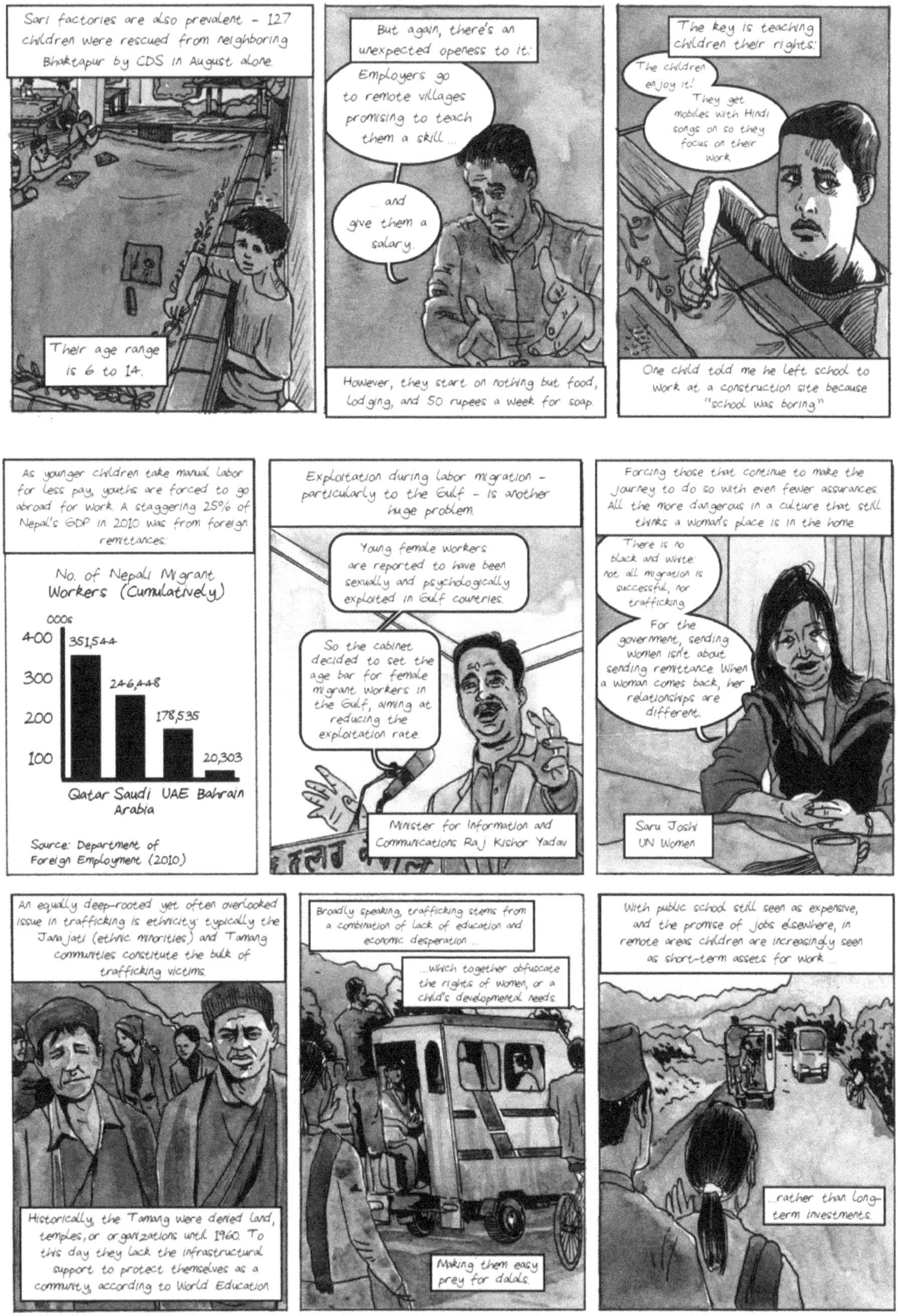
Sari factories are also prevalent – 127 children were rescued from neighboring Bhaktapur by CDS in August alone.
Their age range is 6 to 14.
But again, there's an unexpected openess to it:
Employers go to remote villages promising to teach them a skill ...
... and give them a salary.
However, they start on nothing but food, lodging, and 50 rupees a week for soap.
The key is teaching children their rights:
The children enjoy it!
They get mobiles with Hindi songs on so they focus on their work
One child told me he left school to work at a construction site because "school was boring"
As younger children take manual labor for less pay, youths are forced to go abroad for work. A staggering 25% of Nepal's GDP in 2010 was from foreign remittances:
No. of Nepali Migrant Workers (Cumulatively)
000s
400
300
200
100
351,544
246,448
178,535
20,303
Qatar
Saudi Arabia
UAE
Bahrain
Source: Department of Foreign Employment (2010)
Exploitation during labor migration – particularly to the Gulf – is another huge problem.
Young female workers are reported to have been sexually and psychologically exploited in Gulf countries.
So the cabinet decided to set the age bar for female migrant workers in the Gulf, aiming at reducing the exploitation rate.
Minister for Information and Communications Raj Kishor Yadav
Forcing those that continue to make the journey to do so with even fewer assurances. All the more dangerous in a culture that still thinks a woman's place is in the home.
There is no black and white: not all migration is successful, nor trafficking.
For the government, sending women isn't about sending remittance. When a woman comes back, her relationships are different.
Saru Joshi UN Women
An equally deep-rooted yet often overlooked issue in trafficking is ethnicity: typically the Janajati (ethnic minorities) and Tamang communities constitute the bulk of trafficking victims.
Historically, the Tamang were denied land, temples, or organizations until 1960. To this day they lack the infrastructural support to protect themselves as a community, according to World Education.
Broadly speaking, trafficking stems from a combination of lack of education and economic desperation ...
...which together obfuscate the rights of women, or a child's developmental needs.
Making them easy prey for dalals.
With public school still seen as expensive, and the promise of jobs elsewhere, in remote areas children are increasingly seen as short-term assets for work ...
...rather than long-term investments.

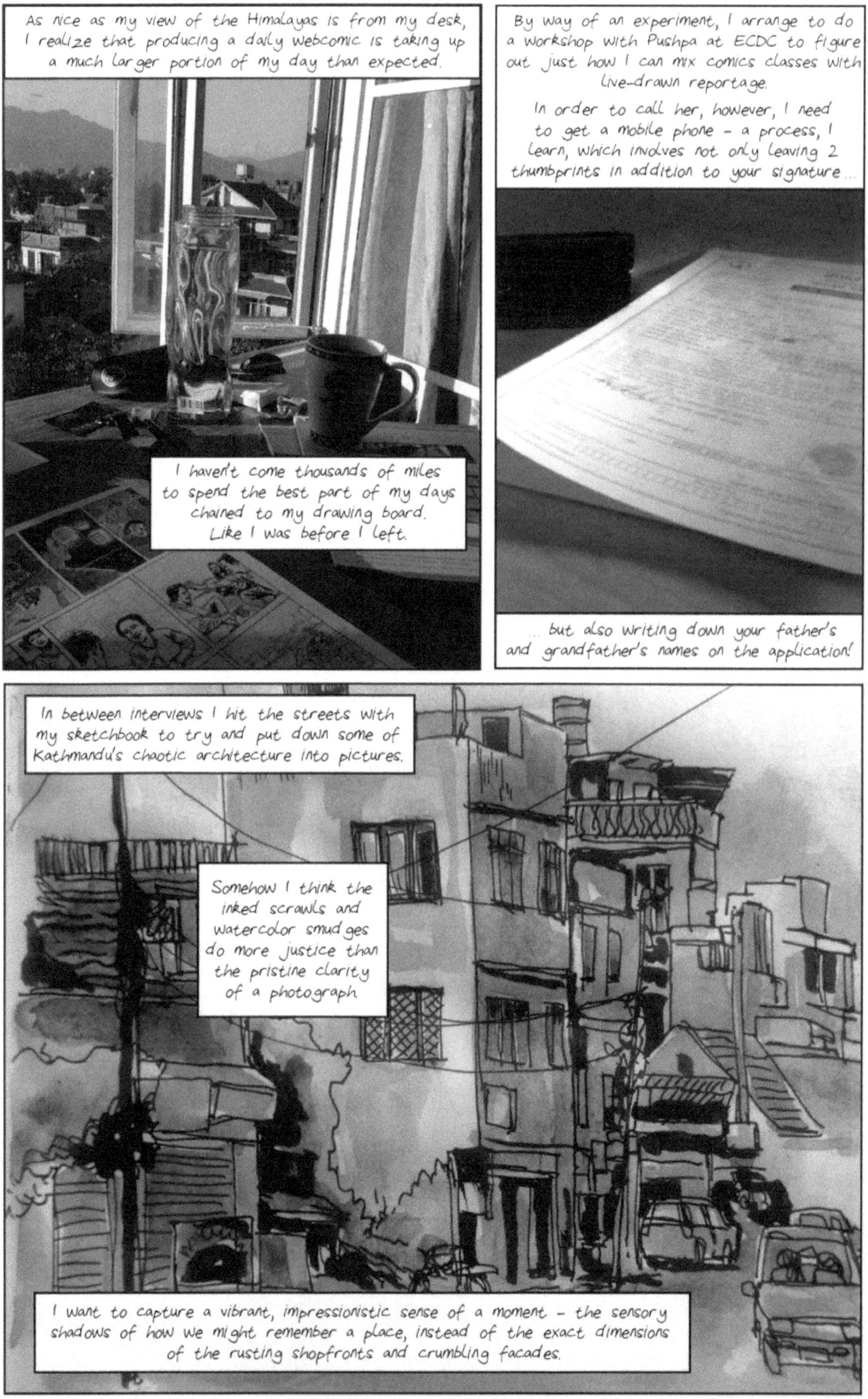
As nice as my view of the Himalayas is from my desk, I realize that producing a daily webcomic is taking up a much larger portion of my day than expected.
I haven't come thousands of miles to spend the best part of my days chained to my drawing board. Like I was before I left.
By way of an experiment, I arrange to do a workshop with Pushpa at ECDC to figure out just how I can mix comics classes with live-drawn reportage.
In order to call her, however, I need to get a mobile phone – a process, I learn, which involves not only leaving 2 thumbprints in addition to your signature...
... but also writing down your father's and grandfather's names on the application!
In between interviews I hit the streets with my sketchbook to try and put down some of Kathmandu's chaotic architecture into pictures.
Somehow I think the inked scrawls and watercolor smudges do more justice than the pristine clarity of a photograph
I want to capture a vibrant, impressionistic sense of a moment – the sensory shadows of how we might remember a place, instead of the exact dimensions of the rusting shopfronts and crumbling facades.

Next we visit Charimaya Tamang, one of the founders of the anti-trafficking NGO Shakti Samuha ("Group Power)." After speaking to her I feel like it's time to see what the situation is like outside the confines of Kathmandu.

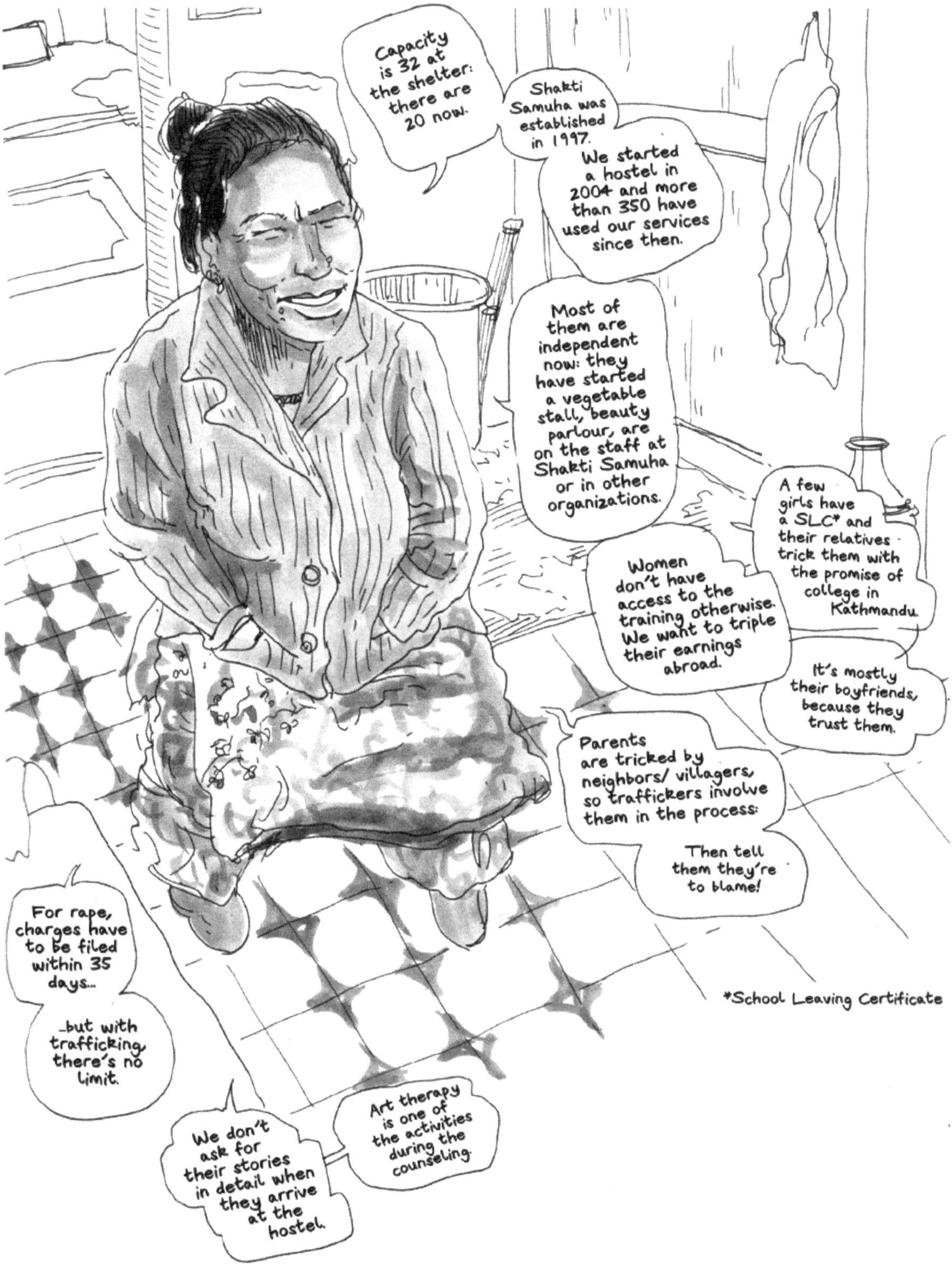
Capacity is 32 at the shelter: there are 20 now.
Shakti Samuha was established in 1997.
We started a hostel in 2004 and more than 350 have used our services since then.
Most of them are independent now: they have started a vegetable stall, beauty parlour, are on the staff at Shakti Samuha or in other organizations.
Women don't have access to the training otherwise. We want to triple their earnings abroad.
A few girls have a SLC* and their relatives trick them with the promise of college in Kathmandu.
It's mostly their boyfriends, because they trust them.
Parents are tricked by neighbors/ villagers, so traffickers involve them in the process.
Then tell them they're to blame!
For rape, charges have to be filed within 35 days...
...but with trafficking, there's no limit.
We don't ask for their stories in detail when they arrive at the hostel.
Art therapy is one of the activities during the counseling.
*School Leaving Certificate

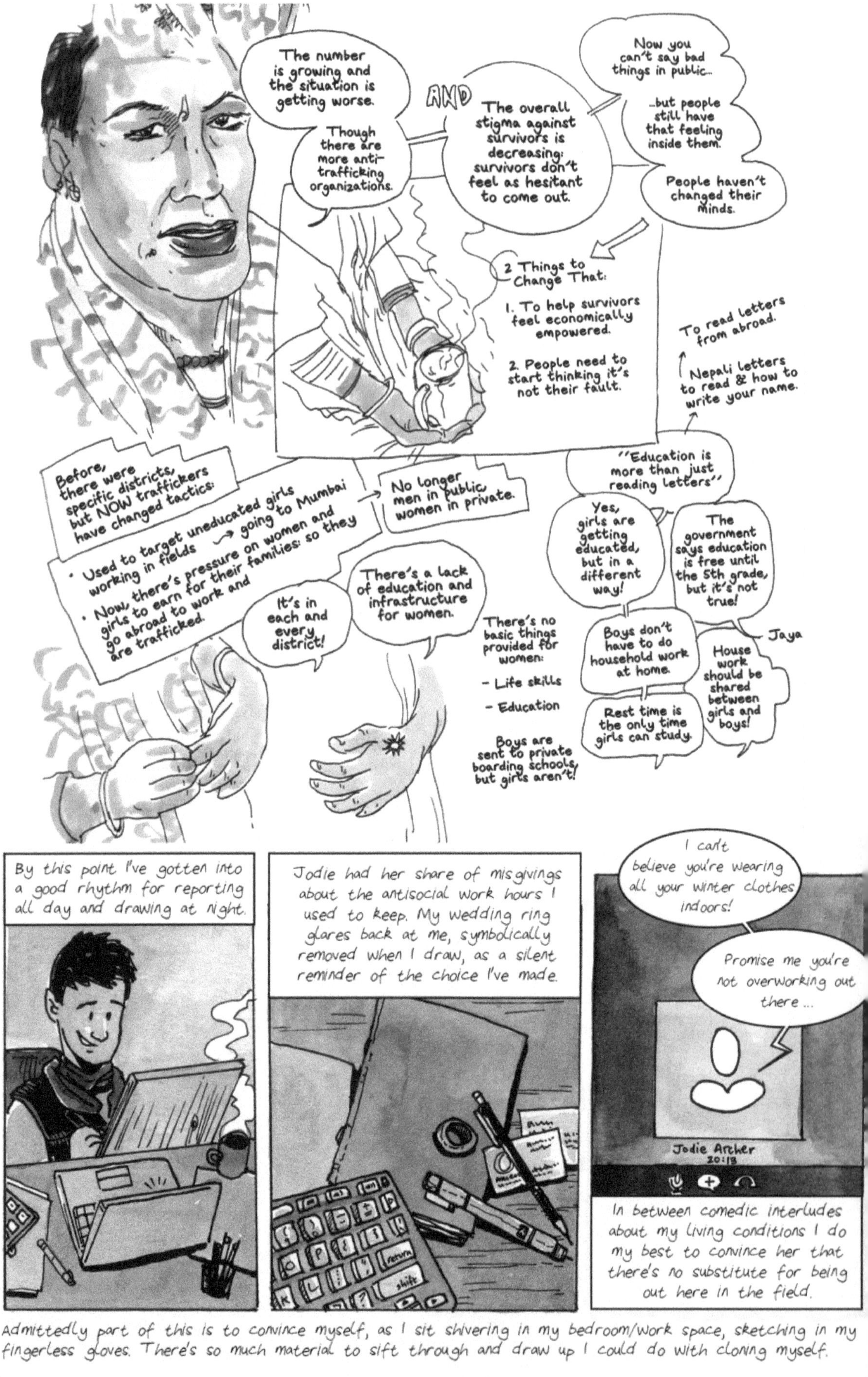
The number is growing and the situation is getting worse.
Though there are more anti-trafficking organizations.
AND
The overall stigma against survivors is decreasing: survivors don't feel as hesitant to come out.
Now you can't say bad things in public...
...but people still have that feeling inside them.
People haven't changed their minds.
2 Things to Change That:
1. To help survivors feel economically empowered.
2. People need to start thinking it's not their fault.
Before, there were specific districts, but NOW traffickers have changed tactics:
• Used to target uneducated girls working in fields → going to Mumbai
• Now, there's pressure on women and girls to earn for their families: so they go abroad to work and are trafficked.
No longer men in public, women in private.
It's in each and every district!
There's a lack of education and infrastructure for women.
There's no basic things provided for women:
- Life skills
- Education
Boys are sent to private boarding schools, but girls aren't!
"Education is more than just reading letters"
To read letters from abroad.
Nepali letters to read & how to write your name.
Yes, girls are getting educated, but in a different way!
The government says education is free until the 5th grade, but it's not true!
Jaya
Boys don't have to do household work at home.
House work should be shared between girls and boys!
Rest time is the only time girls can study.
By this point I've gotten into a good rhythm for reporting all day and drawing at night.
Jodie had her share of misgivings about the antisocial work hours I used to keep. My wedding ring glares back at me, symbolically removed when I draw, as a silent reminder of the choice I've made.
I can't believe you're wearing all your winter clothes indoors!
Promise me you're not overworking out there ...
Jodie Archer
20:13
In between comedic interludes about my living conditions I do my best to convince her that there's no substitute for being out here in the field.

Admittedly part of this is to convince myself, as I sit shivering in my bedroom/work space, sketching in my fingerless gloves. There's so much material to sift through and draw up I could do with cloning myself.

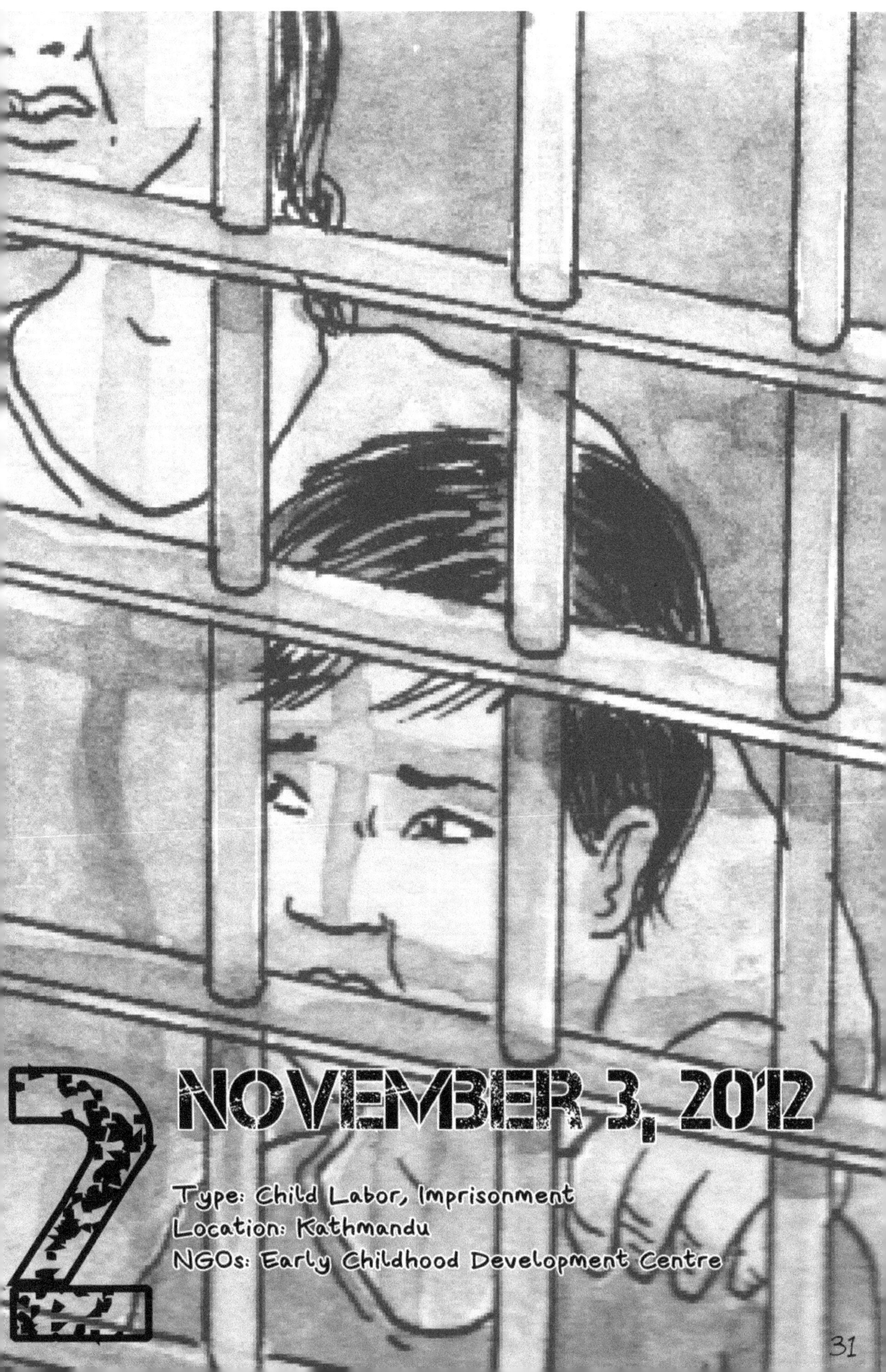

2 NOVEMBER 3, 2012

Type: Child Labor, Imprisonment
Location: Kathmandu
NGOs: Early Childhood Development Centre

EARLY CHILDHOOD DEVELOPMENT CENTRE

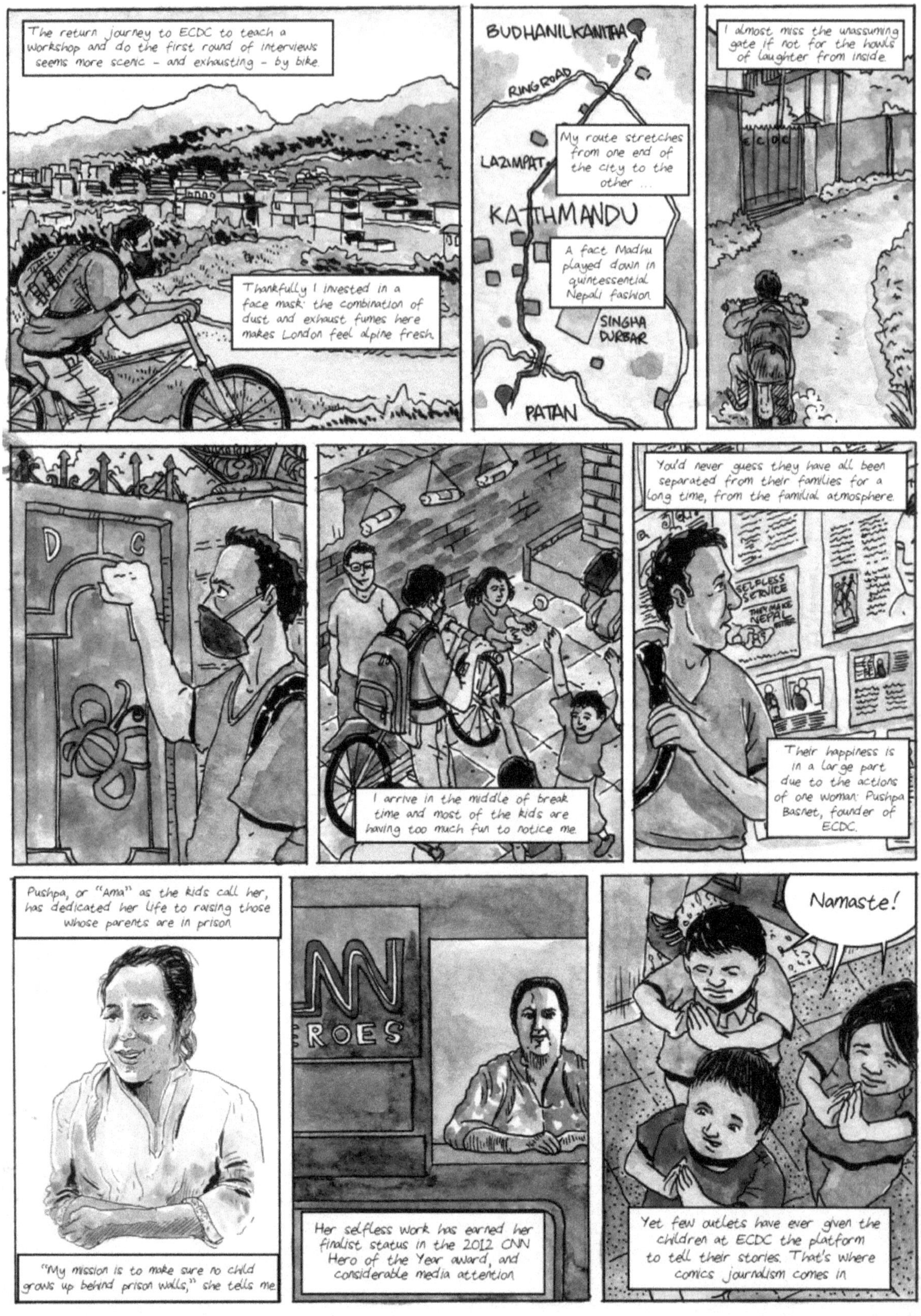

The return journey to ECDC to teach a workshop and do the first round of interviews seems more scenic – and exhausting – by bike.
Thankfully I invested in a face mask: the combination of dust and exhaust fumes here makes London feel alpine fresh.
BUDHANILKANTHA
RING ROAD
LAZIMPAT
KATHMANDU
SINGHA DURBAR
PATAN
My route stretches from one end of the city to the other ...
A fact Madhu played down in quintessential Nepali fashion.
I almost miss the unassuming gate if not for the howls of laughter from inside.
I arrive in the middle of break time and most of the kids are having too much fun to notice me.
You'd never guess they have all been separated from their families for a long time, from the familial atmosphere.
SELFLESS SERVICE
Their happiness is in a large part due to the actions of one woman: Pushpa Basnet, founder of ECDC.
Pushpa, or "Ama" as the kids call her, has dedicated her life to raising those whose parents are in prison.
"My mission is to make sure no child grows up behind prison walls," she tells me.
EROES
Her selfless work has earned her finalist status in the 2012 CNN Hero of the Year award, and considerable media attention.
Namaste!
Yet few outlets have ever given the children at ECDC the platform to tell their stories. That's where comics journalism comes in.

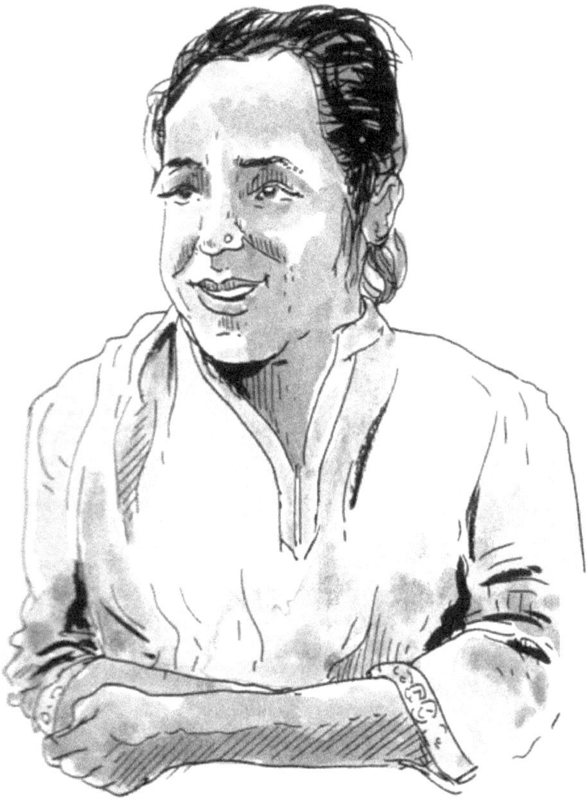

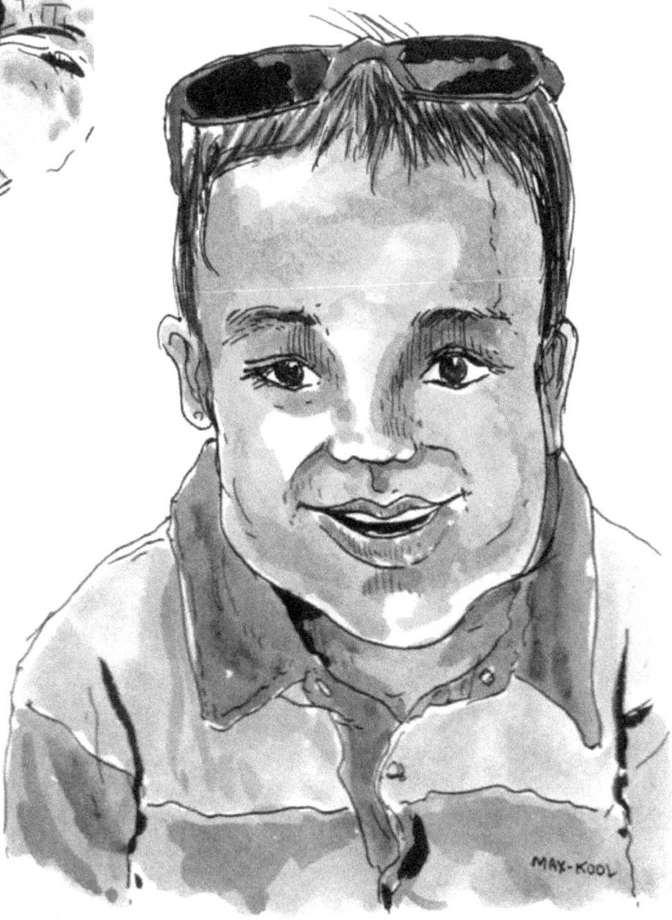
MAX-KOOL

"DRIVER"

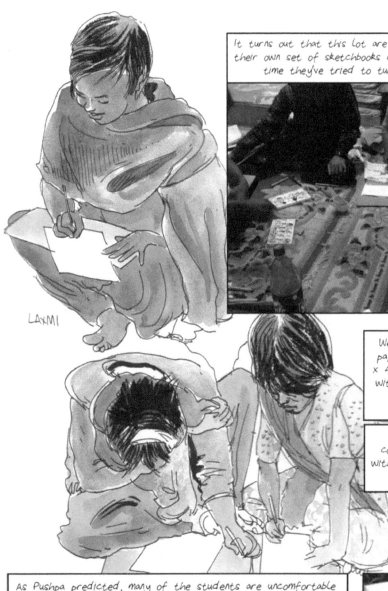

It turns out that this lot are dab hands at sketching, and all ha[ve] their own set of sketchbooks and watercolors. But this is the fir[st] time they've tried to turn their own stories into comics.

LAXMI

We start by thumbnailing our pages, which means drawing 3 x 4 inch mini versions of pages with stick figures, acting like a blueprint for the final artwork.

The silence of total concentration fills the room, with only intermittent questions preceded by "Uncle!"

As Pushpa predicted, many of the students are uncomfortable directly confronting the truth of their parents' incarcerations.

Yet in the wider context of a story about how they came to ECDC, the truth begins to seep out into their comics, slowly but surely. The therapeutic value is clear to see.

They are hungry to learn new skills and keen to experiment with 1-point perspective almost before I've even finished giving my demonstration

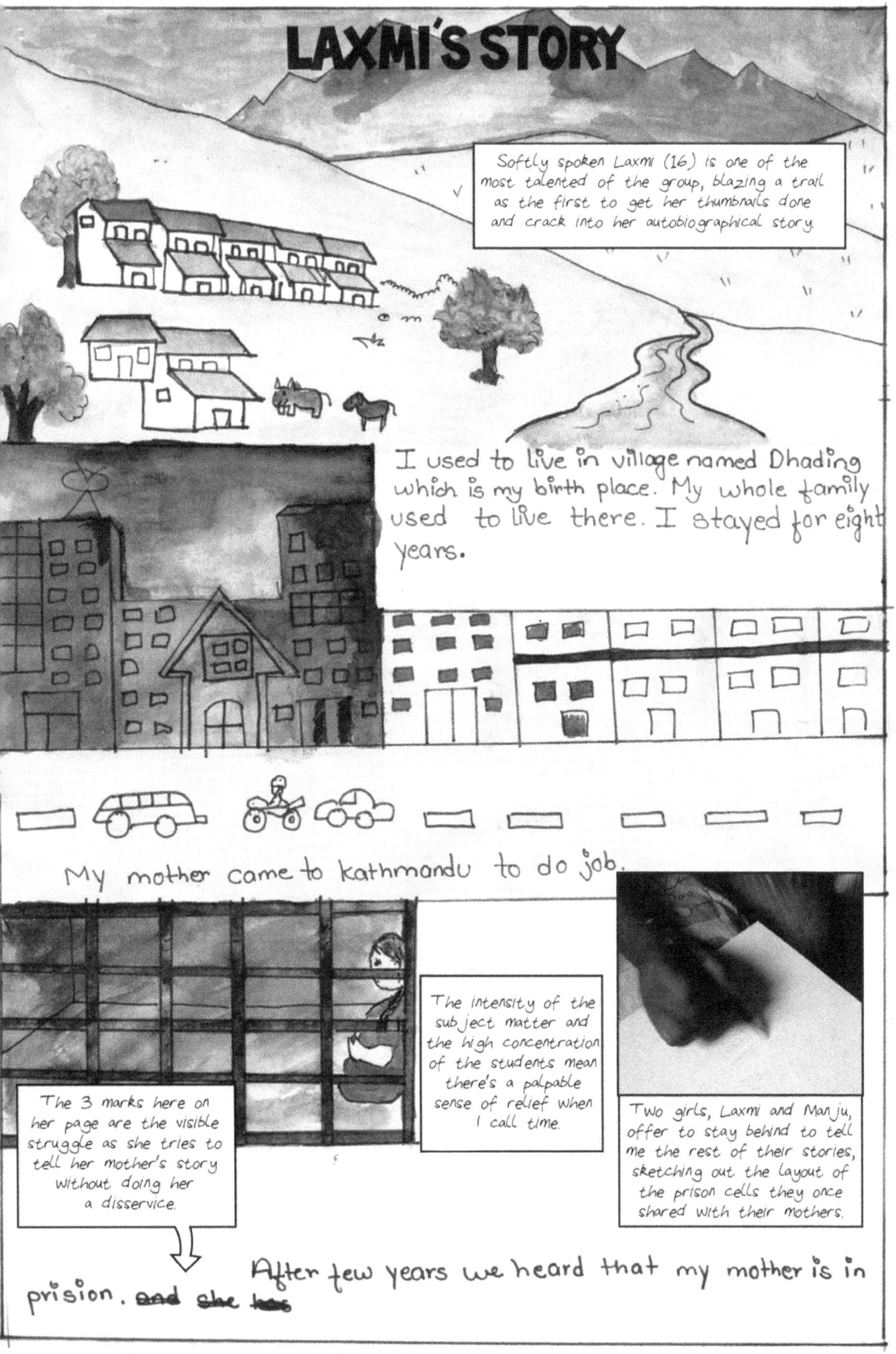

LAXMI'S STORY
Softly spoken Laxmi (16) is one of the most talented of the group, blazing a trail as the first to get her thumbnails done and crack into her autobiographical story.
I used to live in village named Dhading which is my birth place. My whole family used to live there. I stayed for eight years.
My mother came to kathmandu to do job.
The intensity of the subject matter and the high concentration of the students mean there's a palpable sense of relief when I call time.
Two girls, Laxmi and Manju, offer to stay behind to tell me the rest of their stories, sketching out the layout of the prison cells they once shared with their mothers.
The 3 marks here on her page are the visible struggle as she tries to tell her mother's story without doing her a disservice.
After few years we heard that my mother is in prision. and she has

Here's my take on their stories. All of the text below is taken from direct quotes. The images are based on Laxmi's descriptions of her family members and environments.

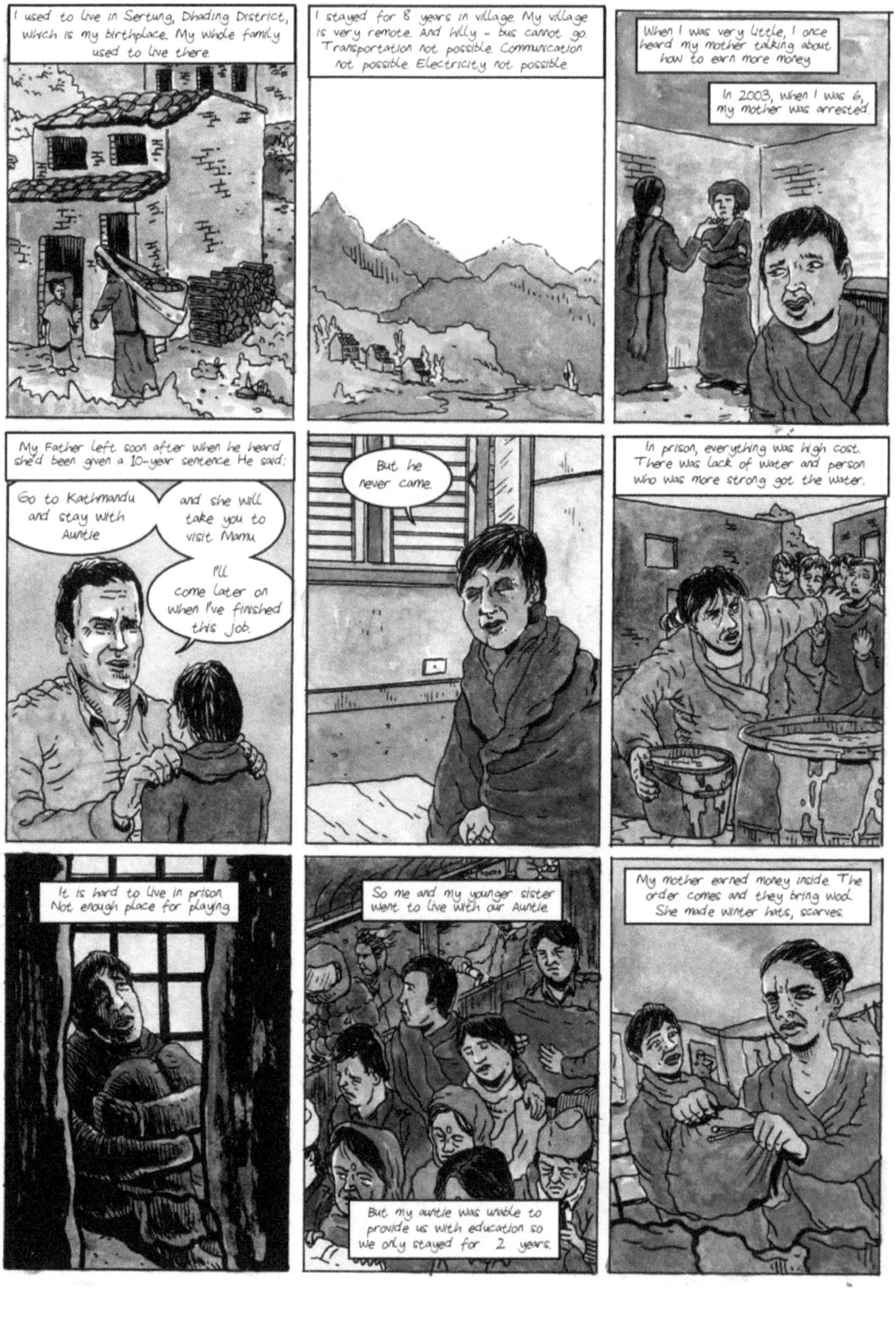
I used to live in Sertung, Dhading District, which is my birthplace. My whole family used to live there.
I stayed for 8 years in village. My village is very remote. And hilly - bus cannot go. Transportation not possible. Communication not possible. Electricity not possible.
When I was very little, I once heard my mother talking about how to earn more money.
In 2003, when I was 6, my mother was arrested.
My Father left soon after when he heard she'd been given a 10-year sentence. He said:
Go to Kathmandu and stay with Auntie
and she will take you to visit Mamu
I'll come later on when I've finished this job.
But he never came.
In prison, everything was high cost. There was lack of water and person who was more strong got the water.
It is hard to live in prison. Not enough place for playing.
So me and my younger sister went to live with our Auntie.
But my auntie was unable to provide us with education so we only stayed for 2 years.
My mother earned money inside. The order comes and they bring wool. She made winter hats, scarves.

There were 8 adults to a room. Children weren't included in the room count, and there were 3 kids, so 11 total.

There was a hospital too, and school for mothers, but not children.

My mother's now in class 3 (of 5), but she can only read and write her name in Nepali. She only knows "a b c d" in English.

The food was dhal baat. The government gave 200 NRs to every prisoner for buying dhal and rice.

Every room has a leader, and the room leader got all the money to distribute the food.

There wasn't an alarm or fixed schedule, but sometimes when we got up early, the older prisoners shouted at us.

There were more old people who didn't have relatives to come and help them. I used to help them carry water.

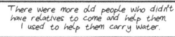

I stayed for 1 month in prison.

My mother said to head of the prison for us to go for school, so she contacted Mamu.

My small sister and me came to ECDC. I got the chance to study.

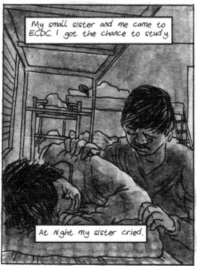

At night my sister cried.

After 1 year my mother will be released from prison I want to make my mother happy.

37

Next is Manju, another taciturn girl with an impish smile. She's buoyed by listening to Laxmi's story and as a result becomes more confident as she gets into her storytelling stride.

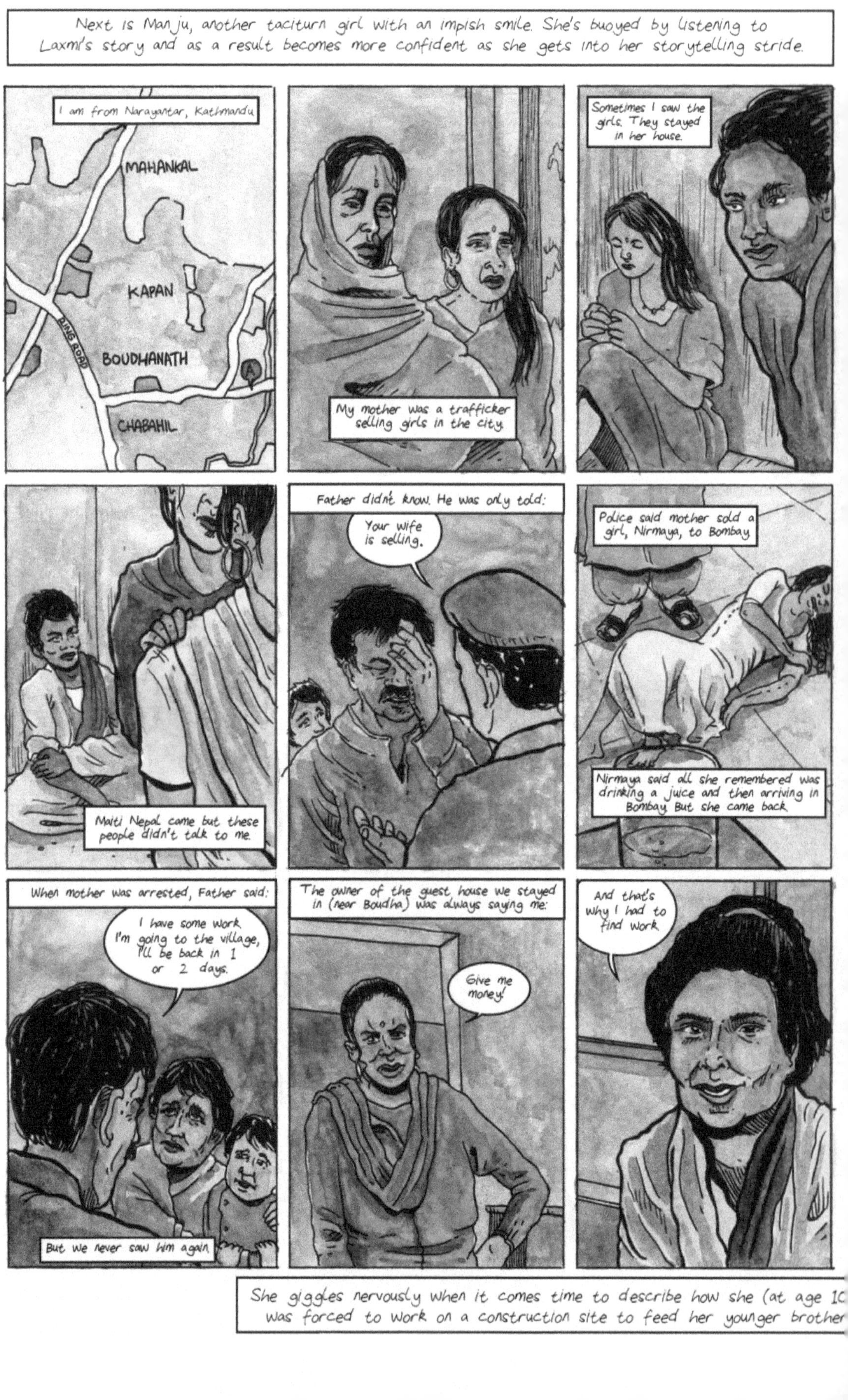
I am from Narayantar, Kathmandu
MAHANKAL
KAPAN
RING ROAD
BOUDHANATH
A
CHABAHIL
My mother was a trafficker selling girls in the city.
Sometimes I saw the girls. They stayed in her house.
Maiti Nepal came but these people didn't talk to me.
Father didn't know. He was only told:
Your wife is selling.
Police said mother sold a girl, Nirmaya, to Bombay.
Nirmaya said all she remembered was drinking a juice and then arriving in Bombay. But she came back.
When mother was arrested, Father said:
I have some work. I'm going to the village, I'll be back in 1 or 2 days.
But we never saw him again.
The owner of the guest house we stayed in (near Boudha) was always saying me:
Give me money!
And that's why I had to find work.

She giggles nervously when it comes time to describe how she (at age 10 was forced to work on a construction site to feed her younger brother

MANJU'S STORY

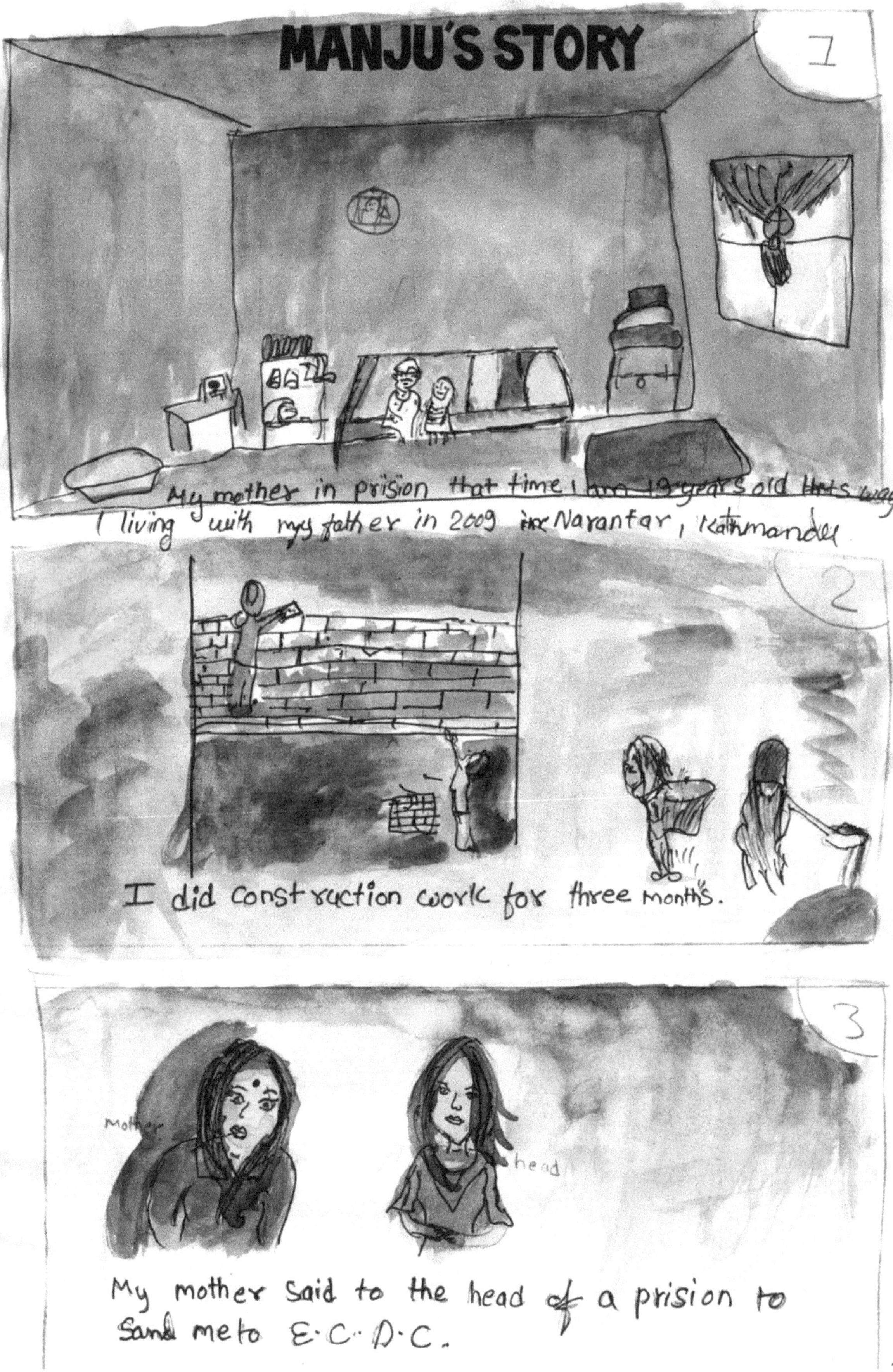
1
My mother in prision that time I am 13 years old thats way I living with my father in 2009 in Narantar, Kathmandu
2
I did construction work for three months.
3
mother
head
My mother said to the head of a prision to sand me to E·C·D·C.

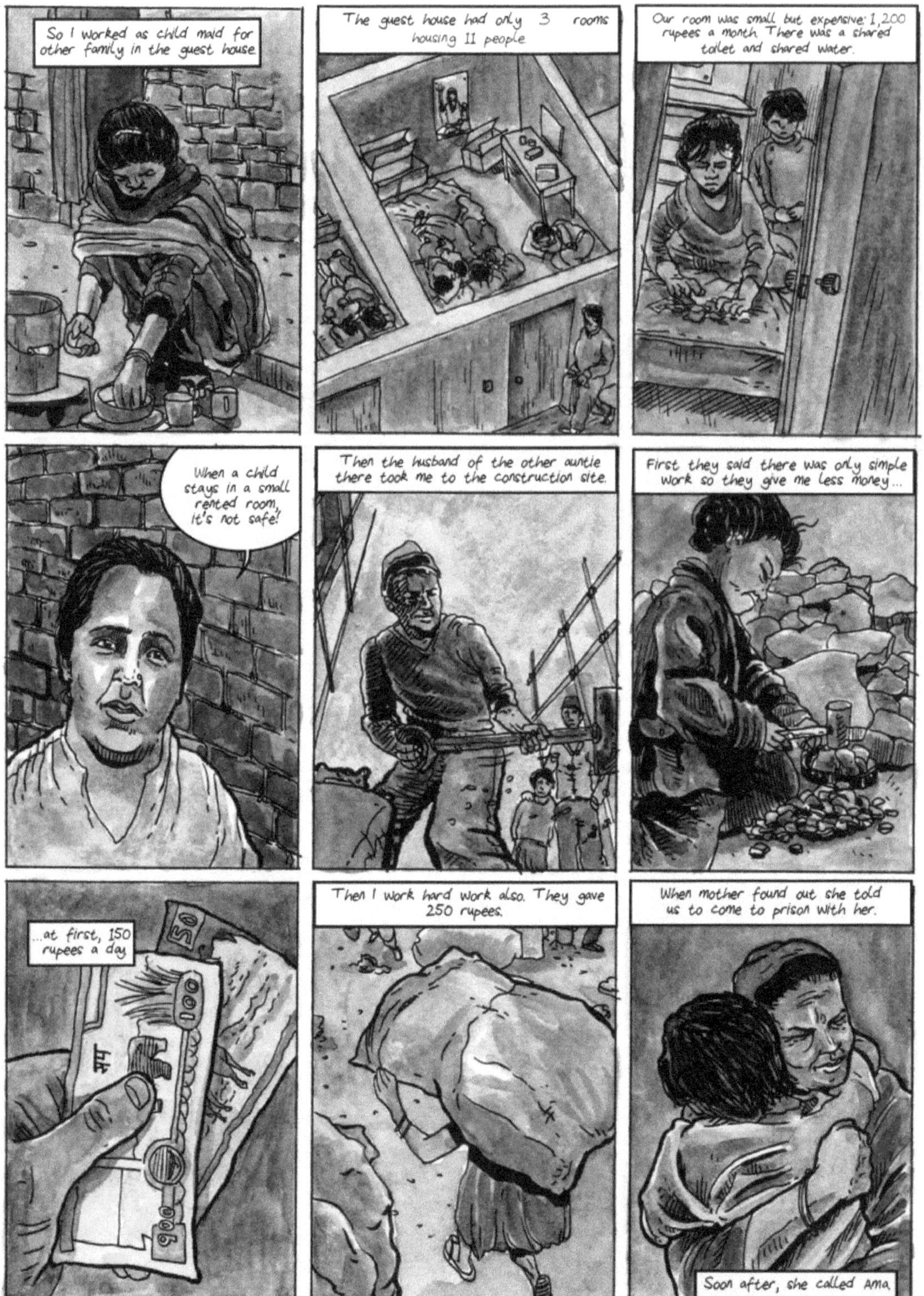
So I worked as child maid for other family in the guest house.
The guest house had only 3 rooms housing 11 people.
Our room was small but expensive: 1,200 rupees a month. There was a shared toilet and shared water.
When a child stays in a small rented room, it's not safe!
Then the husband of the other auntie there took me to the construction site.
First they said there was only simple work so they give me less money...
...at first, 150 rupees a day
Then I work hard work also. They gave 250 rupees.
When mother found out she told us to come to prison with her.
Soon after, she called Ama.

As is so often the case, inadequate state support and lack of services mean that children are either left to fend for themselves or forced to follow in the same footsteps as their parents. The economics of desperation and the instinct to follow whatever glimmer of hope that might lead to a new life is exactly what traffickers take advantage of.

Especially when it involves separating these children from their families in rural areas and sending them to the big city. It was time to follow the trail in reverse and get out of Kathmandu.

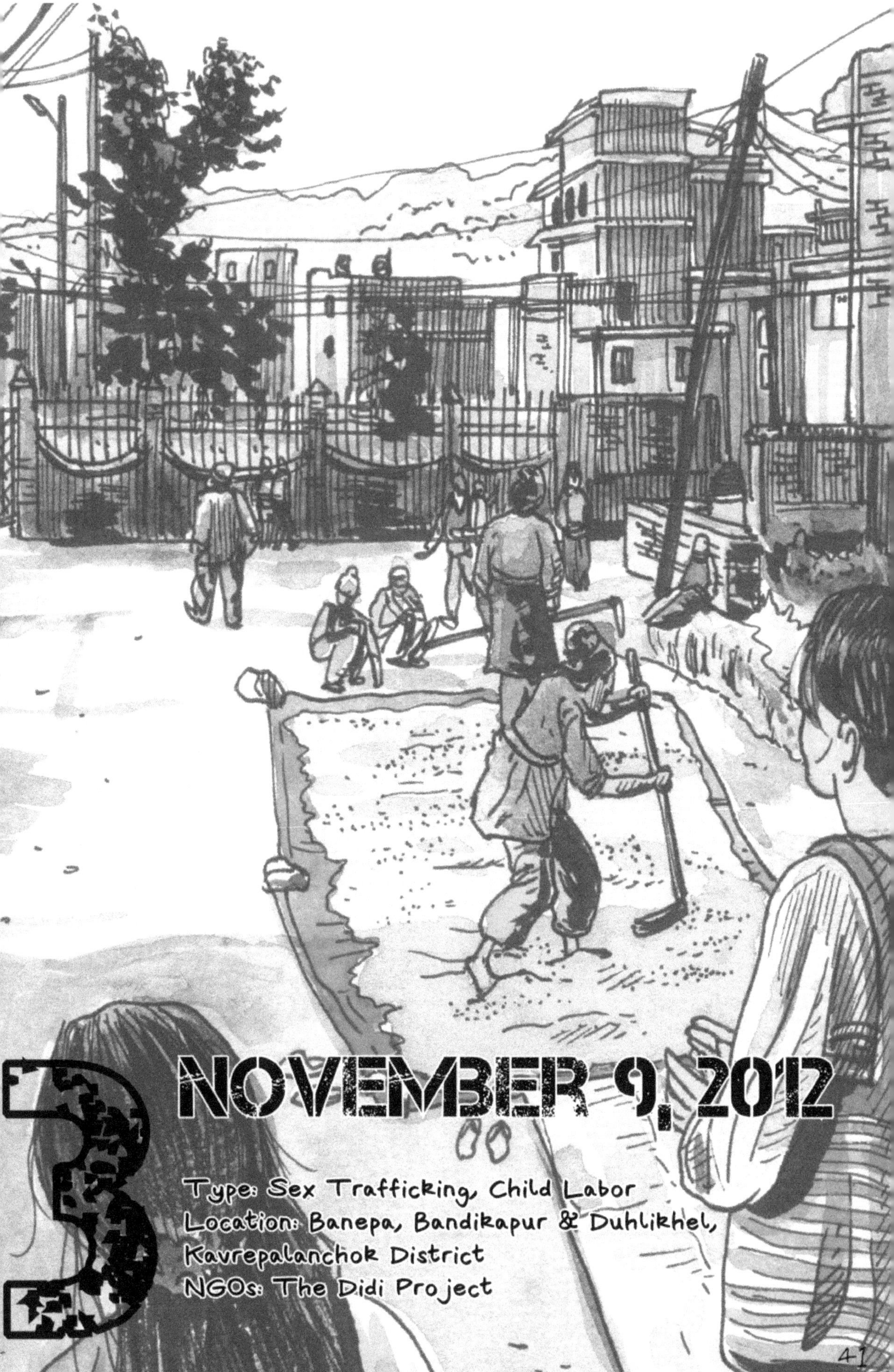

3 NOVEMBER 9, 2012

Type: Sex Trafficking, Child Labor
Location: Banepa, Bandikapur & Duhlikhel, Kavrepalanchok District
NGOs: The Didi Project

THE DIDI PROJECT

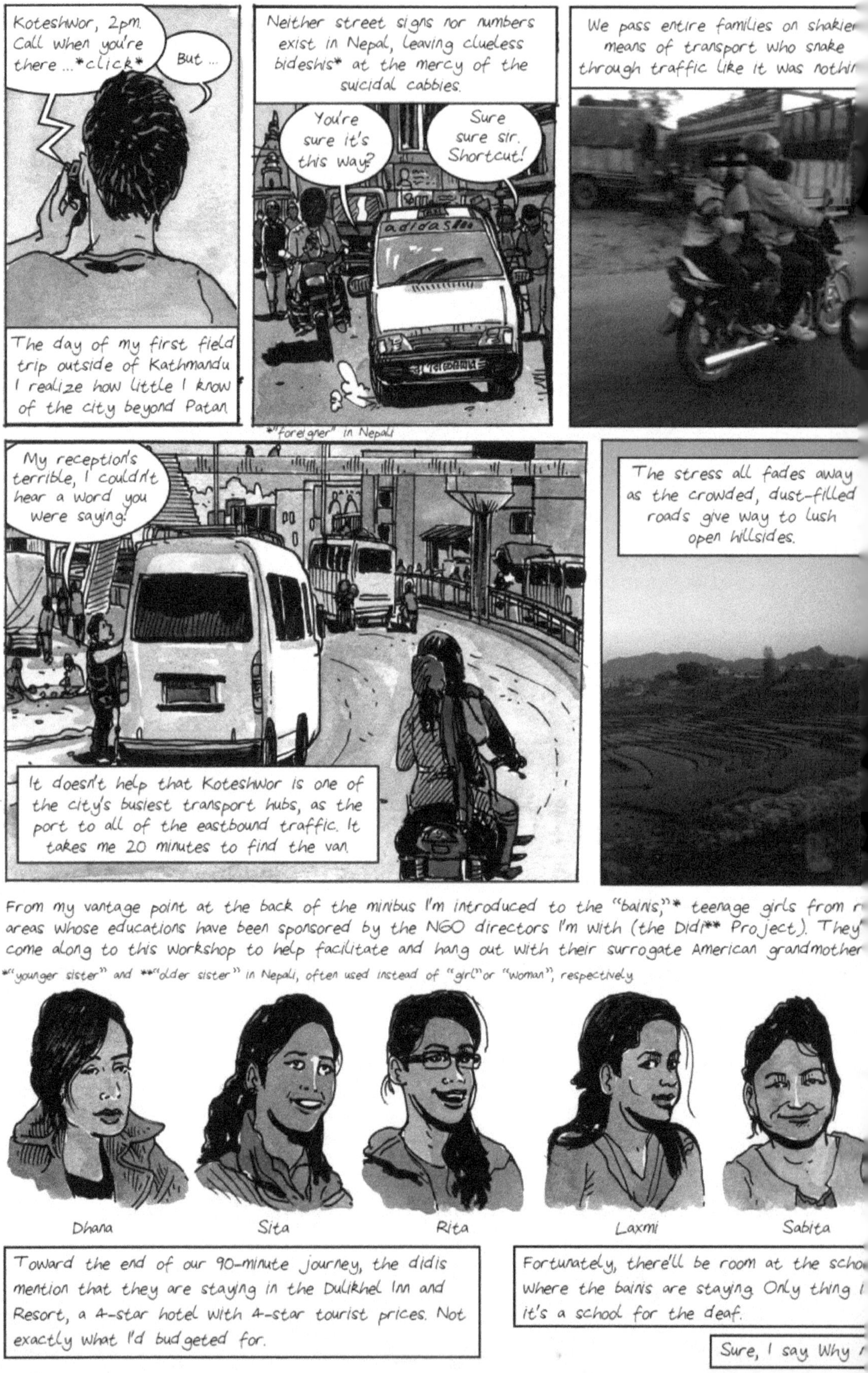

Koteshwor, 2pm. Call when you're there ...*click*
But ...
The day of my first field trip outside of Kathmandu I realize how little I know of the city beyond Patan
Neither street signs nor numbers exist in Nepal, leaving clueless bideshis* at the mercy of the suicidal cabbies.
You're sure it's this way?
Sure sure sir. Shortcut!
adidas
*"foreigner" in Nepali
We pass entire families on shakie means of transport who snake through traffic like it was nothi
My reception's terrible, I couldn't hear a word you were saying!
It doesn't help that Koteshwor is one of the city's busiest transport hubs, as the port to all of the eastbound traffic. It takes me 20 minutes to find the van.
The stress all fades away as the crowded, dust-filled roads give way to lush open hillsides.
From my vantage point at the back of the minibus I'm introduced to the "bainis,"* teenage girls from r areas whose educations have been sponsored by the NGO directors I'm with (the Didi** Project). They come along to this workshop to help facilitate and hang out with their surrogate American grandmother
*"younger sister" and **"older sister" in Nepali, often used instead of "girl" or "woman", respectively
Dhana
Sita
Rita
Laxmi
Sabita
Toward the end of our 90-minute journey, the didis mention that they are staying in the Dulikhel Inn and Resort, a 4-star hotel with 4-star tourist prices. Not exactly what I'd budgeted for.
Fortunately, there'll be room at the scho where the bainis are staying. Only thing i it's a school for the deaf.
Sure, I say. Why

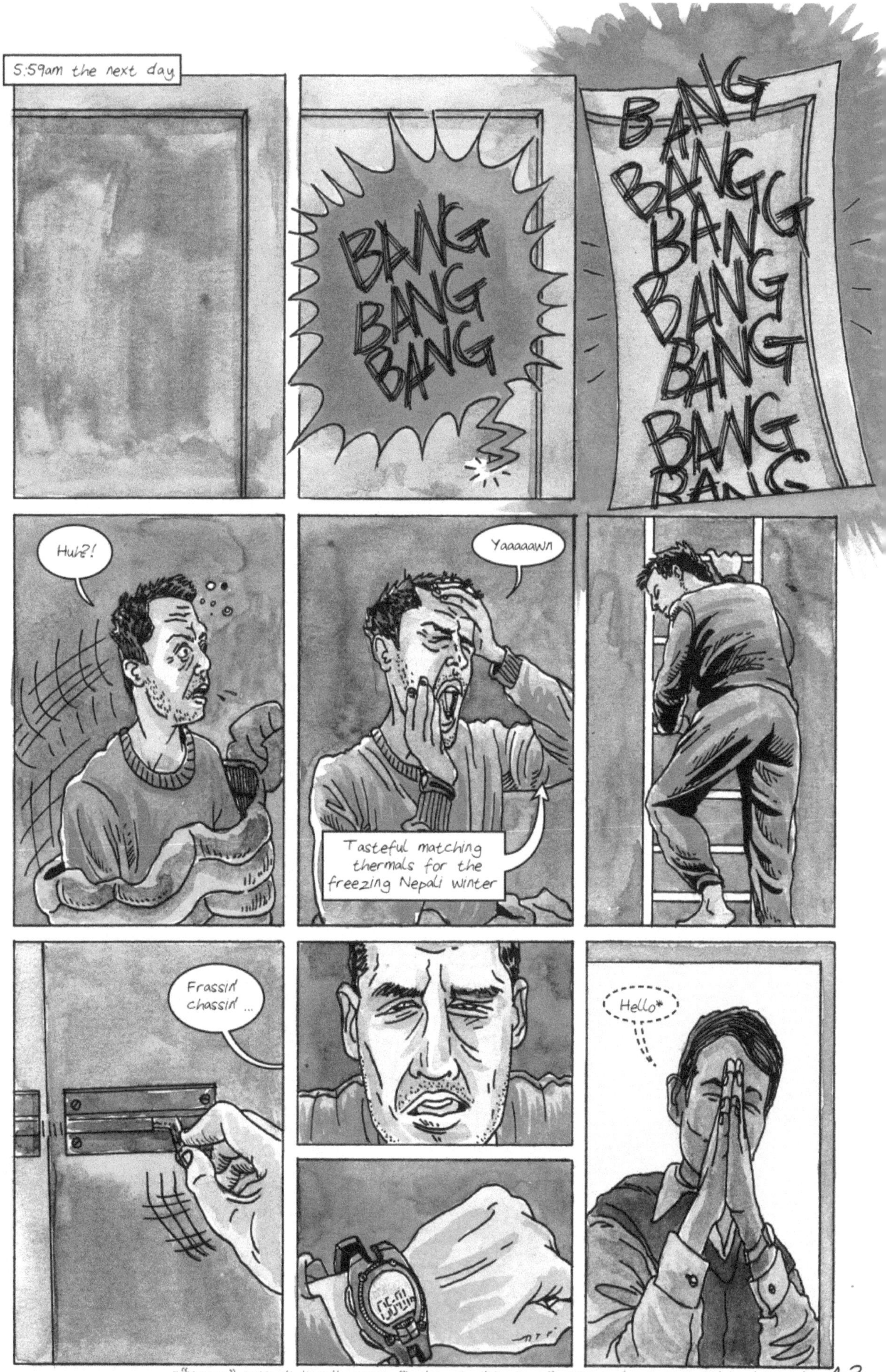

5:59am the next day.
BANG BANG BANG
BANG BANG BANG BANG BANG BANG BANG
Huh?!
Yaaaaawn
Tasteful matching thermals for the freezing Nepali winter
Frassin' chassin' ...
Hello*

* "Namaste" in Nepali, literally meaning "I salute the divine in you," which is always accompanied by joining palms.

One of the downsides about staying at a school for the deaf...

Why so early?

... is that you're the only one on wake-up duty.

Still, it doesn't detract from the joy of hanging out with the kids there ...

(spelling the sign language alphabet for me so we can understand each other)

... who are fascinated by this strange white guy (oglo manche) twice their size.

Endlessly patient, they quickly give me the tools to get my point across:

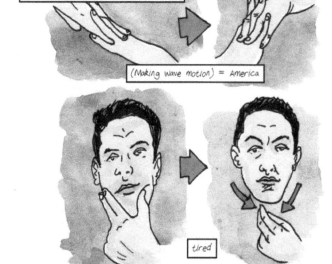

(Making wave motion) = America

tired

confused

clever

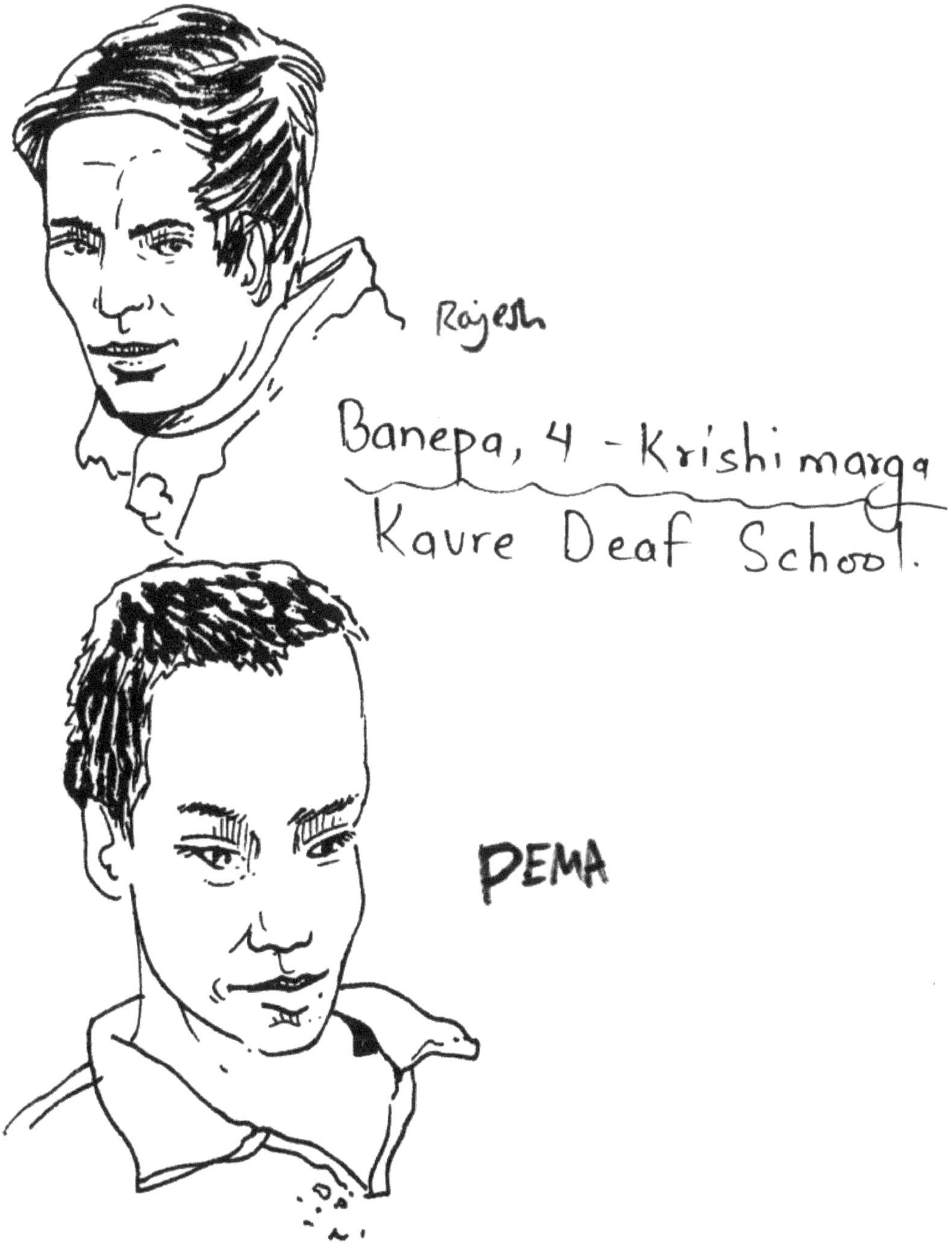
Rajesh
Banepa, 4 - Krishimarga
Kaure Deaf School.
PEMA

Once again, live sketching builds a bridge between us that no words would have been able to.

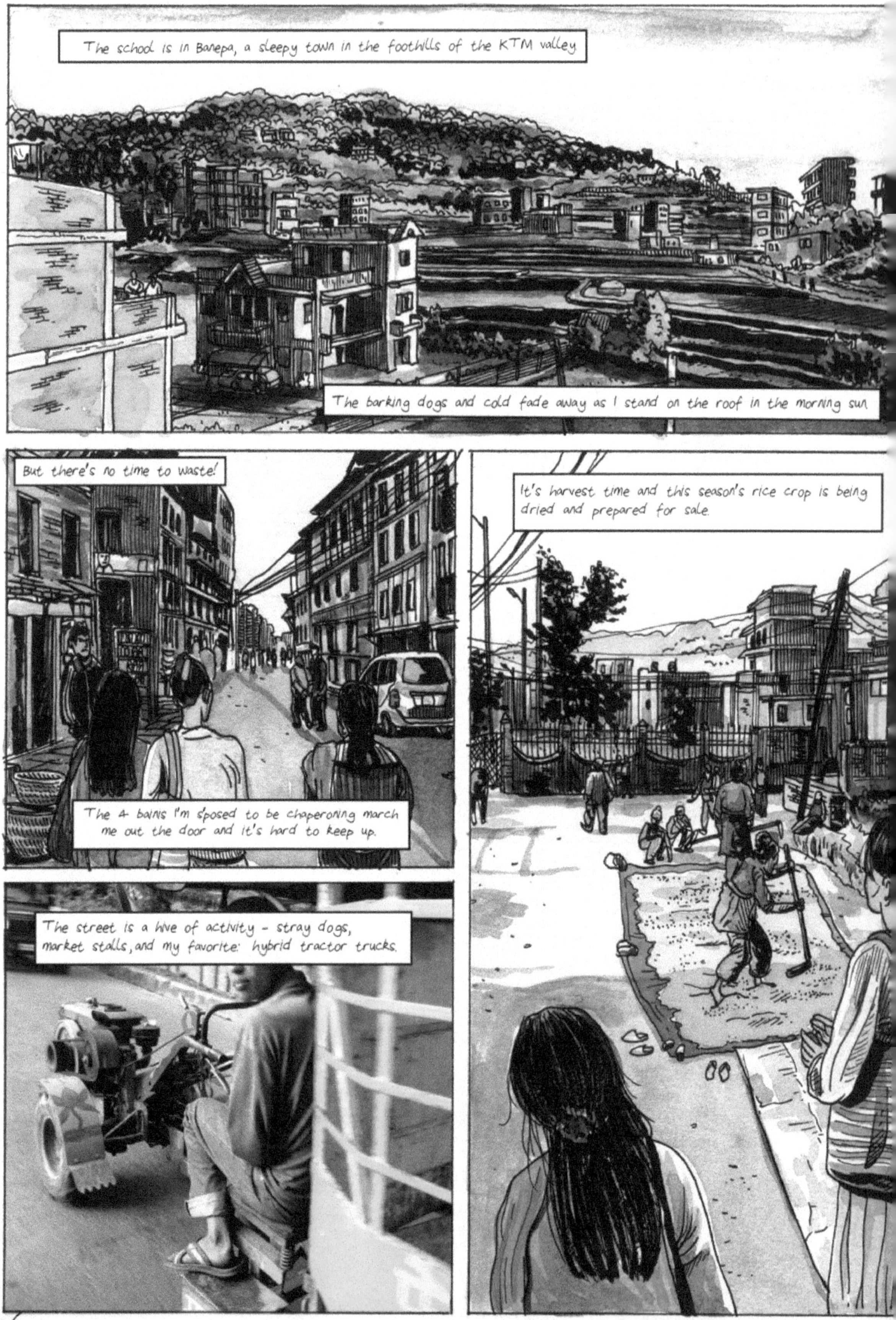
The school is in Banepa, a sleepy town in the foothills of the KTM valley.
The barking dogs and cold fade away as I stand on the roof in the morning sun
But there's no time to waste!
The 4 bainis I'm s'posed to be chaperoning march me out the door and it's hard to keep up.
The street is a hive of activity - stray dogs, market stalls, and my favorite: hybrid tractor trucks.
It's harvest time and this season's rice crop is being dried and prepared for sale.

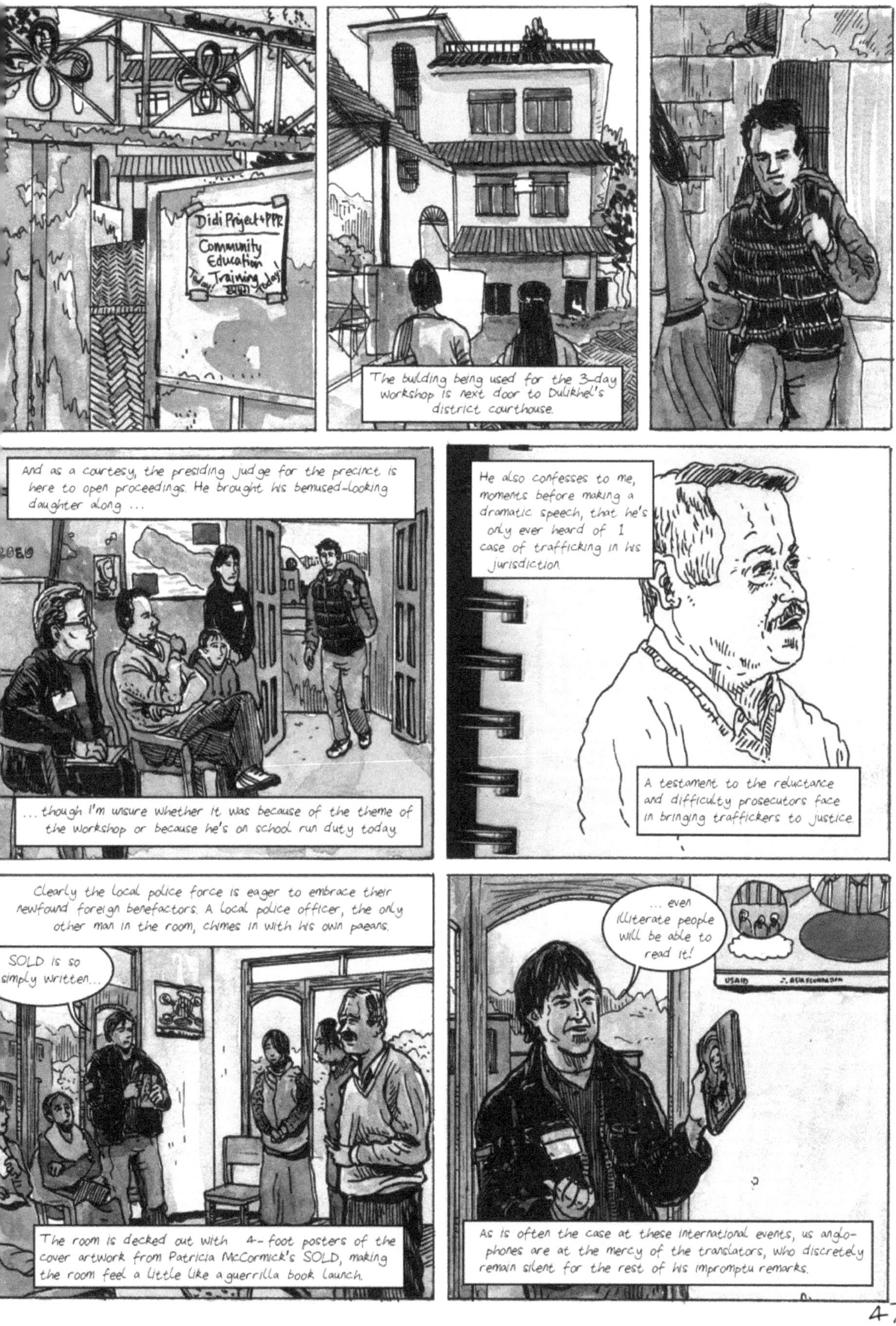
Didi Project+PPR
Community Education Training
Today! Today!
The building being used for the 3-day workshop is next door to Dulikhel's district courthouse.
And as a courtesy, the presiding judge for the precinct is here to open proceedings. He brought his bemused-looking daughter along ...
... though I'm unsure whether it was because of the theme of the workshop or because he's on school run duty today.
He also confesses to me, moments before making a dramatic speech, that he's only ever heard of 1 case of trafficking in his jurisdiction.
A testament to the reluctance and difficulty prosecutors face in bringing traffickers to justice.
Clearly the local police force is eager to embrace their newfound foreign benefactors. A local police officer, the only other man in the room, chimes in with his own paeans.
SOLD is so simply written...
The room is decked out with 4-foot posters of the cover artwork from Patricia McCormick's SOLD, making the room feel a little like a guerrilla book launch.
... even illiterate people will be able to read it!
USAID
As is often the case at these international events, us anglophones are at the mercy of the translators, who discretely remain silent for the rest of his impromptu remarks.

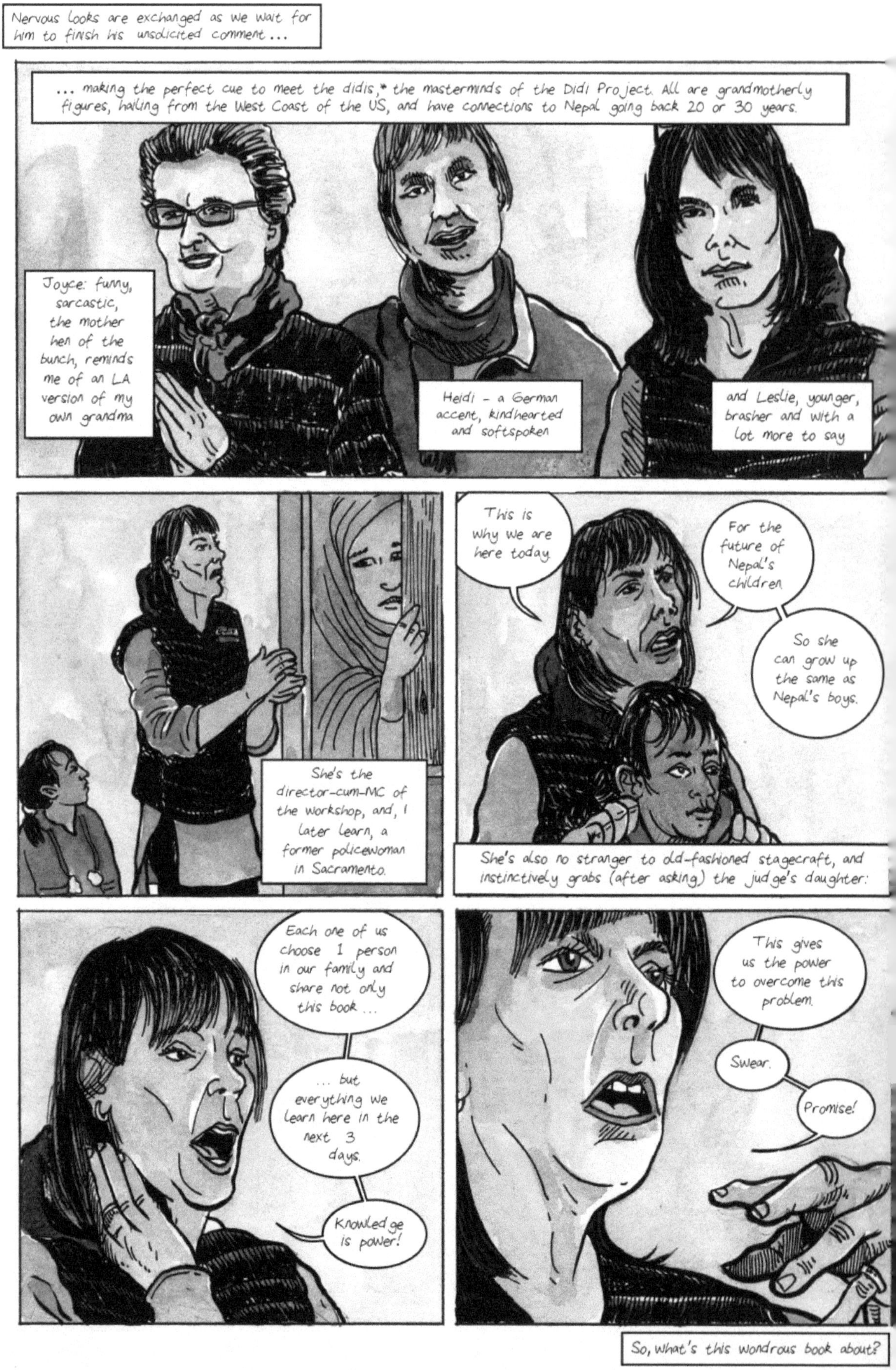
Nervous looks are exchanged as we wait for him to finish his unsolicited comment...
... making the perfect cue to meet the didis,* the masterminds of the Didi Project. All are grandmotherly figures, hailing from the West Coast of the US, and have connections to Nepal going back 20 or 30 years.
Joyce: funny, sarcastic, the mother hen of the bunch, reminds me of an LA version of my own grandma
Heidi - a German accent, kindhearted and softspoken
and Leslie, younger, brasher and with a lot more to say
She's the director-cum-MC of the workshop, and, I later learn, a former policewoman in Sacramento.
This is why we are here today.
For the future of Nepal's children
So she can grow up the same as Nepal's boys.
She's also no stranger to old-fashioned stagecraft, and instinctively grabs (after asking) the judge's daughter:
Each one of us choose 1 person in our family and share not only this book...
... but everything we learn here in the next 3 days.
Knowledge is power!
This gives us the power to overcome this problem.
Swear.
Promise!
So, what's this wondrous book about?

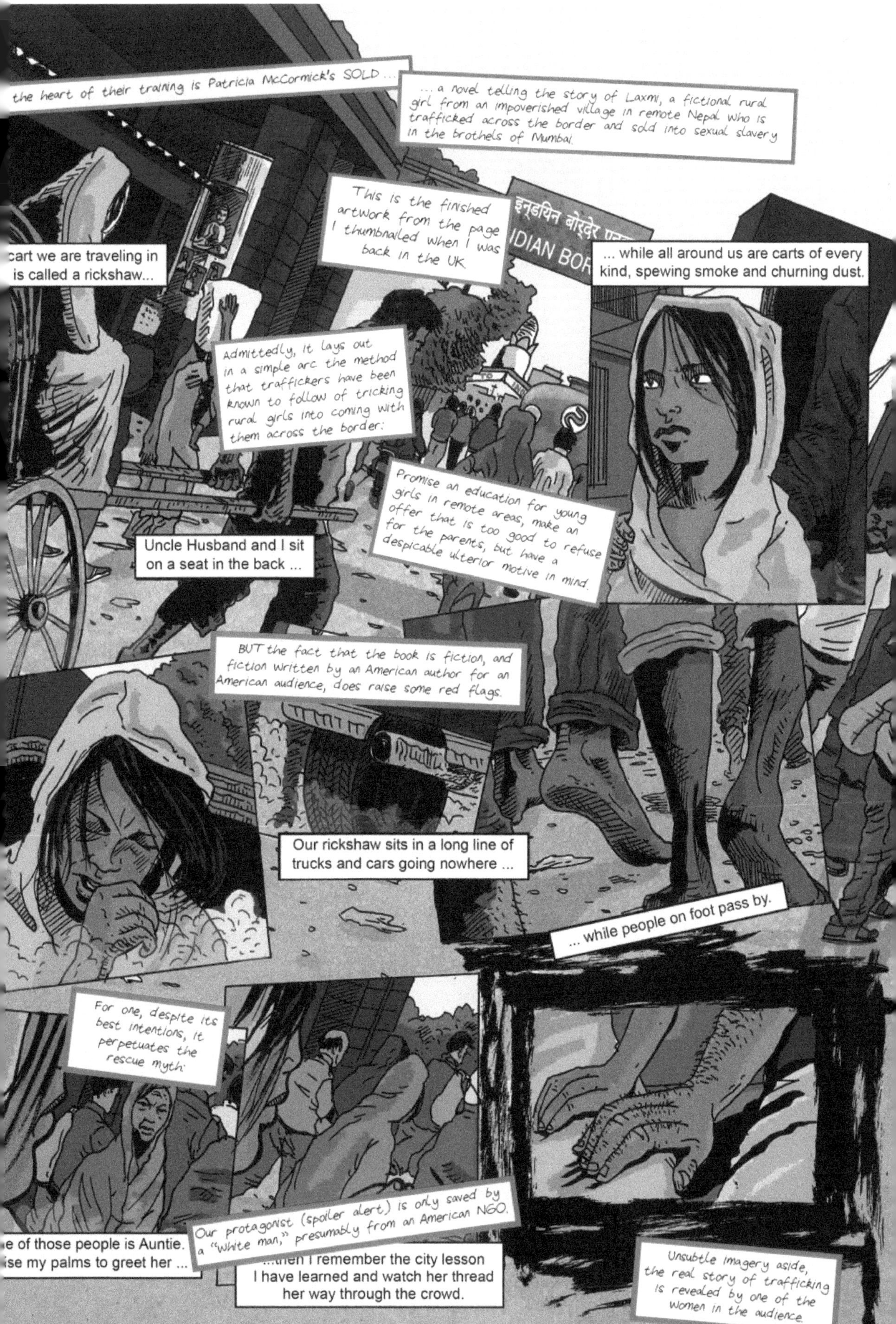

the heart of their training is Patricia McCormick's SOLD ...
... a novel telling the story of Laxmi, a fictional rural girl from an impoverished village in remote Nepal who is trafficked across the border and sold into sexual slavery in the brothels of Mumbai.
This is the finished artwork from the page I thumbnailed when I was back in the UK
cart we are traveling in is called a rickshaw...
IDIAN BOR
... while all around us are carts of every kind, spewing smoke and churning dust.
Admittedly, it lays out in a simple arc the method that traffickers have been known to follow of tricking rural girls into coming with them across the border:
Promise an education for young girls in remote areas, make an offer that is too good to refuse for the parents, but have a despicable ulterior motive in mind.
Uncle Husband and I sit on a seat in the back ...
BUT the fact that the book is fiction, and fiction written by an American author for an American audience, does raise some red flags.
Our rickshaw sits in a long line of trucks and cars going nowhere ...
... while people on foot pass by.
For one, despite its best intentions, it perpetuates the rescue myth:
Our protagonist (spoiler alert) is only saved by a "white man," presumably from an American NGO.
e of those people is Auntie.
se my palms to greet her ...
...then I remember the city lesson I have learned and watch her thread her way through the crowd.
Unsubtle imagery aside, the real story of trafficking is revealed by one of the women in the audience.

EVEN SOME OF THE NEW EDUCATED PEOPLE WANT TO WORK ABROAD — THOUGH THEY KNOW THE RISKS!

PEOPLE MAKE JOKES, SAYING: "LOOK AT YOU WORKING WITH A BASKET ON YOUR BACK!"

Up until this point the testimonials have been anecdotal to say the least.

But then a quiet, unassuming woman called Laxmi steps up.

I was 14 when I was sold.

(What follows are direct quotes from her translator.)

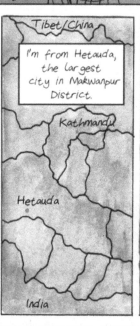

Tibet/China

I'm from Hetauda, the largest city in Makwanpur District.

Kathmandu

Hetauda

India

I wasn't given any education because of the situation in the family.

So I used to take the livestock out.

Sister, where's your home?

I didn't answer.

I was afraid.

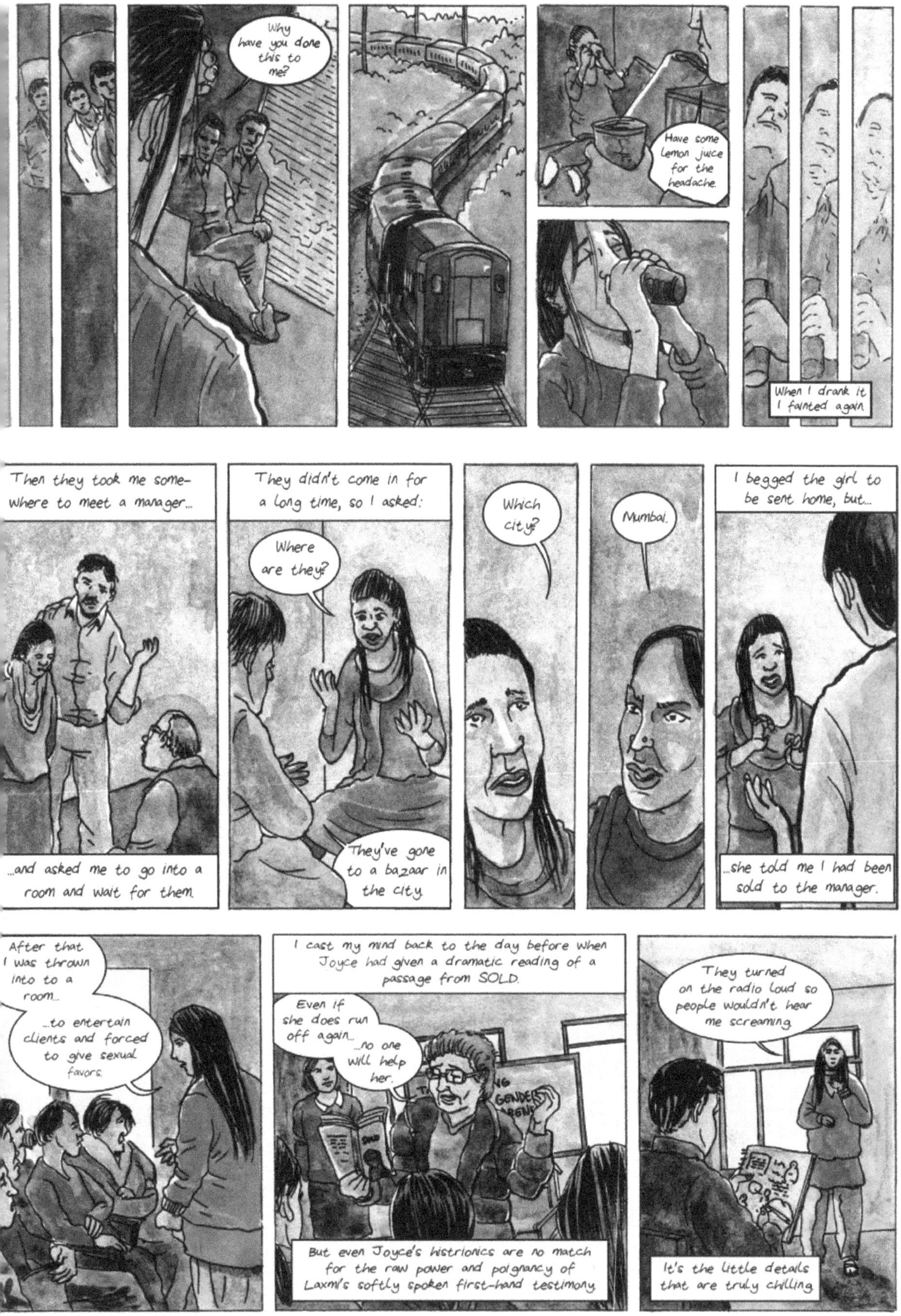

Why have you done this to me?
Have some lemon juice for the headache.
When I drank it I fainted again
Then they took me somewhere to meet a manager...
...and asked me to go into a room and wait for them.
They didn't come in for a long time, so I asked:
Where are they?
They've gone to a bazaar in the city.
Which city?
Mumbai.
I begged the girl to be sent home, but...
...she told me I had been sold to the manager.
After that I was thrown into to a room...
...to entertain clients and forced to give sexual favors.
I cast my mind back to the day before when Joyce had given a dramatic reading of a passage from SOLD.
Even if she does run off again...
...no one will help her.
But even Joyce's histrionics are no match for the raw power and poignancy of Laxmi's softly spoken first-hand testimony.
They turned on the radio loud so people wouldn't hear me screaming.
It's the little details that are truly chilling.

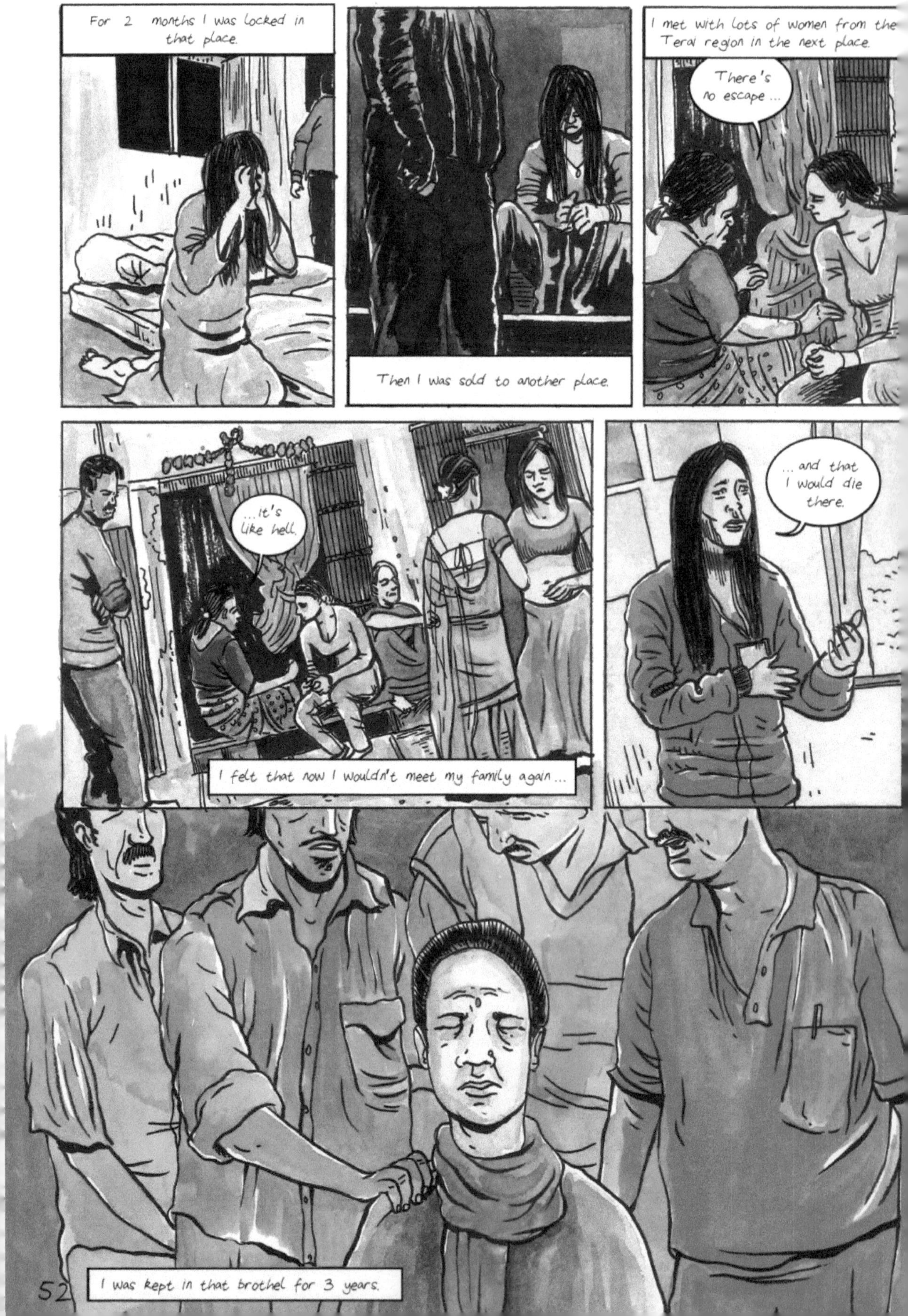
For 2 months I was locked in that place.
Then I was sold to another place.
I met with lots of women from the Terai region in the next place.
There's no escape ...
... it's like hell.
I felt that now I wouldn't meet my family again ...
... and that I would die there.
I was kept in that brothel for 3 years.

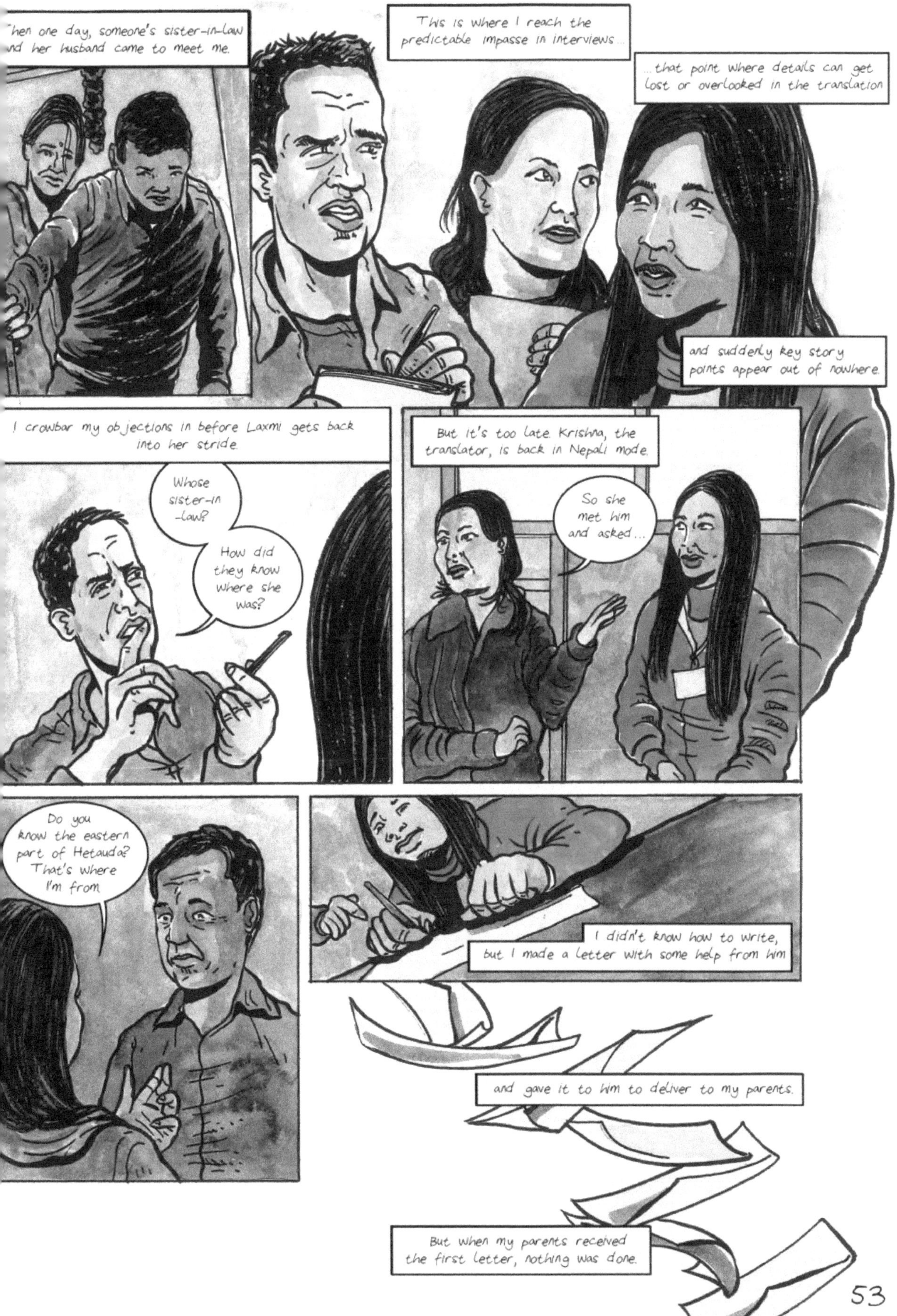
Then one day, someone's sister-in-law and her husband came to meet me.
This is where I reach the predictable impasse in interviews...
...that point where details can get lost or overlooked in the translation
and suddenly key story points appear out of nowhere.
I crowbar my objections in before Laxmi gets back into her stride.
Whose sister-in-law?
How did they know where she was?
But it's too late. Krishna, the translator, is back in Nepali mode.
So she met him and asked...
Do you know the eastern part of Hetauda? That's where I'm from
I didn't know how to write, but I made a letter with some help from him
and gave it to him to deliver to my parents.
But when my parents received the first letter, nothing was done.

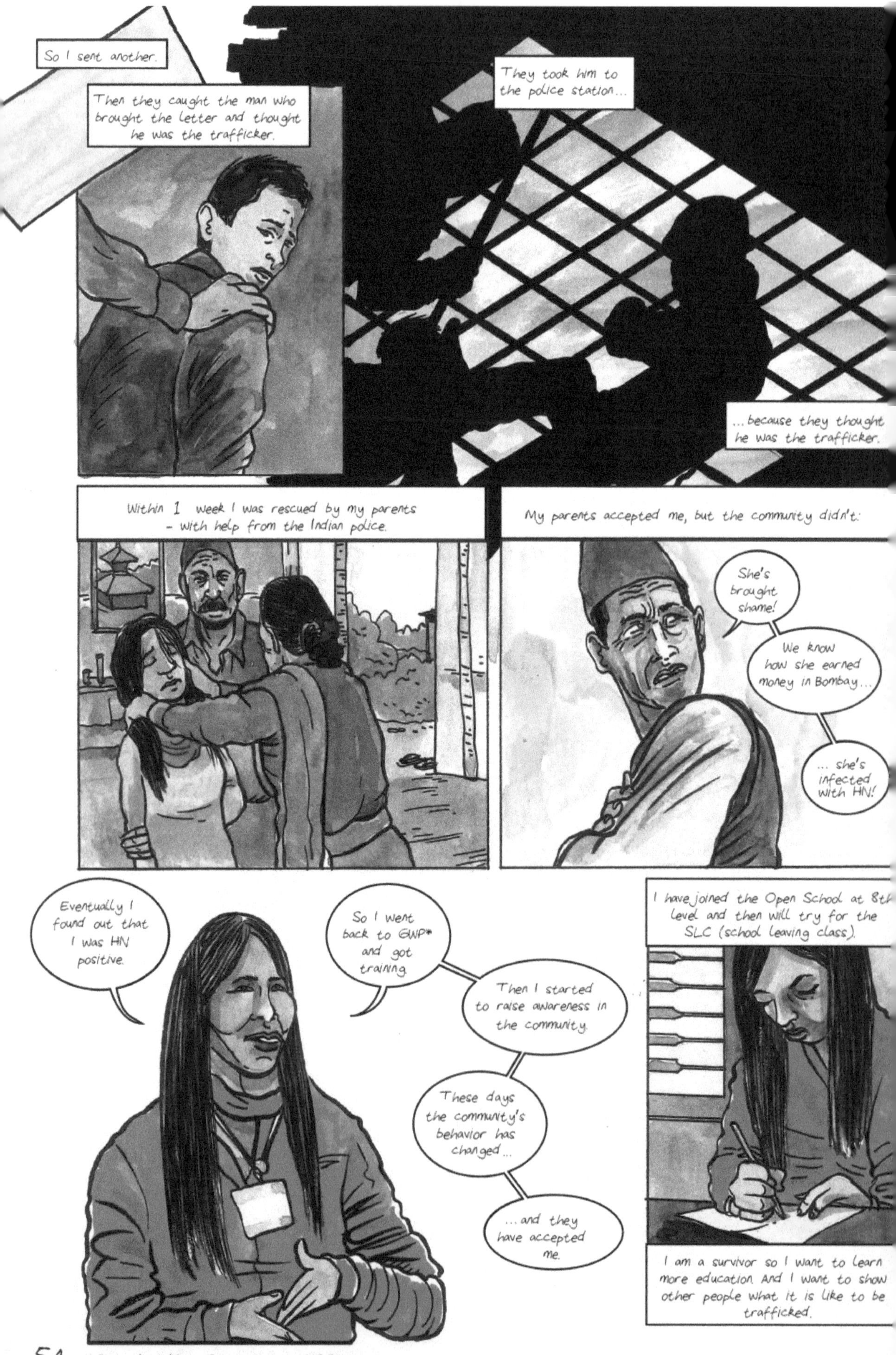
So I sent another.
Then they caught the man who brought the letter and thought he was the trafficker.
They took him to the police station...
...because they thought he was the trafficker.
Within 1 week I was rescued by my parents - with help from the Indian police.
My parents accepted me, but the community didn't:
She's brought shame!
We know how she earned money in Bombay...
... she's infected with HIV!
Eventually I found out that I was HIV positive.
So I went back to GWP* and got training.
Then I started to raise awareness in the community.
These days the community's behavior has changed...
...and they have accepted me.
I have joined the Open School at 8th level and then will try for the SLC (school leaving class).
I am a survivor so I want to learn more education. And I want to show other people what it is like to be trafficked.

 *General Welfare Pratisthan, an NGO

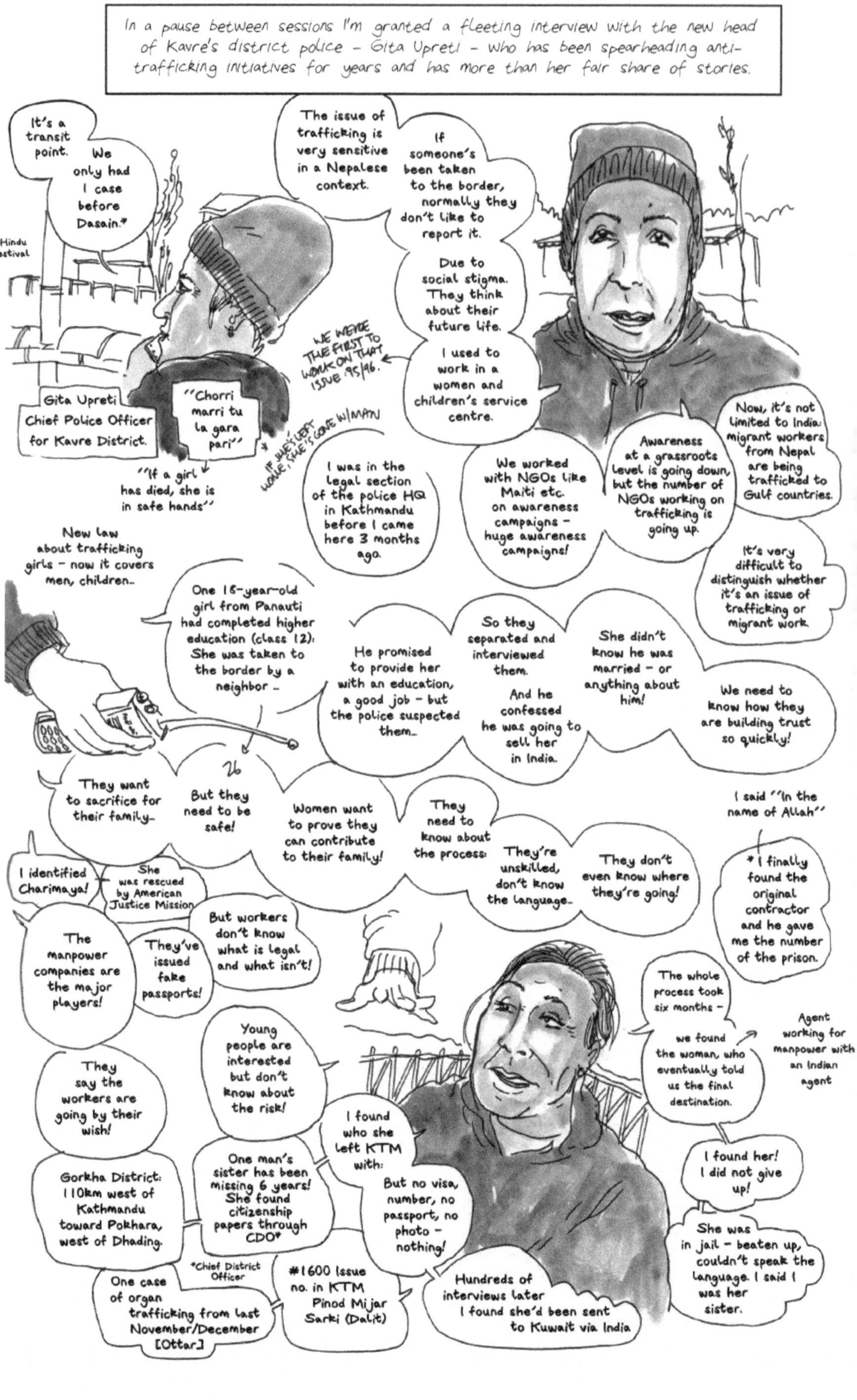
In a pause between sessions I'm granted a fleeting interview with the new head of Kavre's district police – Gita Upreti – who has been spearheading anti-trafficking initiatives for years and has more than her fair share of stories.
It's a transit point.
We only had 1 case before Dasain.*
*Hindu festival
The issue of trafficking is very sensitive in a Nepalese context.
If someone's been taken to the border, normally they don't like to report it.
Due to social stigma. They think about their future life.
I used to work in a women and children's service centre.
WE WERE THE FIRST TO WORK ON THAT ISSUE 95/96.
Gita Upreti Chief Police Officer for Kavre District.
"Chorri marri tu la gara pari"
* IF SHE'S LEFT HOME, SHE'S GONE W/MAN
"If a girl has died, she is in safe hands"
I was in the legal section of the police HQ in Kathmandu before I came here 3 months ago.
We worked with NGOs like Maiti etc. on awareness campaigns – huge awareness campaigns!
Awareness at a grassroots level is going down, but the number of NGOs working on trafficking is going up.
Now, it's not limited to India: migrant workers from Nepal are being trafficked to Gulf countries.
It's very difficult to distinguish whether it's an issue of trafficking or migrant work.
New law about trafficking girls – now it covers men, children...
One 18-year-old girl from Panauti had completed higher education (class 12). She was taken to the border by a neighbor...
He promised to provide her with an education, a good job – but the police suspected them...
So they separated and interviewed them.
And he confessed he was going to sell her in India.
She didn't know he was married – or anything about him!
We need to know how they are building trust so quickly!
26
They want to sacrifice for their family...
But they need to be safe!
Women want to prove they can contribute to their family!
They need to know about the process.
They're unskilled, don't know the language...
They don't even know where they're going!
I said "In the name of Allah"
* I finally found the original contractor and he gave me the number of the prison.
I identified Charimaya!
She was rescued by American Justice Mission
The manpower companies are the major players!
They've issued fake passports!
But workers don't know what is legal and what isn't!
The whole process took six months –
we found the woman, who eventually told us the final destination.
Agent working for manpower with an Indian agent
Young people are interested but don't know about the risk!
They say the workers are going by their wish!
I found who she left KTM with.
But no visa number, no passport, no photo – nothing!
I found her! I did not give up!
She was in jail – beaten up, couldn't speak the language. I said I was her sister.
Gorkha District: 110km west of Kathmandu toward Pokhara, west of Dhading.
One man's sister has been missing 6 years! She found citizenship papers through CDO*
*Chief District Officer
One case of organ trafficking from last November/December [Ottar]
#1600 Issue no. in KTM Pinod Mijar Sarki (Dalit)
Hundreds of interviews later I found she'd been sent to Kuwait via India

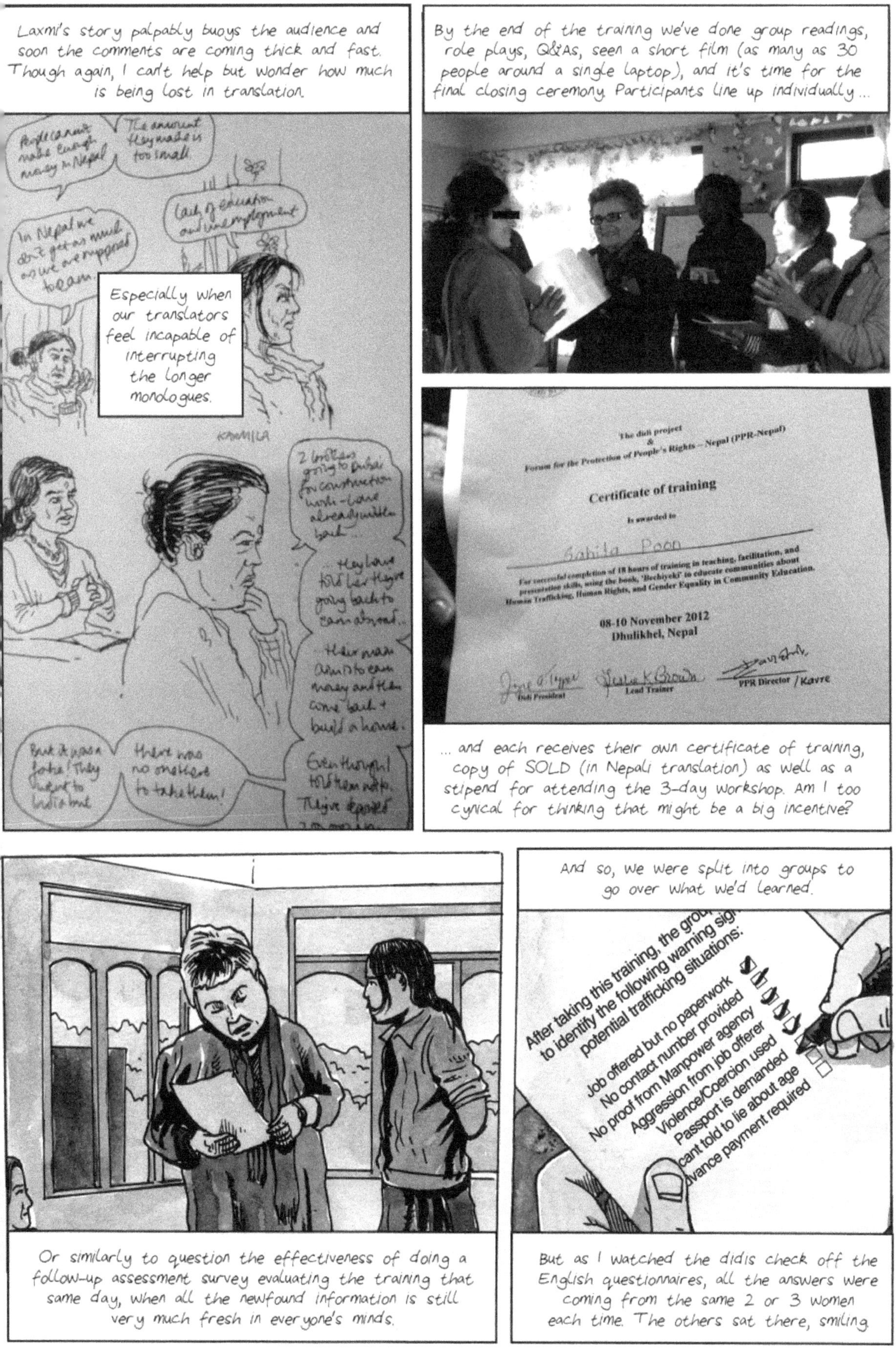
Laxmi's story palpably buoys the audience and soon the comments are coming thick and fast. Though again, I can't help but wonder how much is being lost in translation.
The amount they make is too small.
Lack of education and unemployment
Especially when our translators feel incapable of interrupting the longer monologues.
KAMILA
... their main aim is to earn money and then come back + build a house.
There was no one there to take them!
By the end of the training we've done group readings, role plays, Q&As, seen a short film (as many as 30 people around a single laptop), and it's time for the final closing ceremony. Participants line up individually ...
The didi project
&
Forum for the Protection of People's Rights – Nepal (PPR-Nepal)
Certificate of training
is awarded to
Sabita Poon
For successful completion of 18 hours of training in teaching, facilitation, and presentation skills, using the book, 'Bechiyeki' to educate communities about Human Trafficking, Human Rights, and Gender Equality in Community Education.
08-10 November 2012
Dhulikhel, Nepal
Didi President
Lead Trainer
PPR Director / Kavre
... and each receives their own certificate of training, copy of SOLD (in Nepali translation) as well as a stipend for attending the 3-day workshop. Am I too cynical for thinking that might be a big incentive?
And so, we were split into groups to go over what we'd learned.
After taking this training, the group ... to identify the following warning sig... potential trafficking situations:
Job offered but no paperwork
No contact number provided
No proof from Manpower agency
Aggression from job offerer
Violence/Coercion used
Passport is demanded
...cant told to lie about age
...vance payment required
Or similarly to question the effectiveness of doing a follow-up assessment survey evaluating the training that same day, when all the newfound information is still very much fresh in everyone's minds.
But as I watched the didis check off the English questionnaires, all the answers were coming from the same 2 or 3 women each time. The others sat there, smiling.

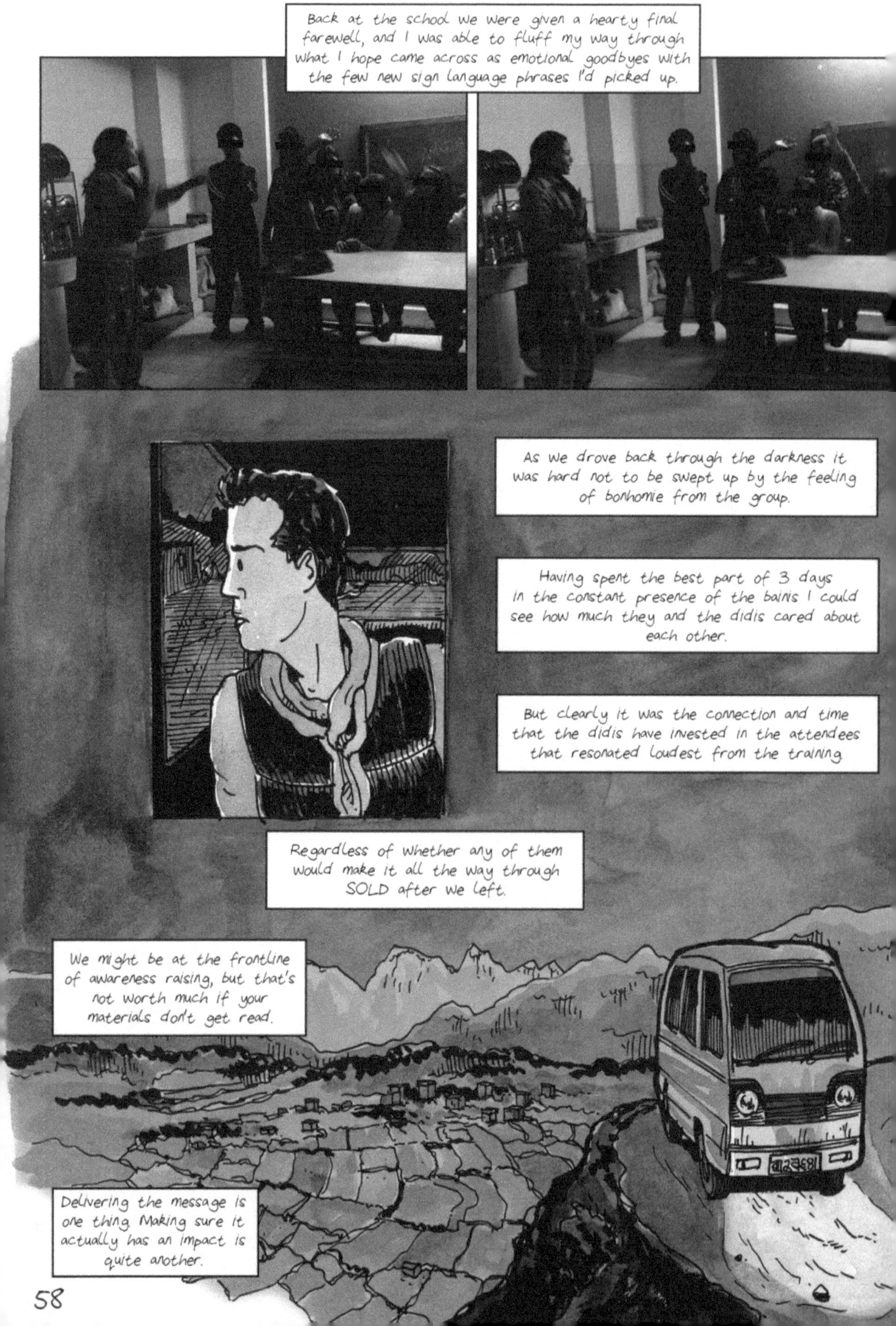
Back at the school we were given a hearty final farewell, and I was able to fluff my way through what I hope came across as emotional goodbyes with the few new sign language phrases I'd picked up.
As we drove back through the darkness it was hard not to be swept up by the feeling of bonhomie from the group.
Having spent the best part of 3 days in the constant presence of the bainis I could see how much they and the didis cared about each other.
But clearly it was the connection and time that the didis have invested in the attendees that resonated loudest from the training
Regardless of whether any of them would make it all the way through SOLD after we left.
We might be at the frontline of awareness raising, but that's not worth much if your materials don't get read.
Delivering the message is one thing. Making sure it actually has an impact is quite another.

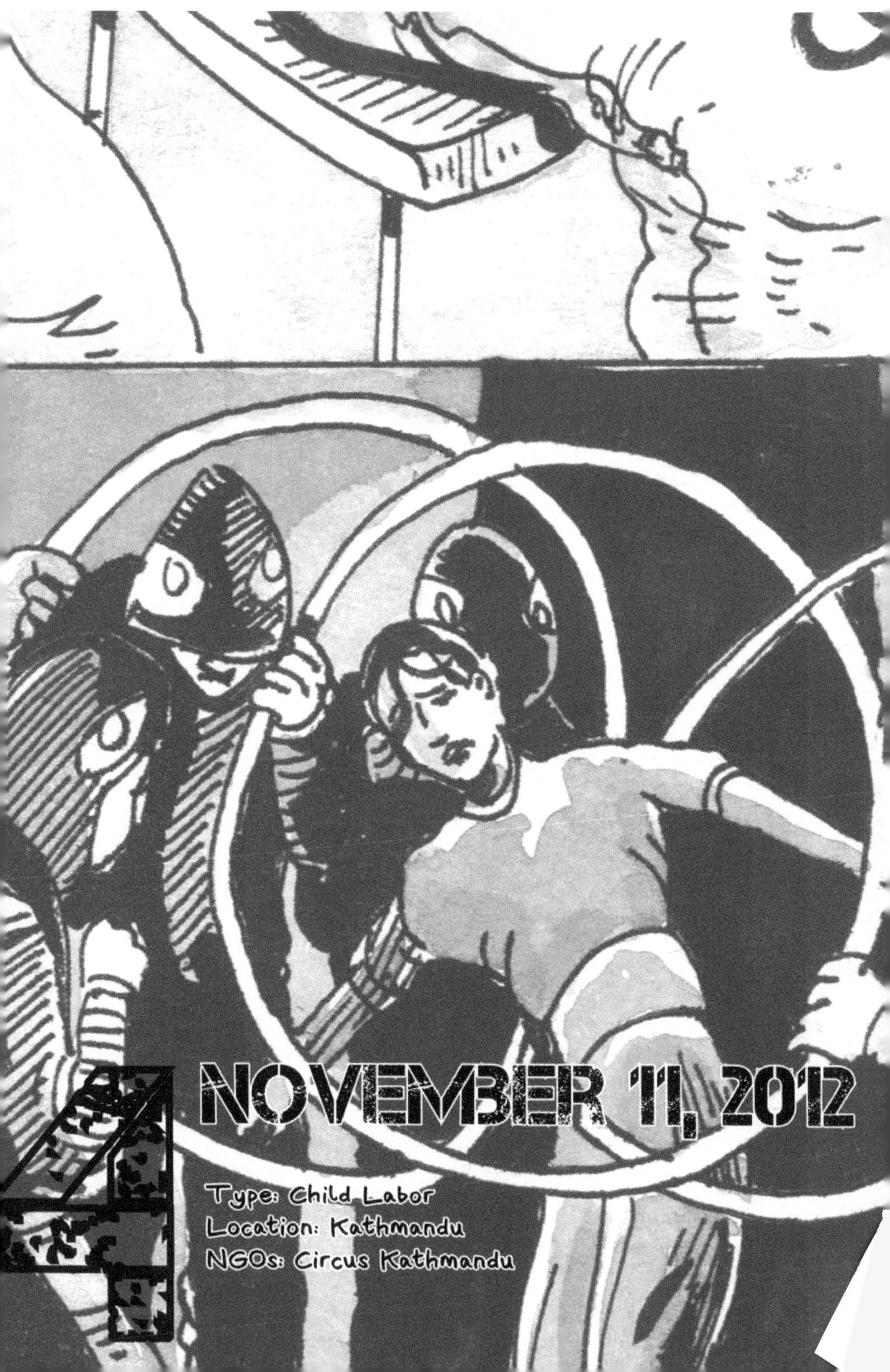

4 NOVEMBER 11, 2012

Type: Child Labor
Location: Kathmandu
NGOs: Circus Kathmandu

CIRCUS KATHMANDU

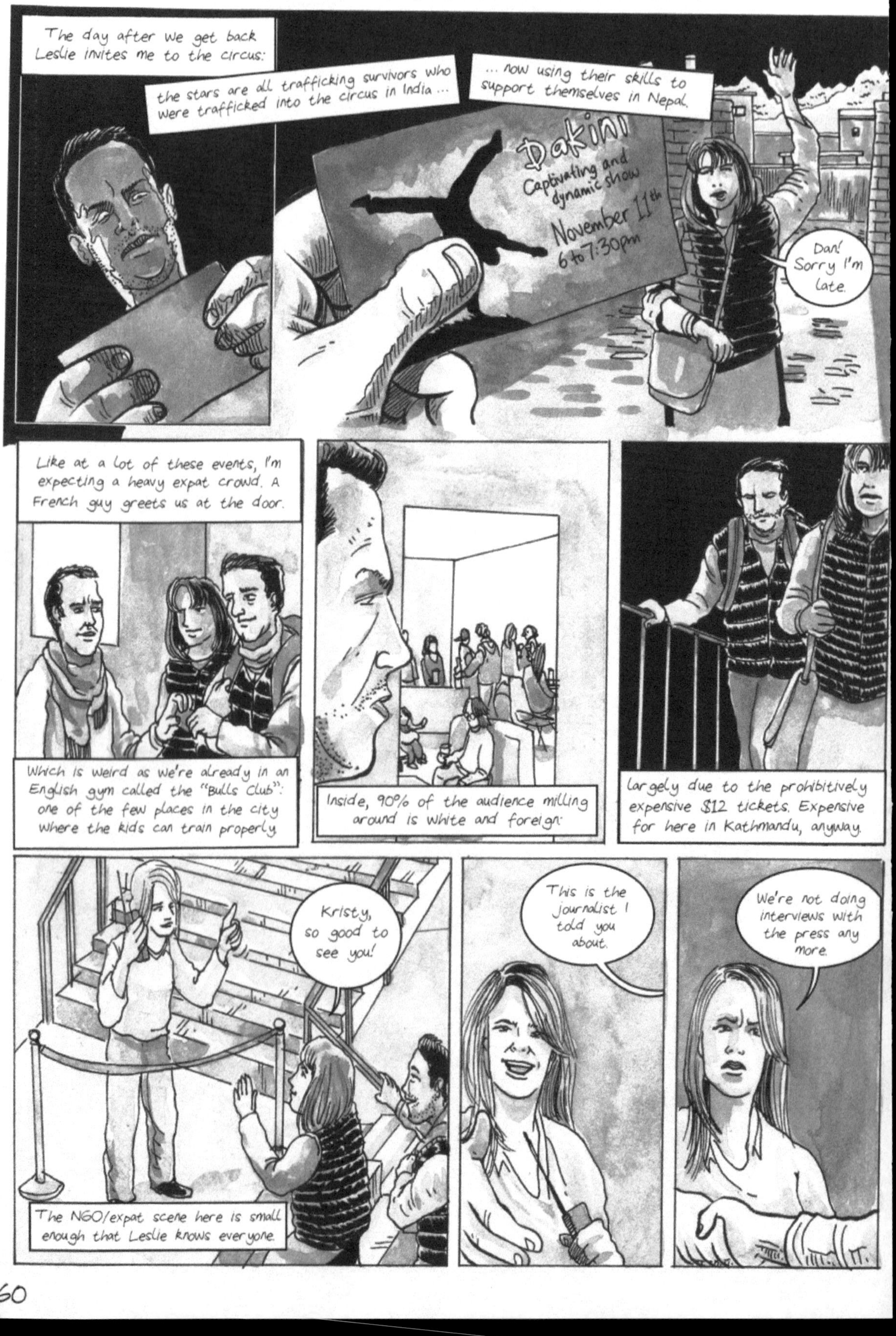
The day after we get back Leslie invites me to the circus:
the stars are all trafficking survivors who were trafficked into the circus in India ...
... now using their skills to support themselves in Nepal.
Dakini
Captivating and dynamic show
November 11th
6 to 7:30pm
Dan! Sorry I'm late.
Like at a lot of these events, I'm expecting a heavy expat crowd. A French guy greets us at the door.
Which is weird as we're already in an English gym called the "Bulls Club": one of the few places in the city where the kids can train properly.
Inside, 90% of the audience milling around is white and foreign:
largely due to the prohibitively expensive $12 tickets. Expensive for here in Kathmandu, anyway.
Kristy, so good to see you!
The NGO/expat scene here is small enough that Leslie knows everyone.
This is the journalist I told you about.
We're not doing interviews with the press any more.

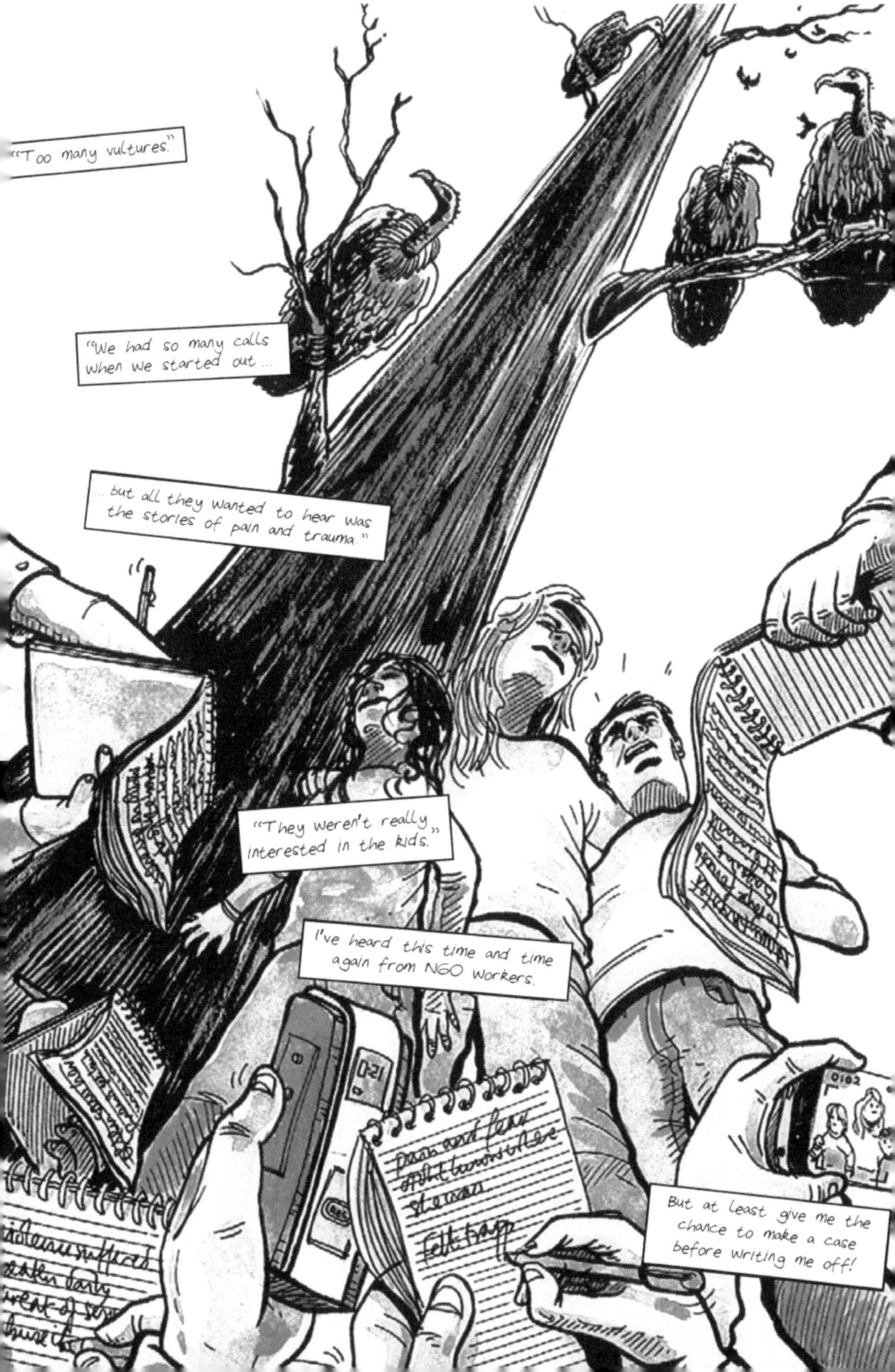
"Too many vultures."
"We had so many calls when we started out ...
... but all they wanted to hear was the stories of pain and trauma."
"They weren't really interested in the kids."
I've heard this time and time again from NGO workers.
But at least give me the chance to make a case before writing me off!

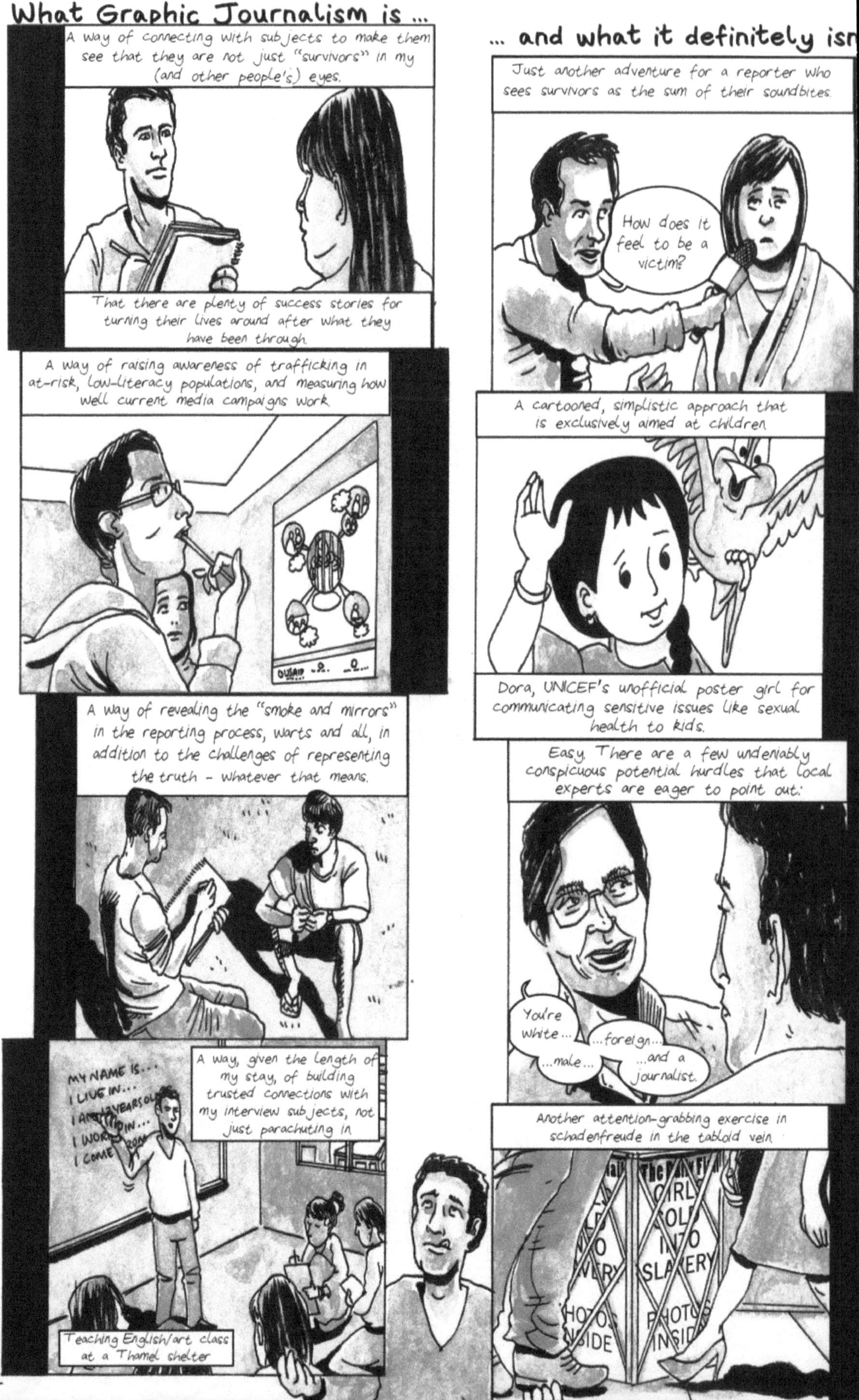
What Graphic Journalism is ...
A way of connecting with subjects to make them see that they are not just "survivors" in my (and other people's) eyes.
That there are plenty of success stories for turning their lives around after what they have been through.
A way of raising awareness of trafficking in at-risk, low-literacy populations, and measuring how well current media campaigns work.
A way of revealing the "smoke and mirrors" in the reporting process, warts and all, in addition to the challenges of representing the truth - whatever that means.
MY NAME IS...
I LIVE IN...
A way, given the length of my stay, of building trusted connections with my interview subjects, not just parachuting in.
Teaching English/art class at a Thamel shelter
... and what it definitely isn
Just another adventure for a reporter who sees survivors as the sum of their soundbites.
How does it feel to be a victim?
A cartooned, simplistic approach that is exclusively aimed at children
Dora, UNICEF's unofficial poster girl for communicating sensitive issues like sexual health to kids.
Easy. There are a few undeniably conspicuous potential hurdles that local experts are eager to point out:
You're white...
...foreign...
...male...
...and a journalist.
Another attention-grabbing exercise in schadenfreude in the tabloid vein
GIRL SOLD INTO SLAVERY
PHOTOS INSIDE

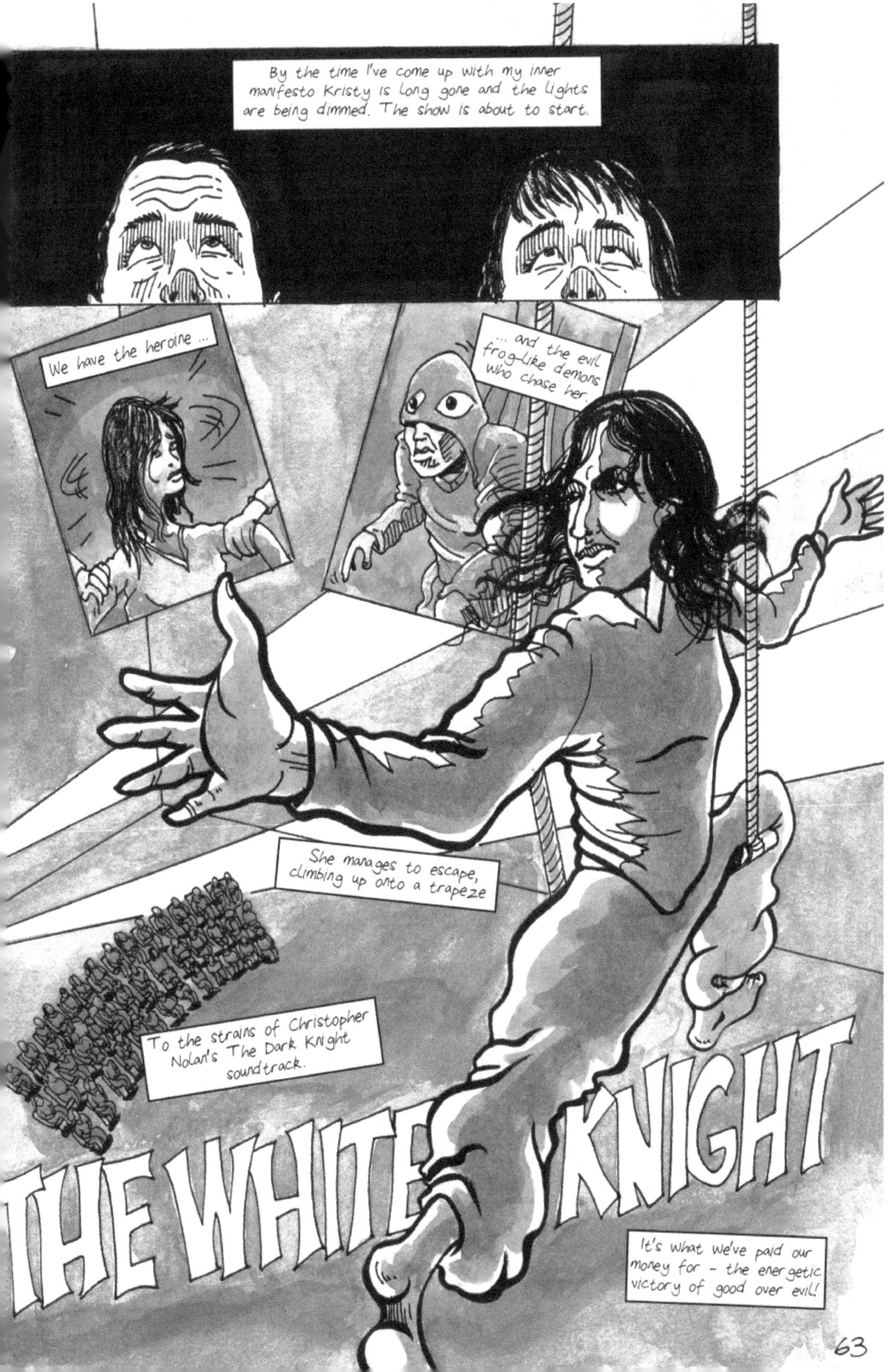

By the time I've come up with my inner manifesto Kristy is long gone and the lights are being dimmed. The show is about to start.
We have the heroine ...
... and the evil frog-like demons who chase her.
She manages to escape, climbing up onto a trapeze
To the strains of Christopher Nolan's The Dark Knight soundtrack.
THE WHITE KNIGHT
It's what we've paid our money for – the energetic victory of good over evil!

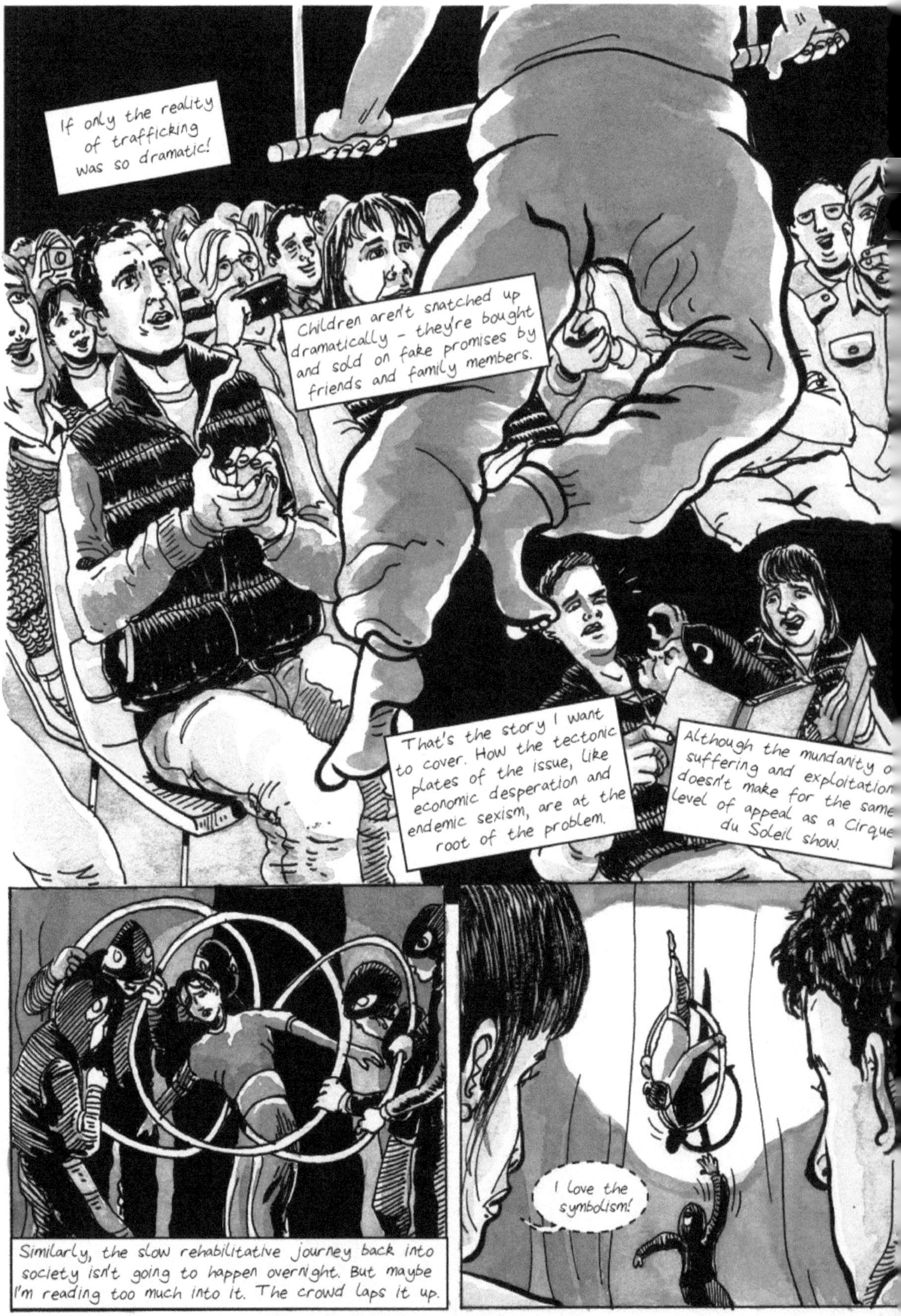

If only the reality of trafficking was so dramatic!
Children aren't snatched up dramatically – they're bought and sold on fake promises by friends and family members.
That's the story I want to cover. How the tectonic plates of the issue, like economic desperation and endemic sexism, are at the root of the problem.
Although the mundanity of suffering and exploitation doesn't make for the same level of appeal as a Cirque du Soleil show.
Similarly, the slow rehabilitative journey back into society isn't going to happen overnight. But maybe I'm reading too much into it. The crowd laps it up.
I love the symbolism!

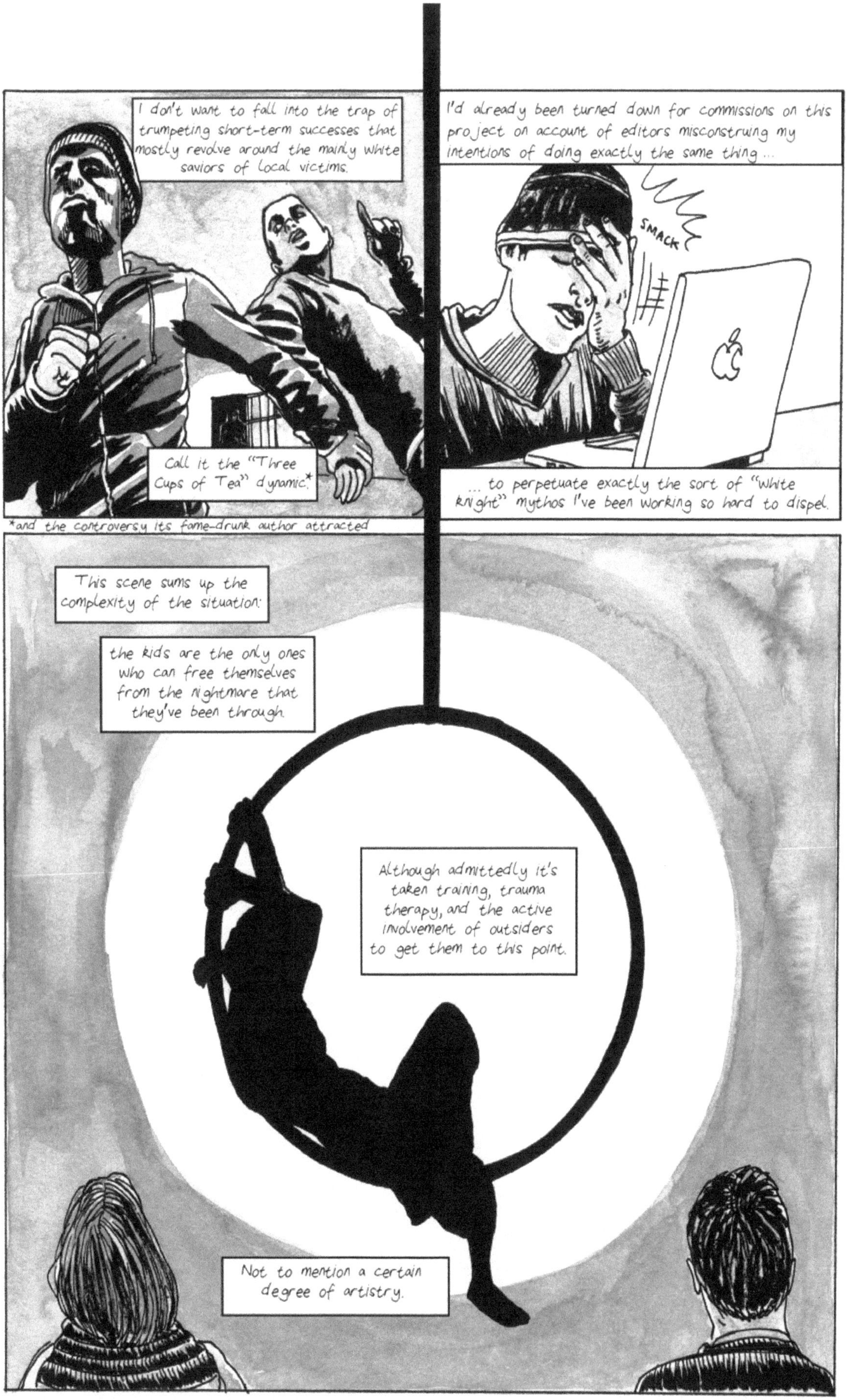

I don't want to fall into the trap of trumpeting short-term successes that mostly revolve around the mainly white saviors of local victims.
Call it the "Three Cups of Tea" dynamic.*
*and the controversy its fame-drunk author attracted
I'd already been turned down for commissions on this project on account of editors misconstruing my intentions of doing exactly the same thing...
SMACK
... to perpetuate exactly the sort of "white knight" mythos I've been working so hard to dispel.
This scene sums up the complexity of the situation:
the kids are the only ones who can free themselves from the nightmare that they've been through.
Although admittedly it's taken training, trauma therapy, and the active involvement of outsiders to get them to this point.
Not to mention a certain degree of artistry.

I stayed in touch with the organizers and, in an attempt to reset the extractive paradigm Kristy mentioned, offered to design their next poster:

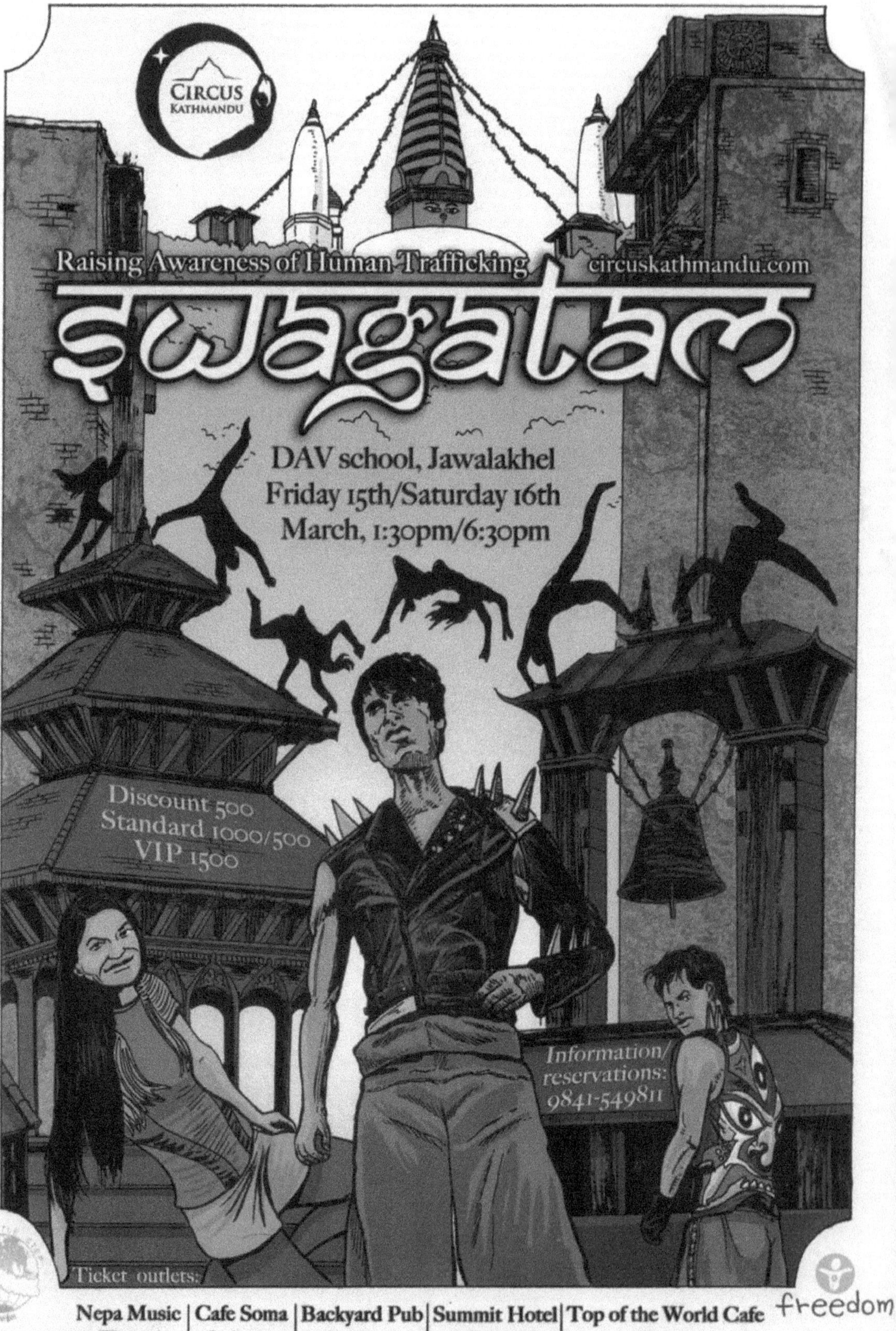
CIRCUS KATHMANDU
Raising Awareness of Human Trafficking
circuskathmandu.com
swagatam
DAV school, Jawalakhel
Friday 15th/Saturday 16th
March, 1:30pm/6:30pm
Discount 500
Standard 1000/500
VIP 1500
Information/
reservations:
9841-549811
Ticket outlets:
freedom
Nepa Music Thamel
Cafe Soma Lalitpur
Backyard Pub Lalitpur
Summit Hotel Sanepa
Top of the World Cafe Sanepa
Poster support from : www.offexploring.com/fergusanderson/blog Poster design: www.archcomix.com

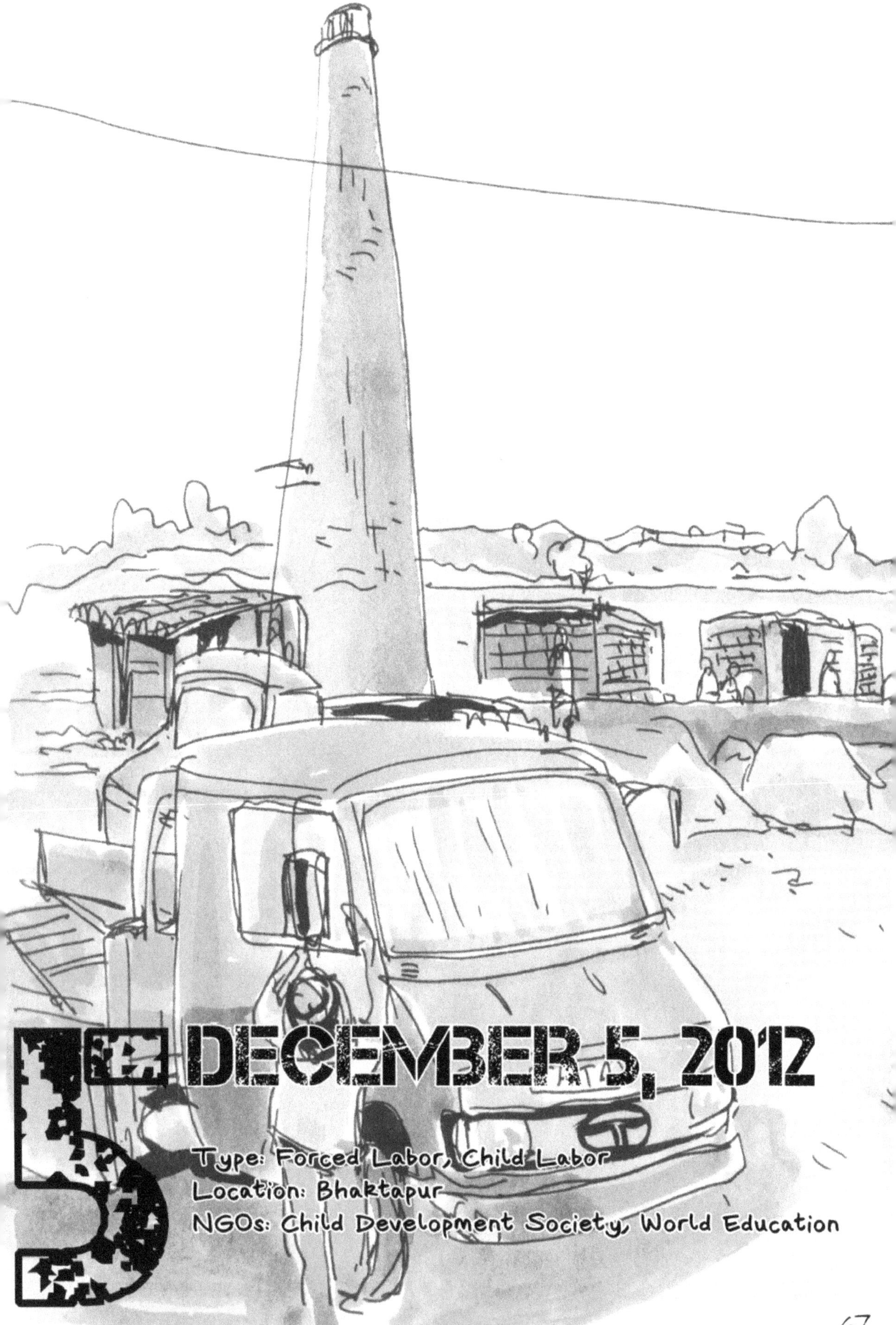

5

DECEMBER 5, 2012

Type: Forced Labor, Child Labor
Location: Bhaktapur
NGOs: Child Development Society, World Education

THE BRICK KILN

Tonight I'm meeting with Youraj Roka from CDS* to talk brick kilns. We've arranged to meet at a restaurant near my place.

You can tell it's swanky as you're saluted on your way in

Which instinctively prompts me to salute back. Like I'm a brigadier general out for dinner.

I sit in a prominent spot near the entrance so I don't miss Youraj.

Which means being slow-smoked by the not-so-swanky outdoor heating system.

*Child Development Society

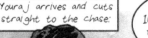

Youraj arrives and cuts straight to the chase:

There are 108 brick kilns in the Kathmandu Valley.

Two closed down because of the mud shortage that they make the bricks from.

The Labor Ministry has provision for 12 national labor inspectors...

...but in the implementation there is a gap.

So there are actually only 6 seats, and only 3 of those are working.

The other 3 have been on leave since 2010. They're not interested in brick kilns.

Brick kilns are traditionally-owned businesses - they don't like changing the technology.

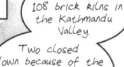

And with that he breaks it down in a sketch:

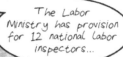

Chimney

Top

Raw bricks baked at the bottom

1 night (24h)

When we do catch kids working in kilns, the owners tell us:

"We're not using the kids: the parents are using them."

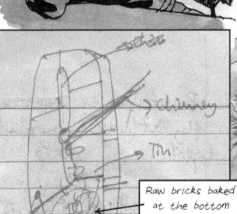

I'm eager to see all this for myself, but wonder about the logistics for sneaking onsite in such a flagrantly abusive work environment.

Youraj nonchalantly waves off those concerns - he's going to escort me personally.

68

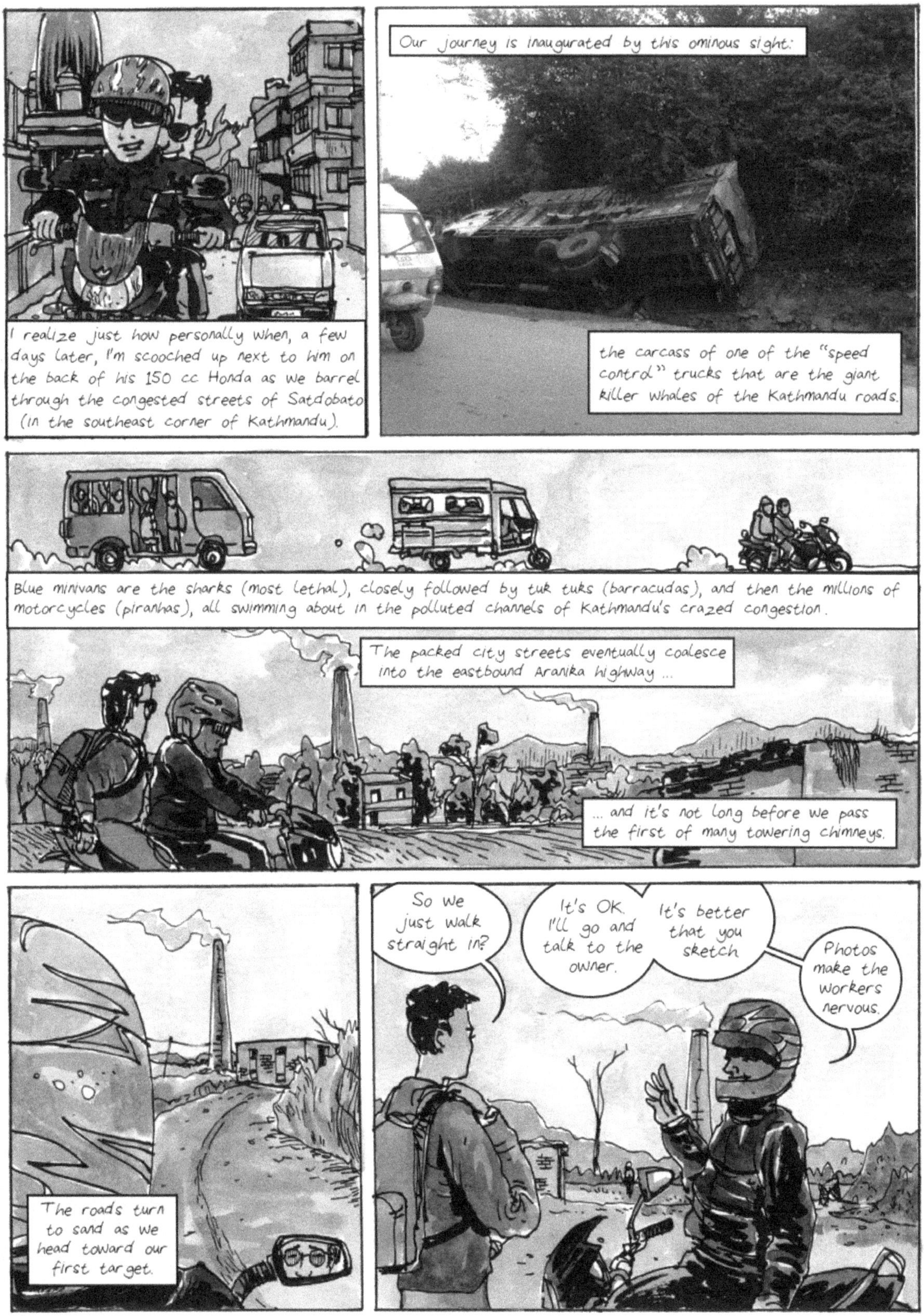
I realize just how personally when, a few days later, I'm scooched up next to him on the back of his 150 cc Honda as we barrel through the congested streets of Satdobato (in the southeast corner of Kathmandu).
Our journey is inaugurated by this ominous sight:
the carcass of one of the "speed control" trucks that are the giant killer whales of the Kathmandu roads.
Blue minivans are the sharks (most lethal), closely followed by tuk tuks (barracudas), and then the millions of motorcycles (piranhas), all swimming about in the polluted channels of Kathmandu's crazed congestion.
The packed city streets eventually coalesce into the eastbound Aranika highway ...
... and it's not long before we pass the first of many towering chimneys.
The roads turn to sand as we head toward our first target.
So we just walk straight in?
It's OK. I'll go and talk to the owner.
It's better that you sketch
Photos make the workers nervous.

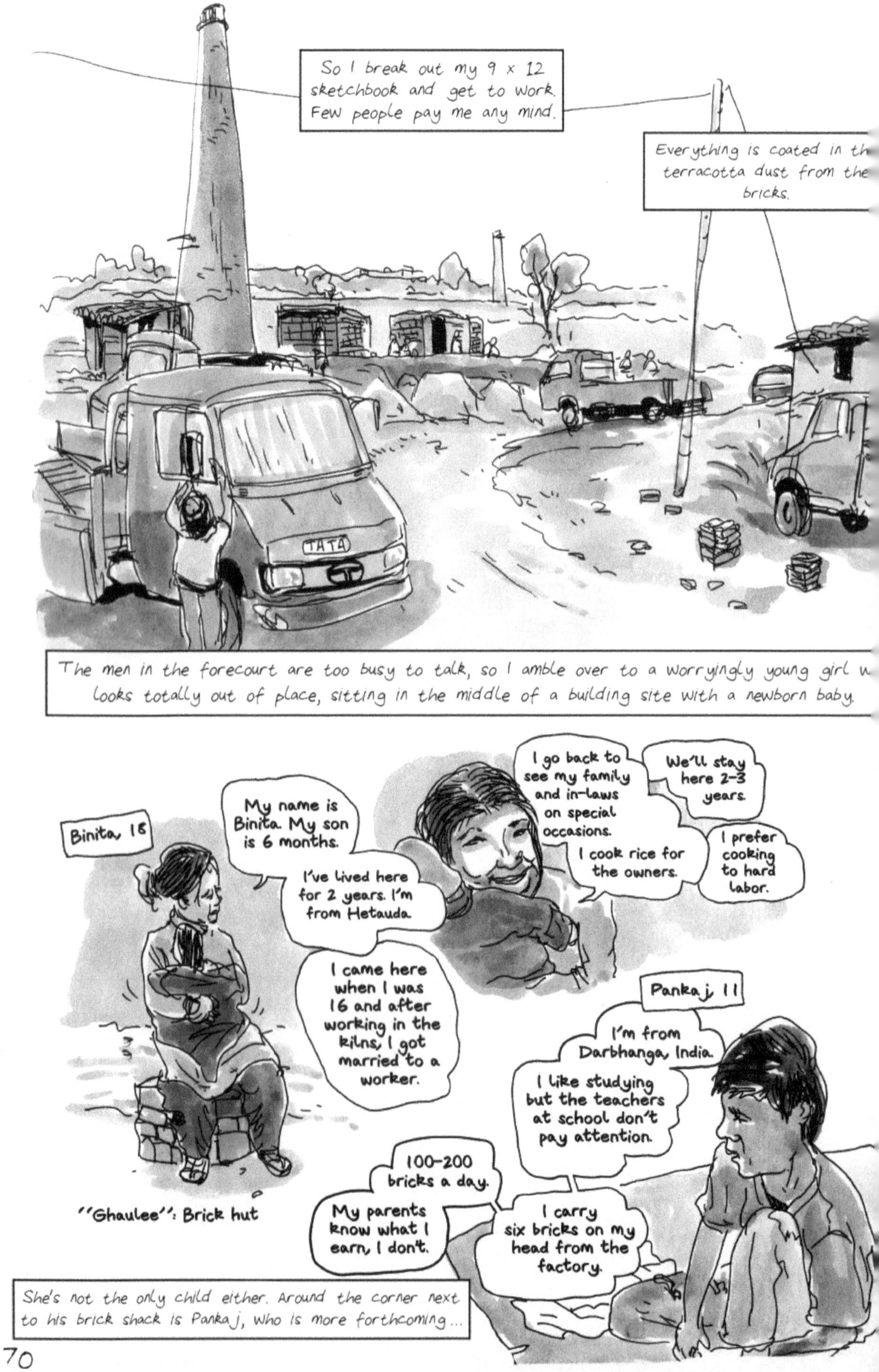

So I break out my 9 x 12 sketchbook and get to work. Few people pay me any mind.
Everything is coated in th terracotta dust from the bricks.
TATA
The men in the forecourt are too busy to talk, so I amble over to a worryingly young girl w looks totally out of place, sitting in the middle of a building site with a newborn baby.
Binita, 18
My name is Binita. My son is 6 months.
I've lived here for 2 years. I'm from Hetauda.
I came here when I was 16 and after working in the kilns, I got married to a worker.
I go back to see my family and in-laws on special occasions.
We'll stay here 2-3 years.
I cook rice for the owners.
I prefer cooking to hard labor.
"Ghaulee": Brick hut
Pankaj, 11
I'm from Darbhanga, India.
I like studying but the teachers at school don't pay attention.
100-200 bricks a day.
I carry six bricks on my head from the factory.
My parents know what I earn, I don't.
She's not the only child either. Around the corner next to his brick shack is Pankaj, who is more forthcoming...

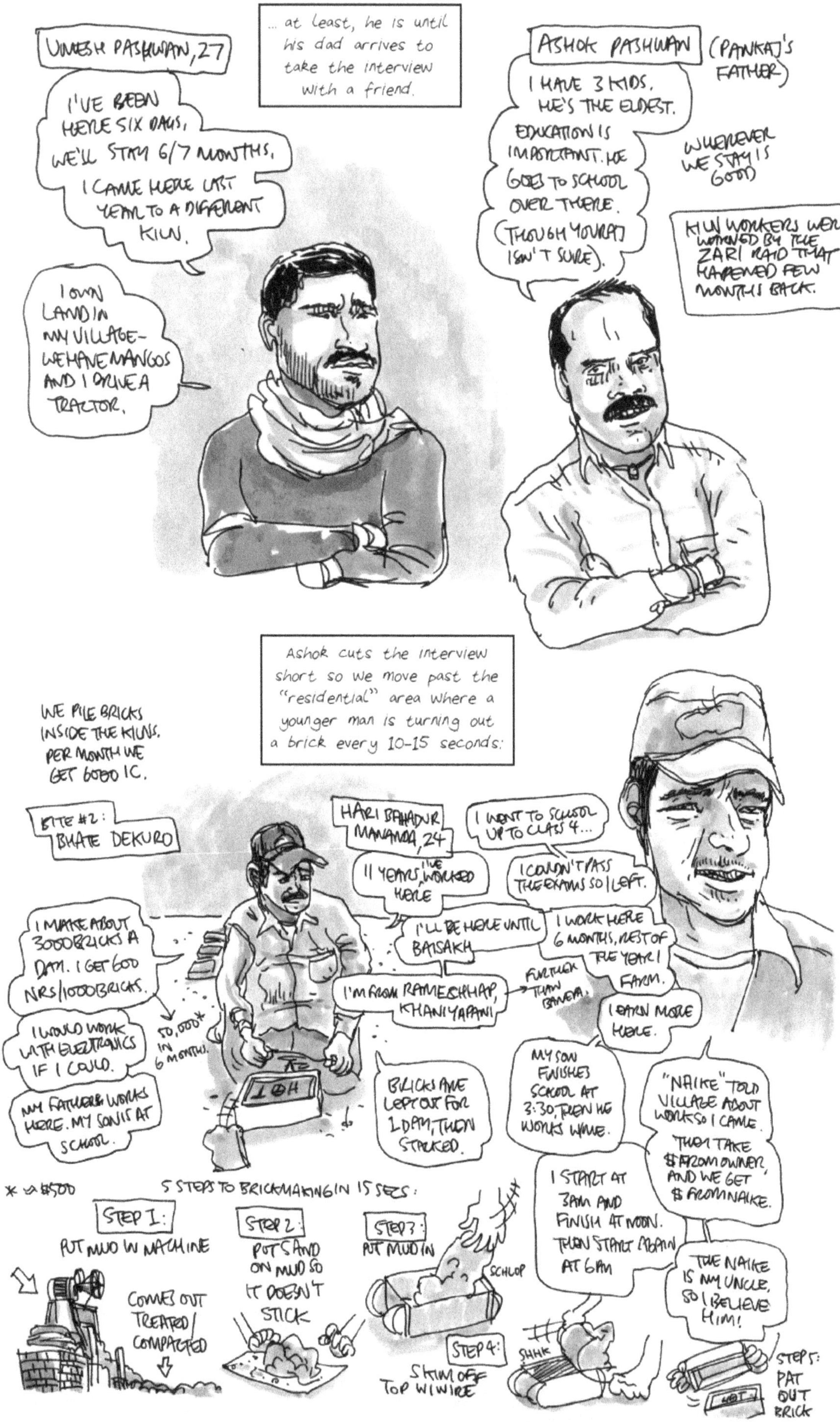
... at least, he is until his dad arrives to take the interview with a friend.
UMESH PASHWAN, 27
I'VE BEEN HERE SIX DAYS, WE'LL STAY 6/7 MONTHS.
I CAME HERE LAST YEAR TO A DIFFERENT KILN.
I OWN LAND IN MY VILLAGE- WE HAVE MANGOS AND I DRIVE A TRACTOR.
ASHOK PASHWAN (PANKAJ'S FATHER)
I HAVE 3 KIDS. HE'S THE ELDEST.
EDUCATION IS IMPORTANT. HE GOES TO SCHOOL OVER THERE. (THOUGH YOURAJ ISN'T SURE).
WHEREVER WE STAY IS GOOD
KILN WORKERS WERE WORRIED BY THE ZARI RAID THAT HAPPENED FEW MONTHS BACK.
Ashok cuts the interview short so we move past the "residential" area where a younger man is turning out a brick every 10-15 seconds:
WE PILE BRICKS INSIDE THE KILNS. PER MONTH WE GET 6000 IC.
SITE #2: BHATE DEKURO
HARI BAHADUR MANANDA, 24
11 YEARS I'VE WORKED HERE
I WENT TO SCHOOL UP TO CLASS 4...
I COULDN'T PASS THE EXAMS SO I LEFT.
I'LL BE HERE UNTIL BAISAKH
I WORK HERE 6 MONTHS, REST OF THE YEAR I FARM.
I'M FROM RAMECHHAP, KHANIYAPANI
FURTHER THAN BANEPA.
I EARN MORE HERE.
I MAKE ABOUT 3000 BRICKS A DAY. I GET 600 NRS/1000 BRICKS.
50,000* IN 6 MONTHS.
I WOULD WORK WITH ELECTRONICS IF I COULD.
MY FATHER WORKS HERE. MY SON IS AT SCHOOL.
BRICKS ARE LEFT OUT FOR 1 DAY, THEN STACKED.
MY SON FINISHES SCHOOL AT 3:30, THEN HE WORKS WITH ME.
"NAIKE" TOLD VILLAGE ABOUT WORK SO I CAME.
THEY TAKE $ FROM OWNER, AND WE GET $ FROM NAIKE.
I START AT 3AM AND FINISH AT NOON. THEN START AGAIN AT 6PM
THE NAIKE IS MY UNCLE, SO I BELIEVE HIM!
* ≈ $500
5 STEPS TO BRICKMAKING IN 15 SECS:
STEP 1: PUT MUD IN MACHINE
COMES OUT TREATED/ COMPACTED
STEP 2: PUT SAND ON MUD SO IT DOESN'T STICK
STEP 3: PUT MUD IN
SCHLOP
STEP 4: SKIM OFF TOP W/ WIRE
SHHK
STEP 5: PAT OUT BRICK

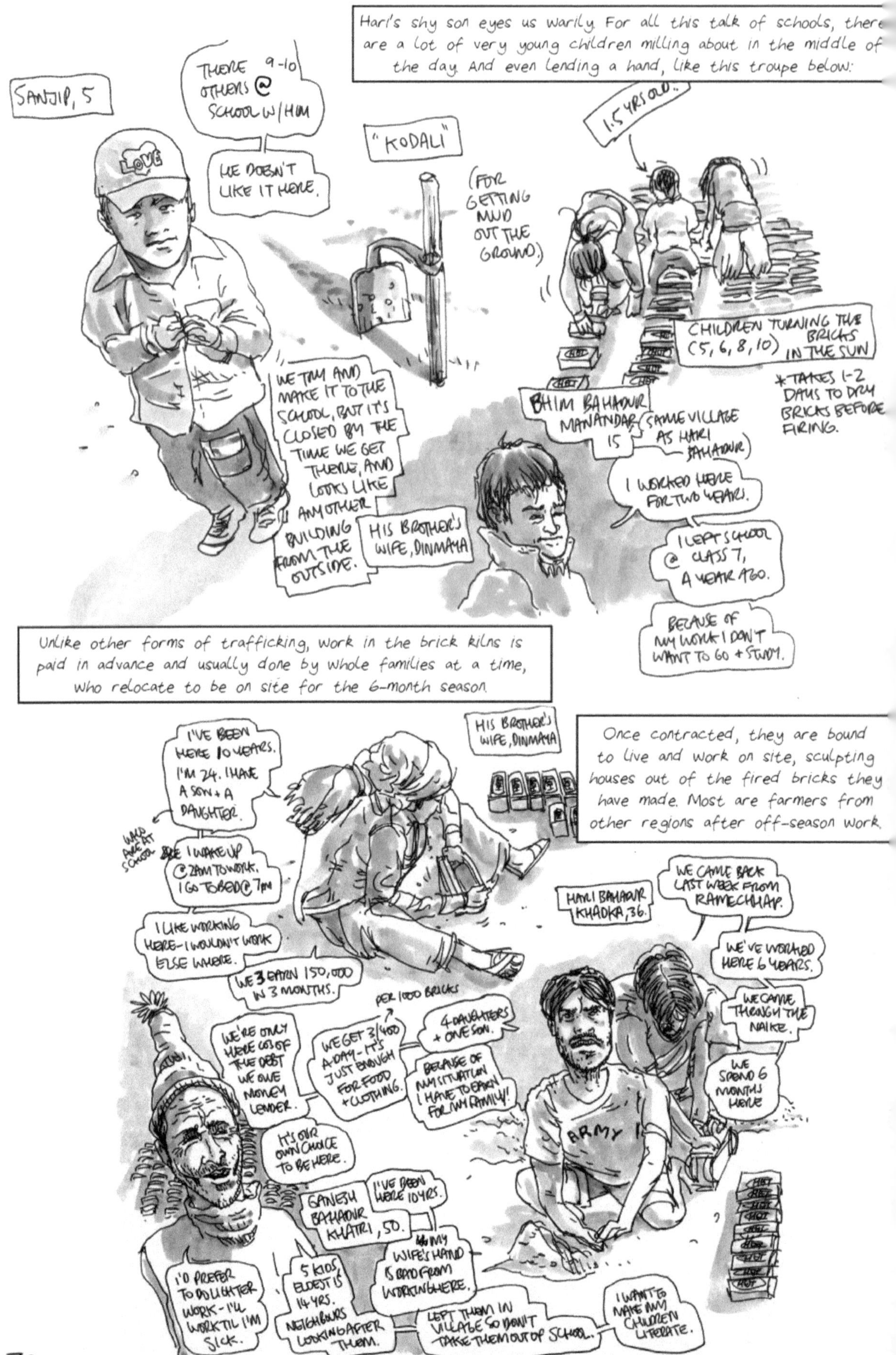

Hari's shy son eyes us warily. For all this talk of schools, there are a lot of very young children milling about in the middle of the day. And even lending a hand, like this troupe below:
SANJIP, 5
THERE 9-10 OTHERS @ SCHOOL W/HIM
HE DOESN'T LIKE IT HERE.
WE TRY AND MAKE IT TO THE SCHOOL, BUT IT'S CLOSED BY THE TIME WE GET THERE, AND LOOKS LIKE ANY OTHER BUILDING FROM THE OUTSIDE.
HIS BROTHER'S WIFE, DINMAYA
"KODALI"
(FOR GETTING MUD OUT THE GROUND.)
1.5 YRS OLD..
CHILDREN TURNING THE BRICKS IN THE SUN (5, 6, 8, 10)
* TAKES 1-2 DAYS TO DRY BRICKS BEFORE FIRING.
BHIM BAHADUR MANANDAR 15
(SAME VILLAGE AS HARI BAHADUR)
I WORKED HERE FOR TWO YEARS.
I LEFT SCHOOL @ CLASS 7, A YEAR AGO.
BECAUSE OF MY WORK I DON'T WANT TO GO + STUDY.
Unlike other forms of trafficking, work in the brick kilns is paid in advance and usually done by whole families at a time, who relocate to be on site for the 6-month season.
HIS BROTHER'S WIFE, DINMAYA
Once contracted, they are bound to live and work on site, sculpting houses out of the fired bricks they have made. Most are farmers from other regions after off-season work.
I'VE BEEN HERE 10 YEARS. I'M 24. I HAVE A SON + A DAUGHTER.
WHO ARE AT SCHOOL
I WAKE UP @ 2AM TO WORK. I GO TO BED @ 7PM
I LIKE WORKING HERE - I WOULDN'T WORK ELSEWHERE.
WE 3 EARN 150,000 IN 3 MONTHS.
HARI BAHADUR KHADKA, 36.
WE CAME BACK LAST WEEK FROM RAMECHHAP.
WE'VE WORKED HERE 6 YEARS.
WE CAME THROUGH THE NAIKE.
WE SPEND 6 MONTHS HERE
PER 1000 BRICKS
WE'RE ONLY HERE COS OF THE DEBT WE OWE MONEY LENDER.
WE GET 3/400 A DAY - IT'S JUST ENOUGH FOR FOOD + CLOTHING.
4 DAUGHTERS + ONE SON.
BECAUSE OF MY SITUATION I HAVE TO EARN FOR MY FAMILY!
IT'S OUR OWN CHOICE TO BE HERE.
GANESH BAHADUR KHATRI, 50.
I'VE BEEN HERE 10 YRS.
I'D PREFER TO DO LIGHTER WORK - I'LL WORK TIL I'M SICK.
5 KIDS, ELDEST IS 14 YRS. NEIGHBOURS LOOKING AFTER THEM.
MY WIFE'S HAND IS BAD FROM WORKING HERE.
LEFT THEM IN VILLAGE SO DON'T TAKE THEM OUT OF SCHOOL.
I WANT TO MAKE MY CHILDREN LITERATE.

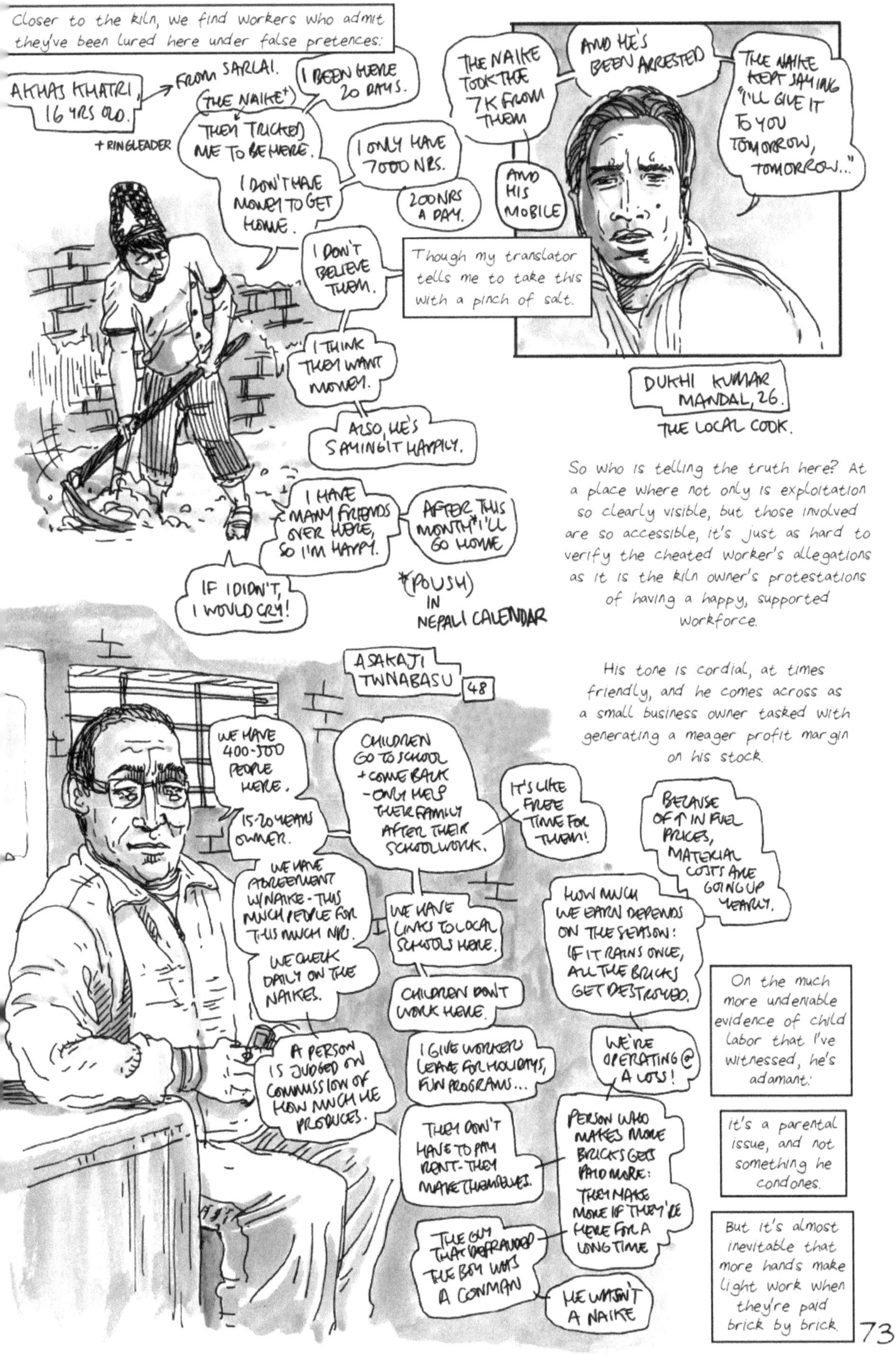
Closer to the kiln, we find workers who admit they've been lured here under false pretences:
AKHAJ KHATRI, 16 YRS OLD.
FROM SARLAI.
+ RINGLEADER
I BEEN HERE 20 DAYS.
(THE NAIKE+) THEY TRICKED ME TO BE HERE.
I ONLY HAVE 7000 NRS.
I DON'T HAVE MONEY TO GET HOME.
200 NRS A DAY.
I DON'T BELIEVE THEM.
Though my translator tells me to take this with a pinch of salt.
I THINK THEY WANT MONEY.
ALSO, HE'S SAYING IT HAPPILY.
I HAVE MANY FRIENDS OVER HERE, SO I'M HAPPY.
AFTER THIS MONTH* I'LL GO HOME
IF I DIDN'T, I WOULD CRY!
*(POUSH) IN NEPALI CALENDAR
THE NAIKE TOOK THE 7K FROM THEM
AND HIS MOBILE
AND HE'S BEEN ARRESTED
THE NAIKE KEPT SAYING "I'LL GIVE IT TO YOU TOMORROW, TOMORROW..."
DUKHI KUMAR MANDAL, 26.
THE LOCAL COOK.
So who is telling the truth here? At a place where not only is exploitation so clearly visible, but those involved are so accessible, it's just as hard to verify the cheated worker's allegations as it is the kiln owner's protestations of having a happy, supported workforce.
His tone is cordial, at times friendly, and he comes across as a small business owner tasked with generating a meager profit margin on his stock.
ASAKAJI TWNABASU 48
WE HAVE 400-500 PEOPLE HERE.
15-20 YEARS OWNER.
CHILDREN GO TO SCHOOL + COME BACK - ONLY HELP THEIR FAMILY AFTER THEIR SCHOOLWORK.
IT'S LIKE FREE TIME FOR THEM!
BECAUSE OF ↑ IN FUEL PRICES, MATERIAL COSTS ARE GOING UP YEARLY.
WE HAVE AGREEMENT W/NAIKE - THIS MUCH PEOPLE FOR THIS MUCH NRS.
WE HAVE LINKS TO LOCAL SCHOOLS HERE.
HOW MUCH WE EARN DEPENDS ON THE SEASON: IF IT RAINS ONCE, ALL THE BRICKS GET DESTROYED.
WE CHECK DAILY ON THE NAIKE.
CHILDREN DON'T WORK HERE.
A PERSON IS JUDGED ON COMMISSION OF HOW MUCH HE PRODUCES.
I GIVE WORKERS LEAVE FOR HOLIDAYS, FUN PROGRAMS...
WE'RE OPERATING @ A LOSS!
THEY DON'T HAVE TO PAY RENT - THEY MAKE THEMSELVES.
PERSON WHO MAKES MORE BRICKS GETS PAID MORE: THEY MAKE MORE IF THEY'RE HERE FOR A LONG TIME
On the much more undeniable evidence of child labor that I've witnessed, he's adamant:
it's a parental issue, and not something he condones.
THE GUY THAT DEFRAUDED THE BOY WAS A CONMAN
HE WASN'T A NAIKE
But it's almost inevitable that more hands make light work when they're paid brick by brick.

THINGS ARE LIKE THAT

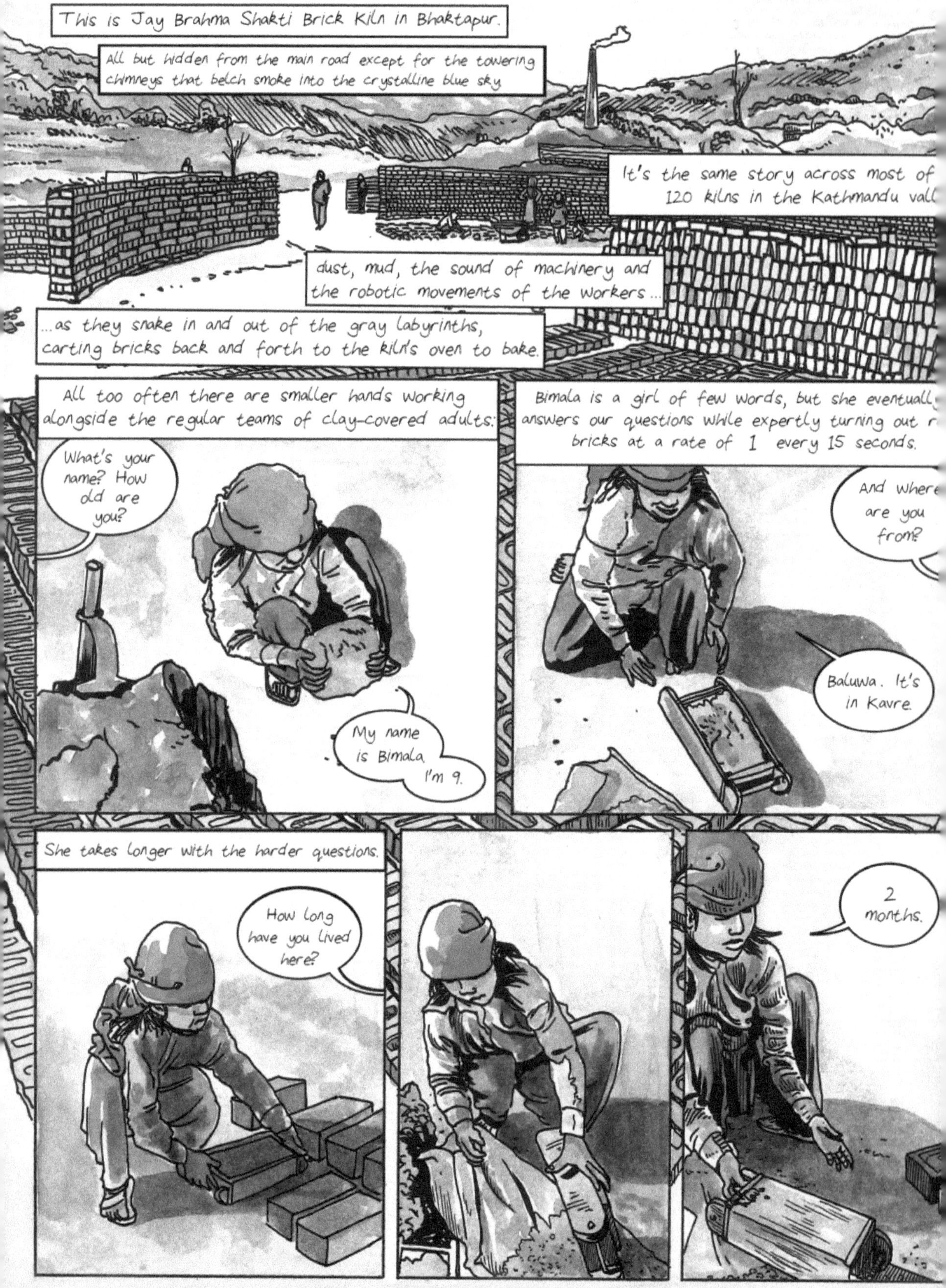

This is Jay Brahma Shakti Brick Kiln in Bhaktapur.
All but hidden from the main road except for the towering chimneys that belch smoke into the crystalline blue sky.
It's the same story across most of 120 kilns in the Kathmandu vall
dust, mud, the sound of machinery and the robotic movements of the workers...
...as they snake in and out of the gray labyrinths, carting bricks back and forth to the kiln's oven to bake.
All too often there are smaller hands working alongside the regular teams of clay-covered adults:
What's your name? How old are you?
My name is Bimala. I'm 9.
Bimala is a girl of few words, but she eventuall answers our questions while expertly turning out r bricks at a rate of 1 every 15 seconds.
And wher are you from?
Baluwa. It's in Kavre.
She takes longer with the harder questions.
How long have you lived here?
2 months.

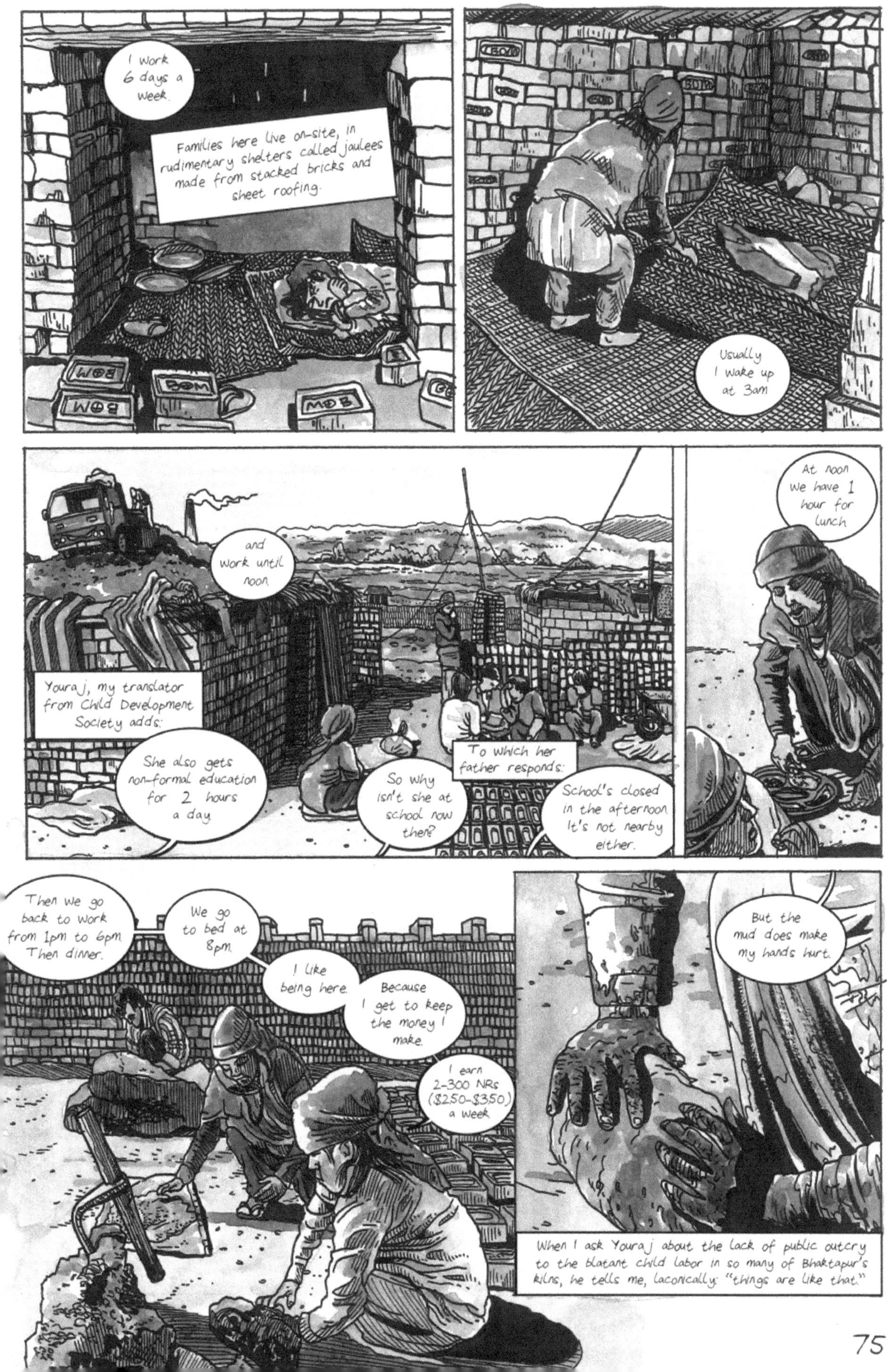

I work 6 days a week.
Families here live on-site, in rudimentary shelters called jaulees made from stacked bricks and sheet roofing.
Usually I wake up at 3am
and work until noon
Youraj, my translator from Child Development Society adds:
She also gets non-formal education for 2 hours a day.
So why isn't she at school now then?
To which her father responds:
School's closed in the afternoon It's not nearby either.
At noon we have 1 hour for lunch
Then we go back to work from 1pm to 6pm. Then dinner.
We go to bed at 8pm.
I like being here.
Because I get to keep the money I make.
I earn 2-300 NRs ($250-$350) a week
But the mud does make my hands hurt.
When I ask Youraj about the lack of public outcry to the blatant child labor in so many of Bhaktapur's kilns, he tells me, laconically: "things are like that."

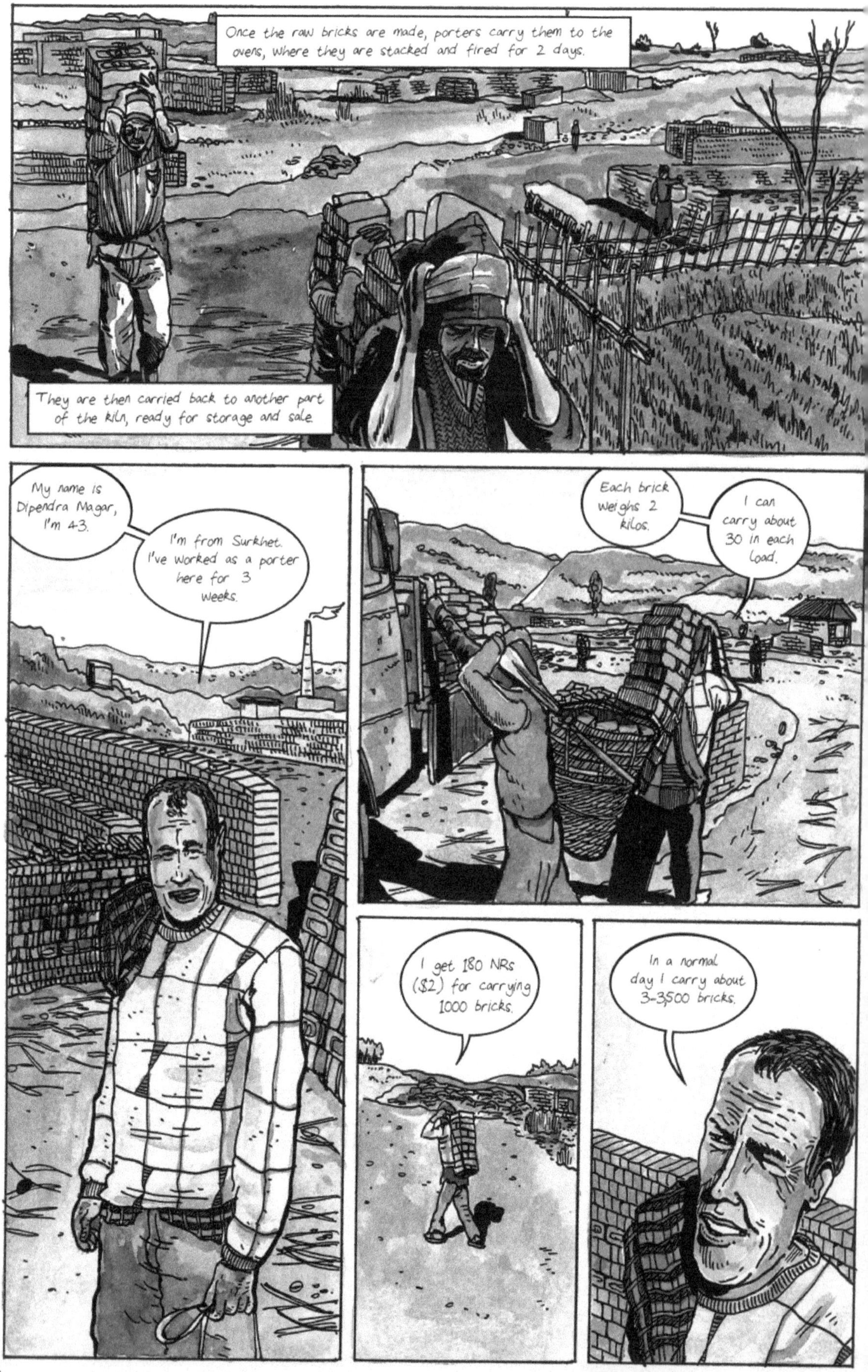
Once the raw bricks are made, porters carry them to the ovens, where they are stacked and fired for 2 days.
They are then carried back to another part of the kiln, ready for storage and sale.
My name is Dipendra Magar, I'm 43.
I'm from Surkhet. I've worked as a porter here for 3 weeks.
Each brick weighs 2 kilos.
I can carry about 30 in each load.
I get 180 NRs ($2) for carrying 1000 bricks.
In a normal day I carry about 3-3,500 bricks.

NO ONE TO WATCH OVER US

As part of a grassroots outreach comic I'm commissioned to do for World Education, I seek out an expert opinion from the Kathmandu School of Medicine on exactly what toll life in the kilns is taking on the children whose parents expose them to brick dust for up to 6 months of every year:

In addition to measuring standard physiological data...

Dr Sunil Joshi

... from which we can deduce BMI (Body Mass Index)...

... and levels of malnutrition...

... we're measuring hearing loss with an audiometer.

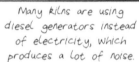

Many kilns are using diesel generators instead of electricity, which produces a lot of noise.

We play sounds at different frequencies and intensities

and the children have to press the button when they can hear them.

Another key piece of tech is the vitalograph COPD, which is used to measure pulmonary (lung) function. It works in 2 ways:

1. To measure Chronic Obstructive Pulmonary Disease, which it does by color.

Green, lime, yellow, and red correspond to normal, mild, moderate, and severe.

It also gives us a reading on the obstructed index, brought about by allergic reactions and dust...

... to show how much their windpipes are shrinking.

77

Statements like these are all the more powerful when you tie the data to actual children with names and faces:

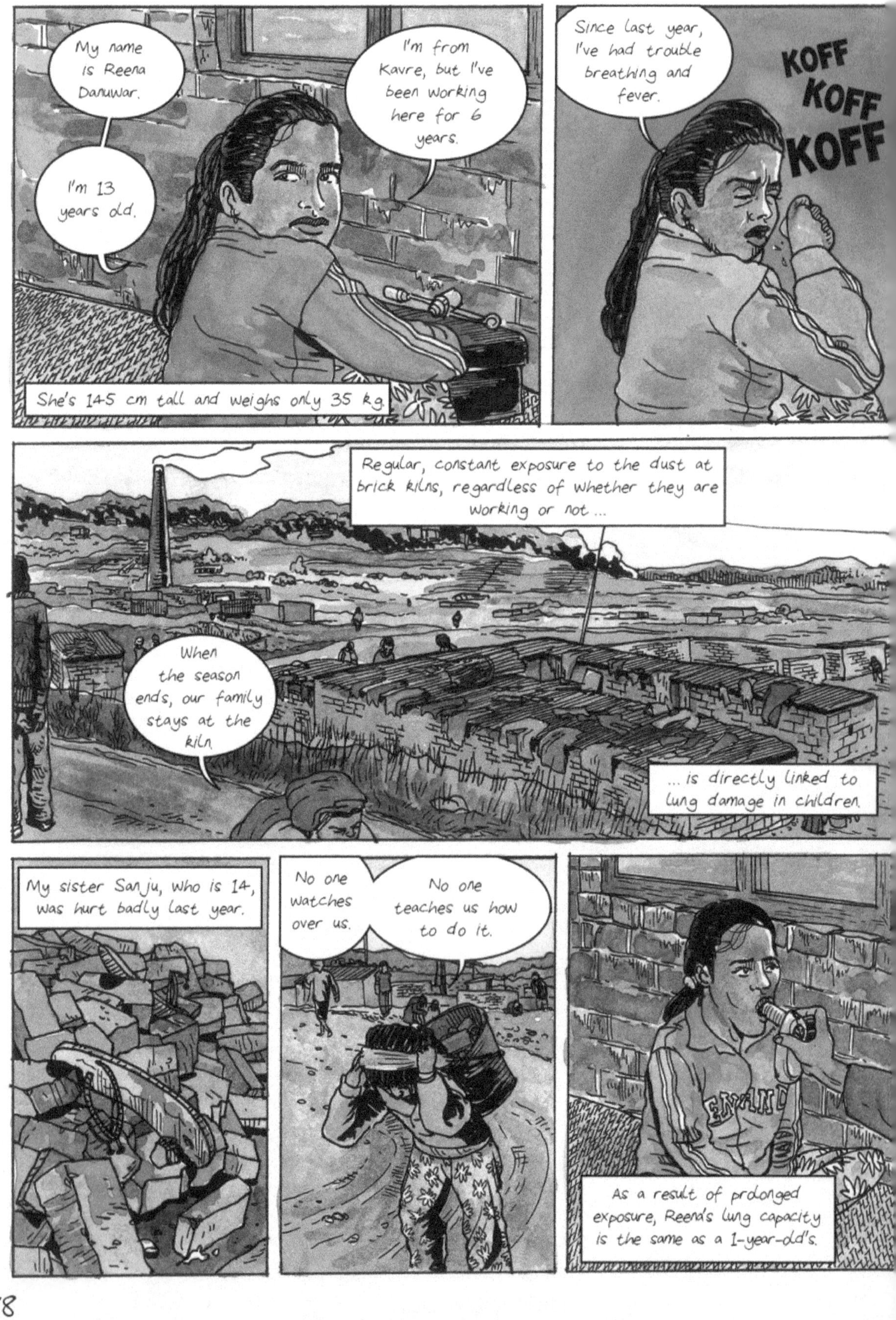
My name is Reena Danuwar.
I'm 13 years old.
I'm from Kavre, but I've been working here for 6 years.
She's 145 cm tall and weighs only 35 kg.
Since last year, I've had trouble breathing and fever.
KOFF KOFF KOFF
Regular, constant exposure to the dust at brick kilns, regardless of whether they are working or not ...
When the season ends, our family stays at the kiln.
... is directly linked to lung damage in children.
My sister Sanju, who is 14, was hurt badly last year.
No one watches over us.
No one teaches us how to do it.
As a result of prolonged exposure, Reena's lung capacity is the same as a 1-year-old's.

My name is Ganesh Giri.

I'm 12 years old, from Dang District in the West.

I've been working for only 1 year, 6 days a week.

I work for 11 hours a day.

In the last year, I fell down from a tree.

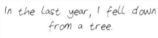

I broke both my arms.

Since then, my neck and back have been hurting me very badly.

There is no medicine for the pain here.

Ganesh also has otitis - ear discharge.

And is suffering from hearing loss.

He's at below 30db, sometimes even below 40.

Some children are more sensitive to the harmful effects than others.

Ganesh's breathing is very bad; it's in the red.

After 1 year of exposure he has the lung capacity of a 4-year-old.

10 db is the norm.

79

It takes time (5-10 years) for the effects of working at kilns to appear. That's why we see reduced capacity in the 15- and 16-year-olds.

Most of them have been coming to the kilns for 5-6 years. Even if they don't do any work, they'll be playing around the kiln and exposed to the dust and different chemicals.

It all depends on the level of exposure:

If they're exposed regularly, lung tissue will get more and more inflamed and the airways will shrink more, restricting airflow.

Mucus deposits

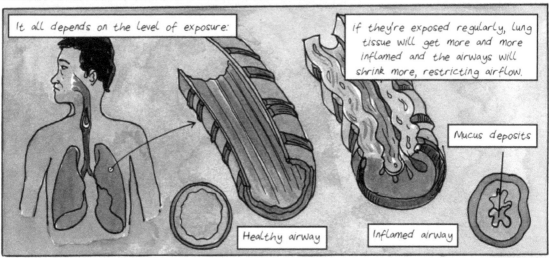

Healthy airway

Inflamed airway

When dealing with small children (6-8) their physiology is totally different: 1. They're growing more and more. Their response to all the exposure could be totally different.

2. Their immunity is a little bit lower than adults because it's not properly developed.

3. Those chemicals don't only affect respiratory systems but also many other bodily systems which are growing very fast in the kids - their bodies are affected differently compared to adults.

The kiln owner said that all the medical expenses are his responsibility. They want a clinic on site so they don't lose workers while they're in hospital!

They shouldn't work at all in such environments.

That's the most important thing.

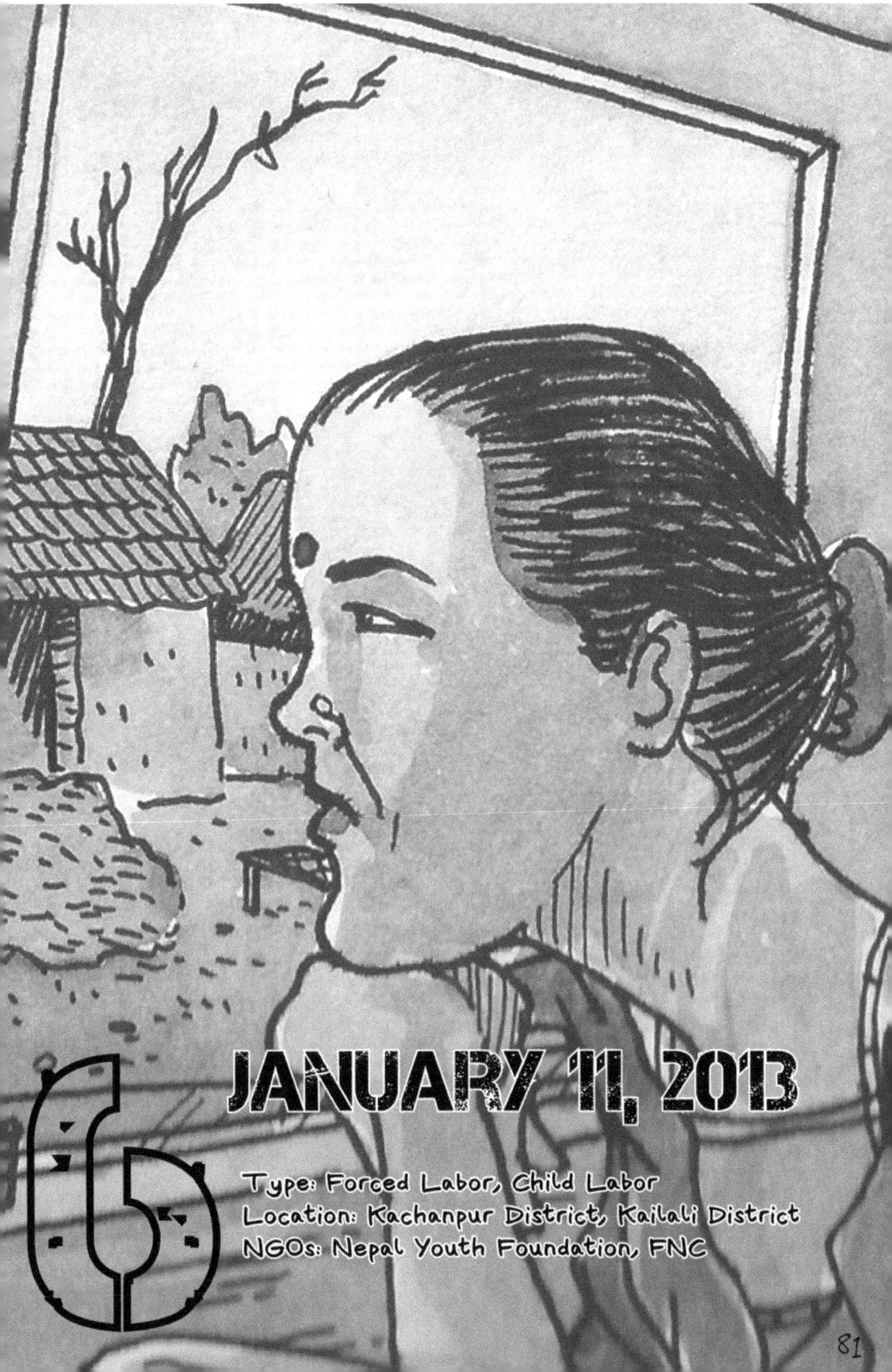

6

JANUARY 11, 2013

Type: Forced Labor, Child Labor
Location: Kachanpur District, Kailali District
NGOs: Nepal Youth Foundation, FNC

FRIENDS OF NEEDY CHILDREN

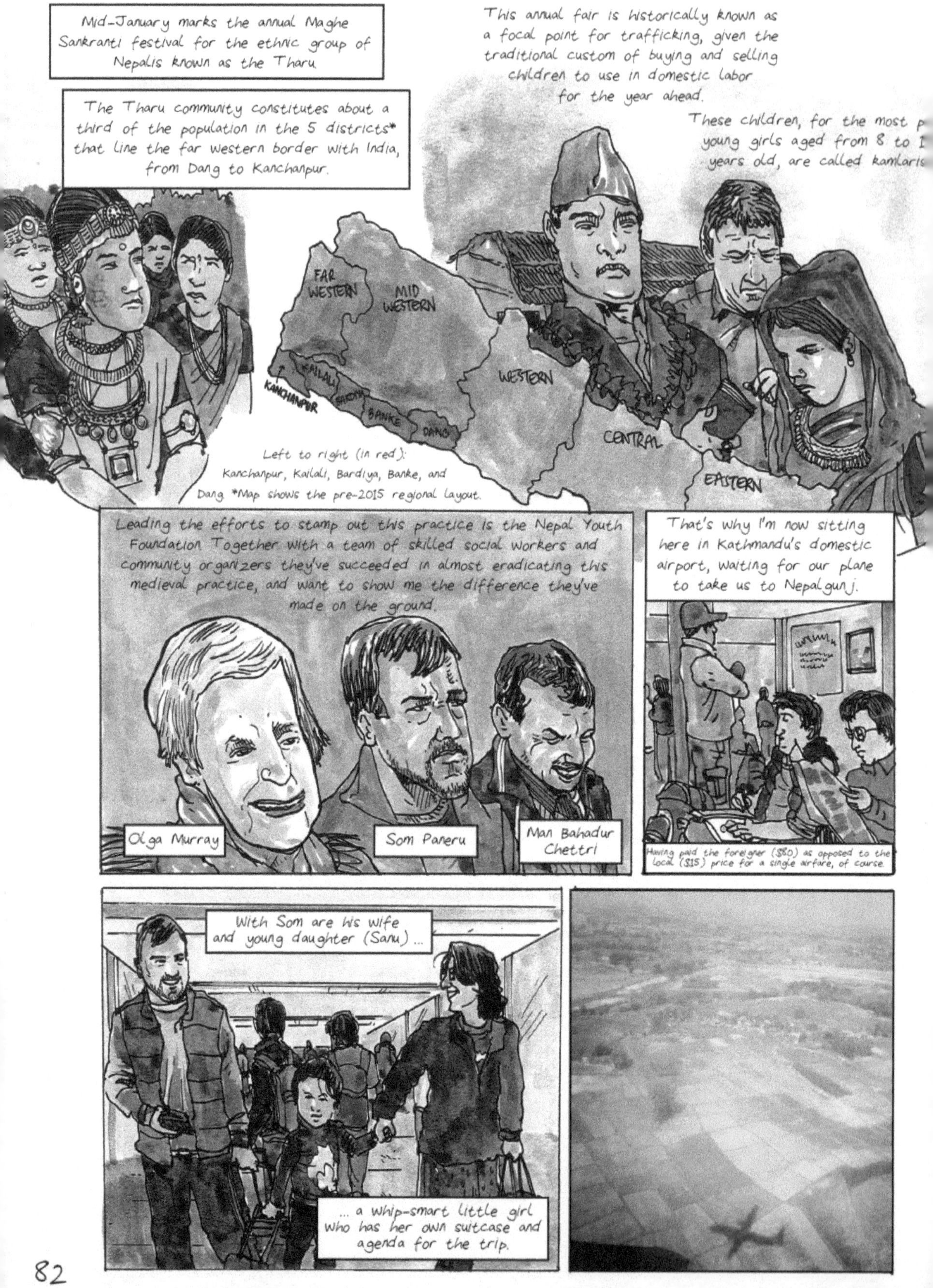

Mid-January marks the annual Maghe Sankranti festival for the ethnic group of Nepalis known as the Tharu.
The Tharu community constitutes about a third of the population in the 5 districts* that line the far western border with India, from Dang to Kanchanpur.
This annual fair is historically known as a focal point for trafficking, given the traditional custom of buying and selling children to use in domestic labor for the year ahead.
These children, for the most p
young girls aged from 8 to 1
years old, are called kamlaris
FAR WESTERN
MID WESTERN
WESTERN
CENTRAL
EASTERN
KANCHANPUR
KAILALI
BANKE
DANG
Left to right (in red): Kanchanpur, Kailali, Bardiya, Banke, and Dang *Map shows the pre-2015 regional layout.
Leading the efforts to stamp out this practice is the Nepal Youth Foundation. Together with a team of skilled social workers and community organizers they've succeeded in almost eradicating this medieval practice, and want to show me the difference they've made on the ground.
Olga Murray
Som Paneru
Man Bahadur Chettri
That's why I'm now sitting here in Kathmandu's domestic airport, waiting for our plane to take us to Nepalgunj.
Having paid the foreigner ($80) as opposed to the local ($15) price for a single airfare, of course.
With Som are his wife and young daughter (Sanu) ...
... a whip-smart little girl who has her own suitcase and agenda for the trip.

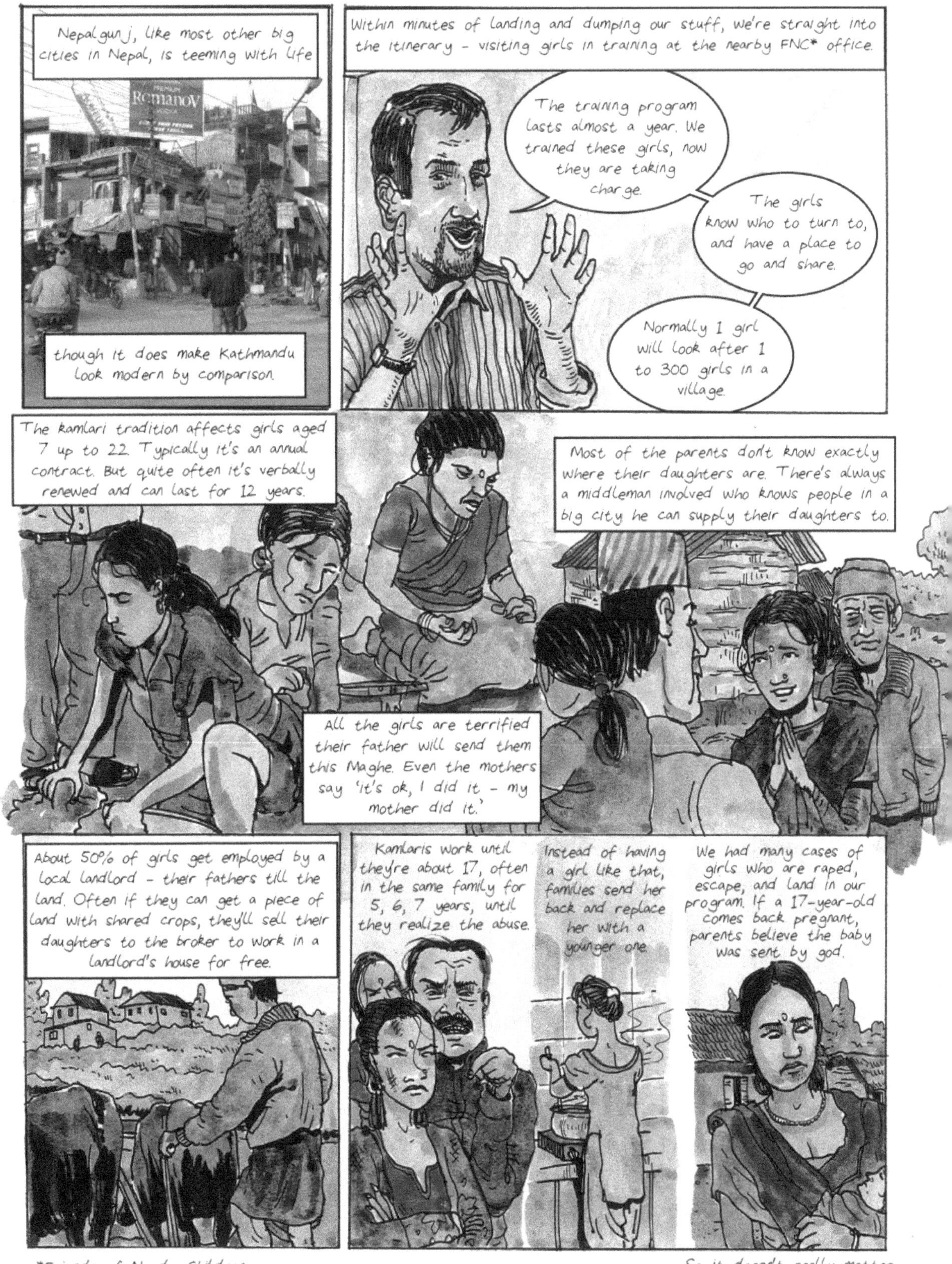
Nepalgunj, like most other big cities in Nepal, is teeming with life
ROMANOV
though it does make Kathmandu look modern by comparison.
Within minutes of landing and dumping our stuff, we're straight into the itinerary - visiting girls in training at the nearby FNC* office.
The training program lasts almost a year. We trained these girls, now they are taking charge.
The girls know who to turn to, and have a place to go and share.
Normally 1 girl will look after 1 to 300 girls in a village.
The kamlari tradition affects girls aged 7 up to 22. Typically it's an annual contract. But quite often it's verbally renewed and can last for 12 years.
Most of the parents don't know exactly where their daughters are. There's always a middleman involved who knows people in a big city he can supply their daughters to.
All the girls are terrified their father will send them this Maghe. Even the mothers say 'it's ok, I did it - my mother did it.'
About 50% of girls get employed by a local landlord - their fathers till the land. Often if they can get a piece of land with shared crops, they'll sell their daughters to the broker to work in a landlord's house for free.
Kamlaris work until they're about 17, often in the same family for 5, 6, 7 years, until they realize the abuse.
Instead of having a girl like that, families send her back and replace her with a younger one.
We had many cases of girls who are raped, escape, and land in our program. If a 17-year-old comes back pregnant, parents believe the baby was sent by god.

*Friends of Needy Children

So it doesn't really matter for most of them.

Many girls have never been to school and are illiterate. It's difficult to integrate them into school: some of them are 14 - we can't just send them to first grade.

So we give them accelerated courses. After a year or two, they are in class with children half their age.

By then, they want to go for vocational training (at 16-18).

This is design training. It started on Dec. 30, and lasts 3 months.

More than garment training, it's designing. They know the tailoring already.

They all want to be self-employed and start their own businesses.

There are 20 of them. Some girls brought their own machine, but most are provided by the training center.

When we started working with these girls, there was no way we could provide support to them all because there were so many of them.

In addition to the 3-month training program, the government provides 10,000 rupees seed money and a machine when they graduate."

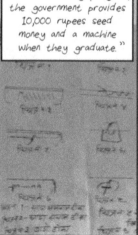

The girls are lightning-focused on the job in hand, though a few agree to be interviewed.

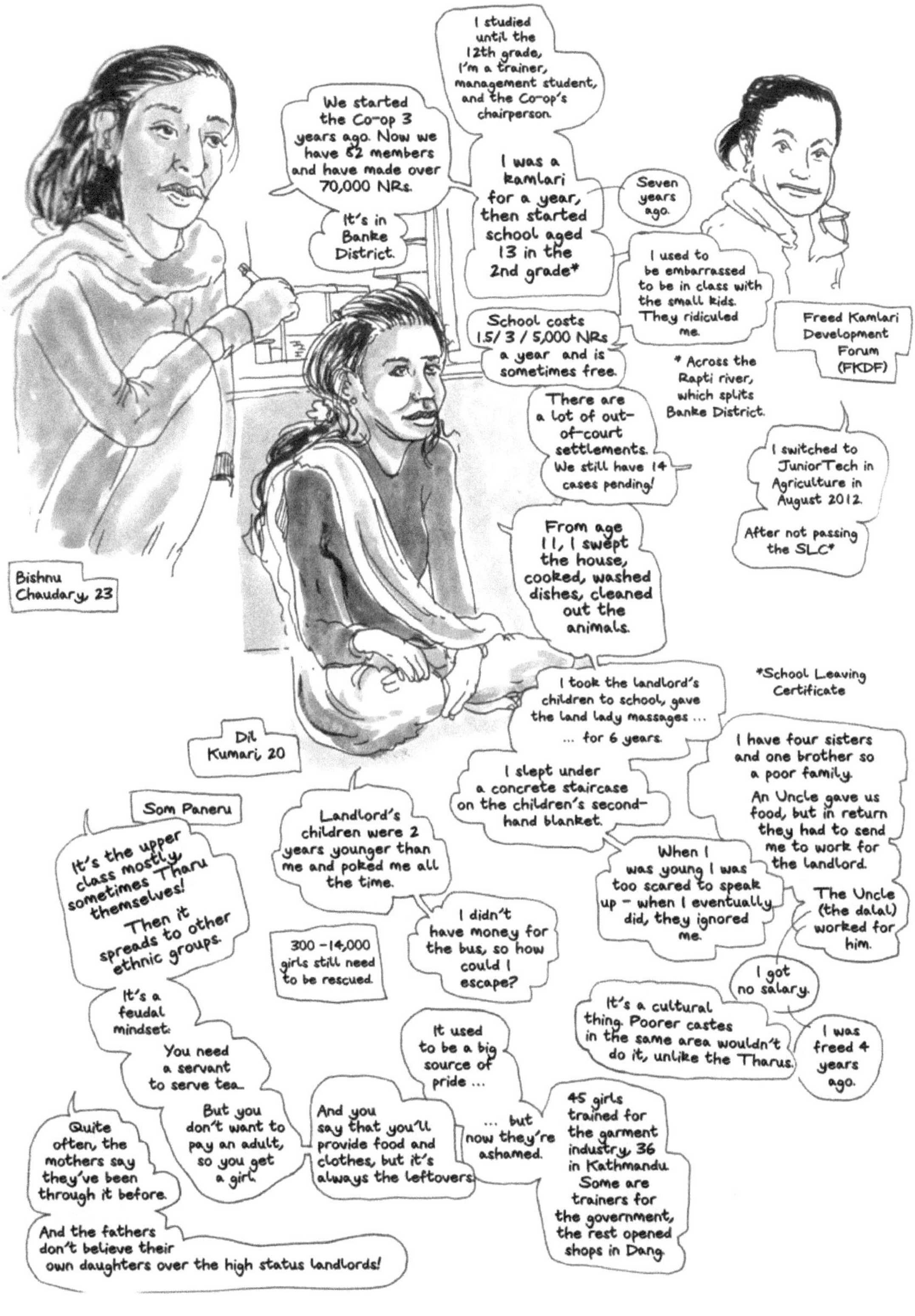
We started the Co-op 3 years ago. Now we have 52 members and have made over 70,000 NRs.
It's in Banke District.
I studied until the 12th grade, I'm a trainer, management student, and the Co-op's chairperson.
I was a kamlari for a year, then started school aged 13 in the 2nd grade*
Seven years ago.
I used to be embarrassed to be in class with the small kids. They ridiculed me.
School costs 1.5/ 3 / 5,000 NRs a year and is sometimes free.
Freed Kamlari Development Forum (FKDF)
* Across the Rapti river, which splits Banke District.
There are a lot of out-of-court settlements. We still have 14 cases pending!
I switched to JuniorTech in Agriculture in August 2012.
After not passing the SLC*
Bishnu Chaudary, 23
From age 11, I swept the house, cooked, washed dishes, cleaned out the animals.
*School Leaving Certificate
I took the landlord's children to school, gave the land lady massages ... ... for 6 years.
Dil Kumari, 20
I slept under a concrete staircase on the children's second-hand blanket.
I have four sisters and one brother so a poor family.
An Uncle gave us food, but in return they had to send me to work for the landlord.
Som Paneru
It's the upper class mostly, sometimes Tharu themselves!
Then it spreads to other ethnic groups.
Landlord's children were 2 years younger than me and poked me all the time.
When I was young I was too scared to speak up – when I eventually did, they ignored me.
The Uncle (the dalal) worked for him.
300 – 14,000 girls still need to be rescued.
I didn't have money for the bus, so how could I escape?
I got no salary.
It's a feudal mindset.
You need a servant to serve tea.
It's a cultural thing. Poorer castes in the same area wouldn't do it, unlike the Tharus.
I was freed 4 years ago.
It used to be a big source of pride ...
... but now they're ashamed.
But you don't want to pay an adult, so you get a girl.
And you say that you'll provide food and clothes, but it's always the leftovers.
45 girls trained for the garment industry, 36 in Kathmandu. Some are trainers for the government, the rest opened shops in Dang.
Quite often, the mothers say they've been through it before.
And the fathers don't believe their own daughters over the high status landlords!

The following day we're up early to check in on 2 graduates from the scheme who have transformed themselves by starting a small shop on the outskirts of town selling snacks, sweets, and miscellaneous household items. Shy at first, one woman declines to give her name but is happy to talk about her newfound success.

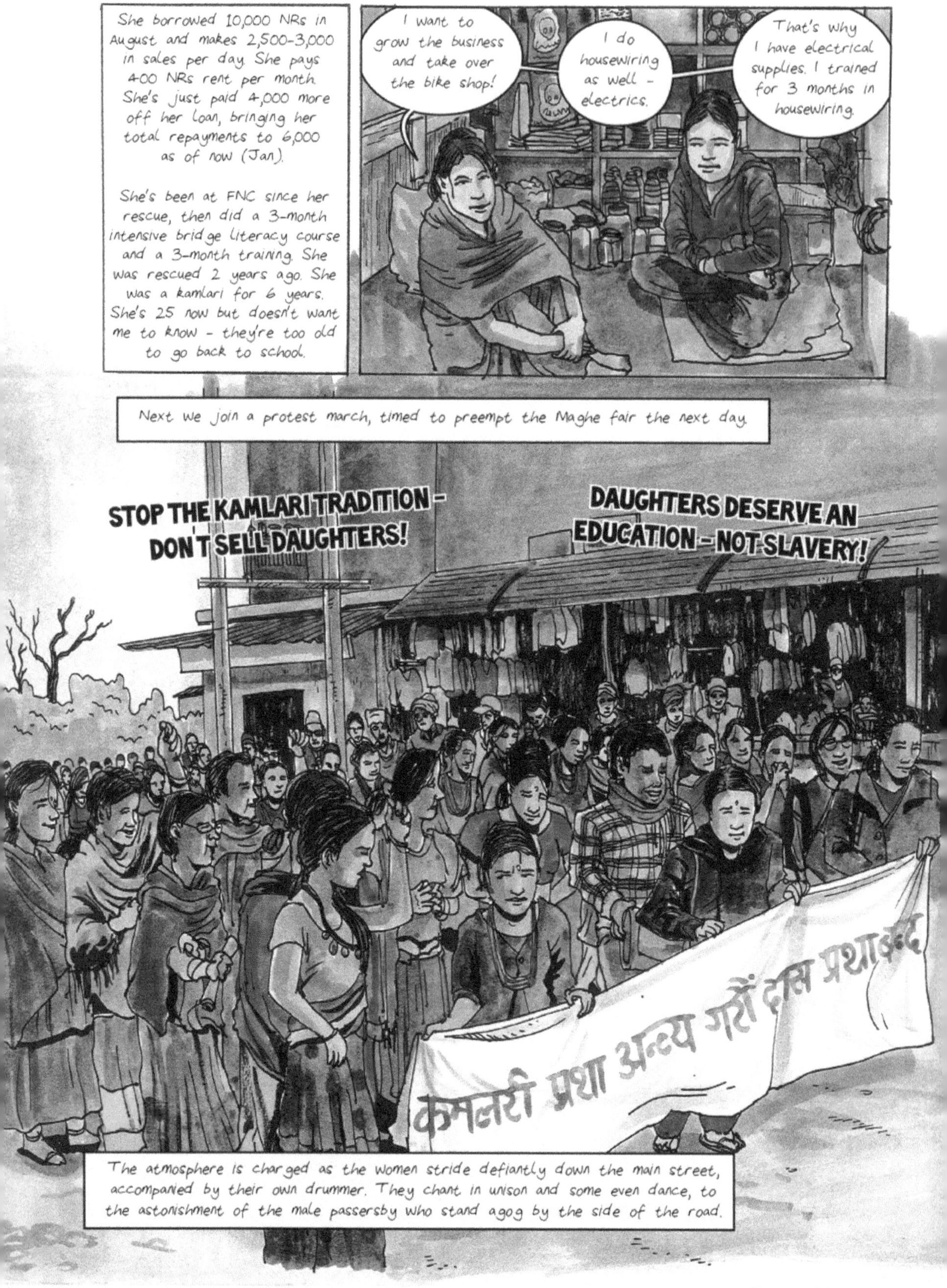
She borrowed 10,000 NRs in August and makes 2,500-3,000 in sales per day. She pays 400 NRs rent per month. She's just paid 4,000 more off her loan, bringing her total repayments to 6,000 as of now (Jan).
She's been at FNC since her rescue, then did a 3-month intensive bridge literacy course and a 3-month training. She was rescued 2 years ago. She was a kamlari for 6 years. She's 25 now but doesn't want me to know - they're too old to go back to school.
I want to grow the business and take over the bike shop!
I do housewiring as well - electrics.
That's why I have electrical supplies. I trained for 3 months in housewiring.
Next we join a protest march, timed to preempt the Maghe fair the next day.
STOP THE KAMLARI TRADITION - DON'T SELL DAUGHTERS!
DAUGHTERS DESERVE AN EDUCATION - NOT SLAVERY!
कमलरी प्रथा अन्त्य गरौं दास प्रथा बन्द
The atmosphere is charged as the women stride defiantly down the main street, accompanied by their own drummer. They chant in unison and some even dance, to the astonishment of the male passersby who stand agog by the side of the road.

Next we head to a smaller village to put faces to the names of families who felt forced to sell their daughters into the tradition. Most are the heads of families who scarcely stop working to talk to us.

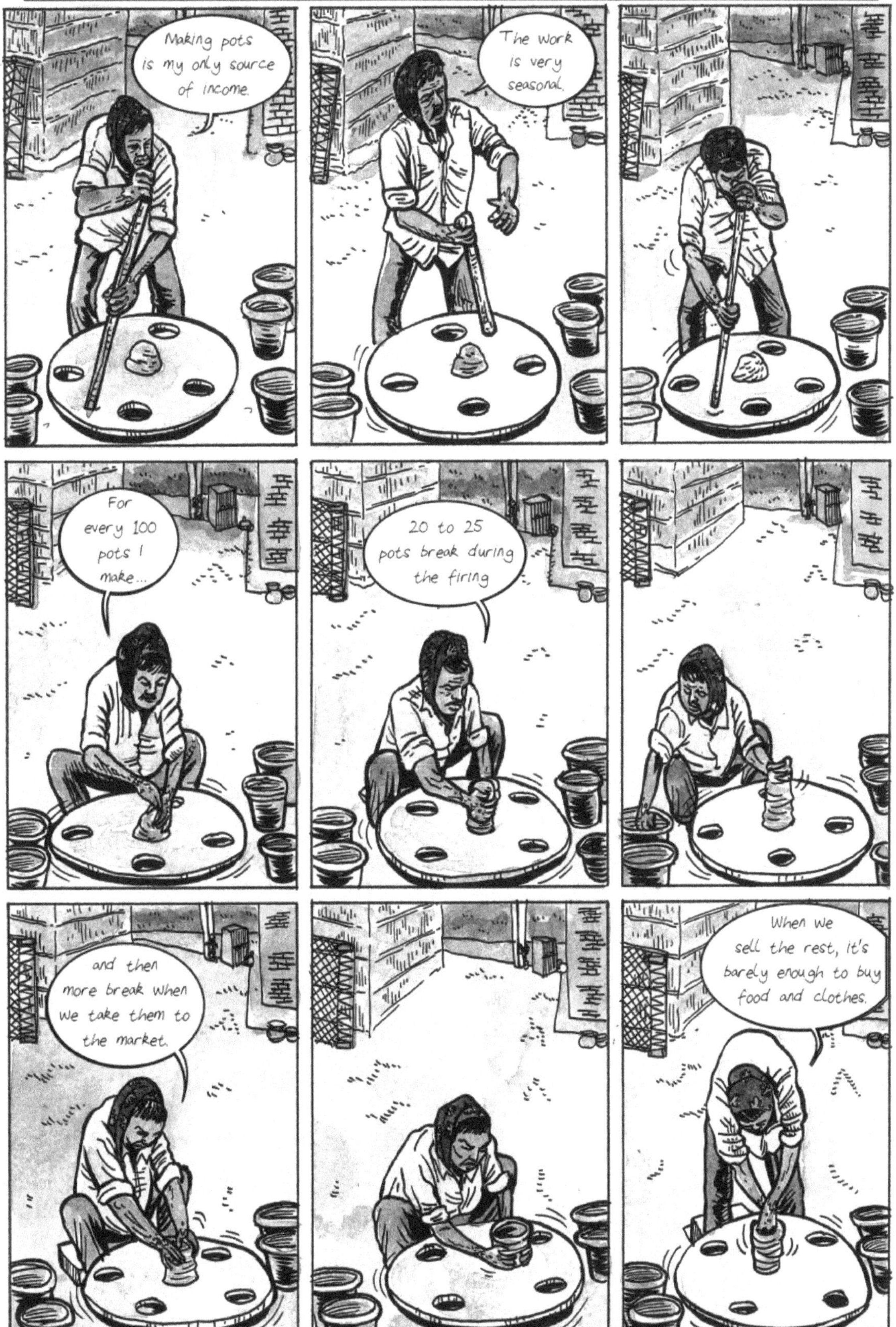

Making pots is my only source of income.
The work is very seasonal.
For every 100 pots I make...
20 to 25 pots break during the firing
and then more break when we take them to the market.
When we sell the rest, it's barely enough to buy food and clothes.

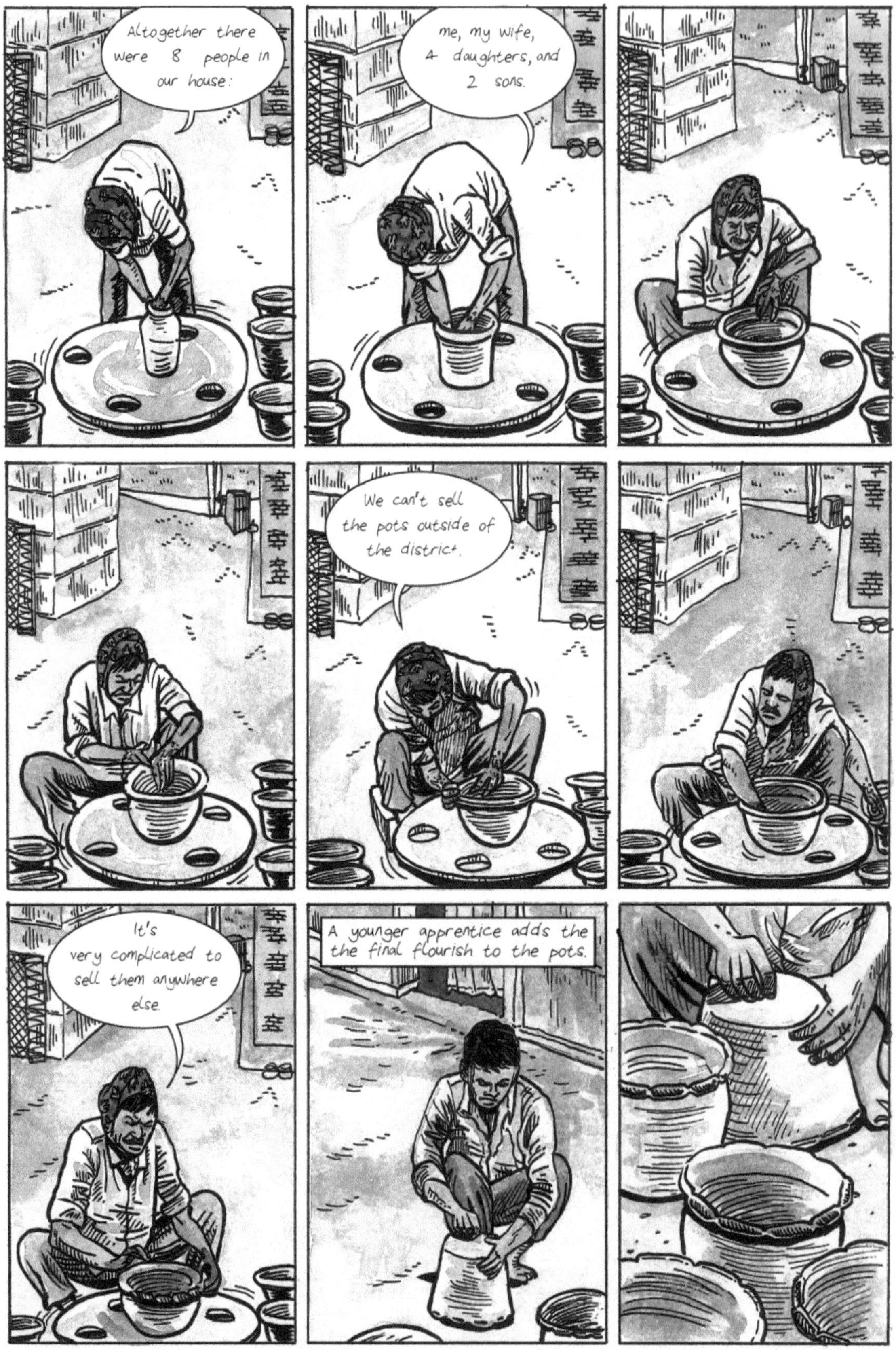
Altogether there were 8 people in our house:
me, my wife, 4 daughters, and 2 sons.
We can't sell the pots outside of the district.
It's very complicated to sell them anywhere else.
A younger apprentice adds the the final flourish to the pots.

I'm here in the western region with a mini delegation from Nepal Youth Foundation, who are checking in on the progress of their anti-kamlari activities.

The outdoor "oven" for firing pots

We visit Ghorahi in Dang District as well as freed Kamaya villages like Tikapur in Kailali.

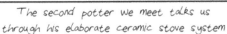

The second potter we meet talks us through his elaborate ceramic stove system

before admitting that he first sold his daughter 12 years ago when she was 7.

I don't remember how long she worked for.

And he goes silent when I ask him why he felt he had to sell his daughters.

Duda Tharu Kumar, 60

I would never sell a son

Sons do the labor work

I am not a literate man

89

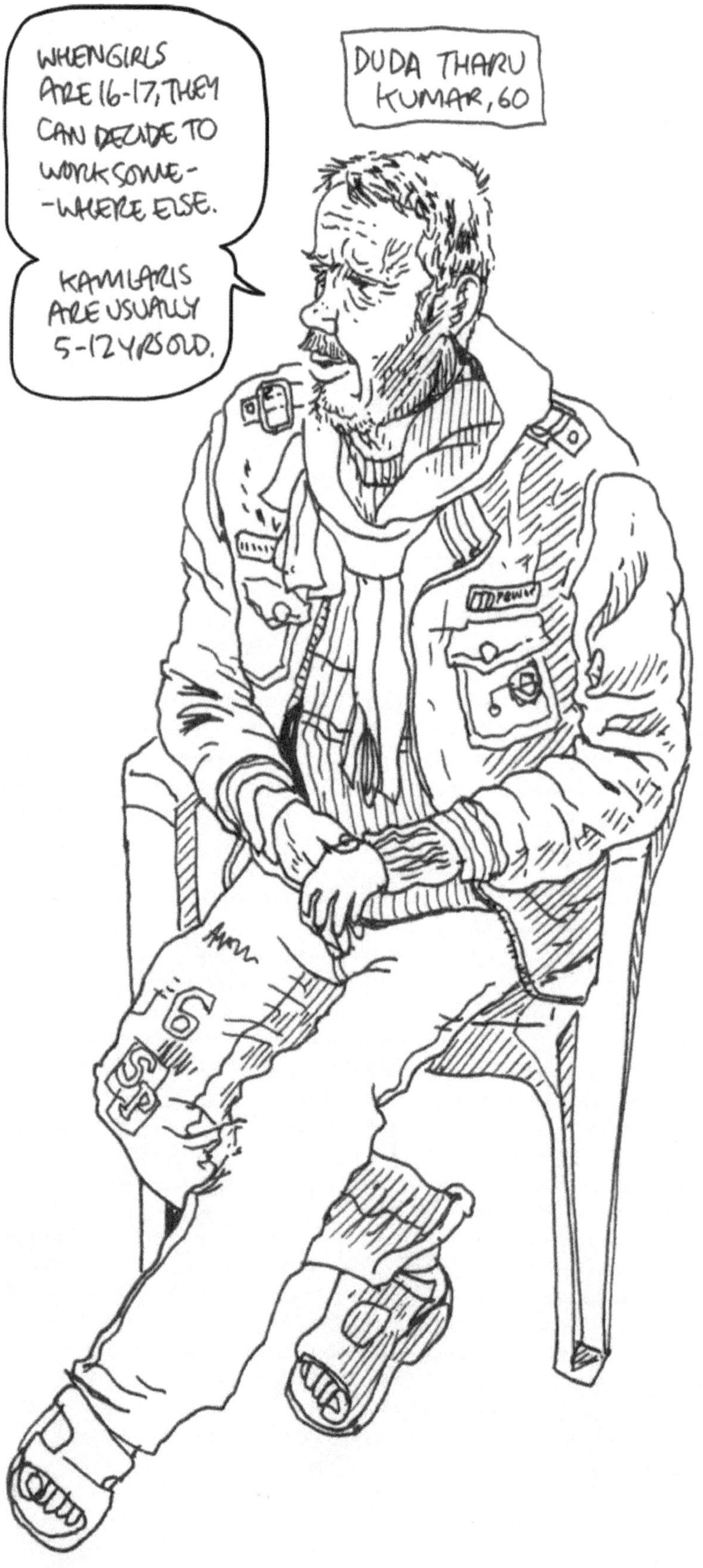
WHEN GIRLS ARE 16-17, THEY CAN DECIDE TO WORK SOME- -WHERE ELSE.
KAMLARIS ARE USUALLY 5-12 YRS OLD.
DUDA THARU KUMAR, 60

In this Tharu community it's the culture to sell their daughters.

No one owns land; it's a long process to get the certificates.

The landlord came to our village, that's how we found him.

He came during the Maghe.

He drove here by car and took the daughters to Butwal.

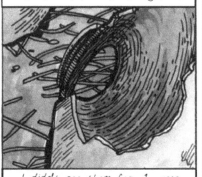

It made my heart beat faster when I sold my daughters. I was worried about what he might do.

I didn't see them for 1 year. We don't know whether he will behave with them or not.

We did the deal. 3,000 rupees per girl for 1 year.

His Daughter, Sangita Tharu Kumar, 24

I was so small I don't know how much I was paid.

I worked as a kamlari for 1 year when I was 12

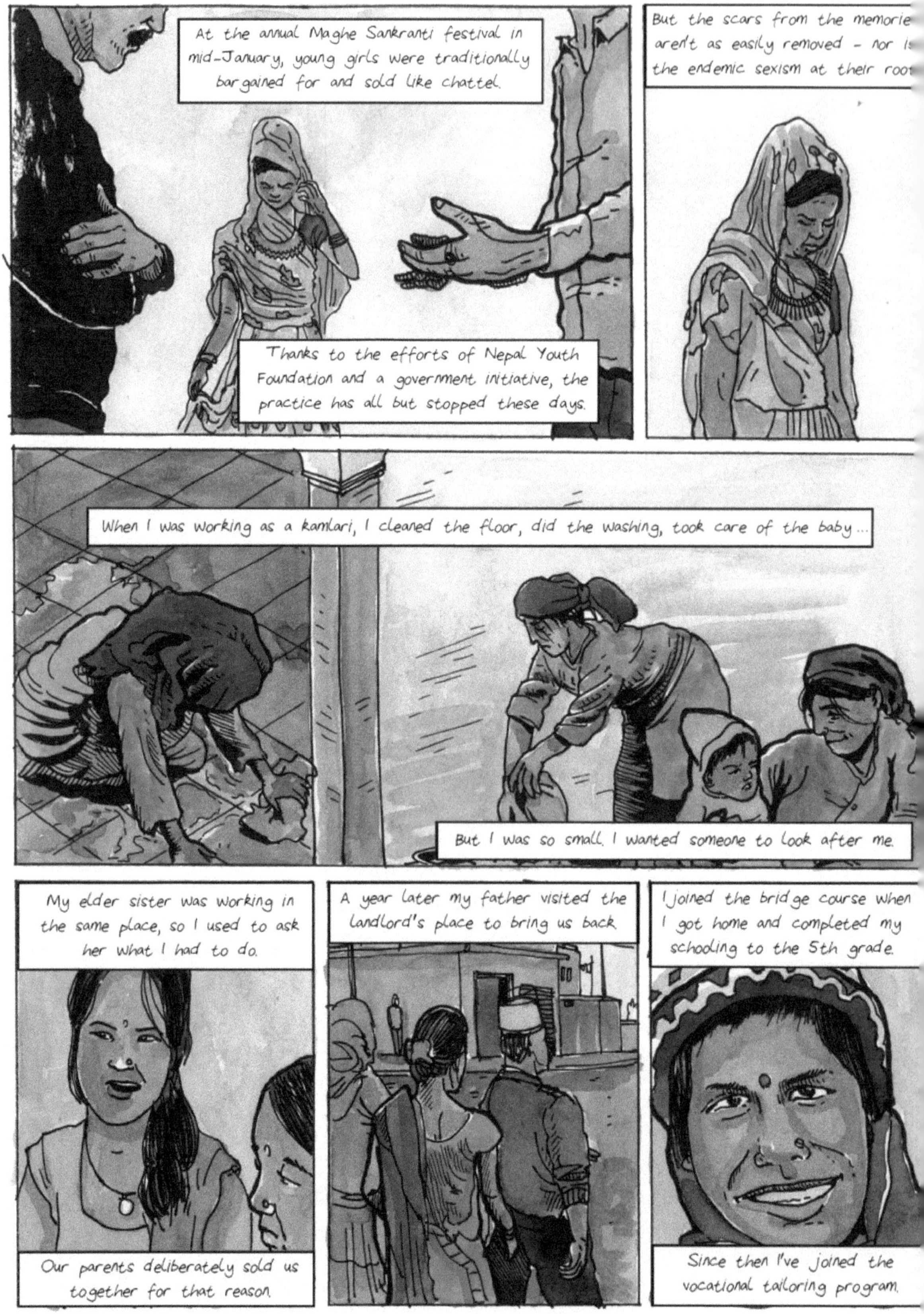
At the annual Maghe Sankranti festival in mid-January, young girls were traditionally bargained for and sold like chattel.
Thanks to the efforts of Nepal Youth Foundation and a government initiative, the practice has all but stopped these days.
But the scars from the memorie
aren't as easily removed – nor i
the endemic sexism at their roo
When I was working as a kamlari, I cleaned the floor, did the washing, took care of the baby...
But I was so small. I wanted someone to look after me.
My elder sister was working in the same place, so I used to ask her what I had to do.
Our parents deliberately sold us together for that reason.
A year later my father visited the landlord's place to bring us back.
I joined the bridge course when I got home and completed my schooling to the 5th grade.
Since then I've joined the vocational tailoring program.

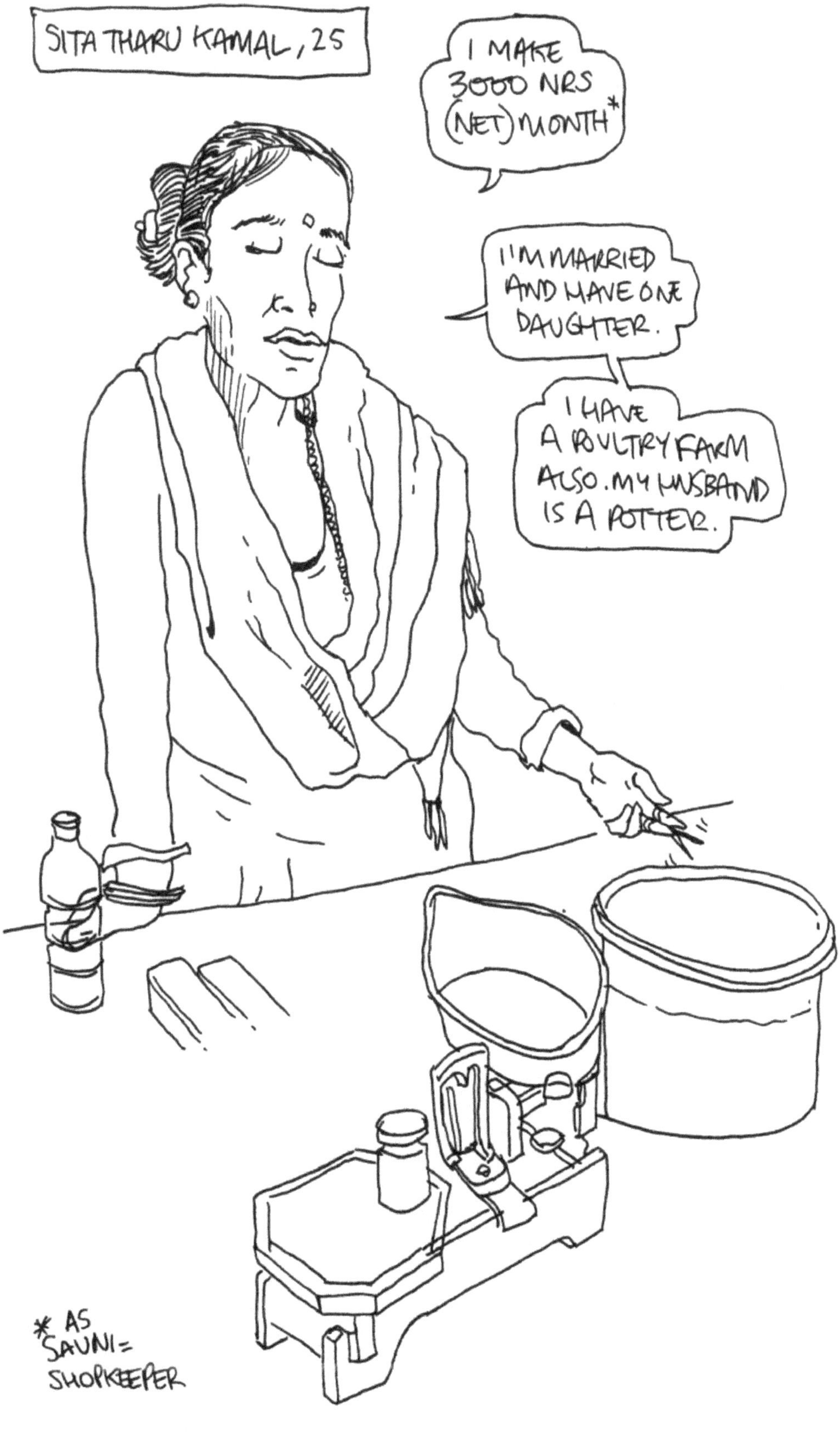
SITA THARU KAMAL, 25
I MAKE 3000 NRS (NET) MONTH*
I'M MARRIED AND HAVE ONE DAUGHTER.
I HAVE A POULTRY FARM ALSO. MY HUSBAND IS A POTTER.
* AS SAUNI = SHOPKEEPER

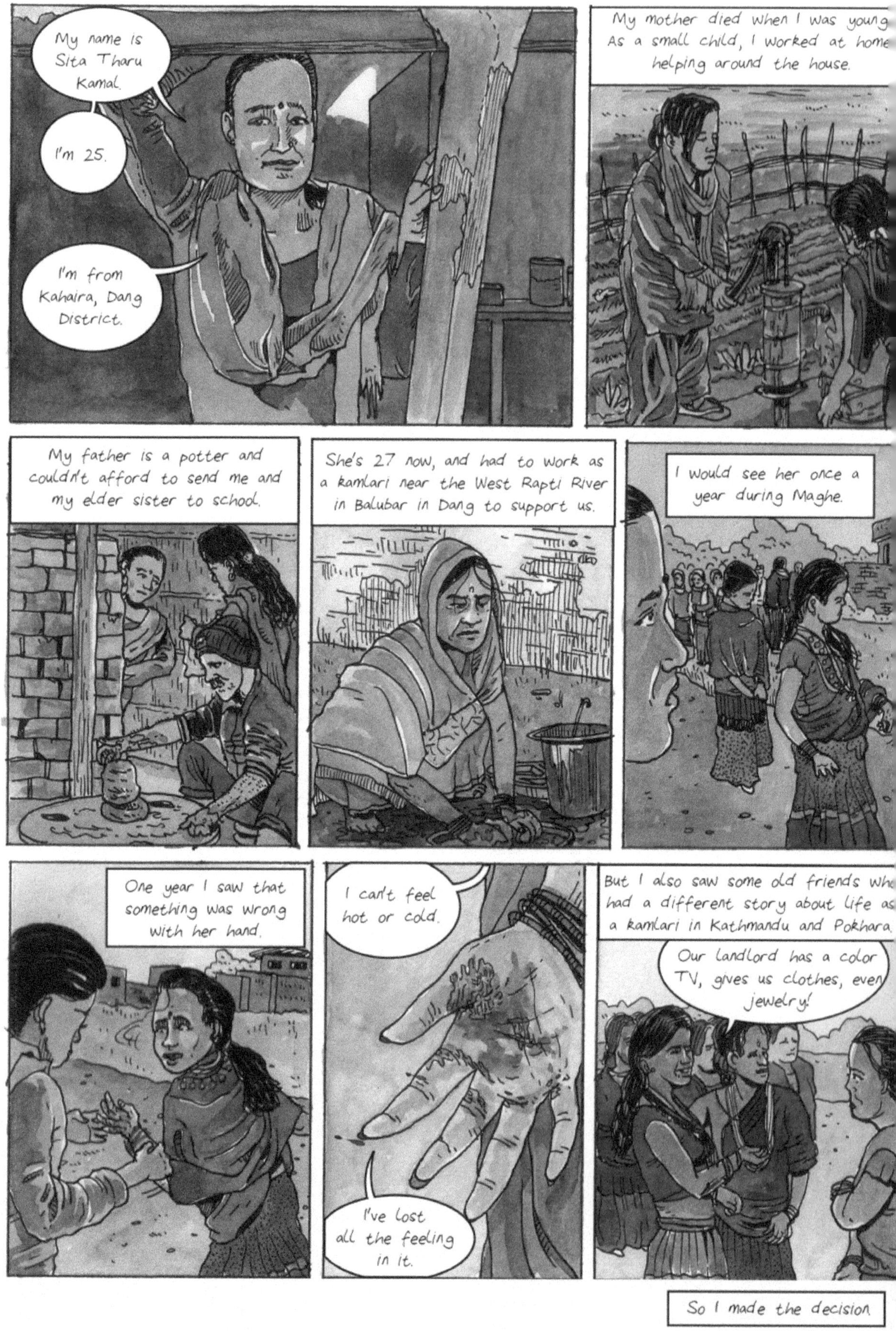
My name is Sita Tharu Kamal.
I'm 25.
I'm from Kahaira, Dang District.
My mother died when I was young. As a small child, I worked at home helping around the house.
My father is a potter and couldn't afford to send me and my elder sister to school.
She's 27 now, and had to work as a kamlari near the West Rapti River in Balubar in Dang to support us.
I would see her once a year during Maghe.
One year I saw that something was wrong with her hand.
I can't feel hot or cold.
I've lost all the feeling in it.
But I also saw some old friends who had a different story about life as a kamlari in Kathmandu and Pokhara.
Our landlord has a color TV, gives us clothes, even jewelry!
So I made the decision

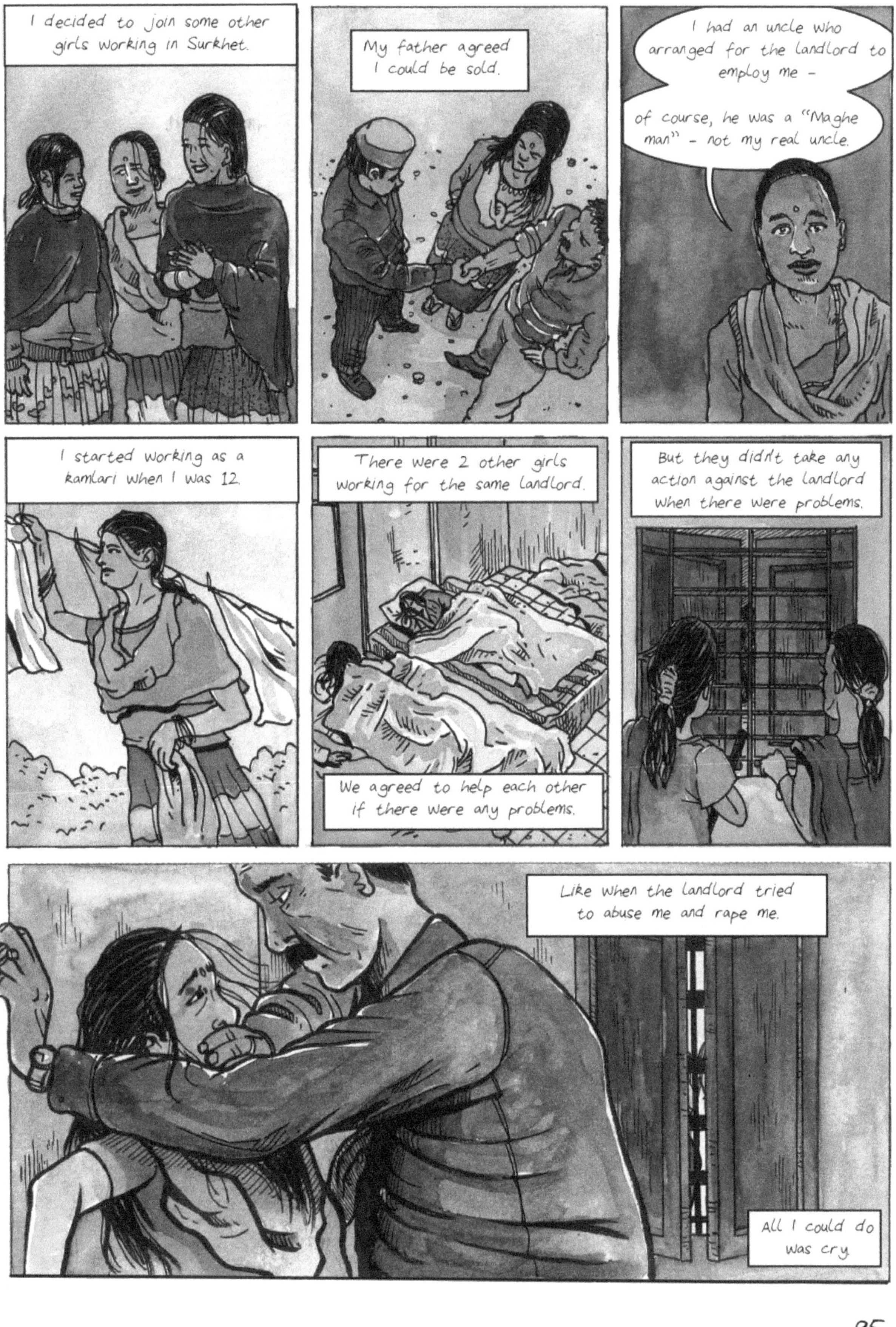
I decided to join some other girls working in Surkhet.
My father agreed I could be sold.
I had an uncle who arranged for the landlord to employ me -
of course, he was a "Maghe man" - not my real uncle.
I started working as a kamlari when I was 12.
There were 2 other girls working for the same landlord.
We agreed to help each other if there were any problems.
But they didn't take any action against the landlord when there were problems.
Like when the landlord tried to abuse me and rape me.
All I could do was cry

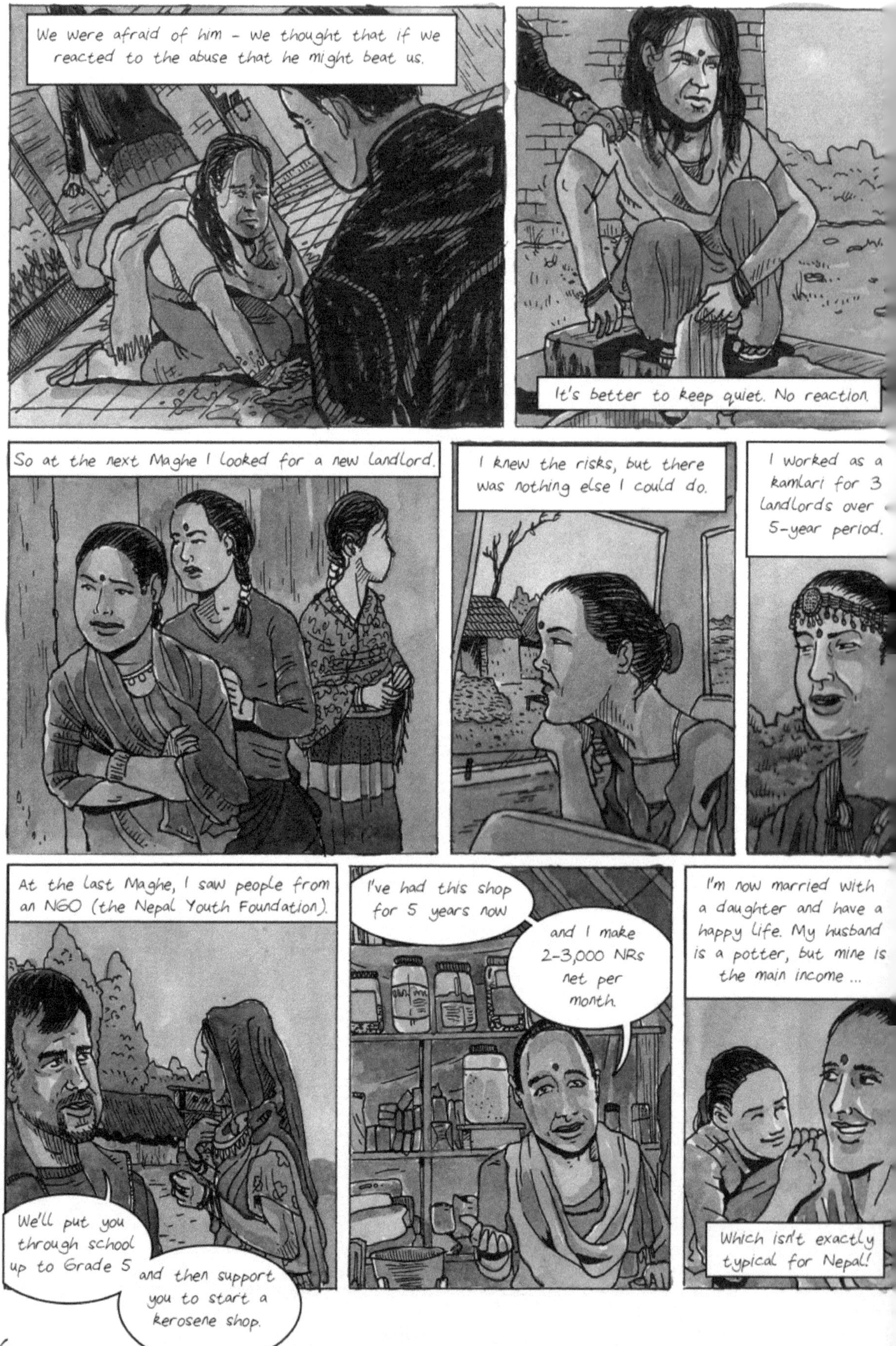
We were afraid of him - we thought that if we reacted to the abuse that he might beat us.
It's better to keep quiet. No reaction.
So at the next Maghe I looked for a new landlord.
I knew the risks, but there was nothing else I could do.
I worked as a kamlari for 3 landlords over 5-year period.
At the last Maghe, I saw people from an NGO (the Nepal Youth Foundation).
We'll put you through school up to Grade 5
and then support you to start a kerosene shop.
I've had this shop for 5 years now
and I make 2-3,000 NRs net per month.
I'm now married with a daughter and have a happy life. My husband is a potter, but mine is the main income ...
Which isn't exactly typical for Nepal!

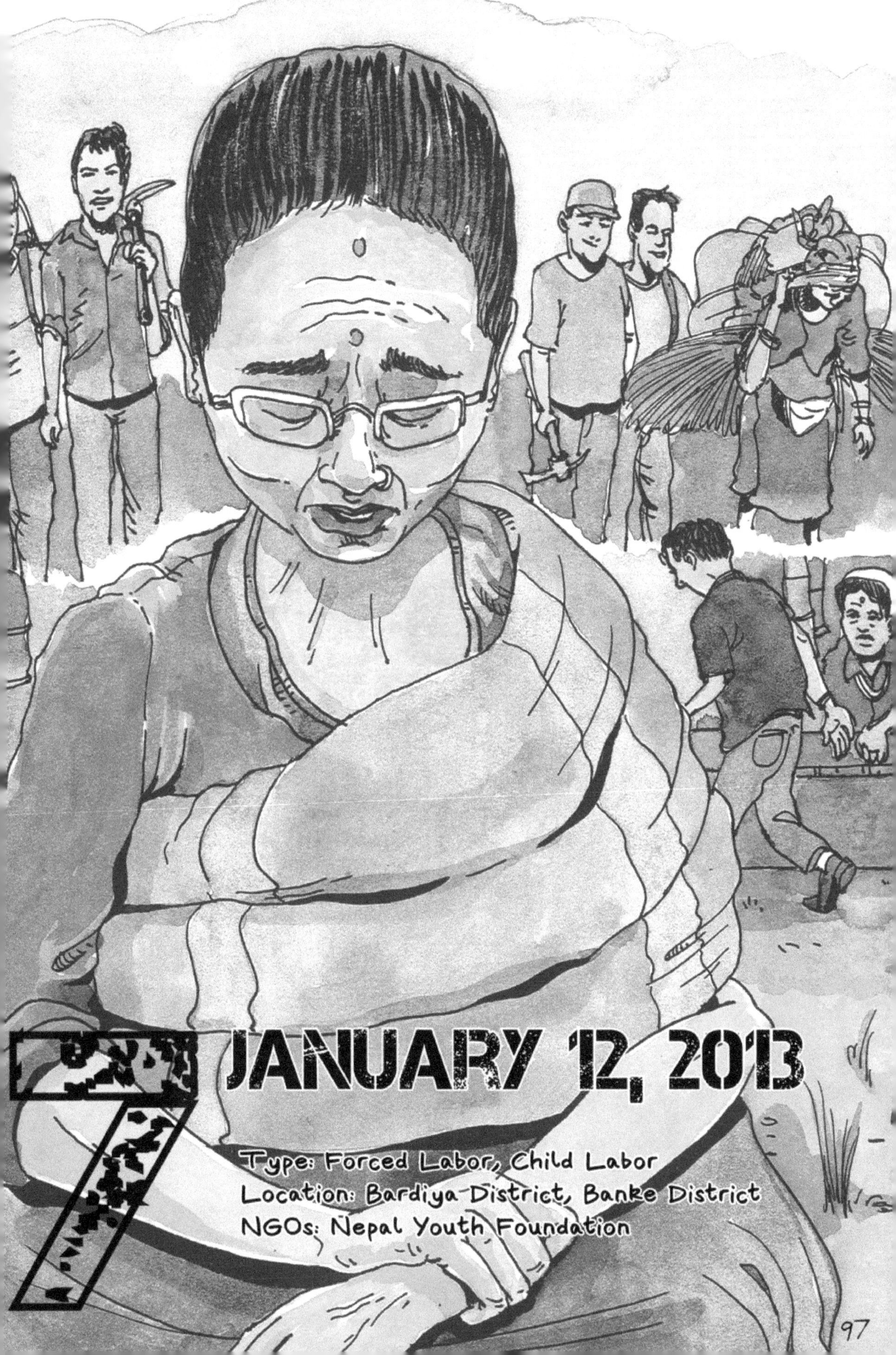

7 JANUARY 12, 2013

Type: Forced Labor, Child Labor
Location: Bardiya District, Banke District
NGOs: Nepal Youth Foundation

THE ANNUAL CHILD SLAVE FAIR

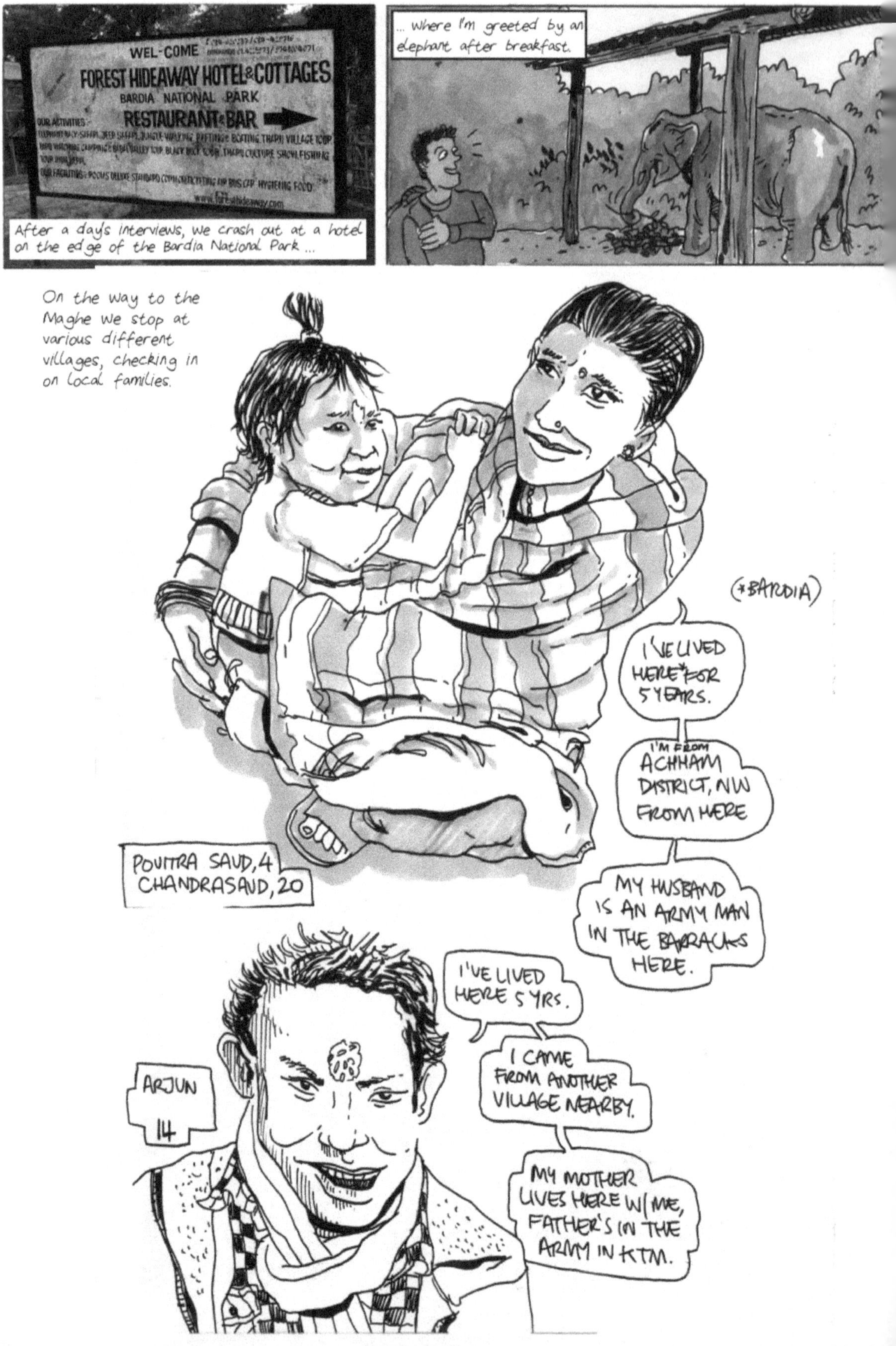
WEL-COME
FOREST HIDEAWAY HOTEL&COTTAGES
BARDIA NATIONAL PARK
RESTAURANT&BAR
After a day's interviews, we crash out at a hotel on the edge of the Bardia National Park ...
... where I'm greeted by an elephant after breakfast.
On the way to the Maghe we stop at various different villages, checking in on local families.
POVITRA SAUD, 4
CHANDRASAUD, 20
I'VE LIVED HERE* FOR 5 YEARS.
(*BARDIA)
I'M FROM ACHHAM DISTRICT, NW FROM HERE
MY HUSBAND IS AN ARMY MAN IN THE BARRACKS HERE.
ARJUN
14
I'VE LIVED HERE 5 YRS.
I CAME FROM ANOTHER VILLAGE NEARBY.
MY MOTHER LIVES HERE W/ ME, FATHER'S IN THE ARMY IN KTM.

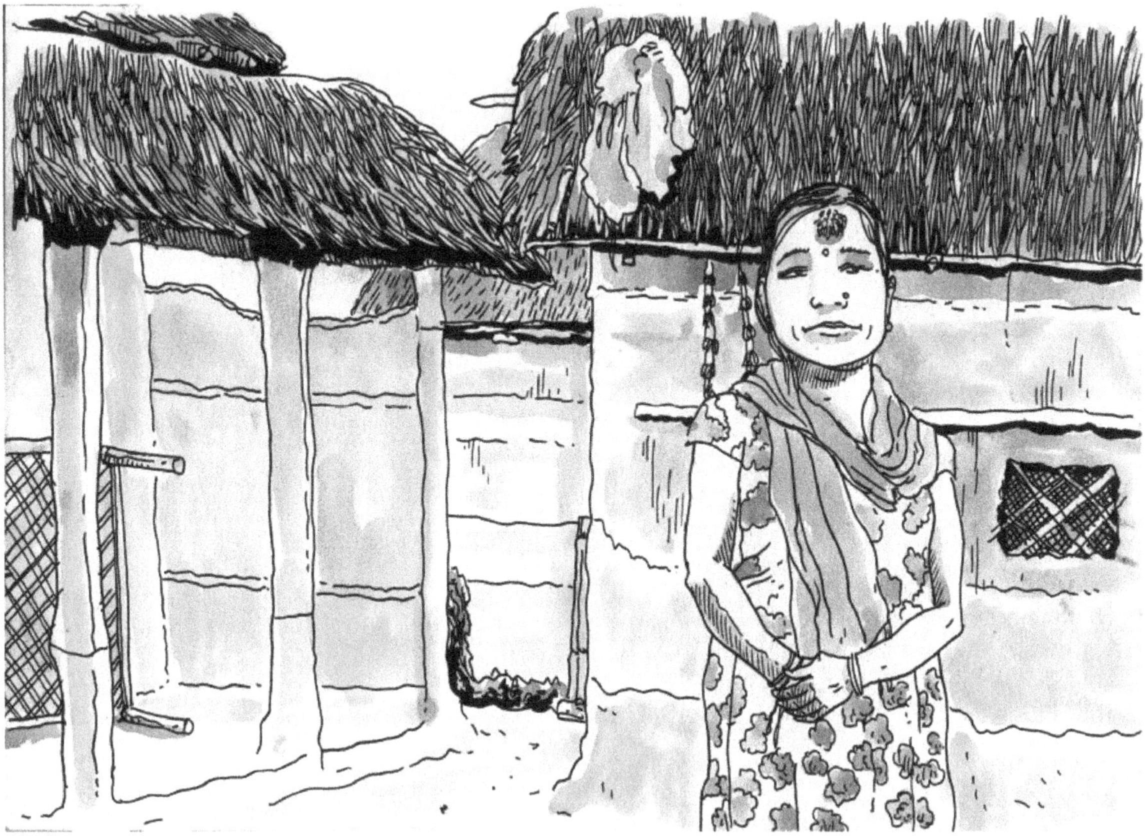

People are intrigued
and delighted to get
their portraits drawn

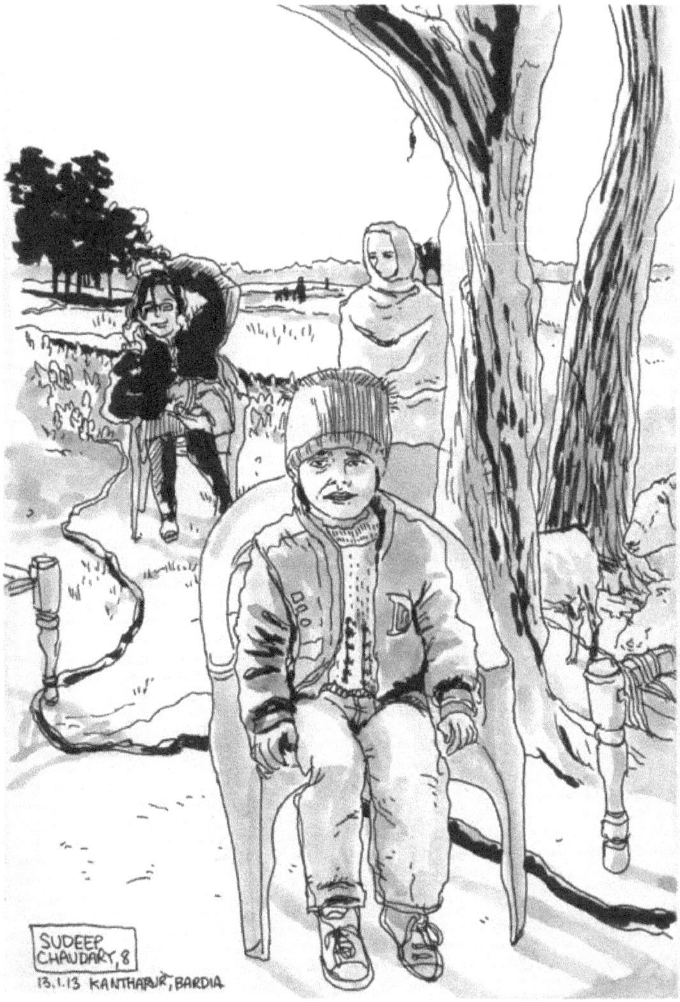
SUDEEP CHAUDARY, 8
13.1.13 KANTHAPUR, BARDIA

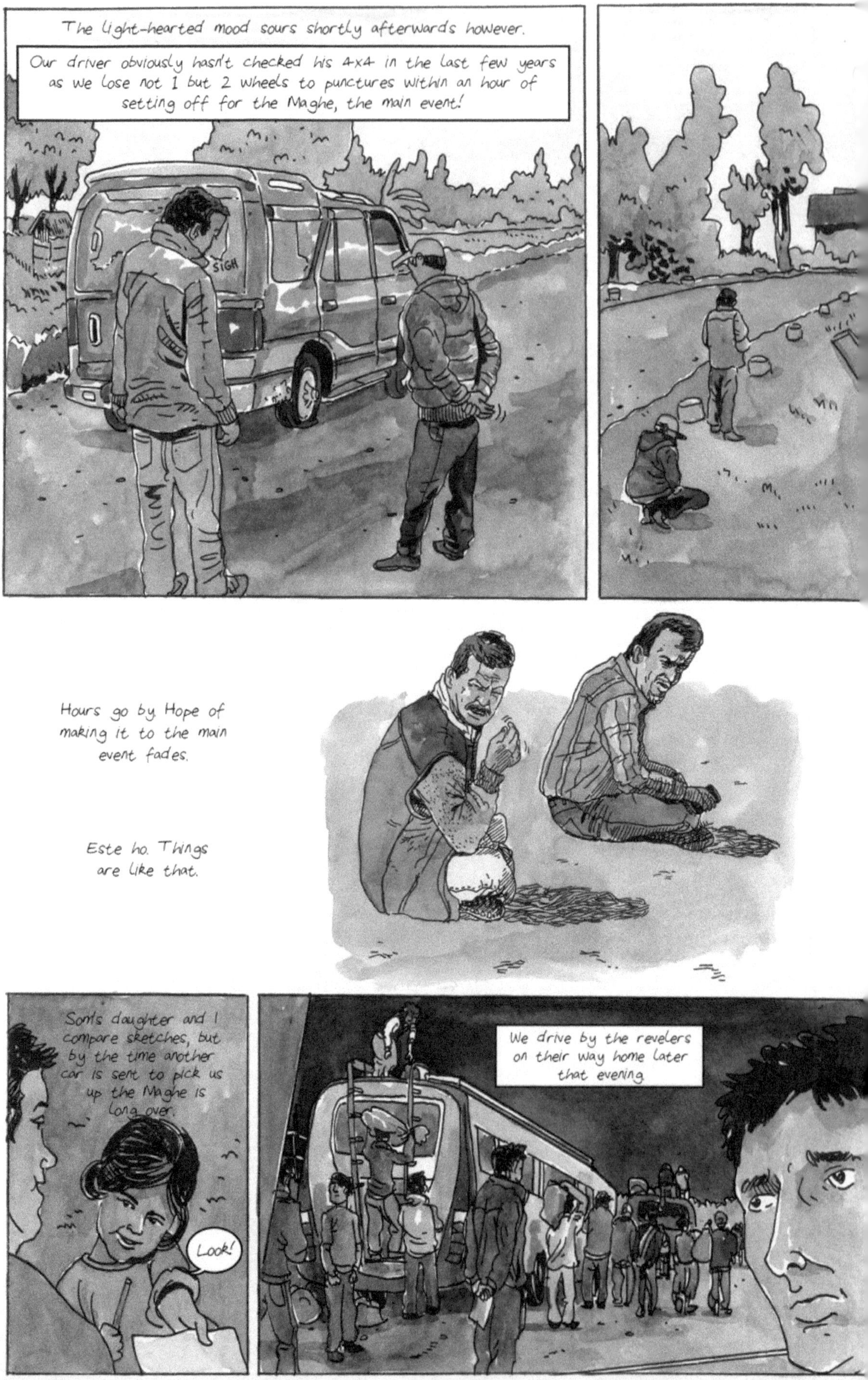
The light-hearted mood sours shortly afterwards however.
Our driver obviously hasn't checked his 4x4 in the last few years as we lose not 1 but 2 wheels to punctures within an hour of setting off for the Maghe, the main event!
SIGH
Hours go by. Hope of making it to the main event fades.
Este ho. Things are like that.
Soni's daughter and I compare sketches, but by the time another car is sent to pick us up the Maghe is long over.
Look!
We drive by the revelers on their way home later that evening.

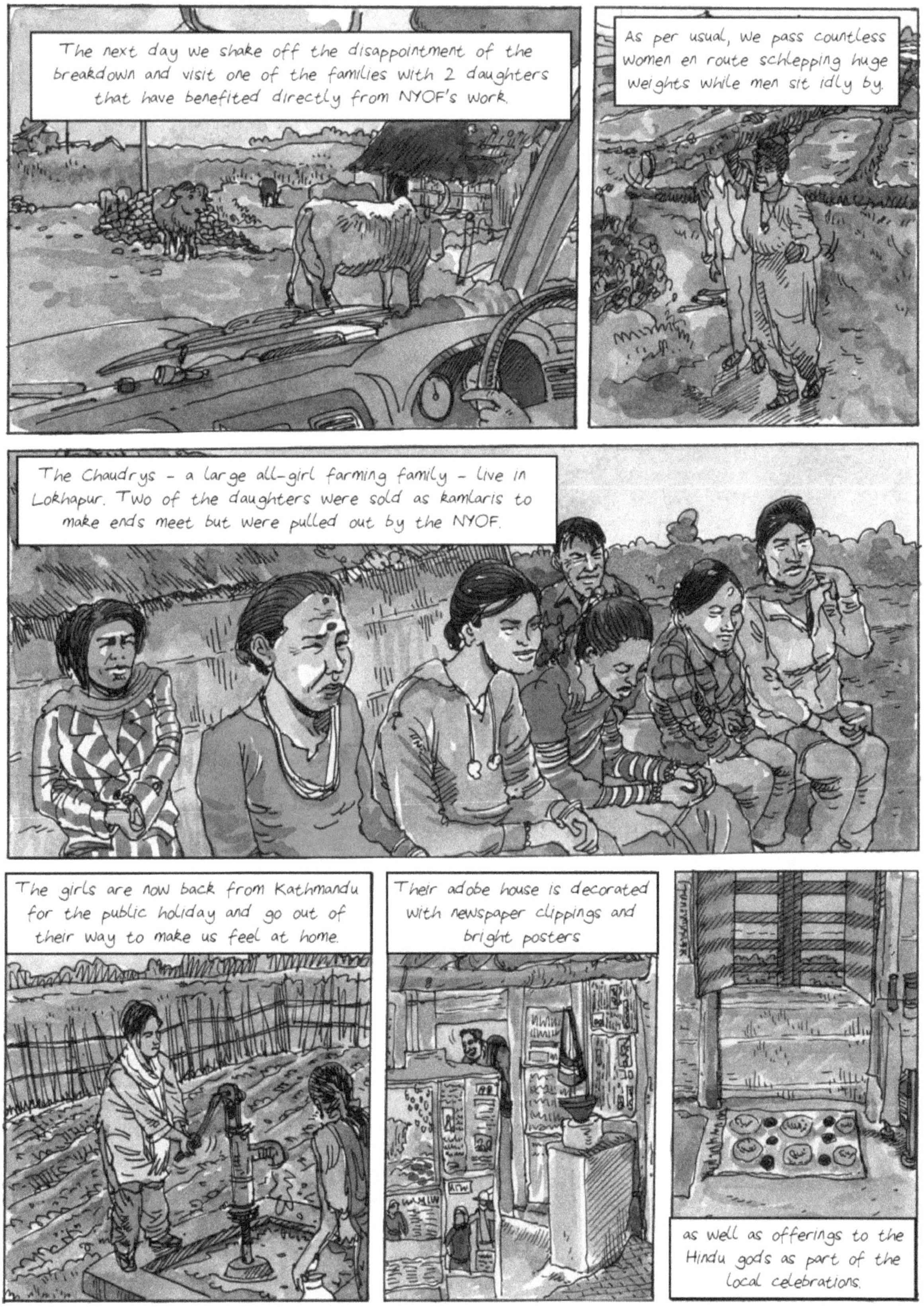
The next day we shake off the disappointment of the breakdown and visit one of the families with 2 daughters that have benefited directly from NYOF's work.
As per usual, we pass countless women en route schlepping huge weights while men sit idly by.
The Chaudrys - a large all-girl farming family - live in Lokhapur. Two of the daughters were sold as kamlaris to make ends meet but were pulled out by the NYOF.
The girls are now back from Kathmandu for the public holiday and go out of their way to make us feel at home.
Their adobe house is decorated with newspaper clippings and bright posters
as well as offerings to the Hindu gods as part of the local celebrations.

Manjita is currently working for Som and his family in Kathmandu as a domestic worker. She overcome her horrendous experience of being abused as a kamlari and set up a cooperative for fellow ex-kamlaris some years ago. She is a living testament to the success of Olga's scheme whereby families are incentivized to not sell their daughters by being given a goat to care for and sell.

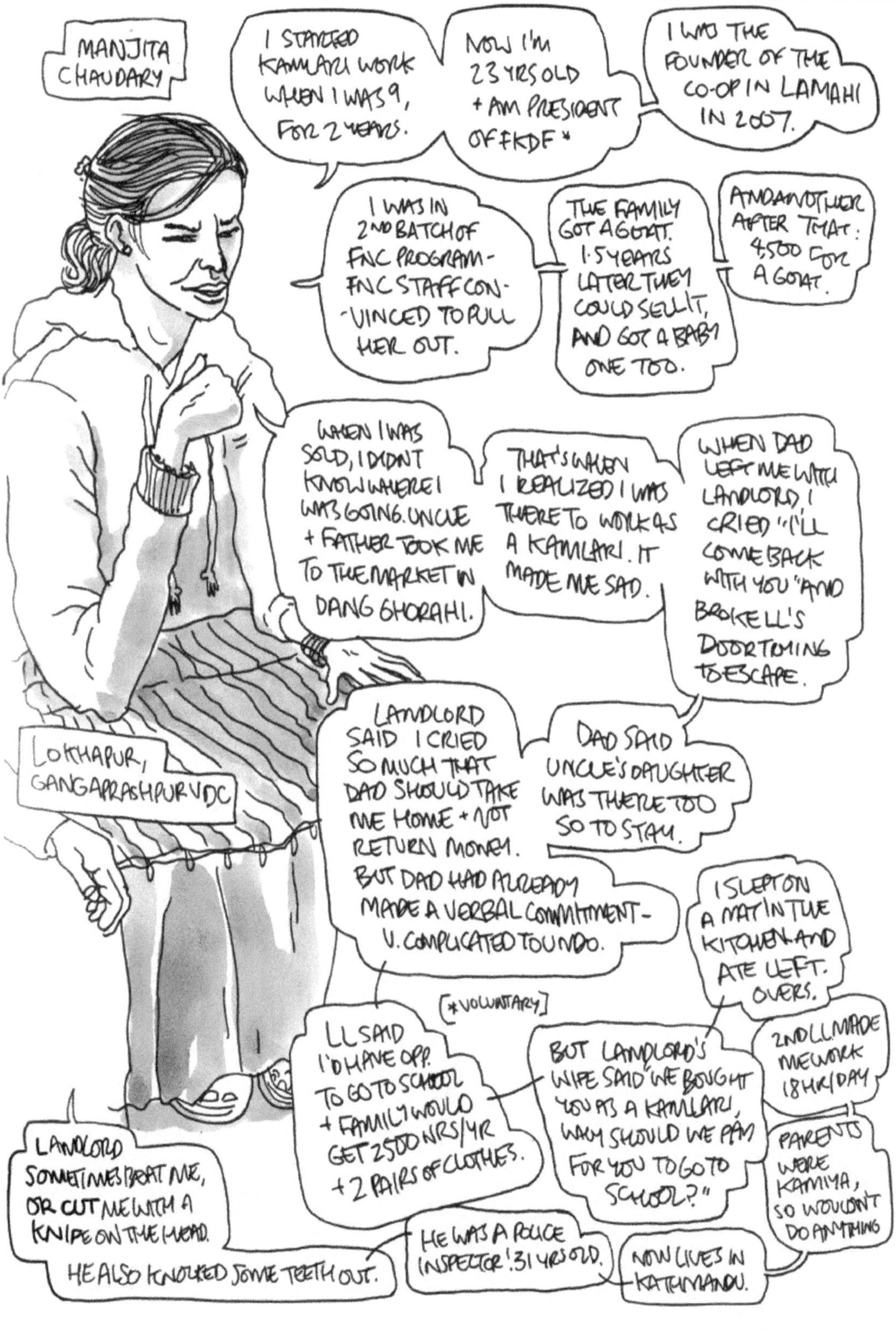

MANJITA CHAUDARY
I STARTED KAMLARI WORK WHEN I WAS 9, FOR 2 YEARS.
NOW I'M 23 YRS OLD + AM PRESIDENT OF FKDF*
I WAS THE FOUNDER OF THE CO-OP IN LAMAHI IN 2007.
I WAS IN 2ND BATCH OF FNC PROGRAM - FNC STAFF CON-VINCED TO PULL HER OUT.
THE FAMILY GOT A GOAT. 1.5 YEARS LATER THEY COULD SELL IT, AND GOT A BABY ONE TOO.
AND ANOTHER AFTER THAT: 4,500 FOR A GOAT.
WHEN I WAS SOLD, I DIDN'T KNOW WHERE I WAS GOING. UNCLE + FATHER TOOK ME TO THE MARKET IN DANG GHORAHI.
THAT'S WHEN I REALIZED I WAS THERE TO WORK AS A KAMLARI. IT MADE ME SAD.
WHEN DAD LEFT ME WITH LANDLORD, I CRIED "I'LL COME BACK WITH YOU" AND BROKE LL'S DOOR TRYING TO ESCAPE.
LOKHAPUR, GANGAPRASHPUR VDC
LANDLORD SAID I CRIED SO MUCH THAT DAD SHOULD TAKE ME HOME + NOT RETURN MONEY. BUT DAD HAD ALREADY MADE A VERBAL COMMITMENT - V. COMPLICATED TO UNDO.
DAD SAID UNCLE'S DAUGHTER WAS THERE TOO SO TO STAY.
I SLEPT ON A MAT IN THE KITCHEN AND ATE LEFT-OVERS.
[*VOLUNTARY]
LL SAID I'D HAVE OPP. TO GO TO SCHOOL + FAMILY WOULD GET 2500 NRS/YR + 2 PAIRS OF CLOTHES.
BUT LANDLORD'S WIFE SAID "WE BOUGHT YOU AS A KAMLARI, WHY SHOULD WE PAY FOR YOU TO GO TO SCHOOL?"
2ND LL MADE ME WORK 18 HR/DAY
PARENTS WERE KAMIYA, SO WOULDN'T DO ANYTHING
LANDLORD SOMETIMES BEAT ME, OR CUT ME WITH A KNIFE ON THE HEAD.
HE ALSO KNOCKED SOME TEETH OUT.
HE WAS A POLICE INSPECTOR! 31 YRS OLD.
NOW LIVES IN KATHMANDU.

Likewise, her elder sister is acutely aware of the underlying roots of the problem, and talks eloquently of the endemic sexism and socioeconomic reasons that allow the kamlari tradition to continue. Like her sister, she is impressively adamant about dedicating herself to helping others avoid a similar fate to her and her sister, as well as counseling fellow ex-slaves.

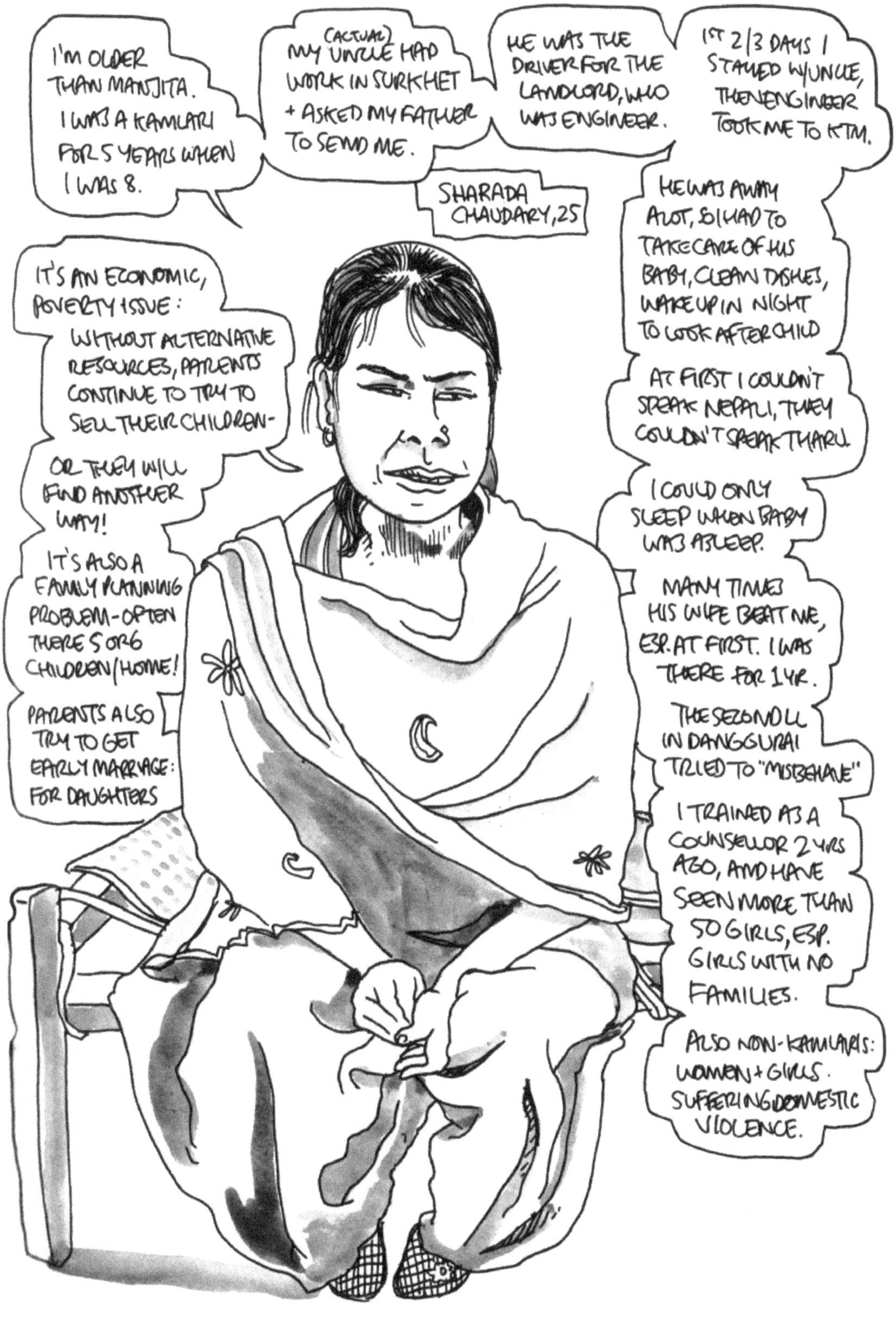

I'M OLDER THAN MANJITA. I WAS A KAMLARI FOR 5 YEARS WHEN I WAS 8.
MY (ACTUAL) UNCLE HAD WORK IN SURKHET + ASKED MY FATHER TO SEND ME.
HE WAS THE DRIVER FOR THE LANDLORD, WHO WAS ENGINEER.
1ST 2/3 DAYS I STAYED W/UNCLE, THEN ENGINEER TOOK ME TO KTM.
SHARADA CHAUDARY, 25
HE WAS AWAY ALOT, SO I HAD TO TAKE CARE OF HIS BABY, CLEAN DISHES, WAKE UP IN NIGHT TO LOOK AFTER CHILD
AT FIRST I COULDN'T SPEAK NEPALI, THEY COULDN'T SPEAK THARU
I COULD ONLY SLEEP WHEN BABY WAS ASLEEP.
MANY TIMES HIS WIFE BEAT ME, ESP. AT FIRST. I WAS THERE FOR 1 YR.
THE SECOND LL IN DANGGURAI TRIED TO "MISBEHAVE"
I TRAINED AS A COUNSELLOR 2 YRS AGO, AND HAVE SEEN MORE THAN 50 GIRLS, ESP. GIRLS WITH NO FAMILIES.
ALSO NON-KAMLARIS: WOMEN + GIRLS. SUFFERING DOMESTIC VIOLENCE.
IT'S AN ECONOMIC, POVERTY ISSUE: WITHOUT ALTERNATIVE RESOURCES, PARENTS CONTINUE TO TRY TO SELL THEIR CHILDREN-
OR THEY WILL FIND ANOTHER WAY!
IT'S ALSO A FAMILY PLANNING PROBLEM-OFTEN THERE 5 OR 6 CHILDREN/HOME!
PARENTS ALSO TRY TO GET EARLY MARRIAGE FOR DAUGHTERS

Our last port of call takes this self-awareness to a whole new level. There we meet Leela, a headstrong character who decided to sell herself (!) in order to finance her education, on her terms. Since then, she received the financial backing from the FNC to start her own telecom shop, where she dispenses electronic advice to the stream of local men who shuffle in and out, proferring their broken phones to her, helplessl

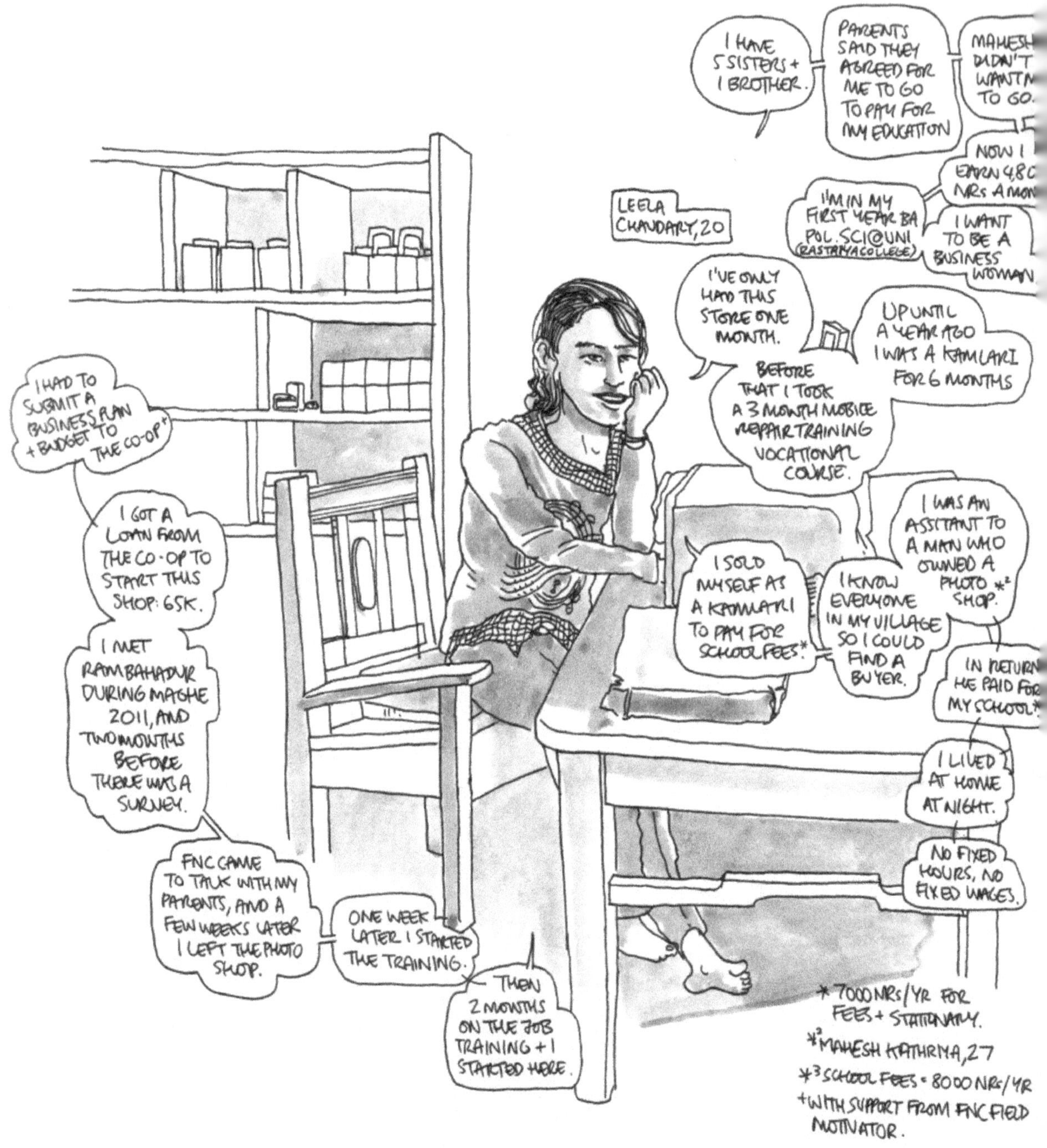
LEELA CHAUDARY, 20
I HAVE 5 SISTERS + 1 BROTHER.
PARENTS SAID THEY AGREED FOR ME TO GO TO PAY FOR MY EDUCATION
MAHESH DIDN'T WANT M TO GO.
NOW I EARN 4,8C NRs A MON
I'M IN MY FIRST YEAR BA POL. SCI@UNI (RASTRIYA COLLEGE)
I WANT TO BE A BUSINESS WOMAN
I'VE ONLY HAD THIS STORE ONE MONTH.
UP UNTIL A YEAR AGO I WAS A KAMLARI FOR 6 MONTHS
BEFORE THAT I TOOK A 3 MONTH MOBILE REPAIR TRAINING VOCATIONAL COURSE.
I SOLD MYSELF AS A KAMLARI TO PAY FOR SCHOOL FEES.*
I KNOW EVERYONE IN MY VILLAGE SO I COULD FIND A BUYER.
I WAS AN ASSITANT TO A MAN WHO OWNED A PHOTO SHOP. *²
IN RETURN HE PAID FOR MY SCHOOL*³
I LIVED AT HOME AT NIGHT.
NO FIXED HOURS, NO FIXED WAGES.
I HAD TO SUBMIT A BUSINESS PLAN + BUDGET TO THE CO-OP⁺
I GOT A LOAN FROM THE CO-OP TO START THIS SHOP: 65K.
I MET RAM BAHADUR DURING MAGHE 2011, AND TWO MONTHS BEFORE THERE WAS A SURVEY.
FNC CAME TO TALK WITH MY PARENTS, AND A FEW WEEKS LATER I LEFT THE PHOTO SHOP.
ONE WEEK LATER I STARTED THE TRAINING.
THEN 2 MONTHS ON THE JOB TRAINING + I STARTED HERE.
* 7000 NRs/YR FOR FEES + STATIONARY.
*² MAHESH KATHRIYA, 27
*³ SCHOOL FEES = 8000 NRs/YR
⁺ WITH SUPPORT FROM FNC FIELD MOTIVATOR.

She's part of the new generation of girls who are aware of the sexist systems of patriarchy and aren't afraid of using them for their own benefit. It's a refreshingly positive note to leave on as we say our farewells and head out toward the border with India

NOBODY'S DAUGHTERS

In Tikapur, Som meets with a group of Badi women, trying to help them in the same way as the kamlari girls.

Badi women are considered to be among the lowest on the caste ladder, aka "untouchables."

As a result, many of them rely on prostitution to support themselves, which only leads to generational cycles of sexual slavery. Som is trying to break them out of this mindset, but it's not easy.

It seems major problems are related to earning a living —

— how's the income from pig rearing?

The main spokeswoman of the community comes forward: Som tells me she's quite political.

The cost of pig feed has gone up.

We rarely earn profits — we save 20 NRs a year!

We prefer finding work in our own country to going to India and suffering,

but only if the government could provide us with satisfactory jobs.

Officials say they send budget for us to VDC*, but we get nothing.

*Village Development Committee

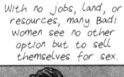

With no jobs, land, or resources, many Badi women see no other option but to sell themselves for sex.

One man on his own, like a husband, is hard enough to bear.

But you can imagine how much you suffer if you have to satisfy 10 to 20 men a day...

It's already been 2 years since the government asked us to change our profession

But we've been given nothing, neither by the government nor by society...

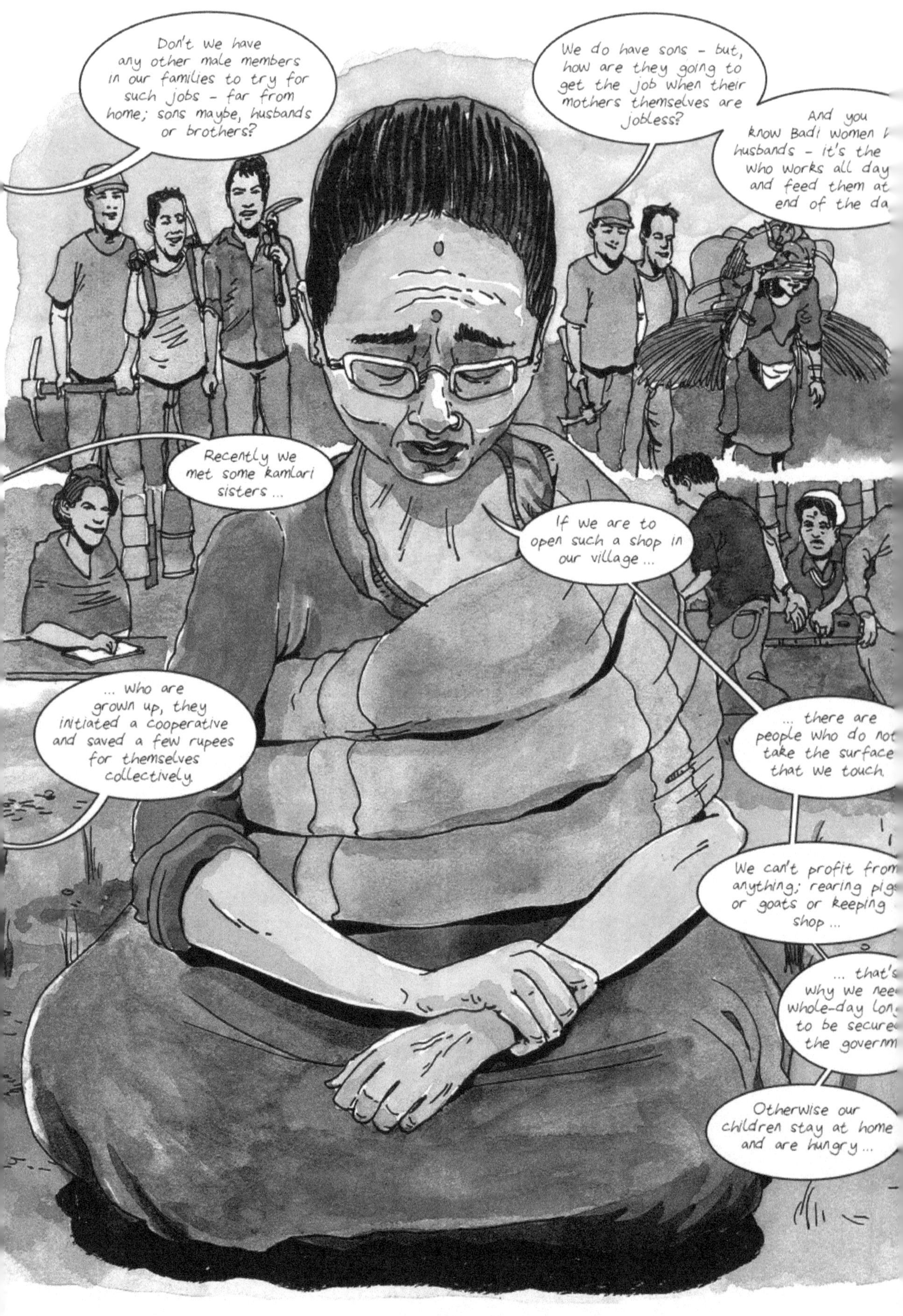
Don't we have any other male members in our families to try for such jobs – far from home; sons maybe, husbands or brothers?
We do have sons – but, how are they going to get the job when their mothers themselves are jobless?
And you know Badi women husbands – it's the who works all day and feed them at end of the
Recently we met some kamlari sisters ...
If we are to open such a shop in our village ...
... who are grown up, they initiated a cooperative and saved a few rupees for themselves collectively.
... there are people who do not take the surface that we touch.
We can't profit from anything; rearing pigs or goats or keeping shop ...
... that's why we whole-day to be the
Otherwise our children stay at home and are hungry ...

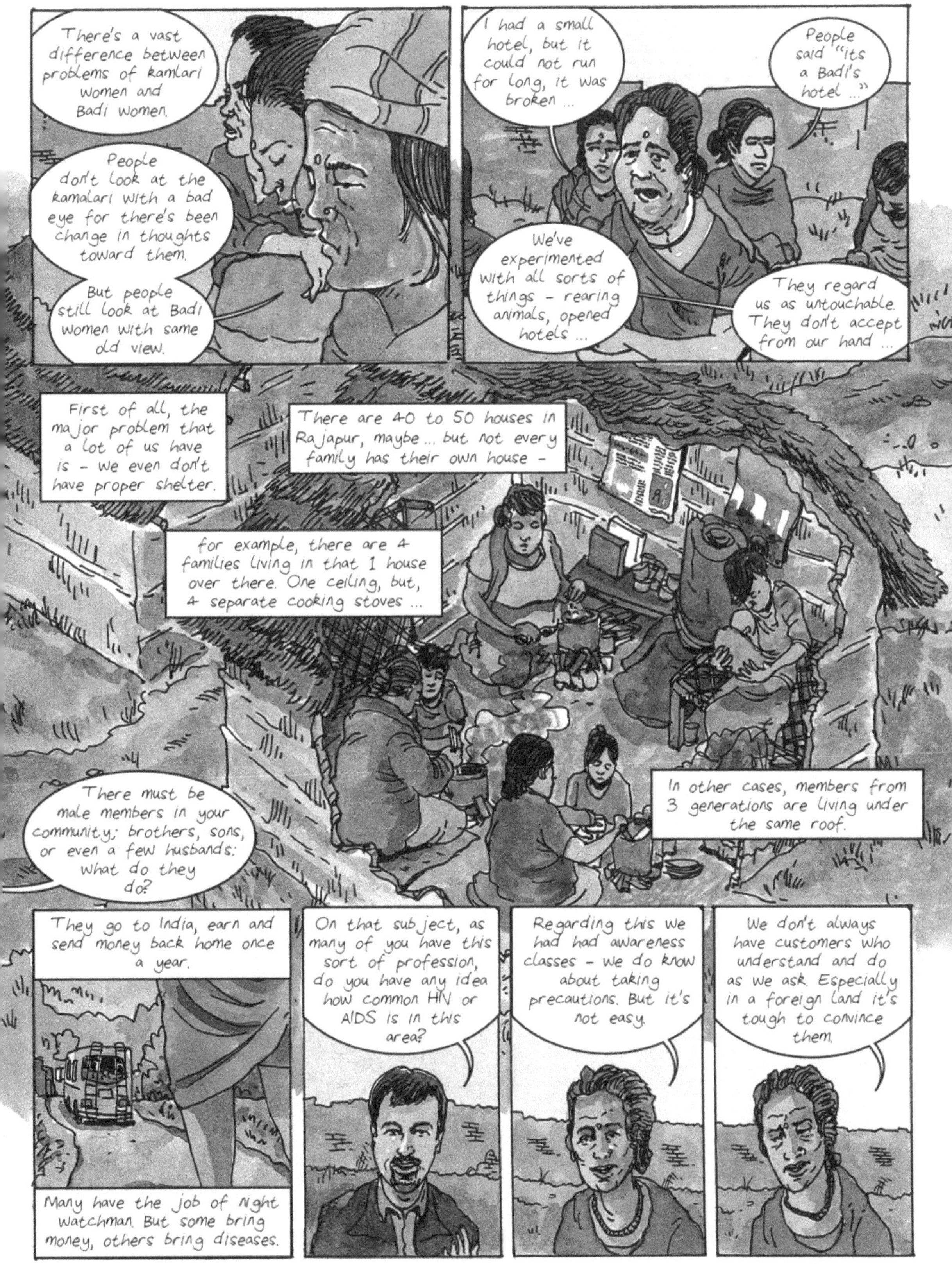
There's a vast difference between problems of kamlari women and Badi women.
People don't look at the kamalari with a bad eye for there's been change in thoughts toward them.
But people still look at Badi women with same old view.
I had a small hotel, but it could not run for long, it was broken ...
People said "its a Badi's hotel ..."
We've experimented with all sorts of things - rearing animals, opened hotels ...
They regard us as untouchable. They don't accept from our hand ...
First of all, the major problem that a lot of us have is - we even don't have proper shelter.
There are 40 to 50 houses in Rajapur, maybe ... but not every family has their own house -
for example, there are 4 families living in that 1 house over there. One ceiling, but, 4 separate cooking stoves ...
In other cases, members from 3 generations are living under the same roof.
There must be male members in your community; brothers, sons, or even a few husbands: what do they do?
They go to India, earn and send money back home once a year.
Many have the job of night watchman. But some bring money, others bring diseases.
On that subject, as many of you have this sort of profession, do you have any idea how common HIV or AIDS is in this area?
Regarding this we had had awareness classes - we do know about taking precautions. But it's not easy.
We don't always have customers who understand and do as we ask. Especially in a foreign land it's tough to convince them.

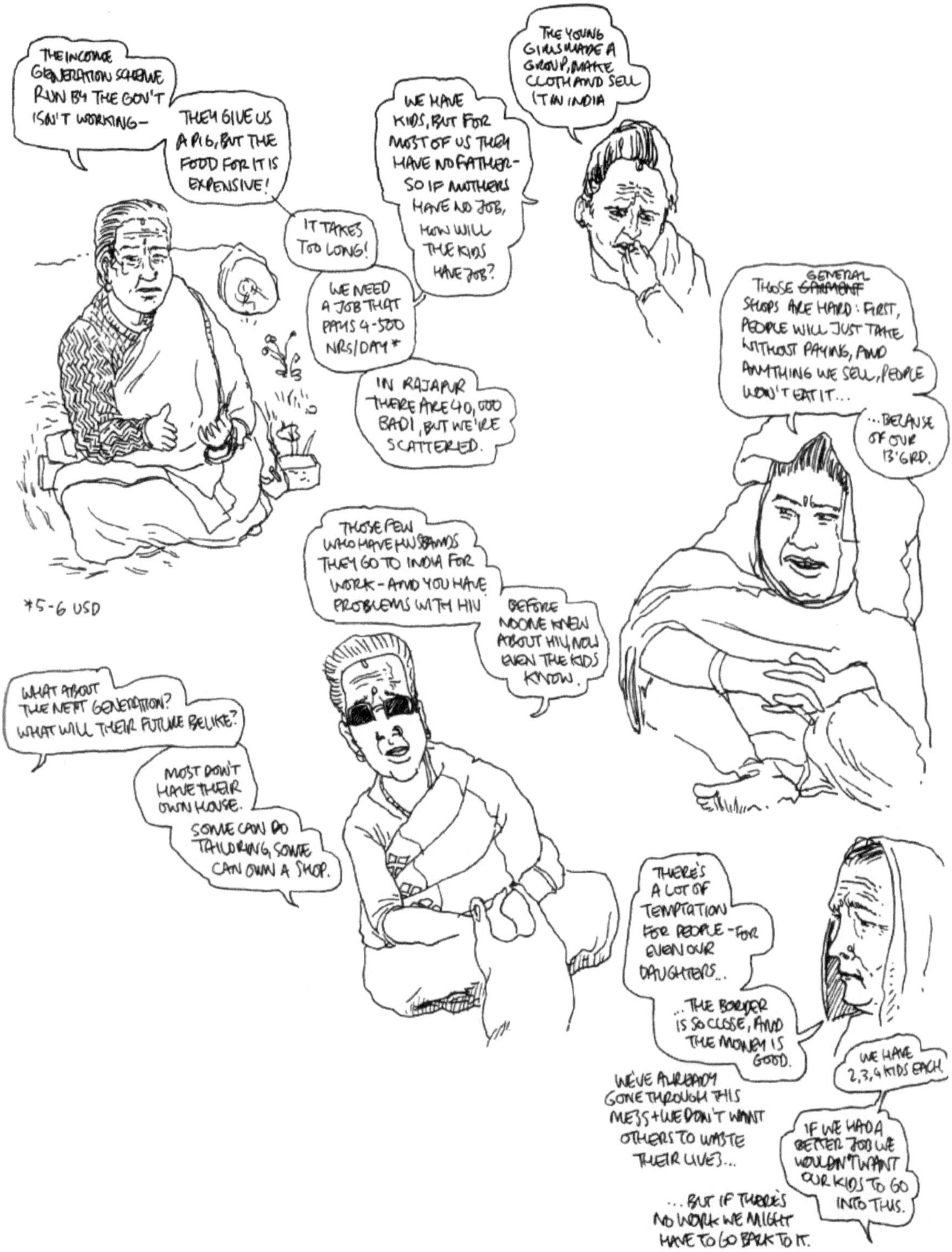
THE INCOME GENERATION SCHEME RUN BY THE GOV'T ISN'T WORKING–
THEY GIVE US A PIG, BUT THE FOOD FOR IT IS EXPENSIVE!
IT TAKES TOO LONG!
WE NEED A JOB THAT PAYS 4-500 NRS/DAY*
IN RAJAPUR THERE ARE 40,000 BADI, BUT WE'RE SCATTERED.
WE HAVE KIDS, BUT FOR MOST OF US THEY HAVE NO FATHER– SO IF MOTHERS HAVE NO JOB, HOW WILL THE KIDS HAVE JOB?
THE YOUNG GIRLS MADE A GROUP, MAKE CLOTH AND SELL IT IN INDIA
THOSE ~~GARMENT~~ GENERAL SHOPS ARE HARD: FIRST, PEOPLE WILL JUST TAKE WITHOUT PAYING, AND ANYTHING WE SELL, PEOPLE WON'T EAT IT...
...BECAUSE OF OUR B'GRD.
THOSE FEW WHO HAVE HUSBANDS THEY GO TO INDIA FOR WORK – AND YOU HAVE PROBLEMS WITH HIV
BEFORE NO ONE KNEW ABOUT HIV, NOW EVEN THE KIDS KNOW.
*5-6 USD
WHAT ABOUT THE NEXT GENERATION? WHAT WILL THEIR FUTURE BE LIKE?
MOST DON'T HAVE THEIR OWN HOUSE.
SOME CAN DO TAILORING, SOME CAN OWN A SHOP.
THERE'S A LOT OF TEMPTATION FOR PEOPLE – FOR EVEN OUR DAUGHTERS...
...THE BORDER IS SO CLOSE, AND THE MONEY IS GOOD.
WE'VE ALREADY GONE THROUGH THIS MESS + WE DON'T WANT OTHERS TO WASTE THEIR LIVES...
...BUT IF THERE'S NO WORK WE MIGHT HAVE TO GO BACK TO IT.
WE HAVE 2,3,4 KIDS EACH.
IF WE HAD A BETTER JOB WE WOULDN'T WANT OUR KIDS TO GO INTO THIS.

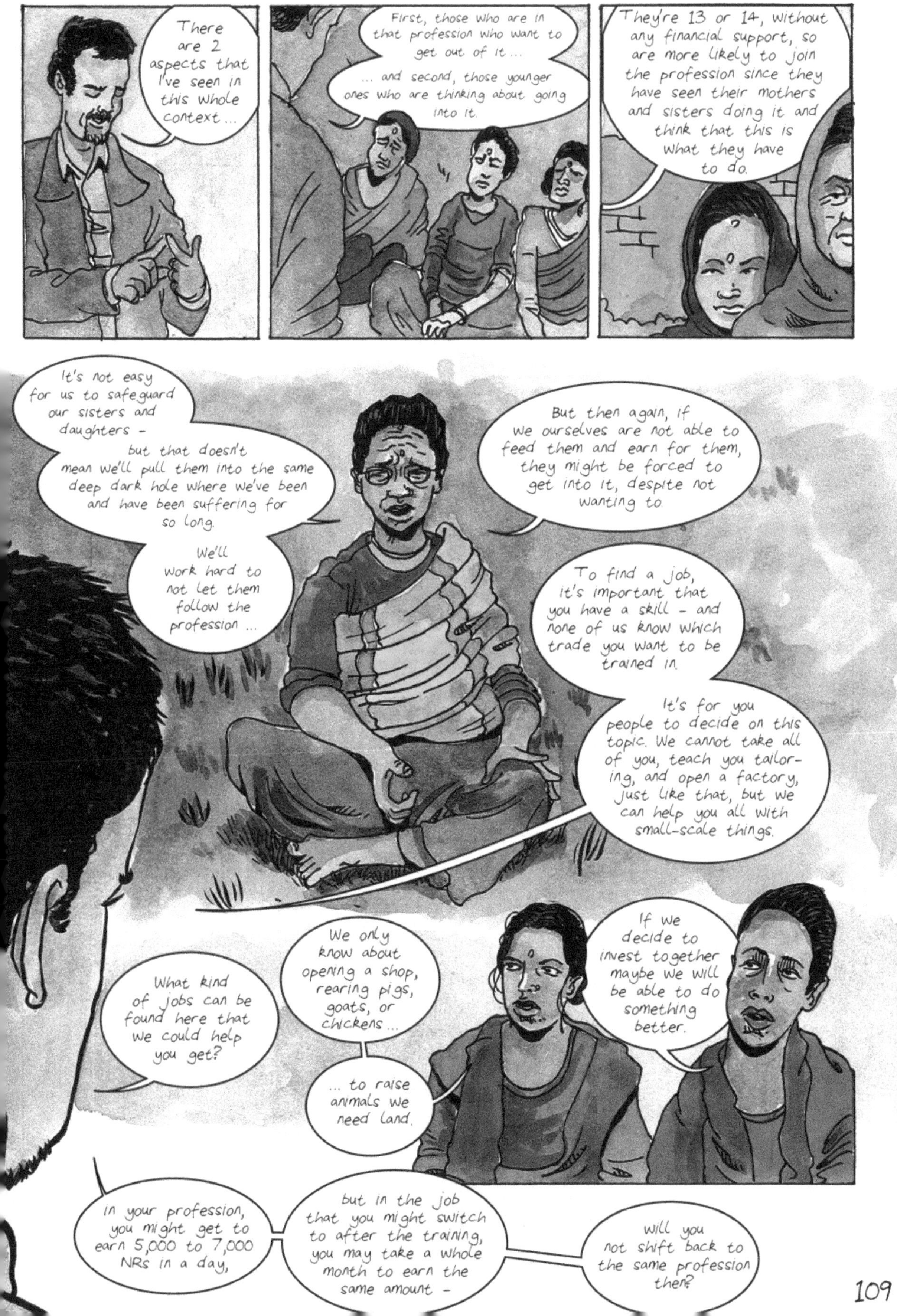
There are 2 aspects that I've seen in this whole context...
First, those who are in that profession who want to get out of it...
... and second, those younger ones who are thinking about going into it.
They're 13 or 14, without any financial support, so are more likely to join the profession since they have seen their mothers and sisters doing it and think that this is what they have to do.
It's not easy for us to safeguard our sisters and daughters -
but that doesn't mean we'll pull them into the same deep dark hole where we've been and have been suffering for so long.
We'll work hard to not let them follow the profession...
But then again, if we ourselves are not able to feed them and earn for them, they might be forced to get into it, despite not wanting to.
To find a job, it's important that you have a skill - and none of us know which trade you want to be trained in.
It's for you people to decide on this topic. We cannot take all of you, teach you tailor-ing, and open a factory, just like that, but we can help you all with small-scale things.
What kind of jobs can be found here that we could help you get?
We only know about opening a shop, rearing pigs, goats, or chickens...
... to raise animals we need land.
If we decide to invest together maybe we will be able to do something better.
In your profession, you might get to earn 5,000 to 7,000 NRs in a day,
but in the job that you might switch to after the training, you may take a whole month to earn the same amount -
will you not shift back to the same profession then?

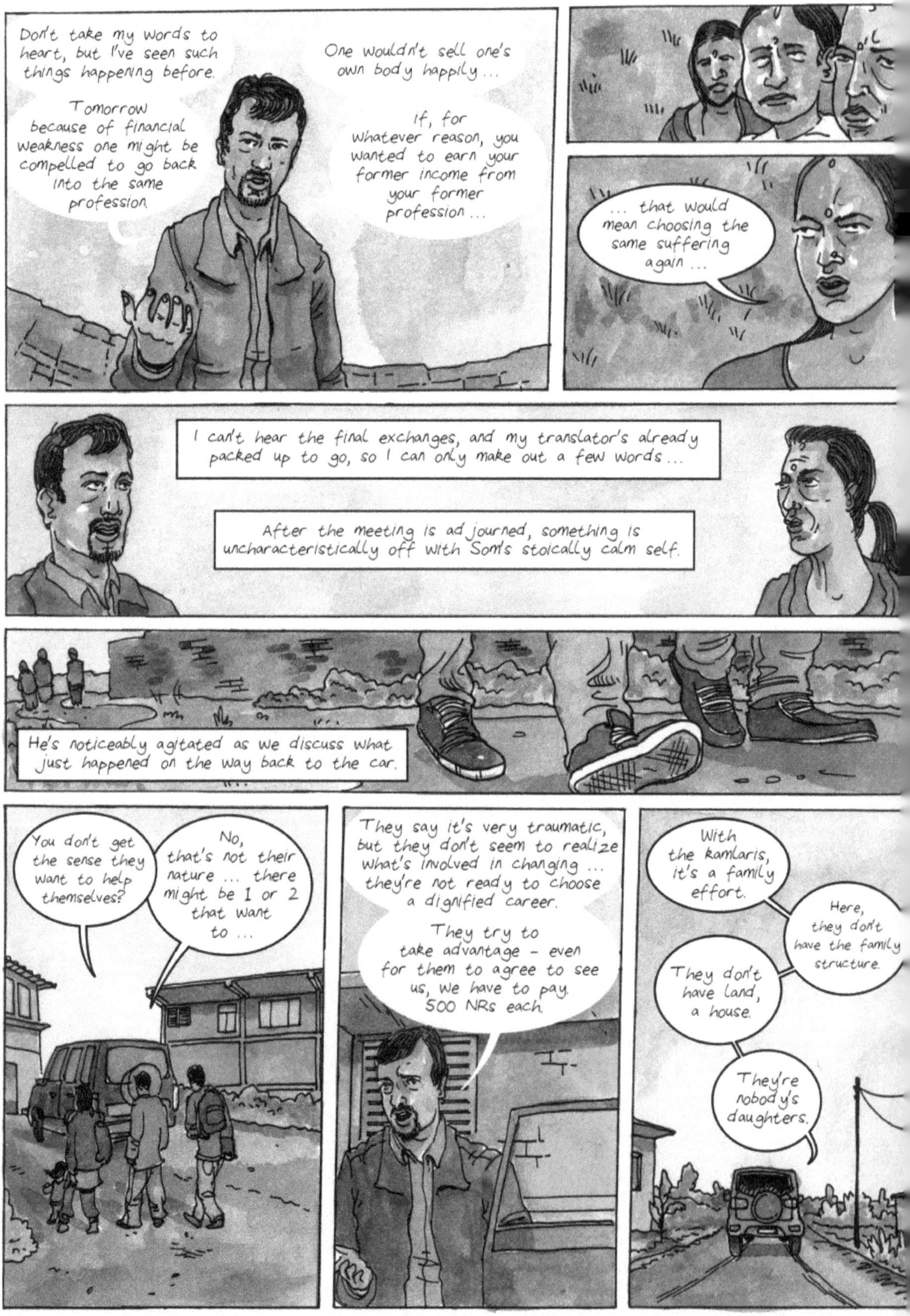
Don't take my words to heart, but I've seen such things happening before.
Tomorrow because of financial weakness one might be compelled to go back into the same profession.
One wouldn't sell one's own body happily ...
if, for whatever reason, you wanted to earn your former income from your former profession ...
... that would mean choosing the same suffering again ...
I can't hear the final exchanges, and my translator's already packed up to go, so I can only make out a few words ...
After the meeting is adjourned, something is uncharacteristically off with Som's stoically calm self.
He's noticeably agitated as we discuss what just happened on the way back to the car.
You don't get the sense they want to help themselves?
No, that's not their nature ... there might be 1 or 2 that want to ...
They say it's very traumatic, but they don't seem to realize what's involved in changing ... they're not ready to choose a dignified career.
They try to take advantage - even for them to agree to see us, we have to pay. 500 NRs each.
With the kamlaris, it's a family effort.
Here, they don't have the family structure.
They don't have land, a house.
They're nobody's daughters.

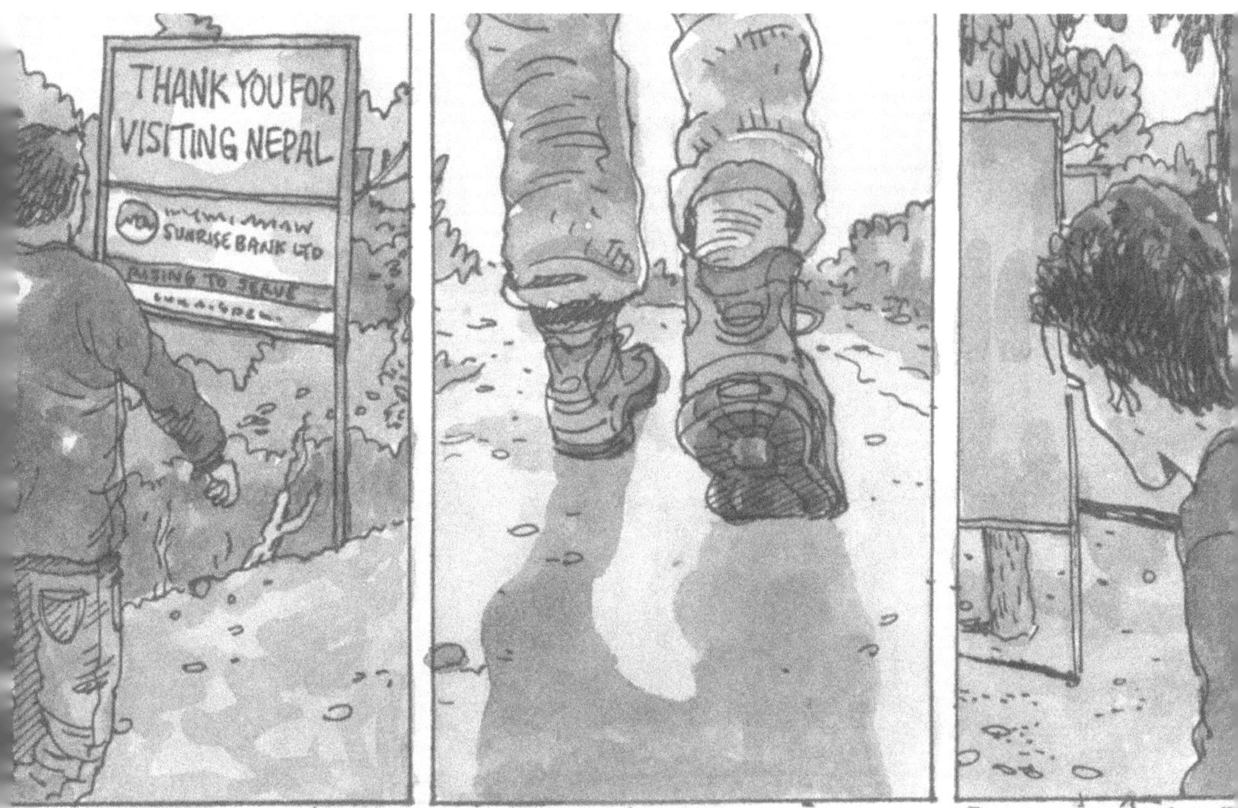
THANK YOU FOR VISITING NEPAL
SUNRISE BANK LTD
RISING TO SERVE

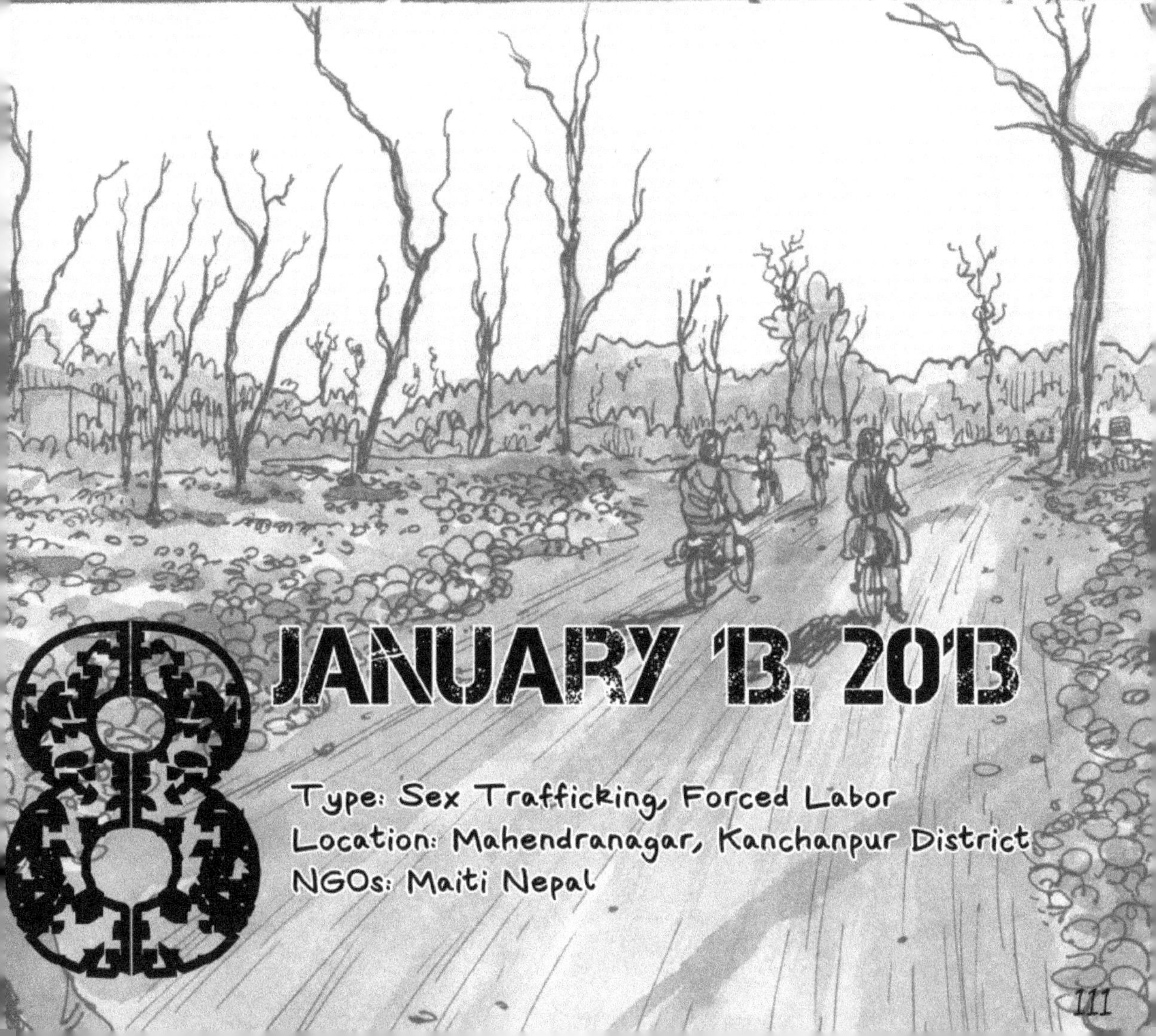

8 JANUARY 13, 2013

Type: Sex Trafficking, Forced Labor
Location: Mahendranagar, Kanchanpur District
NGOs: Maiti Nepal

CROSSING BORDERS

One of the main hotspots for trafficking and primary causes for its infamously high incidence is Nepal's porous border with India.

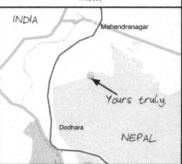

INDIA

Mahendranagar

Yours truly

Dodhara

NEPAL

Today I'm in Mahendranagar, the most western town in Nepal, to get a sense of just how porous.

After saying farewell to Som and family, I head to the local radio station, Shuklaplanta FM.

The director is a huge fan of Madhu's and generally chirpy bloke, happy to lead me around the office and offer me the guest bedroom.

We have our own museum!

It just so happens that the night before my trip there's a wedding celebration outside the station.

BOOM BOOM

2:13am

But the view from my room makes up for it.

I'm accompanied by two of Som's colleagues who are checking on the border and want to ensure my visit there goes smoothly.

Namaste!

I hope you brought your passport!

We bundle into the back of the car and drive the handful of kilometers toward India.

There's 1 main road to the border, first lined with the bustling commerce of a typical border town ...

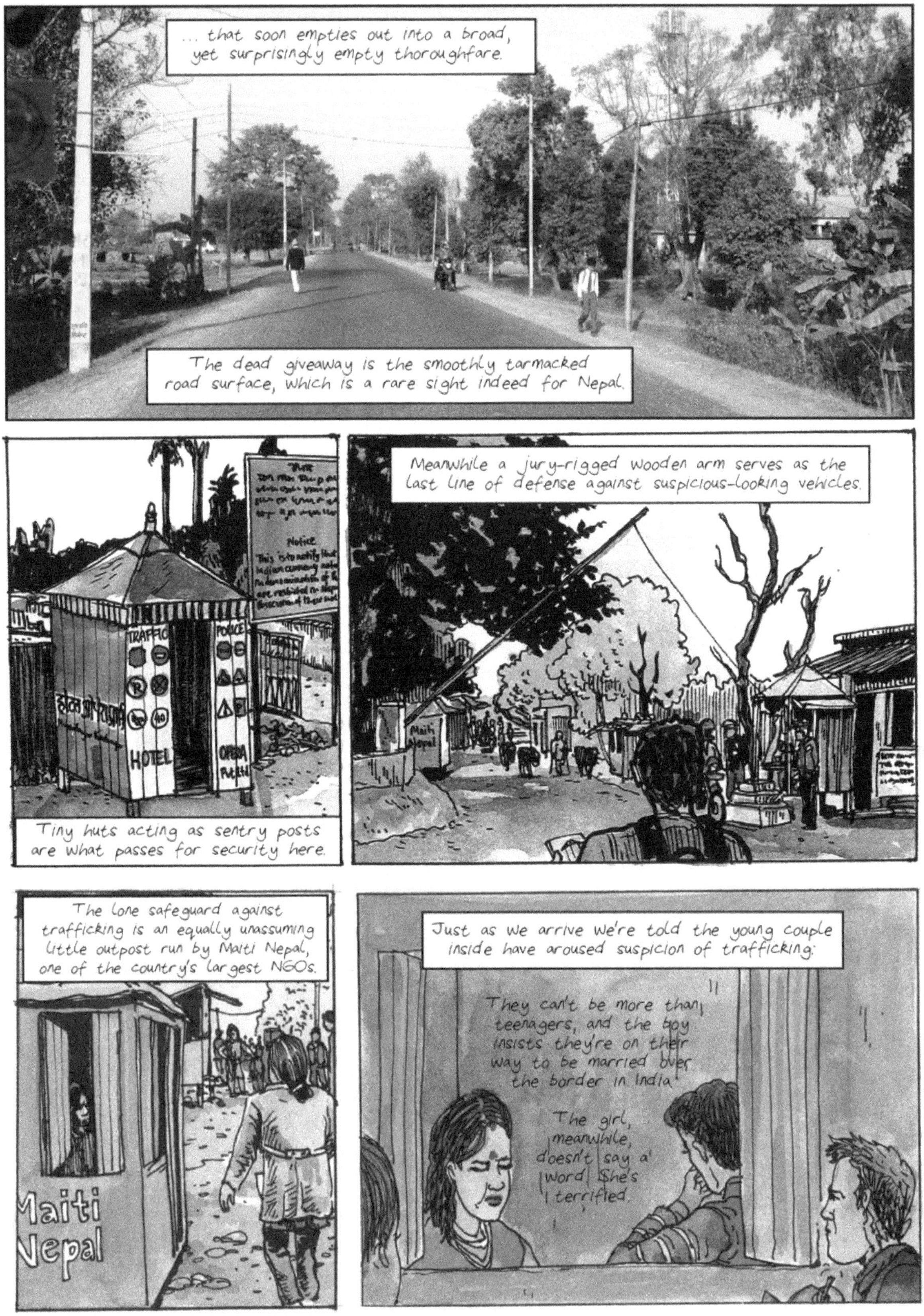
... that soon empties out into a broad, yet surprisingly empty thoroughfare.
The dead giveaway is the smoothly tarmacked road surface, which is a rare sight indeed for Nepal.
Notice
TRAFFIC
POLICE
HOTEL
Tiny huts acting as sentry posts are what passes for security here.
Meanwhile a jury-rigged wooden arm serves as the last line of defense against suspicious-looking vehicles.
Maiti Nepal
The lone safeguard against trafficking is an equally unassuming little outpost run by Maiti Nepal, one of the country's largest NGOs.
Maiti Nepal
Just as we arrive we're told the young couple inside have aroused suspicion of trafficking:
"They can't be more than teenagers, and the boy insists they're on their way to be married over the border in India."
"The girl, meanwhile, doesn't say a word. She's terrified."

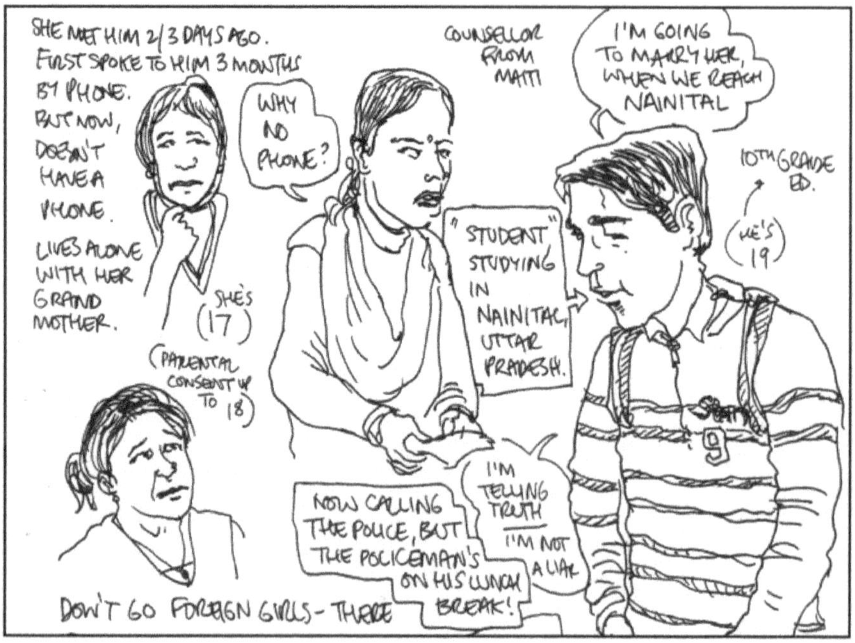
SHE MET HIM 2/3 DAYS AGO. FIRST SPOKE TO HIM 3 MONTHS BY PHONE. BUT NOW, DOESN'T HAVE A PHONE. LIVES ALONE WITH HER GRANDMOTHER.
SHE'S (17)
(PARENTAL CONSENT UP TO 18)
WHY NO PHONE?
COUNSELLOR FROM MAITI
I'M GOING TO MARRY HER, WHEN WE REACH NAINITAL
10TH GRADE ED.
(HE'S 19)
"STUDENT" STUDYING IN NAINITAL, UTTAR PRADESH.
I'M TELLING TRUTH
I'M NOT A LIAR
NOW CALLING THE POLICE, BUT THE POLICEMAN'S ON HIS LUNCH BREAK!
DON'T GO FOREIGN GIRLS - THERE

15:25 Jan 14th: scanned directly from my sketchbook, drawn live.

I scramble frantically to capture the scene as it unfolds.

Two cops eventually show up, but they've just caught a drug smuggler and seem far more interested in that.

Twenty minutes later they tell Maiti to take him to the police station.

Meanwhile Maiti's called the girl's parents and won't let her cross the border without their permission.

Once things have quietened down I interview the Maiti staffers.

They're literally on the frontlines of the fight against trafficking, but are remarkably nonchalant about it all.

These are the real faces of human rights advocates: humble, dedicated women who aren't interested in the spotlight.

Instead, they see their job in very localized, quotidian terms, keenly aware of their own limitations.

I'm truly impressed by their humility and quiet grace in the face of such a seemingly insurmountable challenge.

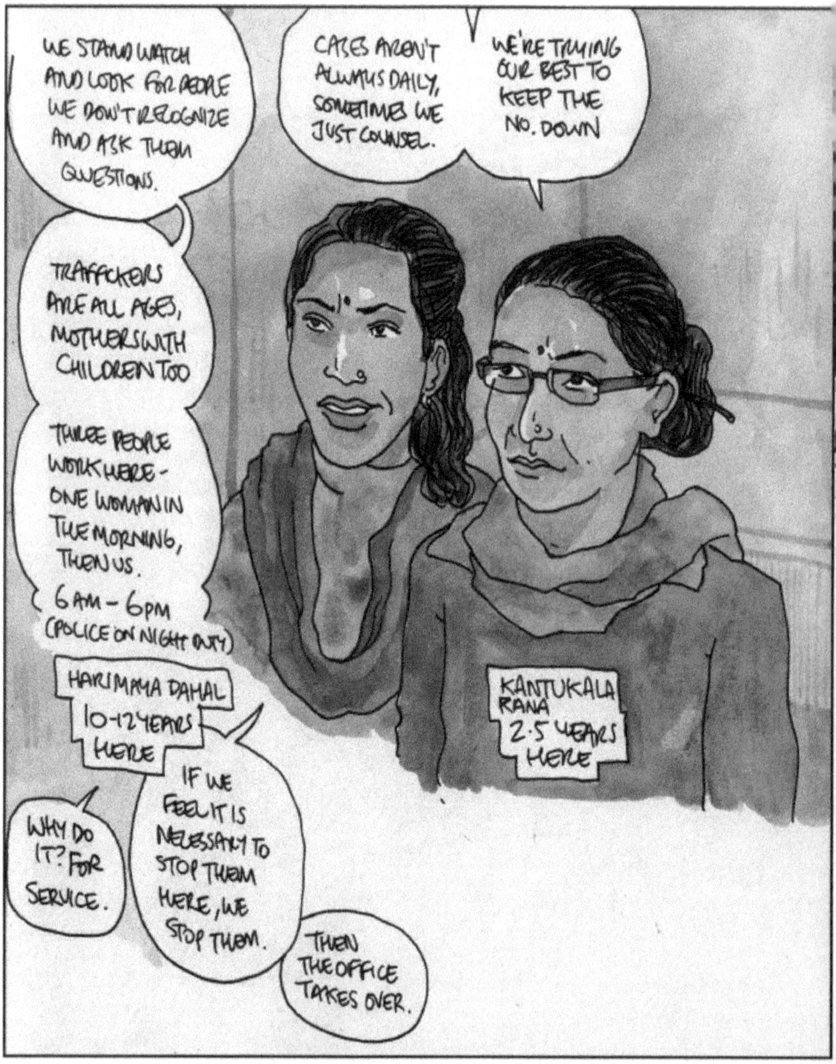
WE STAND WATCH AND LOOK FOR PEOPLE WE DON'T RECOGNIZE AND ASK THEM QUESTIONS.
CASES AREN'T ALWAYS DAILY, SOMETIMES WE JUST COUNSEL.
WE'RE TRYING OUR BEST TO KEEP THE NO. DOWN
TRAFFICKERS ARE ALL AGES, MOTHERS WITH CHILDREN TOO
THREE PEOPLE WORK HERE - ONE WOMAN IN THE MORNING, THEN US.
6AM - 6PM (POLICE ON NIGHT DUTY)
HARIMAYA DAHAL 10-12 YEARS HERE
KANTUKALA RANA 2.5 YEARS HERE
WHY DO IT? FOR SERVICE.
IF WE FEEL IT IS NECESSARY TO STOP THEM HERE, WE STOP THEM.
THEN THE OFFICE TAKES OVER.

A PASSAGE TO INDIA

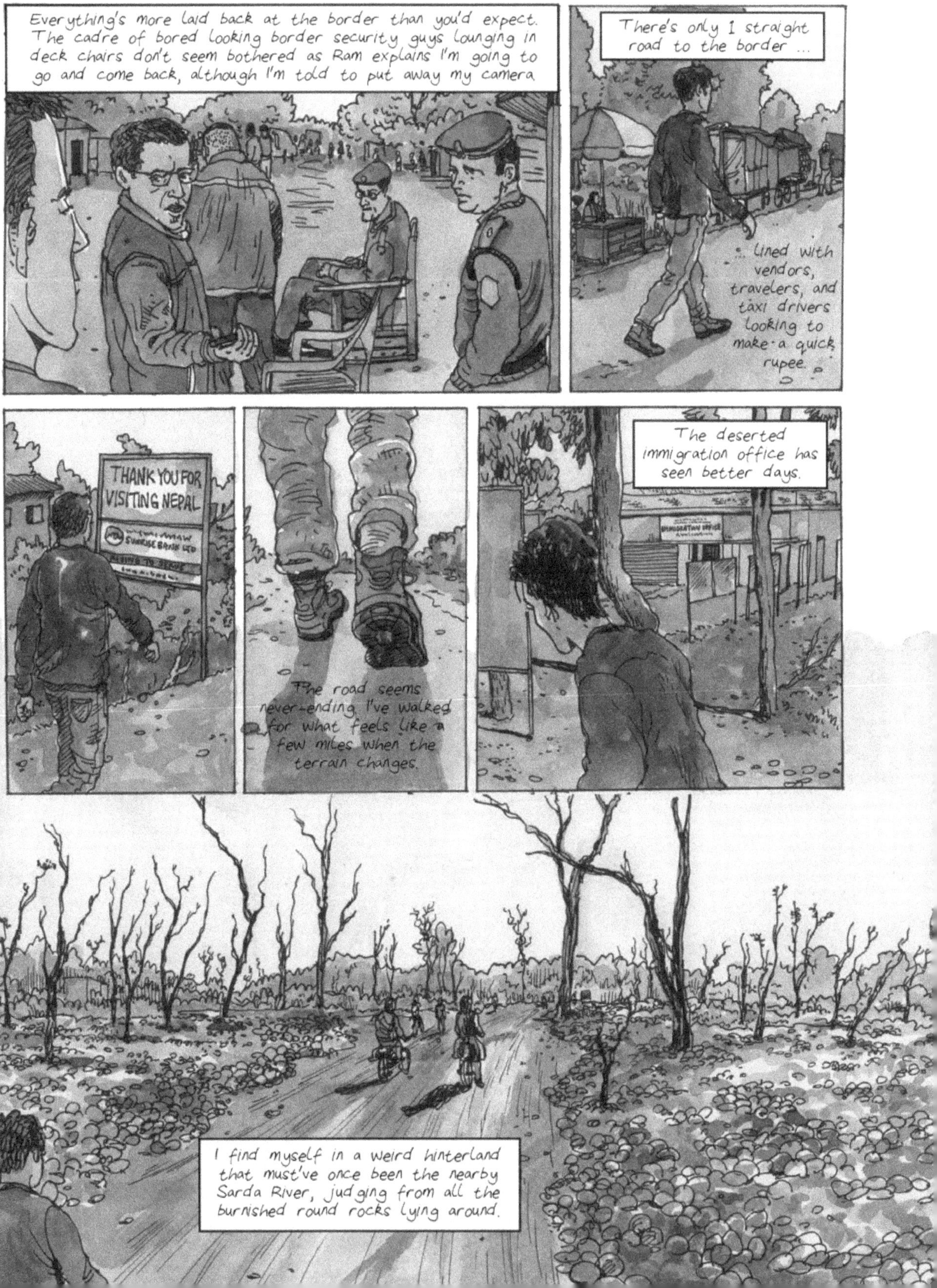
Everything's more laid back at the border than you'd expect. The cadre of bored looking border security guys lounging in deck chairs don't seem bothered as Ram explains I'm going to go and come back, although I'm told to put away my camera
There's only 1 straight road to the border ...
... lined with vendors, travelers, and taxi drivers looking to make a quick rupee.
THANK YOU FOR VISITING NEPAL
The road seems never-ending. I've walked for what feels like a few miles when the terrain changes.
The deserted immigration office has seen better days.
I find myself in a weird hinterland that must've once been the nearby Sarda River, judging from all the burnished round rocks lying around.

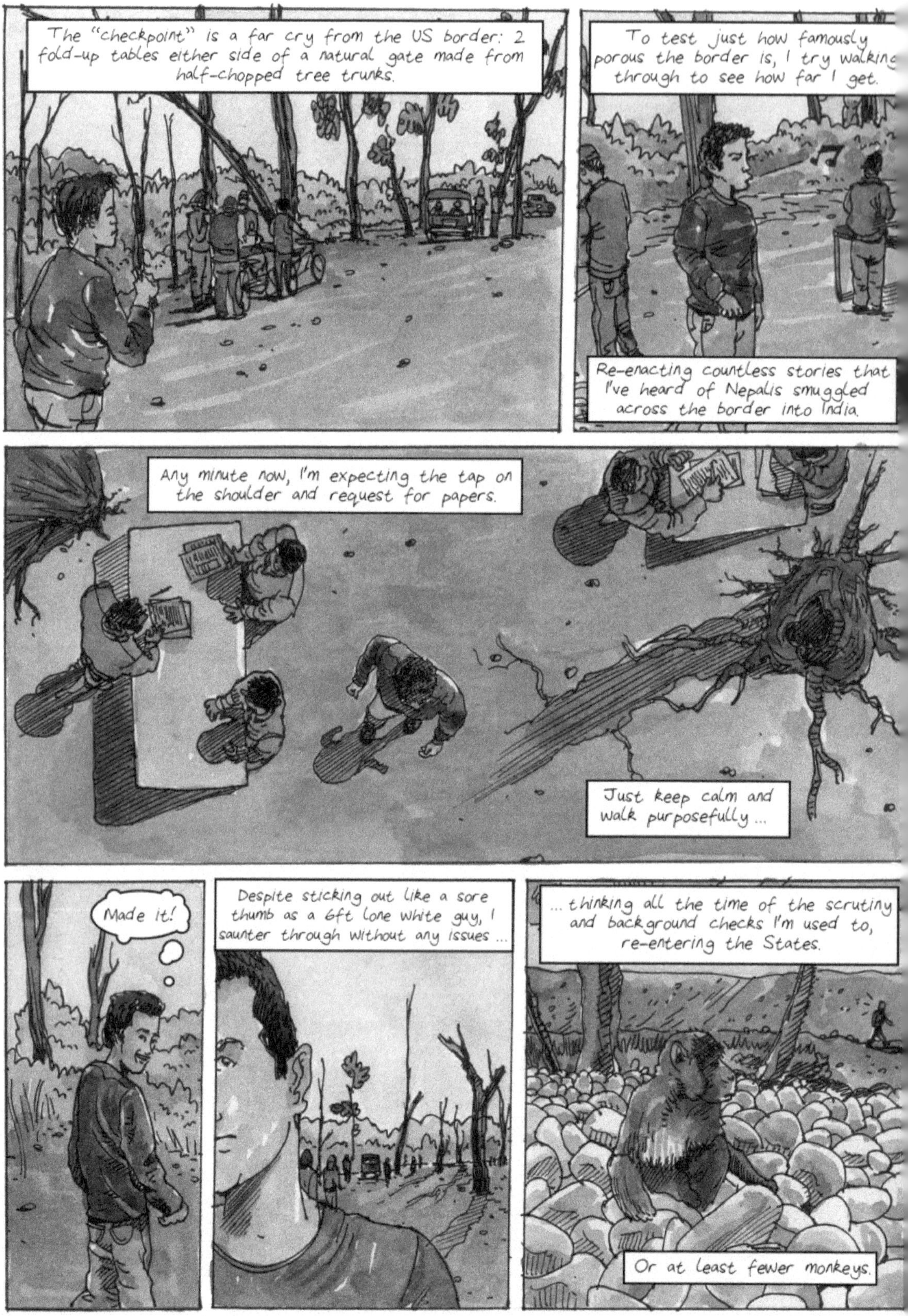

The "checkpoint" is a far cry from the US border: 2 fold-up tables either side of a natural gate made from half-chopped tree trunks.
To test just how famously porous the border is, I try walking through to see how far I get.
Re-enacting countless stories that I've heard of Nepalis smuggled across the border into India.
Any minute now, I'm expecting the tap on the shoulder and request for papers.
Just keep calm and walk purposefully ...
Made it!
Despite sticking out like a sore thumb as a 6ft lone white guy, I saunter through without any issues ...
... thinking all the time of the scrutiny and background checks I'm used to, re-entering the States.
Or at least fewer monkeys.

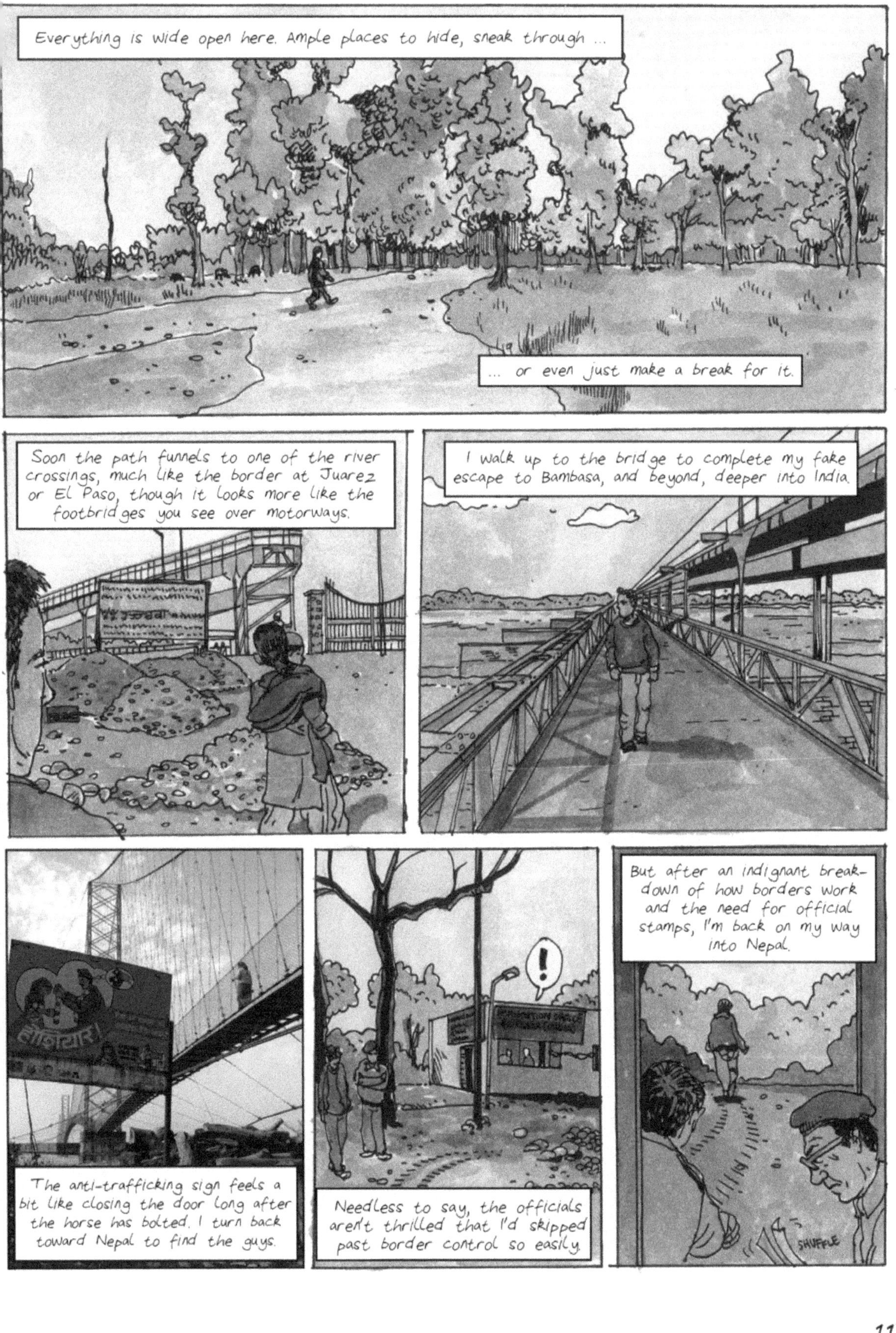
Everything is wide open here. Ample places to hide, sneak through ...
... or even just make a break for it.
Soon the path funnels to one of the river crossings, much like the border at Juarez or El Paso, though it looks more like the footbridges you see over motorways.
I walk up to the bridge to complete my fake escape to Bambasa, and beyond, deeper into India.
The anti-trafficking sign feels a bit like closing the door long after the horse has bolted. I turn back toward Nepal to find the guys.
!
Needless to say, the officials aren't thrilled that I'd skipped past border control so easily.
But after an indignant breakdown of how borders work and the need for official stamps, I'm back on my way into Nepal.
SHUFFLE

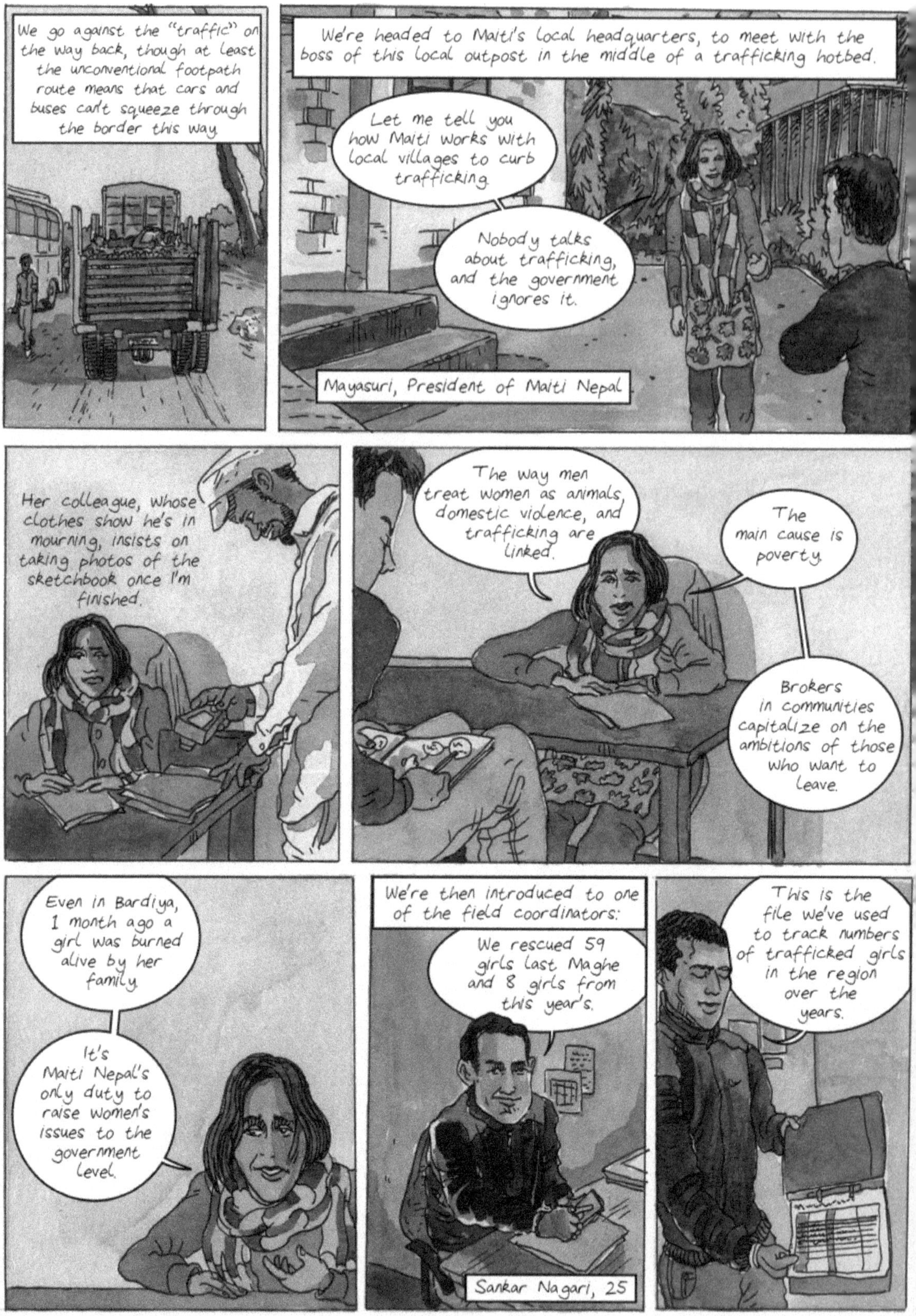
We go against the "traffic" on the way back, though at least the unconventional footpath route means that cars and buses can't squeeze through the border this way.
We're headed to Maiti's local headquarters, to meet with the boss of this local outpost in the middle of a trafficking hotbed.
Let me tell you how Maiti works with local villages to curb trafficking.
Nobody talks about trafficking, and the government ignores it.
Mayasuri, President of Maiti Nepal
Her colleague, whose clothes show he's in mourning, insists on taking photos of the sketchbook once I'm finished.
The way men treat women as animals, domestic violence, and trafficking are linked.
The main cause is poverty.
Brokers in communities capitalize on the ambitions of those who want to leave.
Even in Bardiya, 1 month ago a girl was burned alive by her family.
It's Maiti Nepal's only duty to raise women's issues to the government level.
We're then introduced to one of the field coordinators:
We rescued 59 girls last Maghe and 8 girls from this year's.
Sankar Nagari, 25
This is the file we've used to track numbers of trafficked girls in the region over the years.

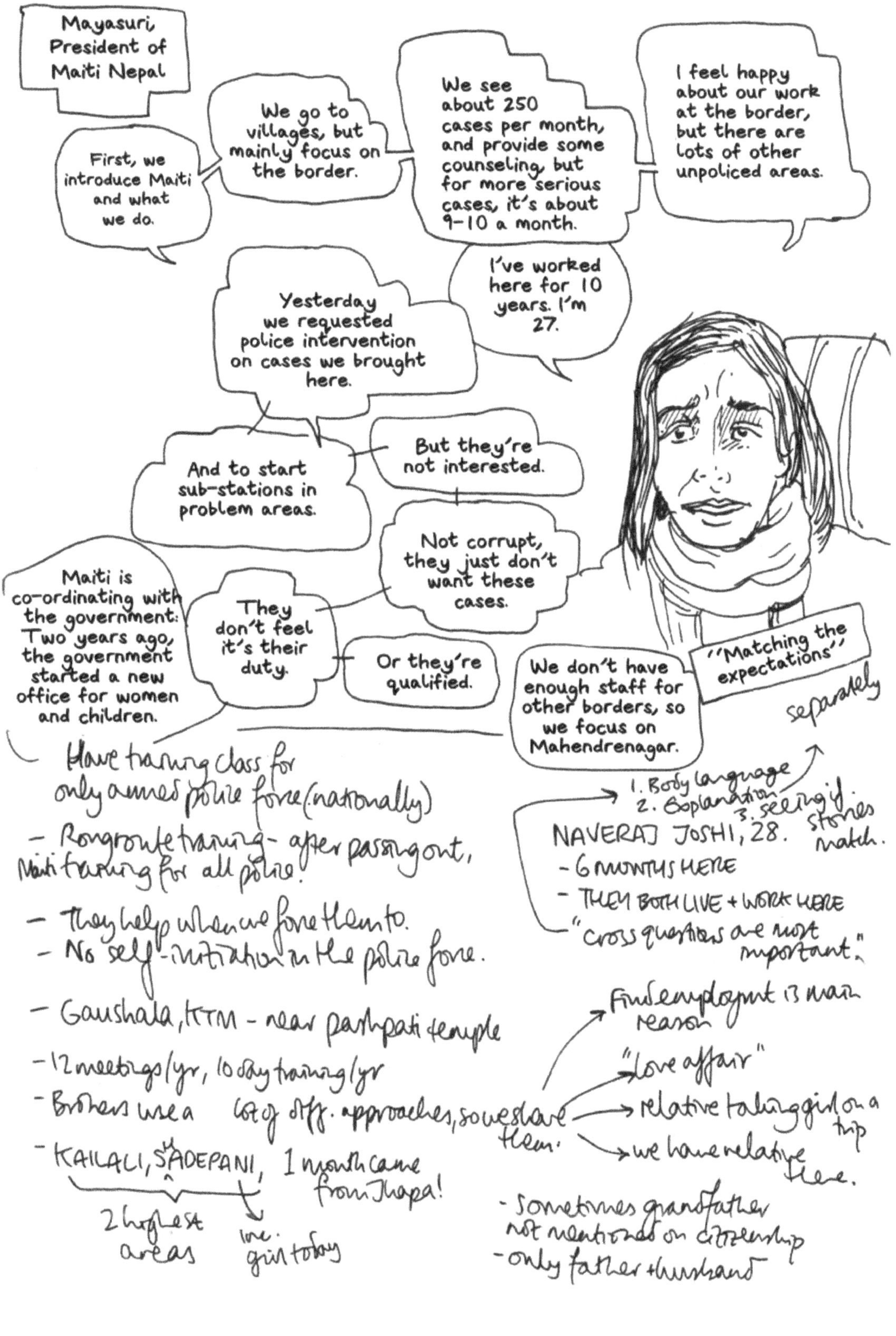
Mayasuri, President of Maiti Nepal
First, we introduce Maiti and what we do.
We go to villages, but mainly focus on the border.
We see about 250 cases per month, and provide some counseling, but for more serious cases, it's about 9–10 a month.
I feel happy about our work at the border, but there are lots of other unpoliced areas.
I've worked here for 10 years. I'm 27.
Yesterday we requested police intervention on cases we brought here.
And to start sub-stations in problem areas.
But they're not interested.
Not corrupt, they just don't want these cases.
Maiti is co-ordinating with the government: Two years ago, the government started a new office for women and children.
They don't feel it's their duty.
Or they're qualified.
We don't have enough staff for other borders, so we focus on Mahendrenagar.
"Matching the expectations"
separately
1. Body language
2. Explanation
3. seeing if stories match.
NAVERAJ JOSHI, 28.
- 6 MONTHS HERE
- THEY BOTH LIVE + WORK HERE
"cross questions are most important."
Have training class for only armed police force (nationally)
Maiti training for all police.
- They help when we force them to.
- No self-initiation in the police force.
- Gaushala, KTM - near pashpati temple
- 12 meetings/yr, 10 day training/yr
- Brothers use a lot of diff. approaches, some slave them.
Find employment is main reason
"Love affair"
relative taking girl on a trip
we have relative there.
- KAILALI, SADEPANI, 1 month came from Jhapa!
2 highest areas
girl today
- Sometimes grandfather not mentioned on citizenship
- only father + husband

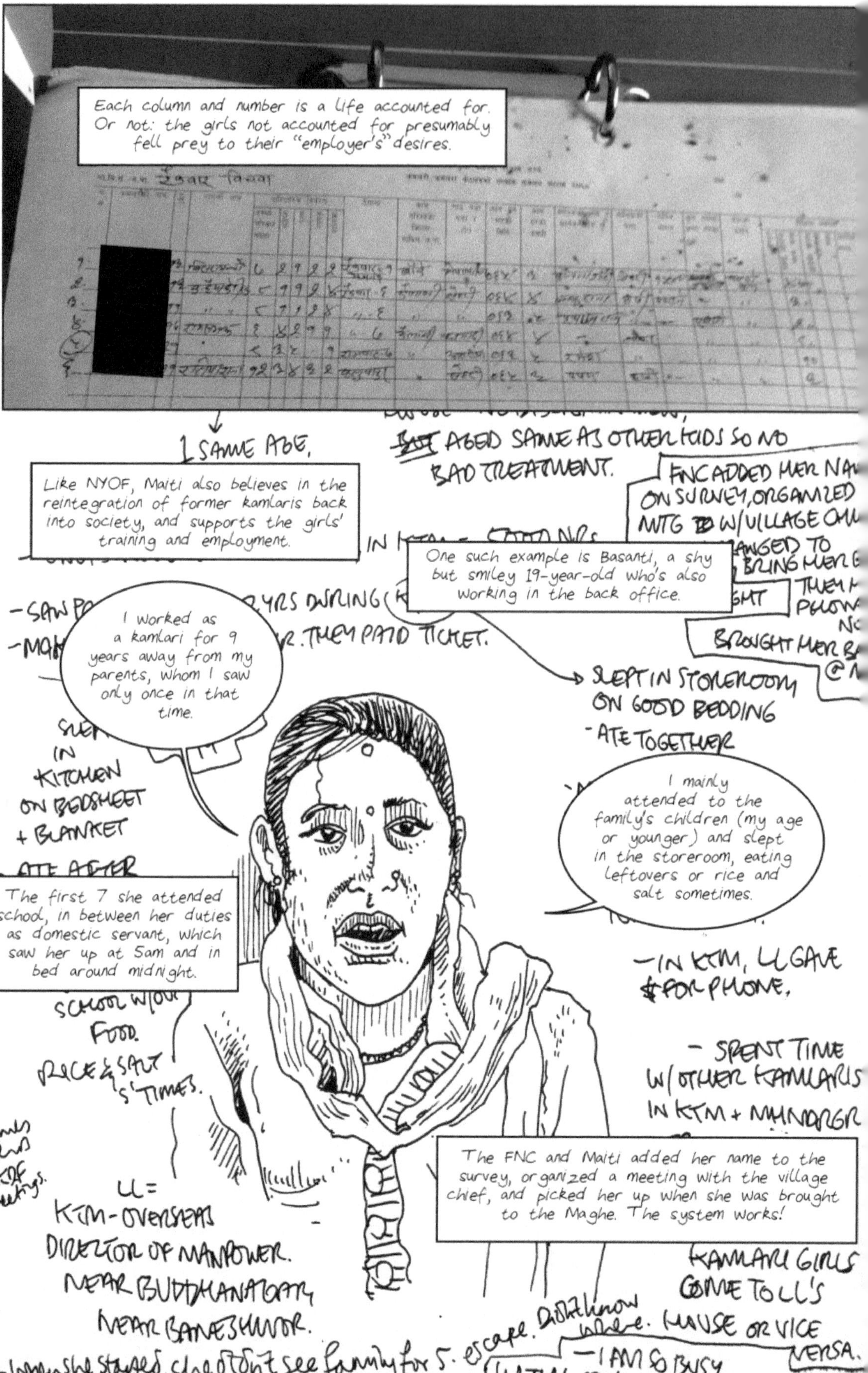

Each column and number is a life accounted for. Or not: the girls not accounted for presumably fell prey to their "employer's" desires.
SAME AGE.
AGED SAME AS OTHER KIDS SO NO BAD TREATMENT.
Like NYOF, Maiti also believes in the reintegration of former kamlaris back into society, and supports the girls' training and employment.
One such example is Basanti, a shy but smiley 19-year-old who's also working in the back office.
I worked as a kamlari for 9 years away from my parents, whom I saw only once in that time.
SLEPT IN STOREROOM ON GOOD BEDDING
-ATE TOGETHER
KITCHEN ON BEDSHEET + BLANKET
I mainly attended to the family's children (my age or younger) and slept in the storeroom, eating leftovers or rice and salt sometimes.
The first 7 she attended school, in between her duties as domestic servant, which saw her up at 5am and in bed around midnight.
FOOD.
RICE & SALT S'TIMES.
-IN KTM, LL GAVE $ FOR PHONE.
- SPENT TIME W/ OTHER KAMLARIS IN KTM + MAHENDRANAGAR
The FNC and Maiti added her name to the survey, organized a meeting with the village chief, and picked her up when she was brought to the Maghe. The system works!
LL = KTM-OVERSEAS DIRECTOR OF MANPOWER. NEAR BUDDHANAGAR NEAR BANESHWOR.
KAMLARI GIRLS COME TO LL'S HOUSE OR VICE VERSA.
-I AM SO BUSY WITH WORK TO TRY TO ESCAPE.

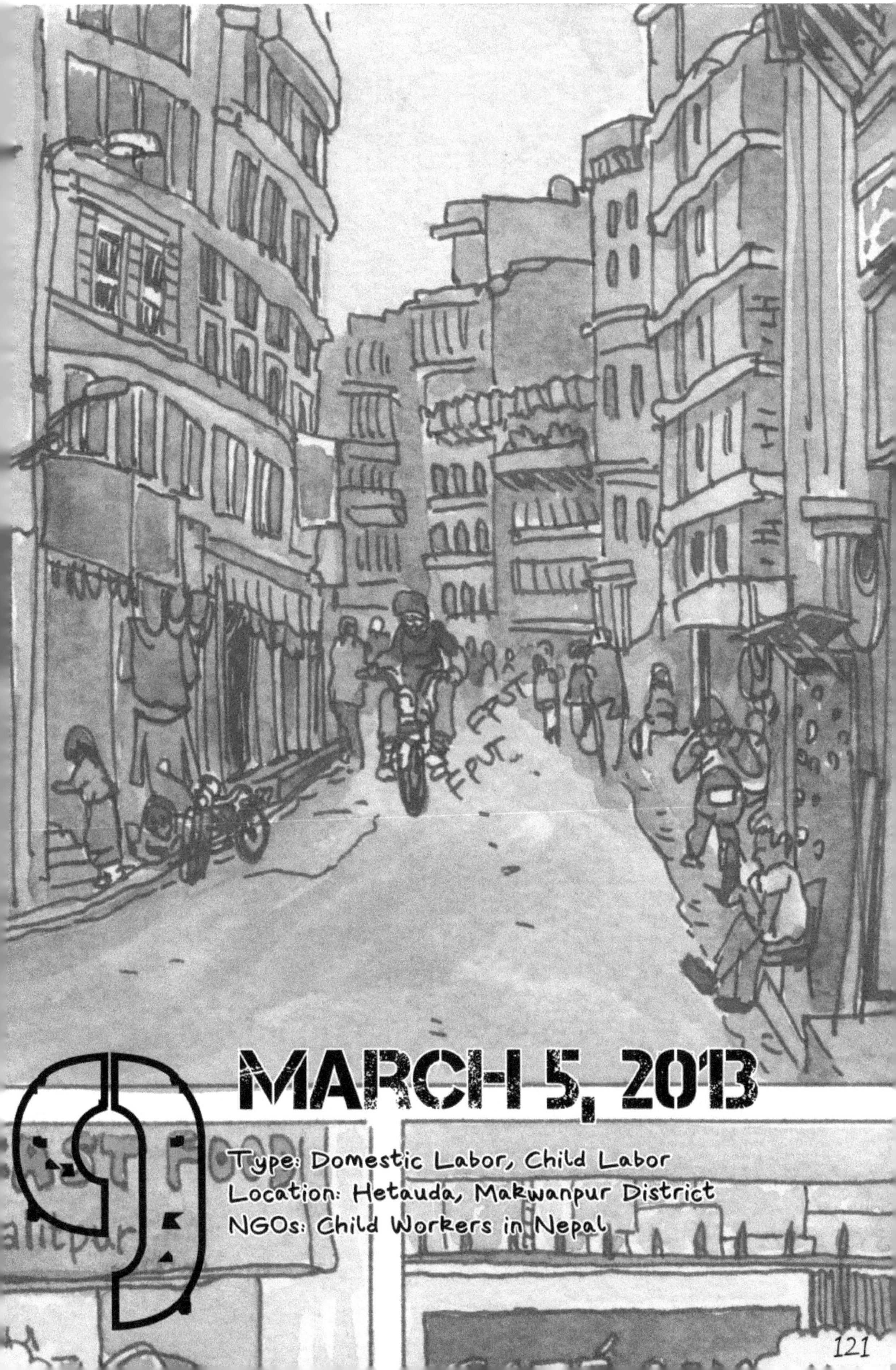

9

MARCH 5, 2013

Type: Domestic Labor, Child Labor

Location: Hetauda, Makwanpur District

NGOs: Child Workers in Nepal

THE HUMAN TRAFFICKING VULNERABILITY PROJECT

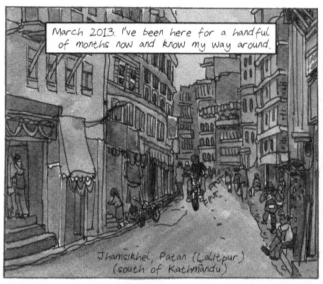

March 2013. I've been here for a handful of months now and know my way around.

Jhamsikhel, Patan (Lalitpur) (south of Kathmandu)

I've moved out of Madhu's office and into what used to be the Goethe Institut.

I've got my go-to lunch spot ...

MMM... FRANKIE ROLLS

My go-to meeting spot ...

MMM... COFFEE

mmm... MOMOS

... and my go-to dinner spot.

momo=Nepalese boiled dumplings

I also finally sorted out a motorbike, albeit 2nd hand.

Turns out the UNHCR boss previous owner sold me a dud.

positive head wobble

(namaste greeting to my landlord next door)

Bathroom   Bedroom

Living room/ work area

(Firing up Skype.)

(Palatial digs compared to the last place)

Kitchen

Odd single slab of stone table

I've also shored up my collaboration with a team of researchers from the US working on a quantitative study of human trafficking.

Hey ladies, can you hear me OK?

Hey Dan!

Cecilia Mo

Margaret Boittin

The project we pitched to USAID is getting traction and Margaret, one of the co-PIs,* is coming to Nepal to help lay the groundwork for it.

122

*co-Principal Investigator

Only a few weeks later, Margaret (whom I've just met in person for the first time) and I are en route to Hetauda, Makwanpur.

THUNK

hanging on for dear life, has never been on a motorbike before

Gas station closures mean we stop when we can to stock up on bottles of petrol.

the shy but curious seller

At around 2,000 m, it's one of the most beautiful, if challenging, rides I've ever been on. Margaret remains amazingly stoic throughout.

Do you mind if we take a break soon?

Despite only being 85 km away, the cliffhanging route makes it a 4.5-hour, white-knuckle ride, especially for 2.

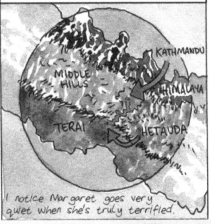

KATHMANDU
MIDDLE HILLS
HIMALAYA
TERAI
HETAUDA

I notice Margaret goes very quiet when she's truly terrified.

Plan Nepal, Makwanpur Program Unit
Demography of Makwanpur District

Makwanpur Program Unit

We're there to cement ties with local anti-trafficking NGOs, collect some interviews with the survivors they're working with, and plan logistics for our project.

We're welcomed in true Nepali style at CWIN,* before we begin the interviews.

*Child Workers in Nepal

Among the interviews there are some grains of hope: in the case of this young girl, she recognized the suspicious circumstances around a "job offer" in India and managed to escape from a brothel.

Unfortunately, the older woman who accompanies her wasn't so lucky: she spent 17 years in sexual slavery in India after being sold across the border.

Of course, it's nothing to do with luck but more a sense of empowerment that perhaps the younger generation feels at being able to challenge their circumstances.

123

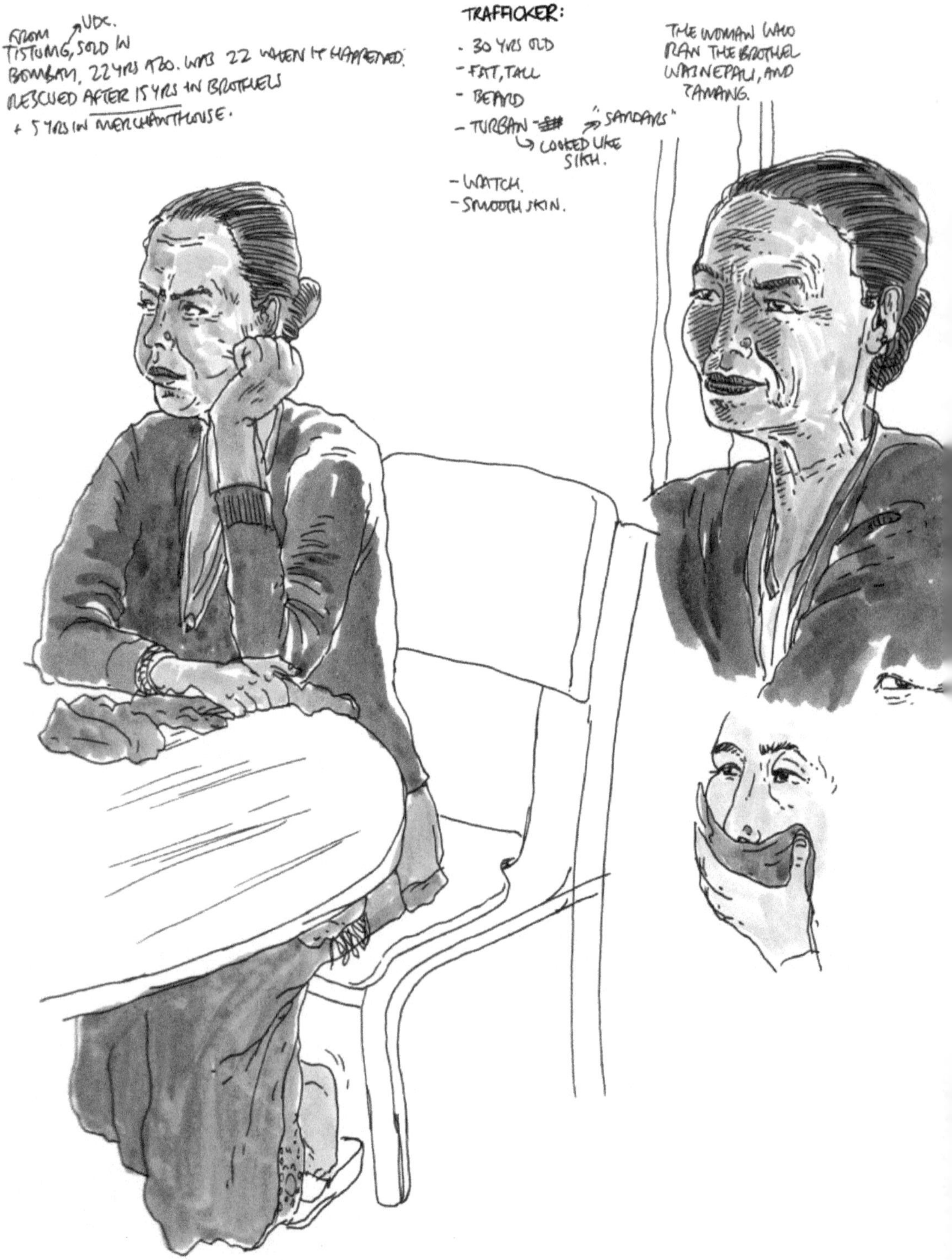
FROM UDX.
TISTUNG, SOLD IN
BOMBAY, 22 YRS AGO. WAS 22 WHEN IT HAPPENED.
RESCUED AFTER 15 YRS IN BROTHELS
+ 5 YRS IN MERCHANTHOUSE.
TRAFFICKER:
- 30 YRS OLD
- FAT, TALL
- BEARD
- TURBAN → LOOKED LIKE SIKH. → "SARDARS"
- WATCH.
- SMOOTH SKIN.
THE WOMAN WHO RAN THE BROTHEL WAS NEPALI, AND TAMANG.

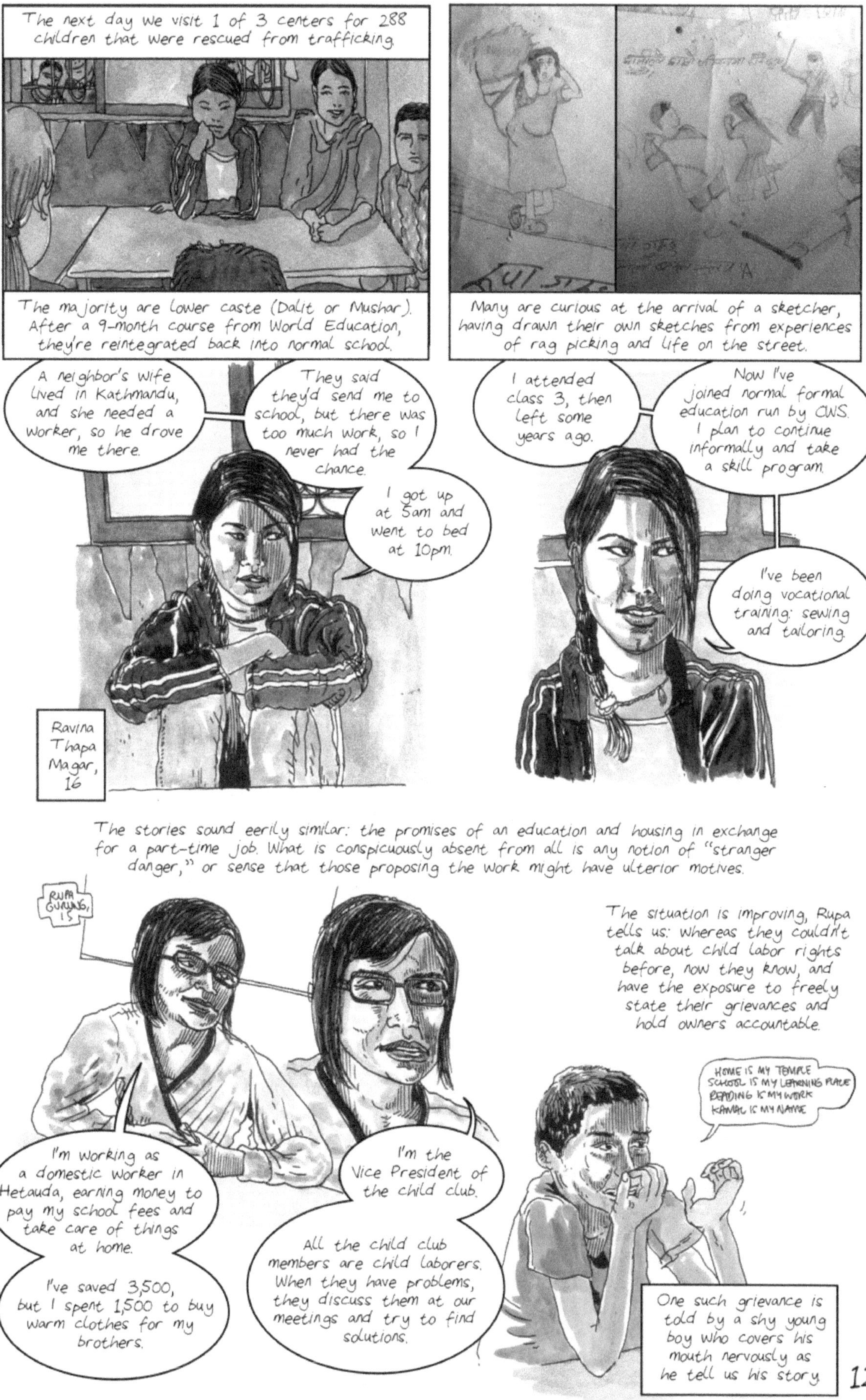
The next day we visit 1 of 3 centers for 288 children that were rescued from trafficking.
The majority are lower caste (Dalit or Mushar). After a 9-month course from World Education, they're reintegrated back into normal school.
Many are curious at the arrival of a sketcher, having drawn their own sketches from experiences of rag picking and life on the street.
A neighbor's wife lived in Kathmandu, and she needed a worker, so he drove me there.
They said they'd send me to school, but there was too much work, so I never had the chance.
I got up at 5am and went to bed at 10pm.
Ravina Thapa Magar, 16
I attended class 3, then left some years ago.
Now I've joined normal formal education run by CWS. I plan to continue informally and take a skill program.
I've been doing vocational training: sewing and tailoring.
The stories sound eerily similar: the promises of an education and housing in exchange for a part-time job. What is conspicuously absent from all is any notion of "stranger danger," or sense that those proposing the work might have ulterior motives.
RUPA GURUNG, 15
The situation is improving, Rupa tells us: whereas they couldn't talk about child labor rights before, now they know, and have the exposure to freely state their grievances and hold owners accountable.
I'm working as a domestic worker in Hetauda, earning money to pay my school fees and take care of things at home.
I've saved 3,500, but I spent 1,500 to buy warm clothes for my brothers.
I'm the Vice President of the child club.
All the child club members are child laborers. When they have problems, they discuss them at our meetings and try to find solutions.
HOME IS MY TEMPLE
SCHOOL IS MY LEARNING PLACE
READING IS MY WORK
KAMAL IS MY NAME
One such grievance is told by a shy young boy who covers his mouth nervously as he tell us his story.

MY HOME IS MY TEMPLE

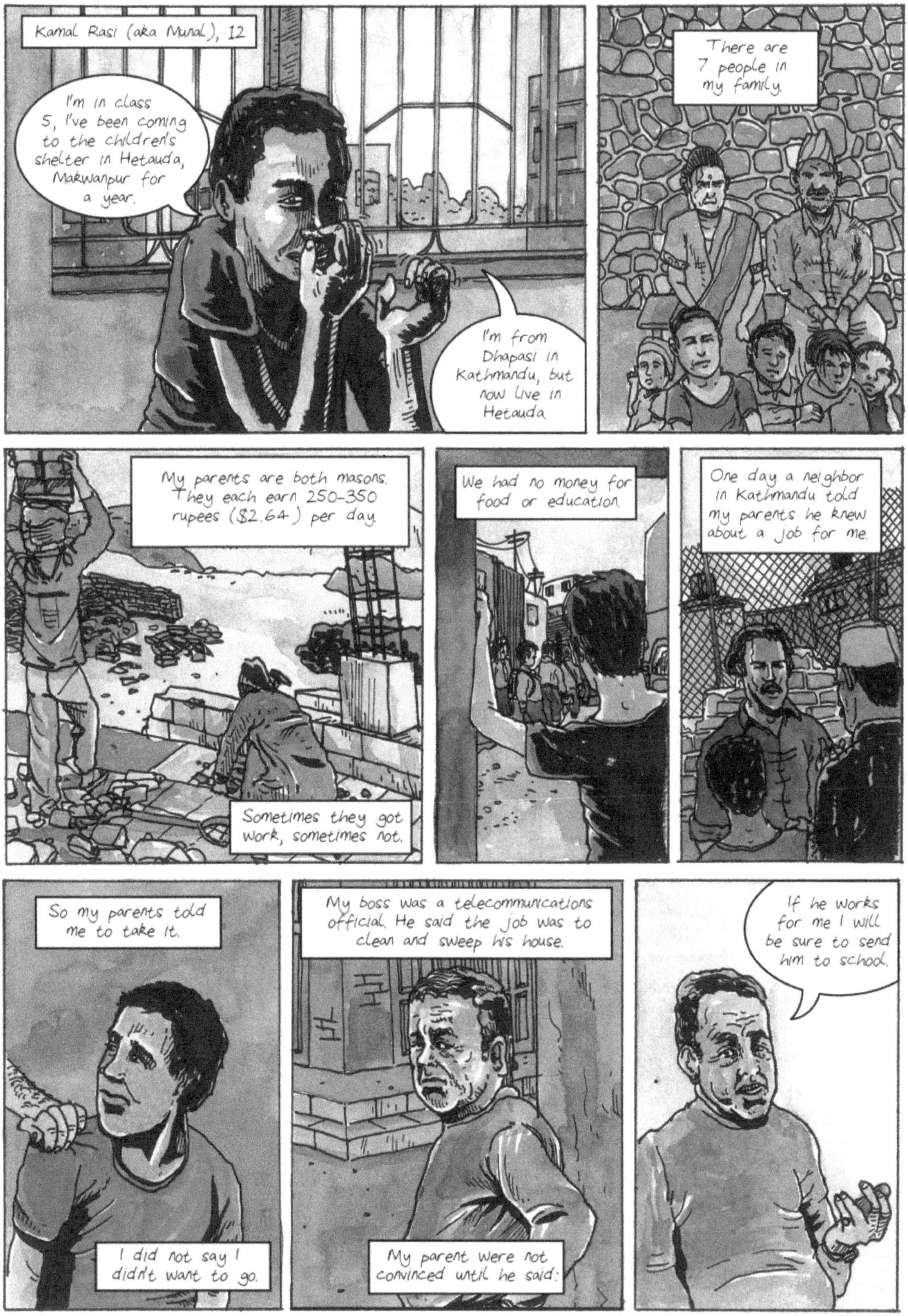
Kamal Rasi (aka Munal), 12
I'm in class 5, I've been coming to the children's shelter in Hetauda, Makwanpur for a year.
I'm from Dhapasi in Kathmandu, but now live in Hetauda.
There are 7 people in my family.
My parents are both masons. They each earn 250-350 rupees ($2.64) per day.
Sometimes they got work, sometimes not.
We had no money for food or education.
One day a neighbor in Kathmandu told my parents he knew about a job for me.
So my parents told me to take it.
I did not say I didn't want to go.
My boss was a telecommunications official. He said the job was to clean and sweep his house.
My parent were not convinced until he said:
If he works for me I will be sure to send him to school.

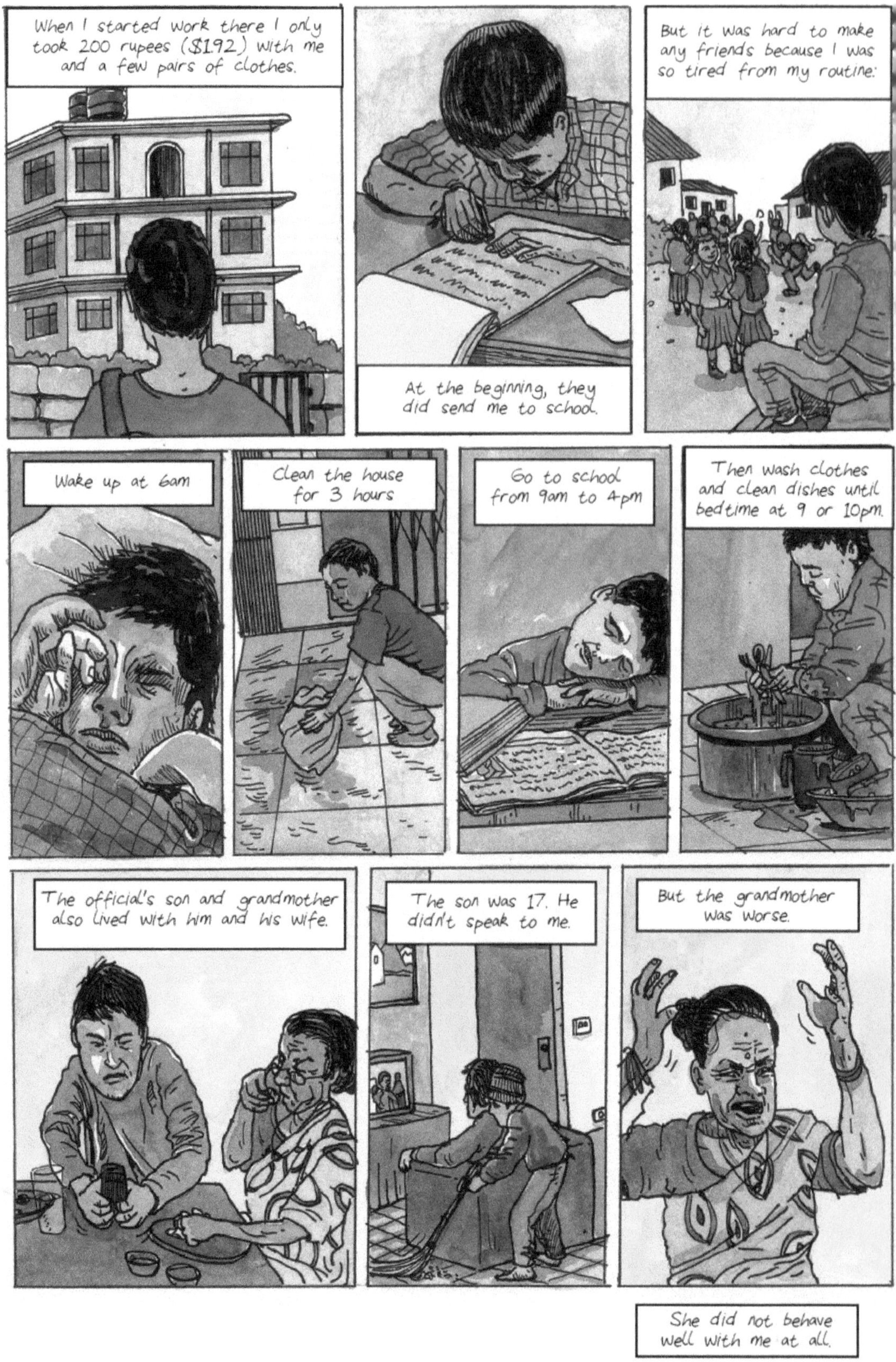
When I started work there I only took 200 rupees ($1.92) with me and a few pairs of clothes.
At the beginning, they did send me to school.
But it was hard to make any friends because I was so tired from my routine:
Wake up at 6am
Clean the house for 3 hours
Go to school from 9am to 4pm
Then wash clothes and clean dishes until bedtime at 9 or 10pm.
The official's son and grandmother also lived with him and his wife.
The son was 17. He didn't speak to me.
But the grandmother was worse.
She did not behave well with me at all.

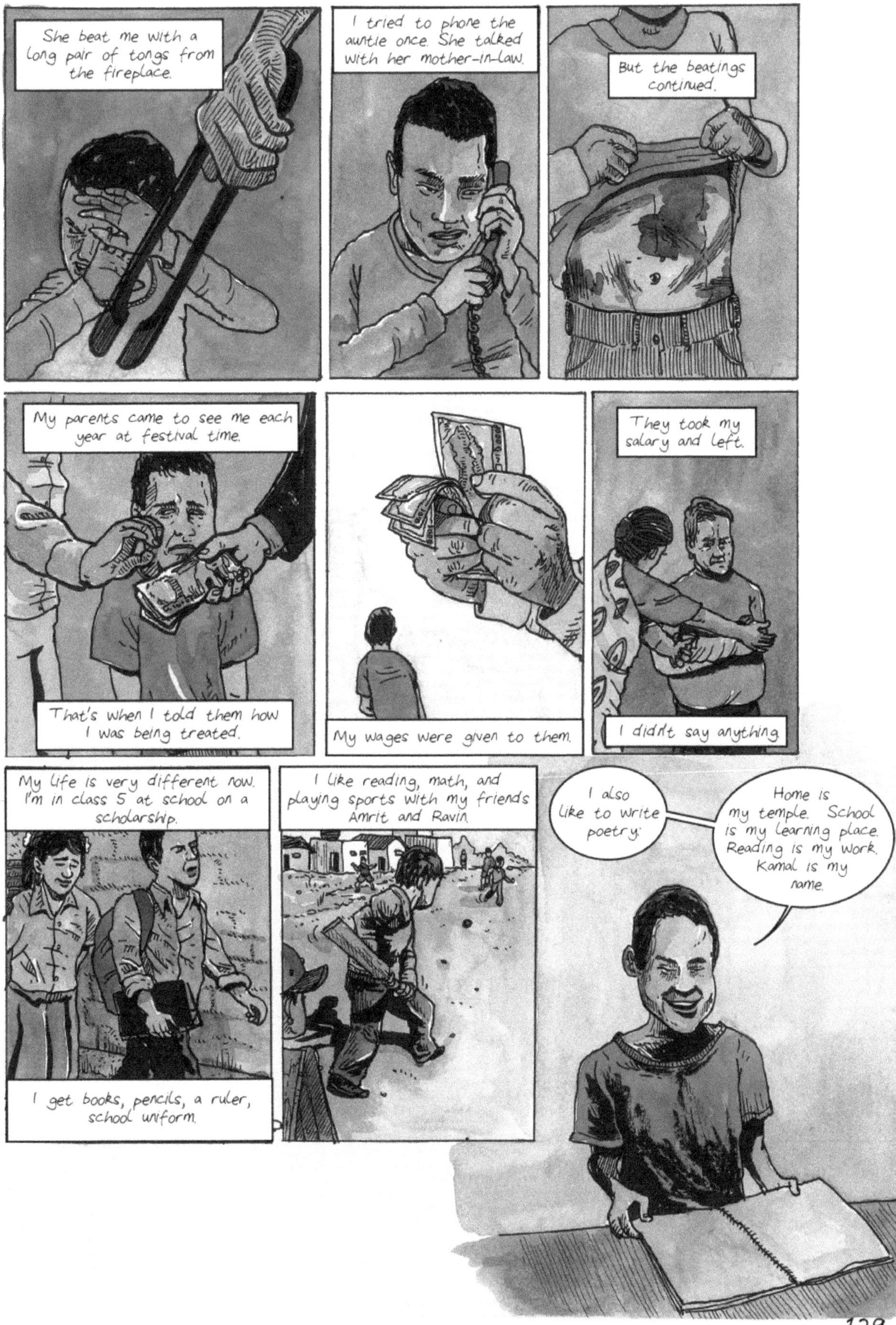

She beat me with a long pair of tongs from the fireplace.
I tried to phone the auntie once. She talked with her mother-in-law.
But the beatings continued.
My parents came to see me each year at festival time.
That's when I told them how I was being treated.
My wages were given to them.
They took my salary and left.
I didn't say anything.
My life is very different now. I'm in class 5 at school on a scholarship.
I get books, pencils, a ruler, school uniform.
I like reading, math, and playing sports with my friends Amrit and Ravin.
I also like to write poetry:
Home is my temple. School is my learning place. Reading is my work. Kamal is my name.

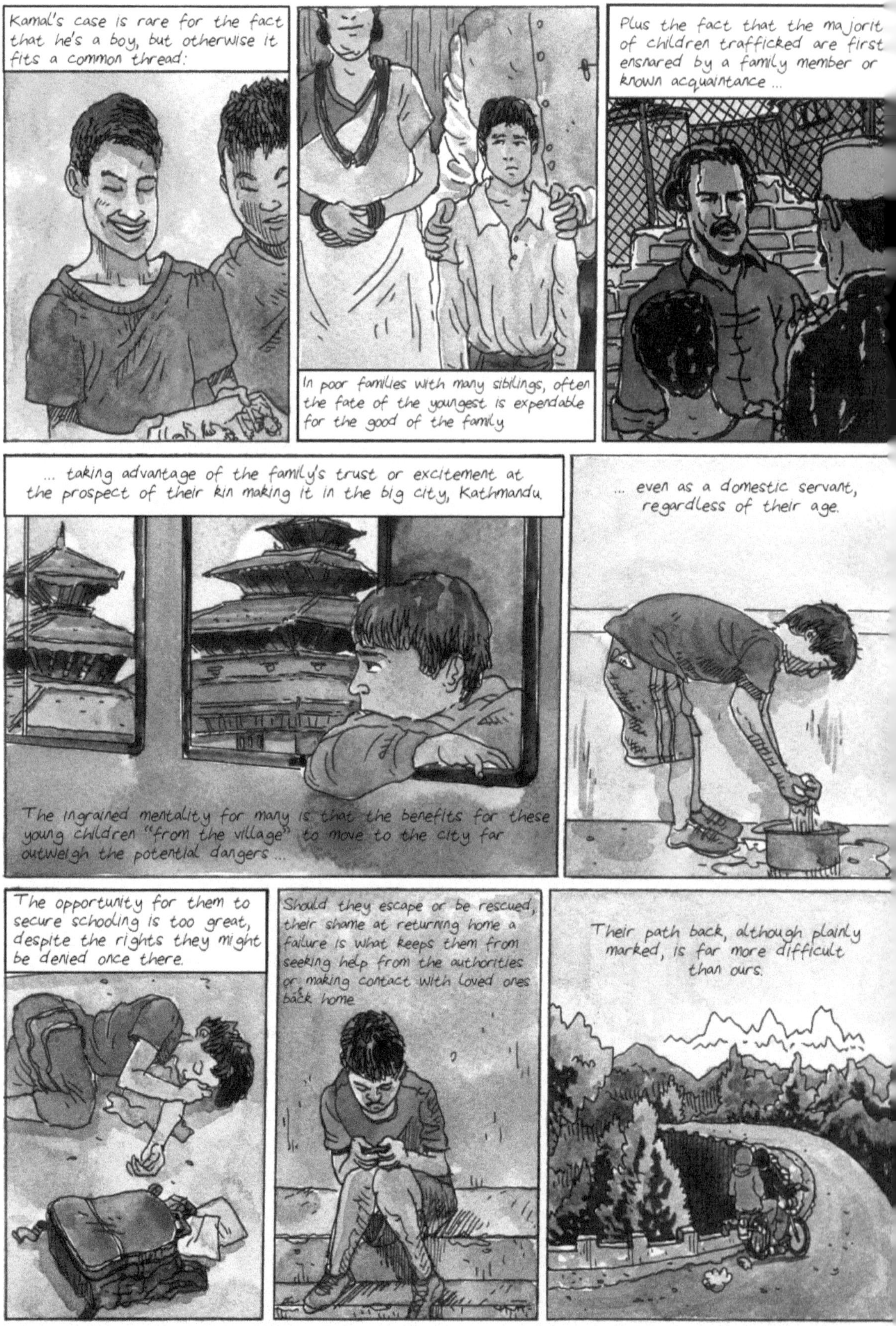
Kamal's case is rare for the fact that he's a boy, but otherwise it fits a common thread:
In poor families with many siblings, often the fate of the youngest is expendable for the good of the family.
Plus the fact that the majorit of children trafficked are first ensnared by a family member or known acquaintance ...
... taking advantage of the family's trust or excitement at the prospect of their kin making it in the big city, Kathmandu.
The ingrained mentality for many is that the benefits for these young children "from the village" to move to the city far outweigh the potential dangers ...
... even as a domestic servant, regardless of their age.
The opportunity for them to secure schooling is too great, despite the rights they might be denied once there.
Should they escape or be rescued, their shame at returning home a failure is what keeps them from seeking help from the authorities or making contact with loved ones back home.
Their path back, although plainly marked, is far more difficult than ours.

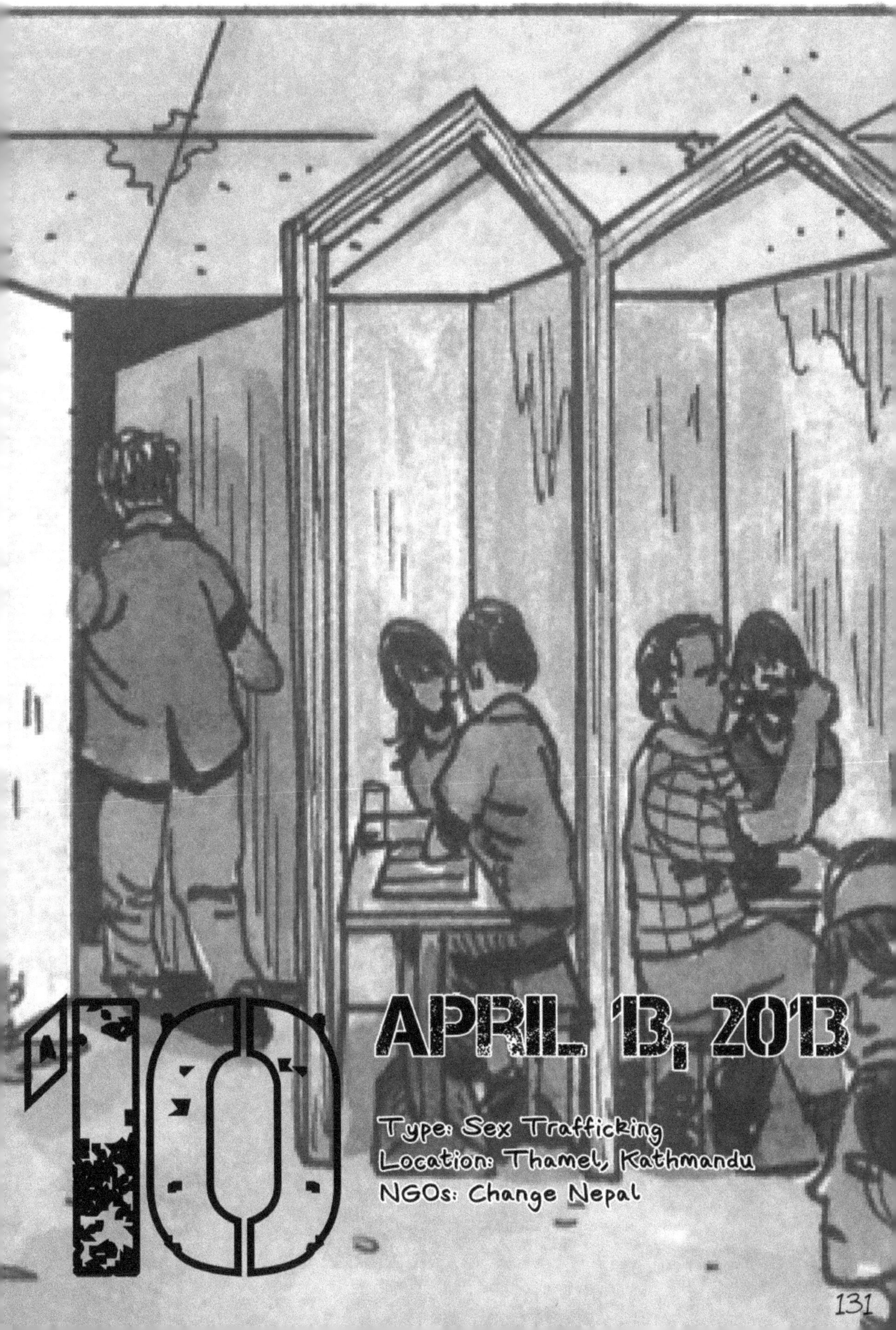

10

APRIL 13, 2013

Type: Sex Trafficking
Location: Thamel, Kathmandu
NGOs: Change Nepal

THE MASSAGE PARLORS

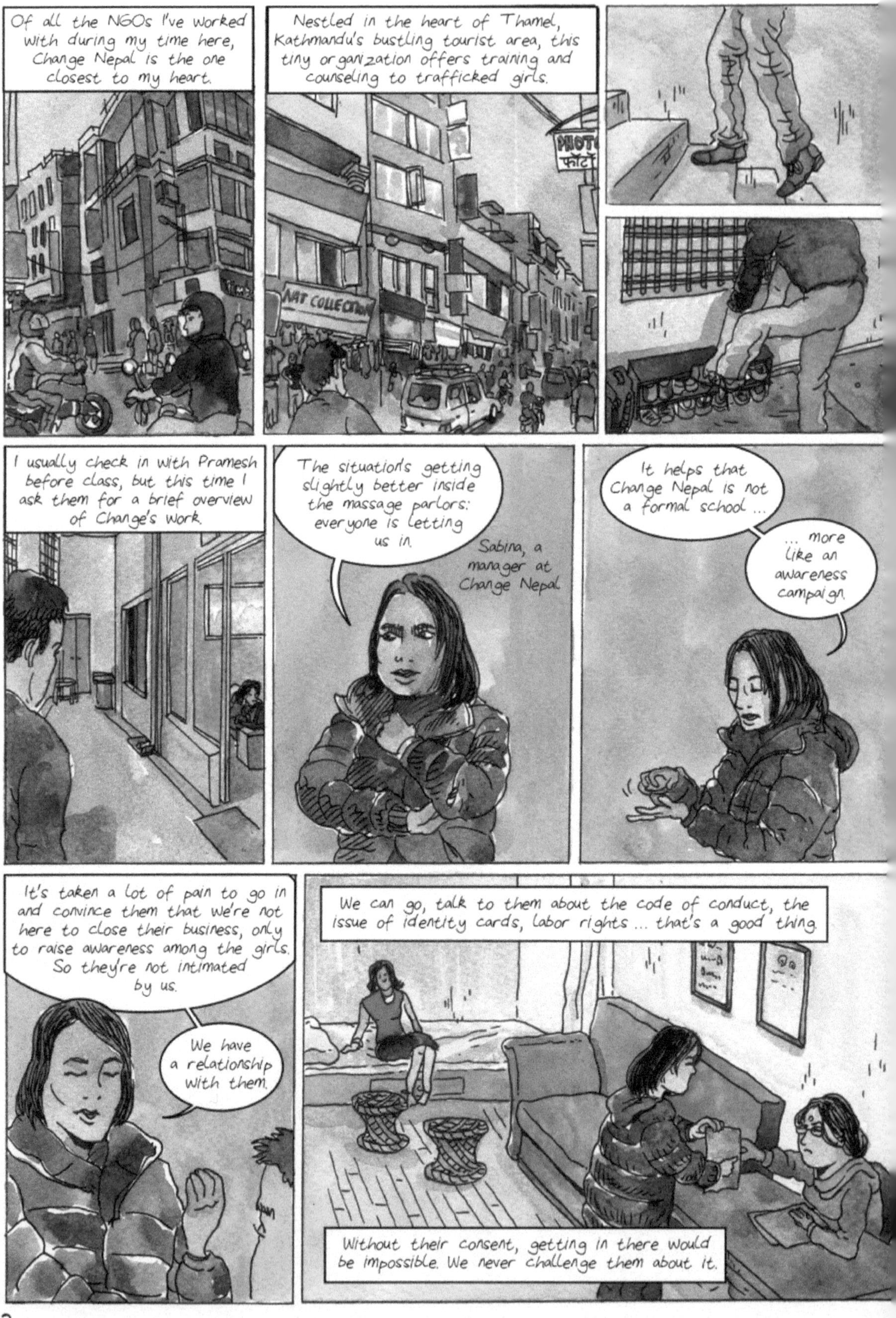

Of all the NGOs I've worked with during my time here, Change Nepal is the one closest to my heart.
Nestled in the heart of Thamel, Kathmandu's bustling tourist area, this tiny organization offers training and counseling to trafficked girls.
NAT COLLECTION
PHOTO
I usually check in with Pramesh before class, but this time I ask them for a brief overview of Change's work.
The situation's getting slightly better inside the massage parlors: everyone is letting us in.
Sabina, a manager at Change Nepal
It helps that Change Nepal is not a formal school ...
... more like an awareness campaign.
It's taken a lot of pain to go in and convince them that we're not here to close their business, only to raise awareness among the girls. So they're not intimated by us.
We have a relationship with them.
We can go, talk to them about the code of conduct, the issue of identity cards, labor rights ... that's a good thing.
Without their consent, getting in there would be impossible. We never challenge them about it.

I take a look at the photos smuggled out of the brothels by some of the girls they're working with

"We tell the owners that this is the duty of a good citizen, you need to send the girls to education classes, allow them access to legal officers," Sabina tells me. Many ignore them.

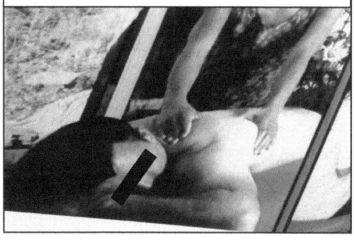

Dance bars are another avenue that is ripe for exploitation, working in much the same way as the strip clubs in the West. The difference being that because conspicuous nudity is so rare here ...

... girls court their clients behind closed doors, at first feigning the hostess role in public (as above), before escorting them to private rooms in the back. There's no protection should the men turn violent.

Thamel is the unofficial home to Nepal's "entertainment industry," with one of the highest concentrations of dance bars, massage parlors, and cabin restaurants in the country.

Pramesh, Change Nepal's director, gives me the guided tour of known "spas" operating as brothels.

All of them are less than a minute away (or, in some cases, directly above) from the stalls selling Buddhist mandalas, Gurkha knives, and Tibetan thangkas* to tourists.

The advertised reality paints a different picture ...

HIMALAYAN
MASSAGE SPA

... from the one that greets us when we step inside.

*ornate devotional Buddhist paintings

133

At the top of the stairs we find a small reception area with 3 young girls* waiting for customers. I pull out my sketchbook to get their likenesses (the main reason I sketch is to protect the identities of survivors I talk to and to try to avoid re-traumatizing them by shoving a telephoto lens in their face):

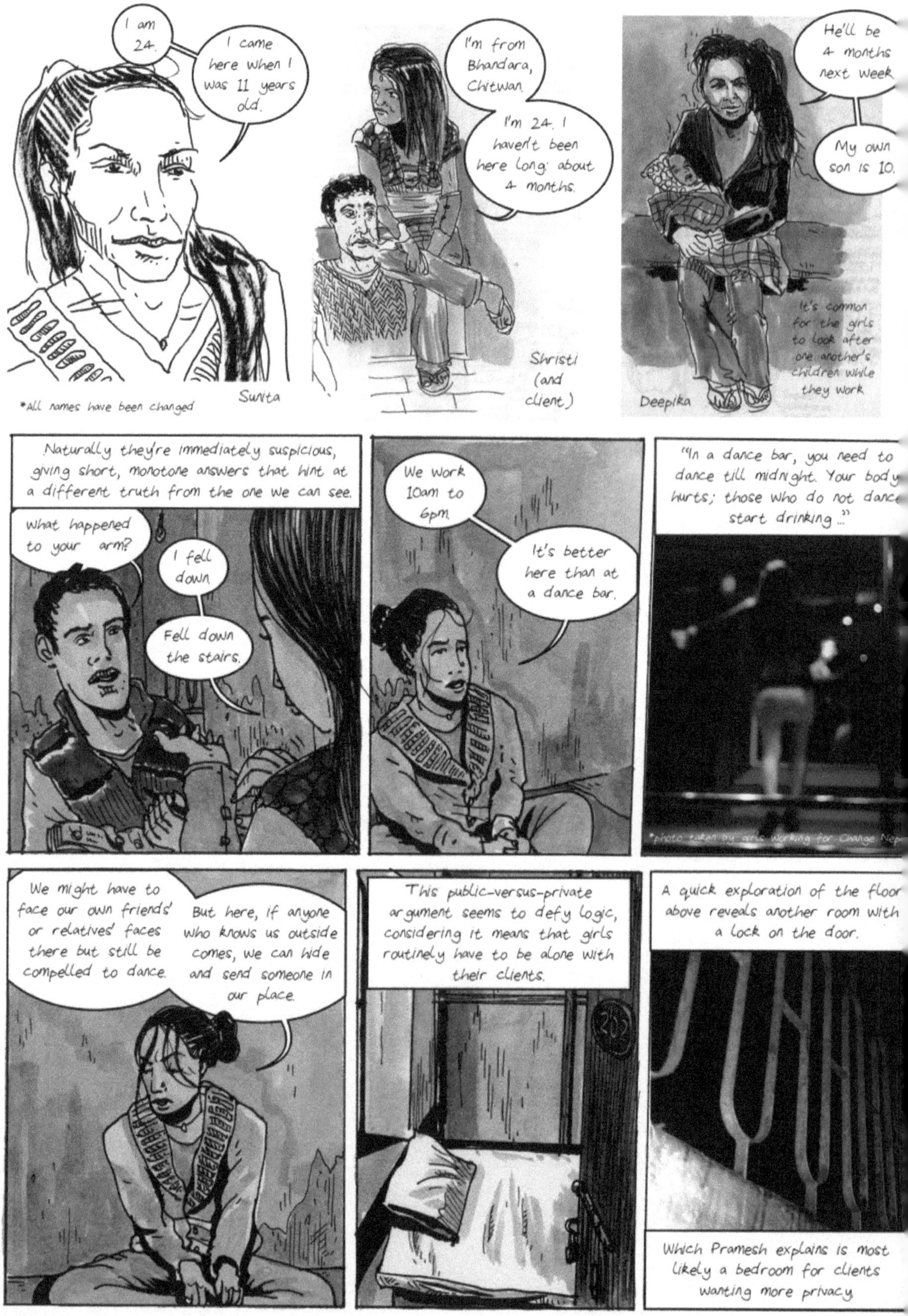
I am 24.
I came here when I was 11 years old.
Sunita
*All names have been changed
I'm from Bhandara, Chitwan.
I'm 24. I haven't been here long: about 4 months.
Shristi (and client)
He'll be 4 months next week.
My own son is 10.
It's common for the girls to look after one another's children while they work
Deepika
Naturally they're immediately suspicious, giving short, monotone answers that hint at a different truth from the one we can see.
What happened to your arm?
I fell down.
Fell down the stairs.
We work 10am to 6pm.
It's better here than at a dance bar.
"In a dance bar, you need to dance till midnight. Your body hurts; those who do not dance start drinking..."
*photo taken by girls working for Change Nep
We might have to face our own friends' or relatives' faces there but still be compelled to dance.
But here, if anyone who knows us outside comes, we can hide and send someone in our place.
This public-versus-private argument seems to defy logic, considering it means that girls routinely have to be alone with their clients.
252
A quick exploration of the floor above reveals another room with a lock on the door.
Which Pramesh explains is most likely a bedroom for clients wanting more privacy.

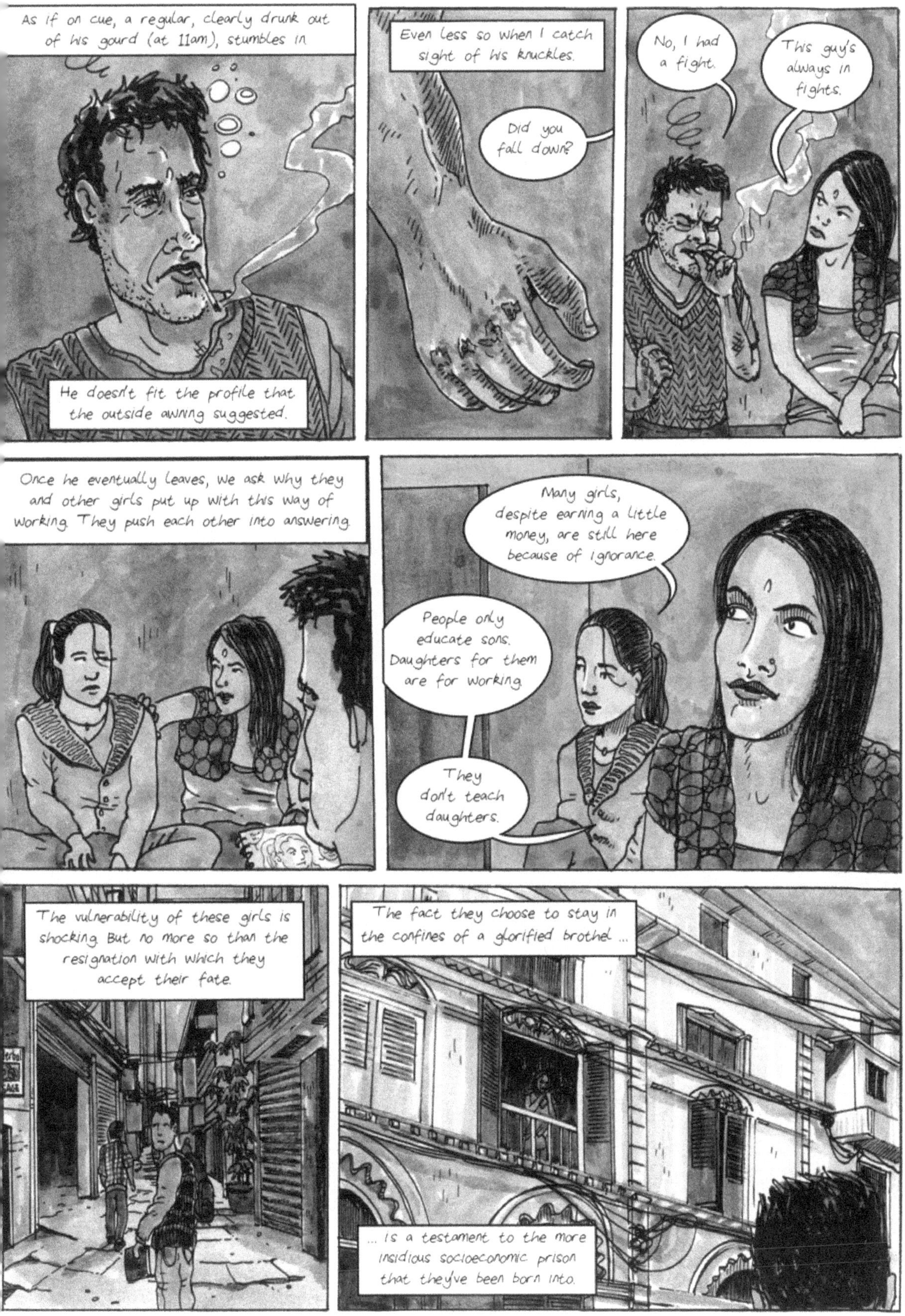
As if on cue, a regular, clearly drunk out of his gourd (at 11am), stumbles in.
He doesn't fit the profile that the outside awning suggested.
Even less so when I catch sight of his knuckles.
Did you fall down?
No, I had a fight.
This guy's always in fights.
Once he eventually leaves, we ask why they and other girls put up with this way of working. They push each other into answering.
Many girls, despite earning a little money, are still here because of ignorance.
People only educate sons. Daughters for them are for working.
They don't teach daughters.
The vulnerability of these girls is shocking. But no more so than the resignation with which they accept their fate.
The fact they choose to stay in the confines of a glorified brothel ...
... is a testament to the more insidious socioeconomic prison that they've been born into.

CABIN (RESTAURANT) FEVER

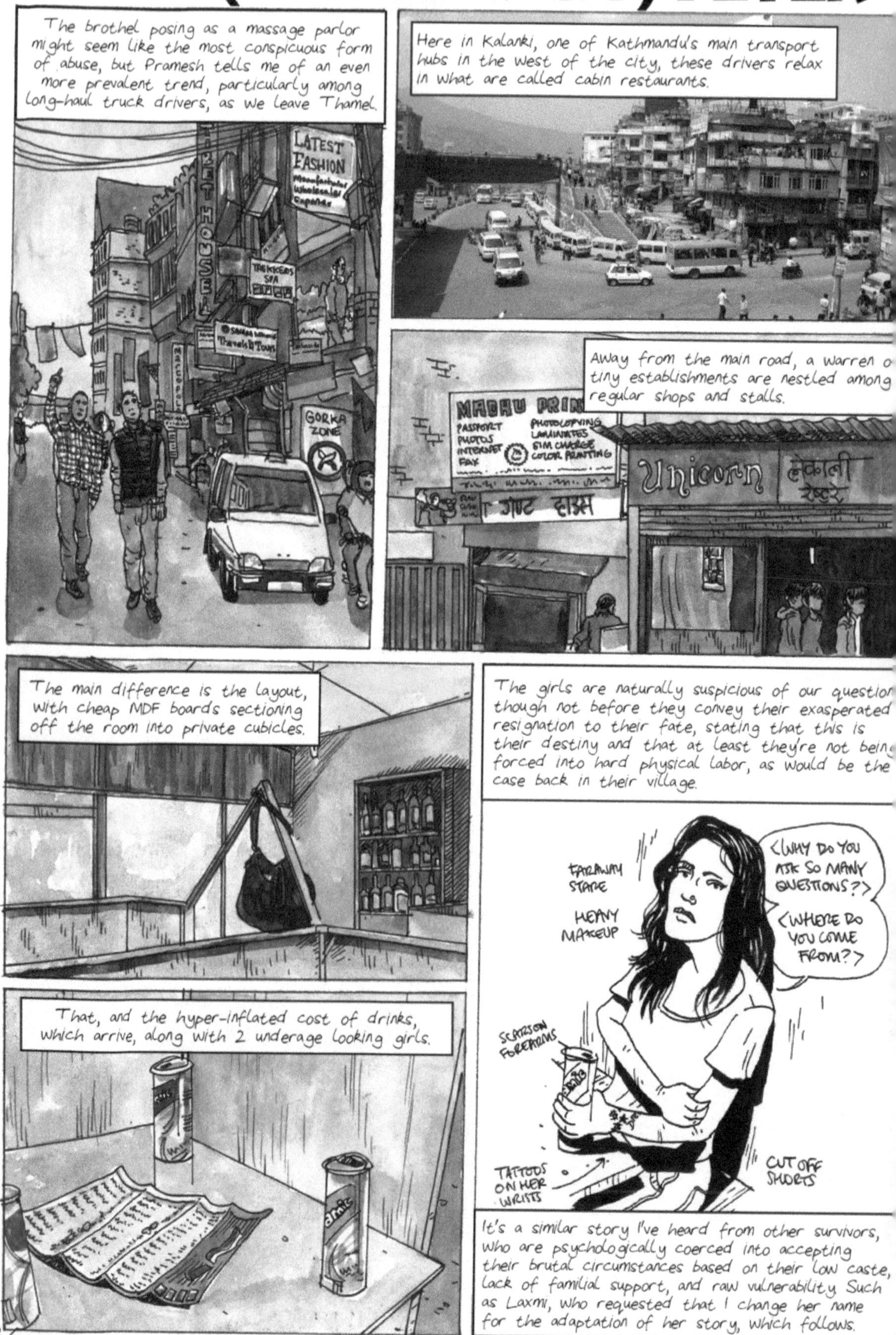
The brothel posing as a massage parlor might seem like the most conspicuous form of abuse, but Pramesh tells me of an even more prevalent trend, particularly among long-haul truck drivers, as we leave Thamel.
LATEST FASHION
GORKA ZONE
Here in Kalanki, one of Kathmandu's main transport hubs in the west of the city, these drivers relax in what are called cabin restaurants.
Away from the main road, a warren o
tiny establishments are nestled among regular shops and stalls.
MADHU PRIN
PASSPORT PHOTOS INTERNET FAX
PHOTOCOPYING LAMINATES SIM CHARGE COLOR PRINTING
Unicorn
The main difference is the layout, with cheap MDF boards sectioning off the room into private cubicles.
The girls are naturally suspicious of our questior though not before they convey their exasperated resignation to their fate, stating that this is their destiny and that at least they're not being forced into hard physical labor, as would be the case back in their village.
FARAWAY STARE
HEAVY MAKEUP
<WHY DO YOU ASK SO MANY QUESTIONS?>
<WHERE DO YOU COME FROM?>
SCARS ON FOREARMS
TATTOOS ON HER WRISTS
CUT OFF SHORTS
That, and the hyper-inflated cost of drinks, which arrive, along with 2 underage looking girls.
It's a similar story I've heard from other survivors, who are psychologically coerced into accepting their brutal circumstances based on their low caste, lack of familial support, and raw vulnerability. Such as Laxmi, who requested that I change her name for the adaptation of her story, which follows.

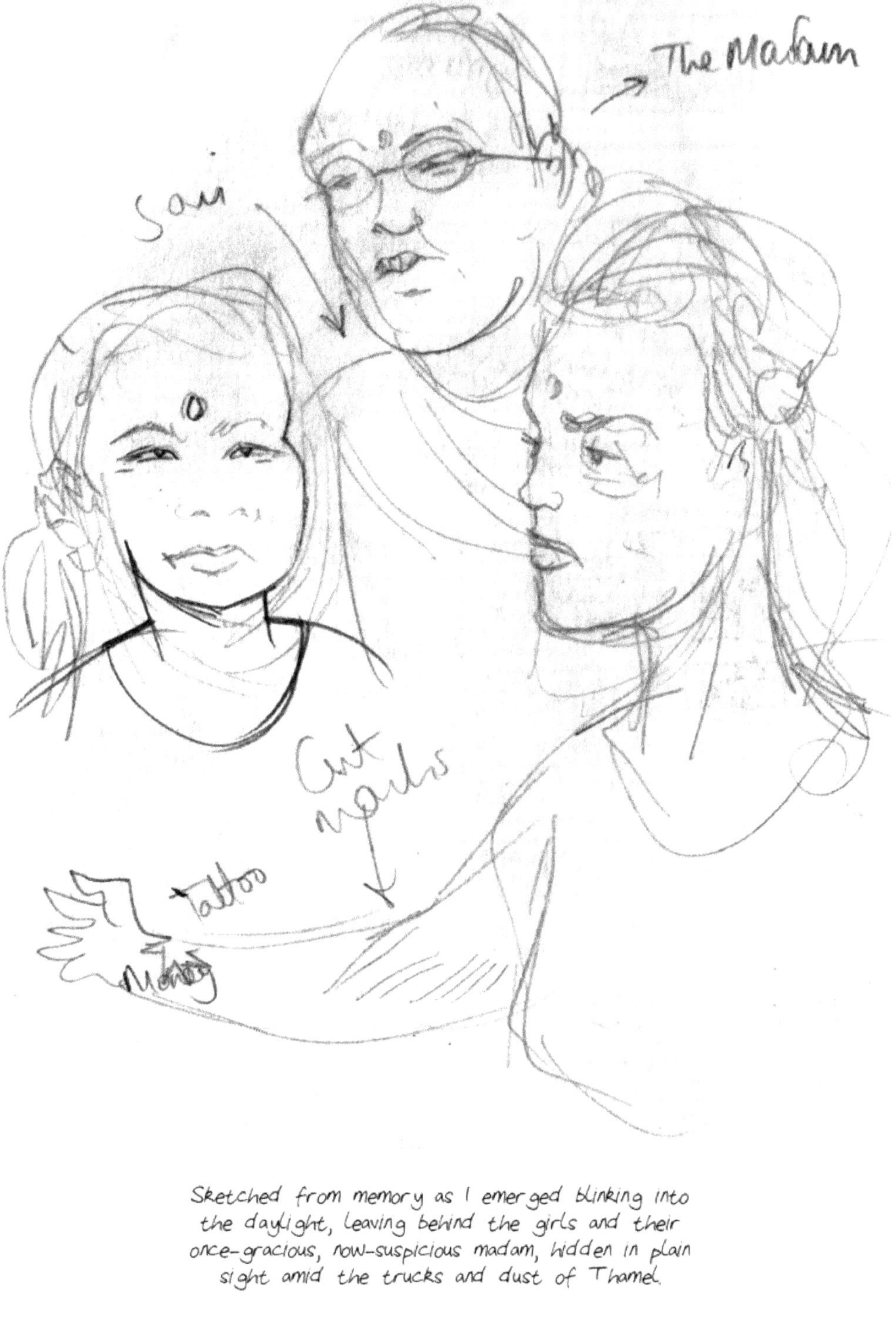
The Madam
Sani
Cut nails
Tattoo

Sketched from memory as I emerged blinking into the daylight, leaving behind the girls and their once-gracious, now-suspicious madam, hidden in plain sight amid the trucks and dust of Thamel.

I take certain details from their responses and combine them with the similar stories of other girls promised better opportunities in the capital.

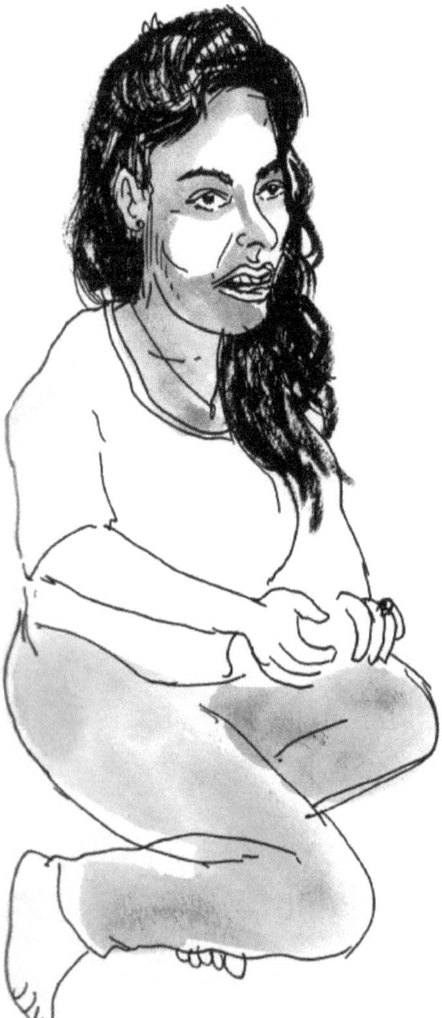

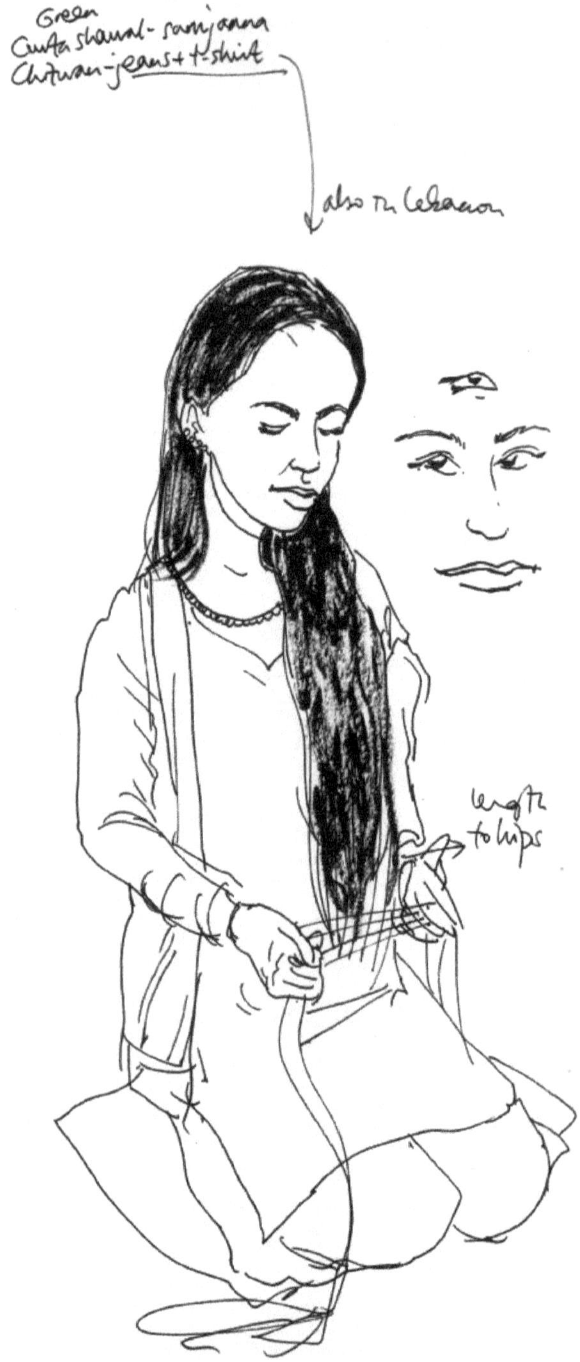
Green
Chitwan - jeans + t-shirt
length to hips

Often composite characters are preferred by our NGO partners as it reduces the likelihood of interviewees being recognized.

This happened 3 years ago, when I was walking 18.*

I'm Dalit, very low caste. We have very few rights in society.

*Nepali term meaning she was going to be 18 at the end of the year, ie., 17.

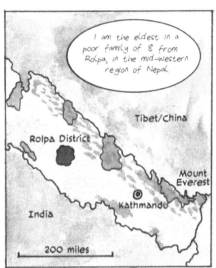

I am the eldest in a poor family of 8 from Rolpa, in the mid-western region of Nepal.

Tibet/China

Rolpa District

Mount Everest

Kathmandu

India

200 miles

My father was jailed for adultery with my mother's sister.

Mother was therefore left to support us by doing manual labor.

As the eldest, I felt a responsibility to support the family (I already dropped out of school in 4th grade).

I came to Kathmandu in 2010 for the first time. In fact it was the first time that I left my village.

My friend paid for me.

The journey cost 1,000 Nepali rupees ($12.)

I liked it when I arrived because of the lighting and electricity.

But in the morning I felt uneasy because it was so crowded.

So many people, so many houses.

We made our way to a brick factory in Thankot, near Santungal.

The friend who had been before had a brother-in-law who worked there.

He got us jobs there and we found a ghailee (hut made of bricks) where we could sleep.

139

I worked there for 6 months, carrying bricks to make money.

I was paid 1 rupee (0.8 of a cent) for each brick I carried.

There were many children, more girls than boys.

As young as 6- and 7-year-olds up to 13-year-olds.

One day the 2 friends I came with disappeared.

A week later

Meera — It's for you.

We're in Balaju — you need to come!

We've started working in a shop that's better than the kiln.

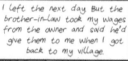

I left the next day. But the brother-in-law took my wages from the owner and said he'd give them to me when I got back to my village.

He never did.

My friends met me at the crossroads in Kalanki and took me to the New Bus Park.

One thing, Meera ...

We all have to work and live here.

I didn't know anyone, have any other choices or any money, so I had nowhere to go.

There were many restaurants of this type.

So many people, so many houses.

My friends had lied to me. Maybe they felt embarrassed about what they were doing.

But everyone there knew what was happening.

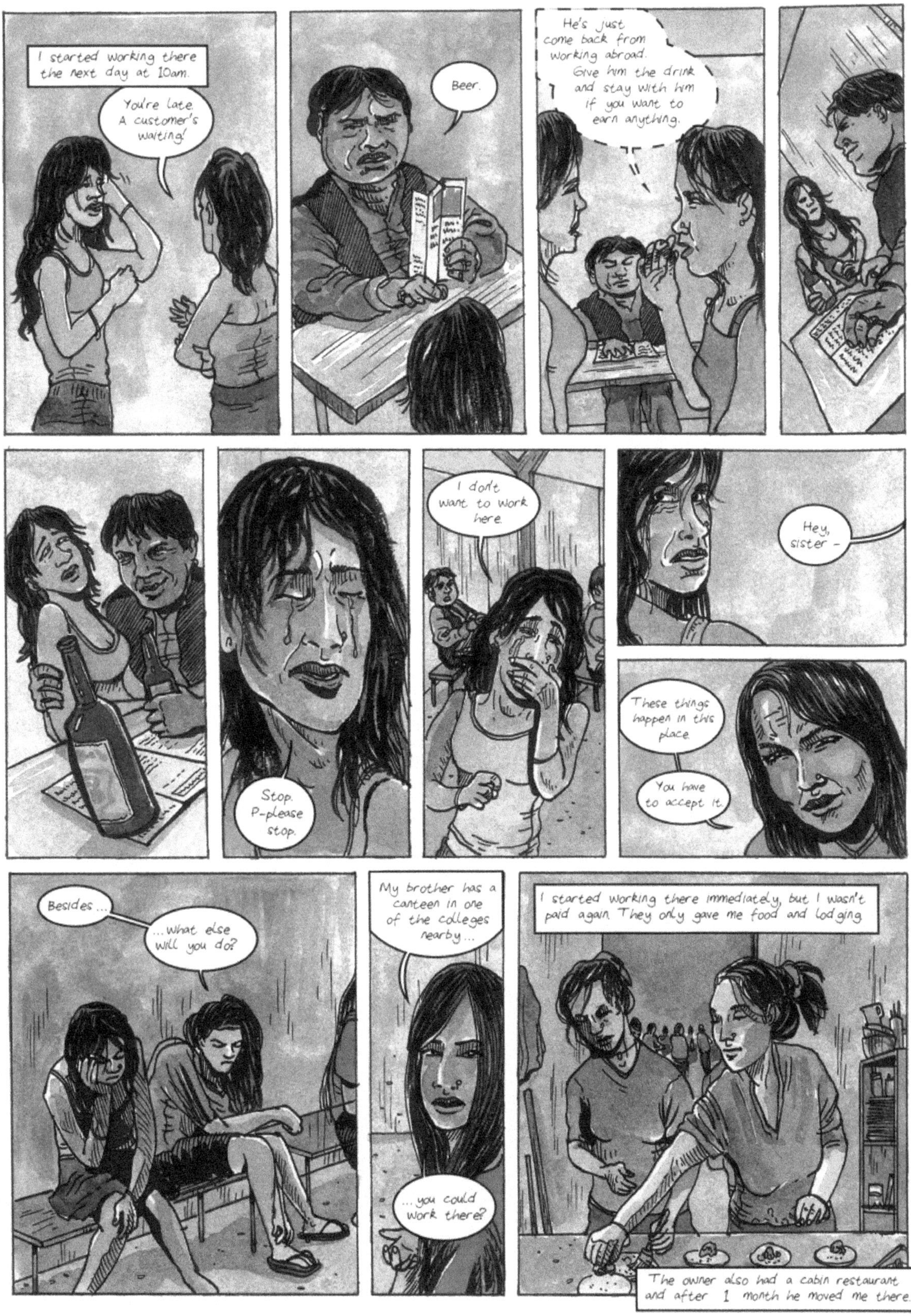
I started working there the next day at 10am.
You're late. A customer's waiting!
Beer.
He's just come back from working abroad. Give him the drink and stay with him if you want to earn anything.
Stop. P-please stop.
I don't want to work here.
Hey, sister -
These things happen in this place.
You have to accept it.
Besides ...
... what else will you do?
My brother has a canteen in one of the colleges nearby ...
... you could work there?
I started working there immediately, but I wasn't paid again. They only gave me food and lodging.
The owner also had a cabin restaurant and after 1 month he moved me there.

I was there for 2 months.

Men misbehaved there again

Here you go, Uncle*

I used to deliver things to the owner. I thought he was on my side.

*typical Nepali honorific.

But the owner's wife said that I had to make the customers happy.

Be more talkative with customers, sit closer to them...

... so they will be happier, eat more, and pay more.

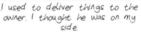

The customers used to misbehave and when the owner's wife was at the cabin I had to do things I didn't want to.

I was there for 2 months, but only got paid for 1 month

I ran away from that place to go to another restaurant, where a friend from the first restaurant was working.

I was there for 1 year.

This was the first time I called my mother.

I'm fine, mother.

I worked from 6am to 9pm. I used to earn 3000 rupees ($35) a month working there.

Most customers had alcohol. Most were drivers or migrant workers. Most were over 35.

I took these jobs because it was my destiny.

Whenever I got the chance to be alone, I would ask myself, why am I here?

Maybe I did wrong deeds in a previous life - maybe I'm paying for it all my life now.

I was pulled out of the last restaurant by workers from an NGO who visited during their fieldwork.

At the shelter I trained as a cook and was told about the cultural factors that influenced the path that I was on

One year after leaving the restaurant, I'm an active member of the shelter staff ...

... and I want to help other girls overcome similar problems.

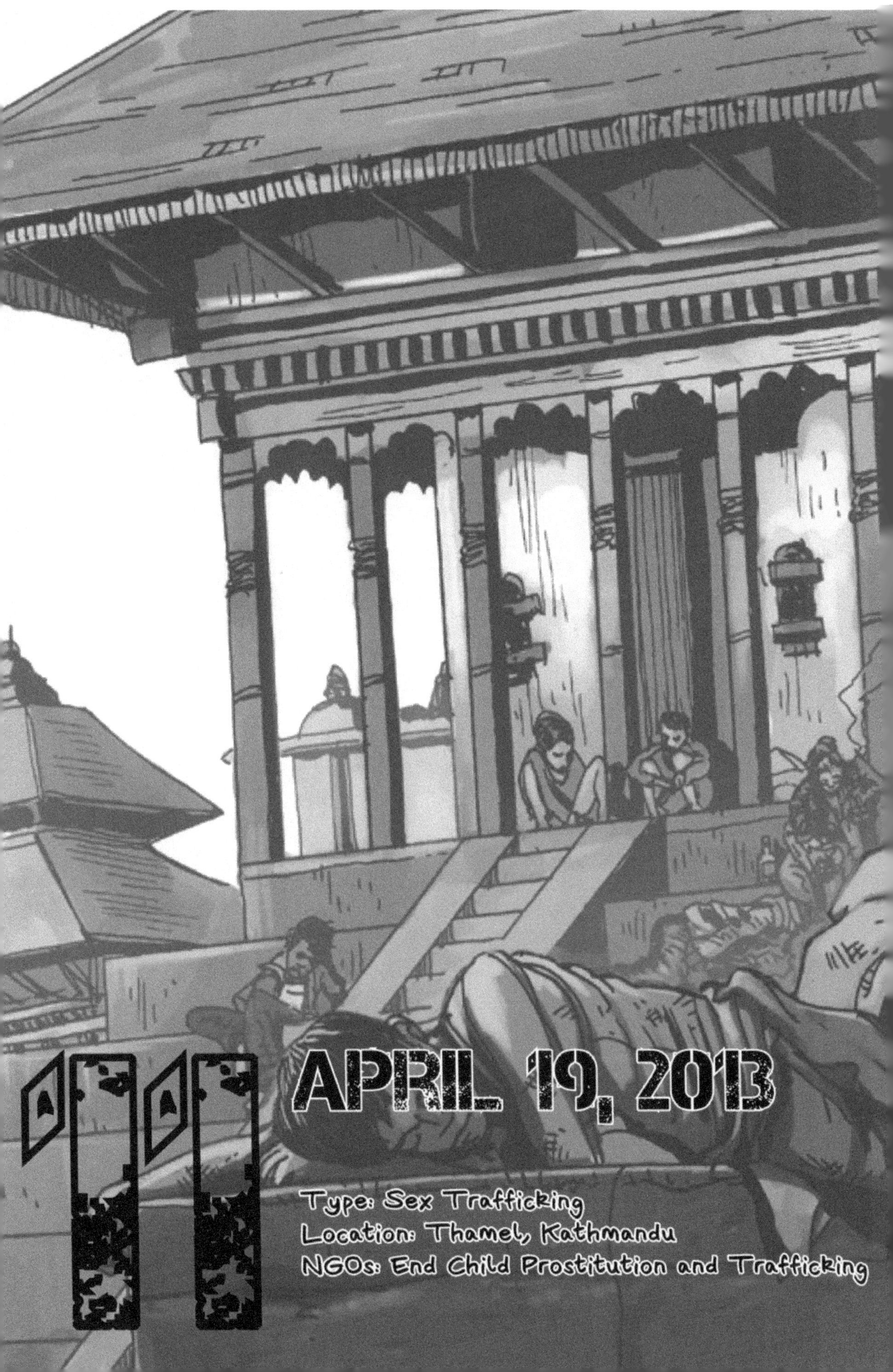

11

APRIL 19, 2013

Type: Sex Trafficking
Location: Thamel, Kathmandu
NGOs: End Child Prostitution and Trafficking

A TRAFFICKER SPEAKS

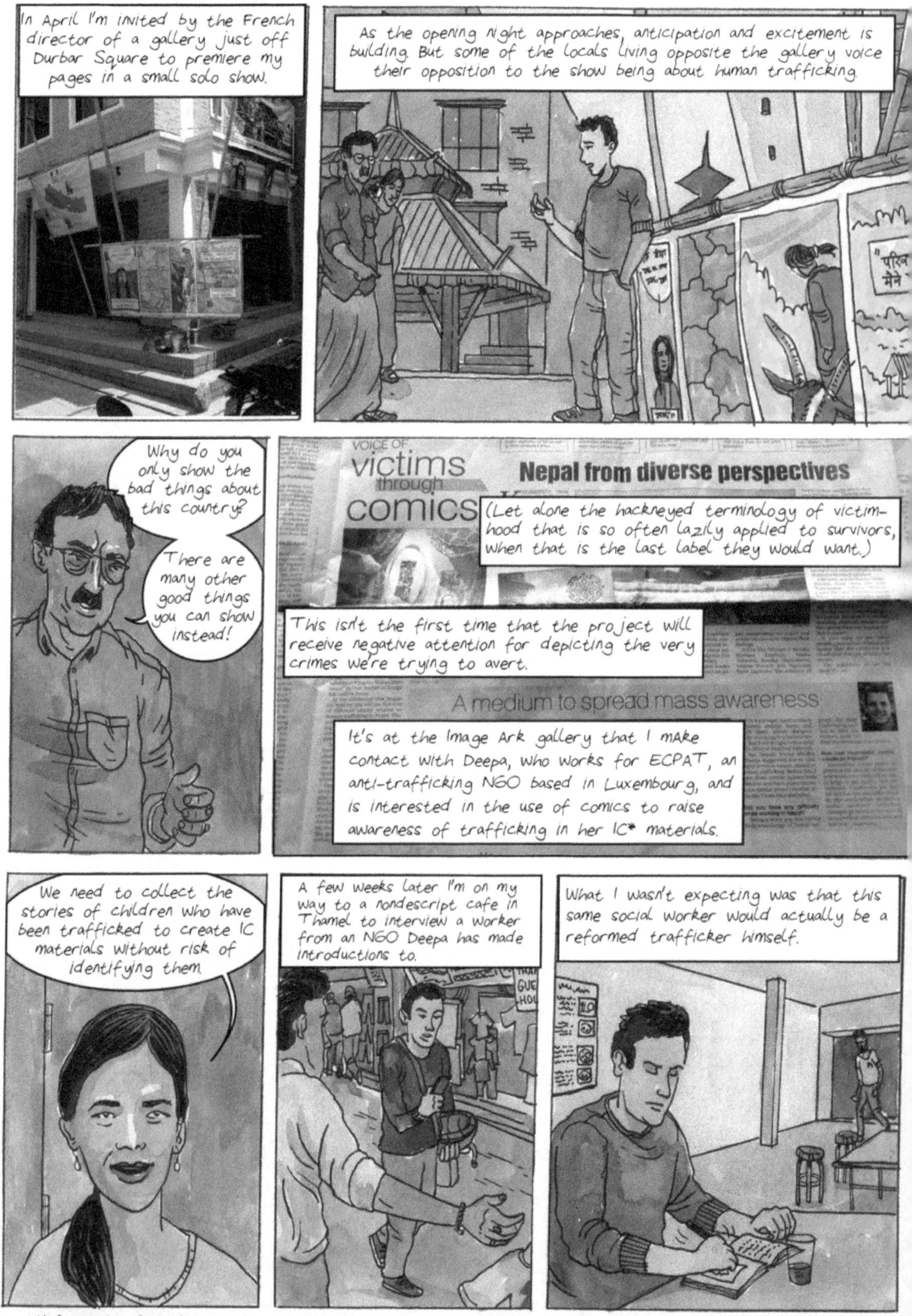
In April I'm invited by the French director of a gallery just off Durbar Square to premiere my pages in a small solo show.
As the opening night approaches, anticipation and excitement is building. But some of the locals living opposite the gallery voice their opposition to the show being about human trafficking.
Why do you only show the bad things about this country?
There are many other good things you can show instead!
VOICE OF victims through comics
Nepal from diverse perspectives
(Let alone the hackneyed terminology of victimhood that is so often lazily applied to survivors, when that is the last label they would want.)
This isn't the first time that the project will receive negative attention for depicting the very crimes we're trying to avert.
A medium to spread mass awareness
It's at the Image Ark gallery that I make contact with Deepa, who works for ECPAT, an anti-trafficking NGO based in Luxembourg, and is interested in the use of comics to raise awareness of trafficking in her IC* materials.
We need to collect the stories of children who have been trafficked to create IC materials without risk of identifying them.
A few weeks later I'm on my way to a nondescript cafe in Thamel to interview a worker from an NGO Deepa has made introductions to.
What I wasn't expecting was that this same social worker would actually be a reformed trafficker himself.

*Information Campaign

I live near Koteshwor. I am 22 years old now. I studied until grade 12.

Twelve years ago I was living with my family in a village in eastern Nepal.

I have 2 elder brothers, 2 younger brothers, and 2 sisters.

Intially my father was selling yak churpi and made a lot of money.

But then he became an alcoholic after a bad investment, and then it became difficult to get food.

One of my brothers left home and went to the city.

So I followed him. During that period we started begging.

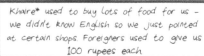

Khaire* used to buy lots of food for us - we didn't know English so we just pointed at certain shops. Foreigners used to give us 100 rupees each.

*literally, "light brown," meaning foreigners

That way it was easy to live on the street.

I stayed 3-4 months at an NGO with my elder brother. There was 1 room - for a drawing you get a simple meal.

There were around 30 to 35 kids there each day.

Substance abuse wasn't such a problem at that time. We were quite disciplined compared to today: no glue (dayn), hash, cigarette, alcohol, or drugs from syringes.

After years on the street, I started smoking because of my brother. You have to have a cigarette to stay warm at night.

We enjoyed life in the Durbar Marg/Kingsway area. In the mornings, we collected the garbage from the restaurants and took them to the dump.

The hotel owners used to give us scraps and leftovers in return.

At that time the elder boys started to take our money.

And when we didn't have money to give them, they cut our hands or forearms.

We used to sleep inside the Hindu temple at night.

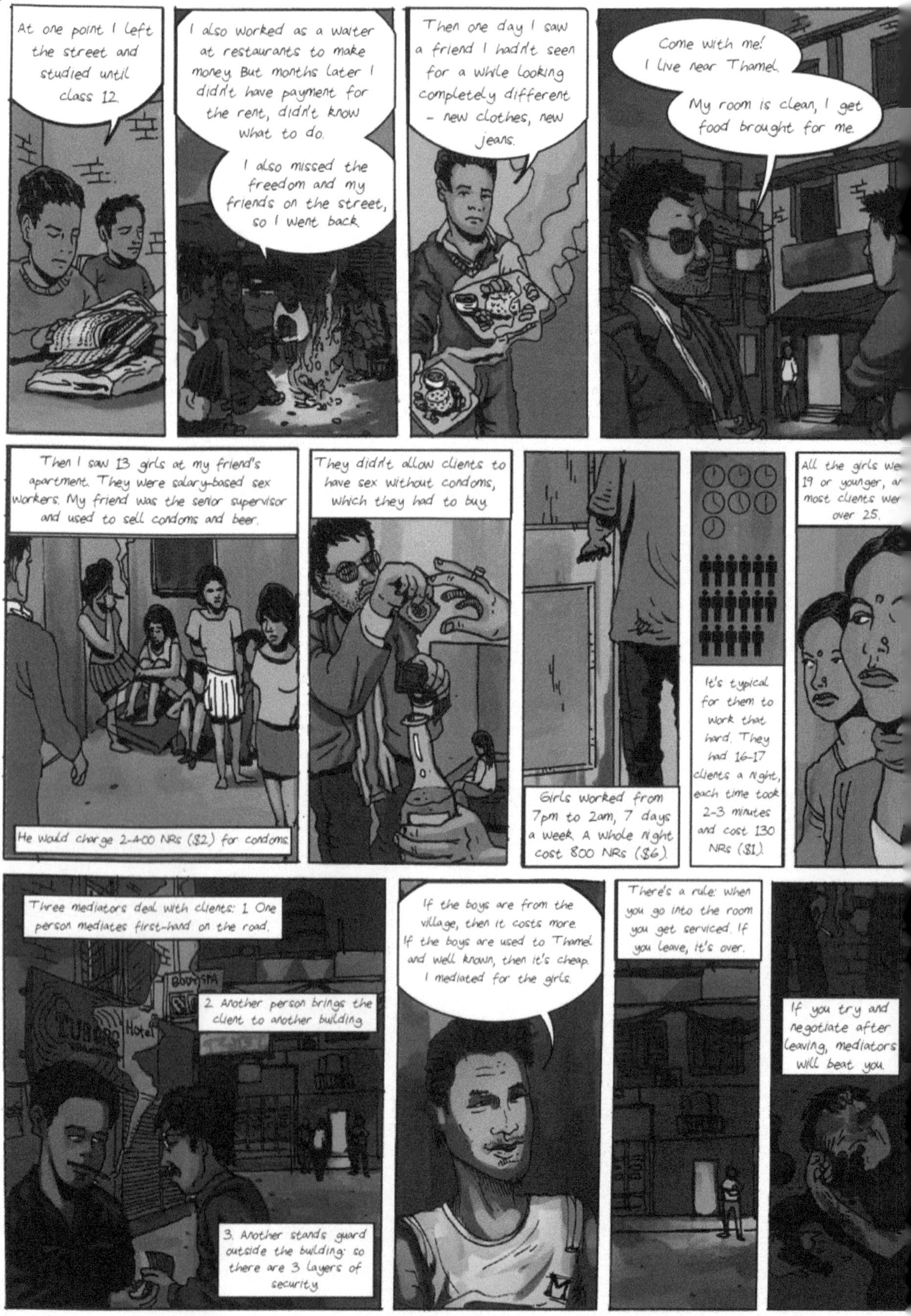
At one point I left the street and studied until class 12.
I also worked as a waiter at restaurants to make money. But months later I didn't have payment for the rent, didn't know what to do.
I also missed the freedom and my friends on the street, so I went back.
Then one day I saw a friend I hadn't seen for a while looking completely different - new clothes, new jeans.
Come with me! I live near Thamel.
My room is clean, I get food brought for me.
Then I saw 13 girls at my friend's apartment. They were salary-based sex workers. My friend was the senior supervisor and used to sell condoms and beer.
He would charge 2-400 NRs ($2) for condoms.
They didn't allow clients to have sex without condoms, which they had to buy.
Girls worked from 7pm to 2am, 7 days a week. A whole night cost 800 NRs ($6).
It's typical for them to work that hard. They had 16-17 clients a night, each time took 2-3 minutes and cost 130 NRs ($1).
All the girls we
19 or younger, a
most clients wer
over 25.
Three mediators deal with clients: 1. One person mediates first-hand on the road.
2. Another person brings the client to another building.
3. Another stands guard outside the building: so there are 3 layers of security.
Hotel
If the boys are from the village, then it costs more. If the boys are used to Thamel and well known, then it's cheap. I mediated for the girls.
There's a rule: when you go into the room you get serviced. If you leave, it's over.
If you try and negotiate after leaving, mediators will beat you.

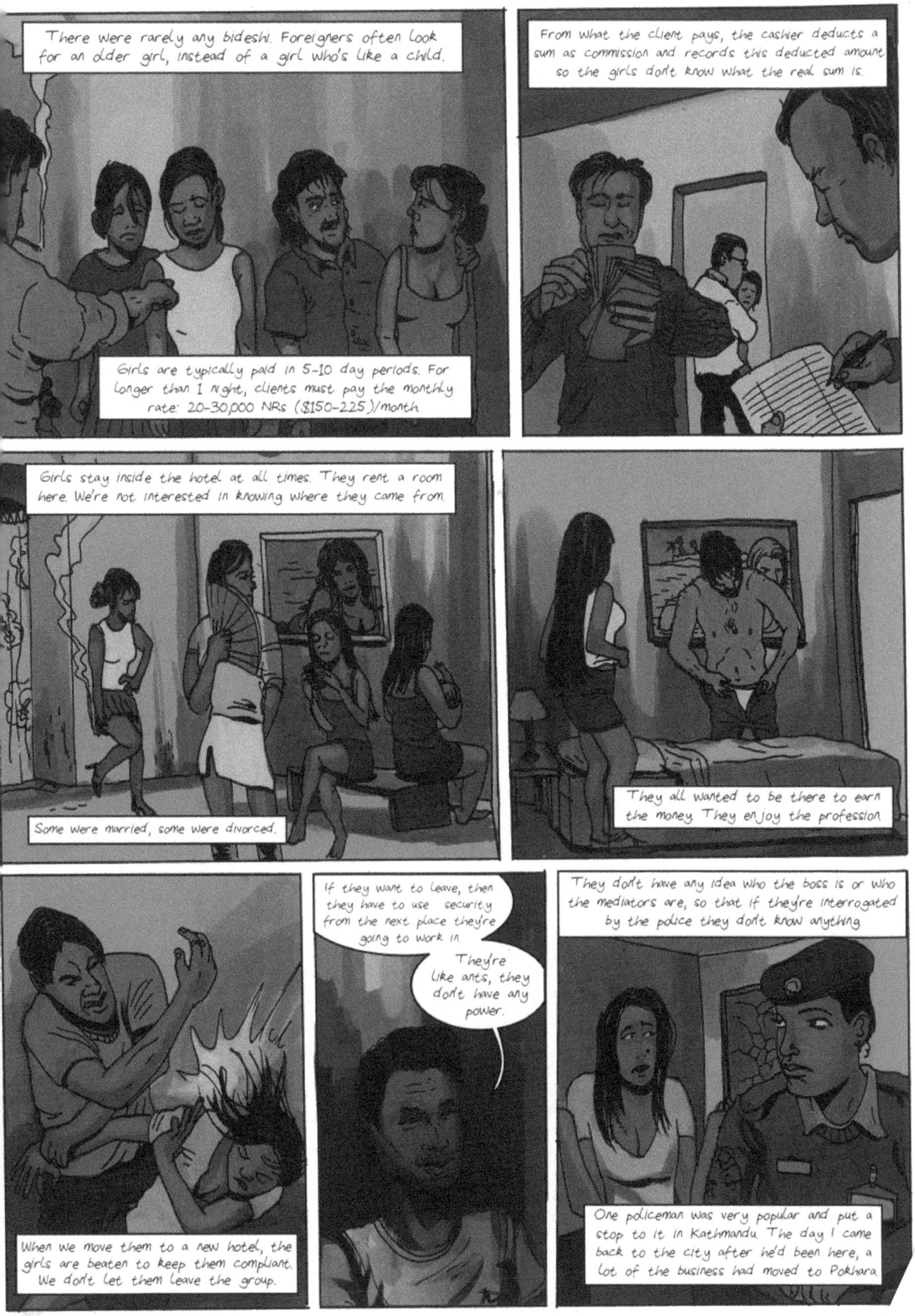
There were rarely any bideshi. Foreigners often look for an older girl, instead of a girl who's like a child.
Girls are typically paid in 5-10 day periods. For longer than 1 night, clients must pay the monthly rate: 20-30,000 NRs ($150-225)/month
From what the client pays, the cashier deducts a sum as commission and records this deducted amount so the girls don't know what the real sum is.
Girls stay inside the hotel at all times. They rent a room here. We're not interested in knowing where they came from.
Some were married, some were divorced.
They all wanted to be there to earn the money. They enjoy the profession
When we move them to a new hotel, the girls are beaten to keep them compliant. We don't let them leave the group.
If they want to leave, then they have to use security from the next place they're going to work in
They're like ants, they don't have any power.
They don't have any idea who the boss is or who the mediators are, so that if they're interrogated by the police they don't know anything
One policeman was very popular and put a stop to it in Kathmandu. The day I came back to the city after he'd been here, a lot of the business had moved to Pokhara

After some time I decided to not work inside a hotel any more. So I began to work on the street instead. It's easier to find clients for girls that way.

That's when I started mediating over the phone, sending girls out to people. To the same clients as before.

When they were interested and they liked the service, they would call again and again.

I also started selling hashish and taking drugs.

One was called saman: a mix of cocaine and I don't know what else.

One day, my friend was admitted to hospital for 3 days.

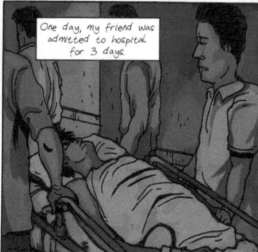

Soon after my sister told me my friend was dead. He was 20.

I did some mediating after that and earned enough money to get married to a working girl.

There was no option to work in restaurants or hotels, so I moved from Thamel to Dulko where rent is cheap.

1.5 years later I returned to the NGO from the beginning and volunteered for a year. I proved myself and have been a social worker there for 2.5 years.

But I still miss my friend. When I realized that he died because of the life he led, I decided to do things differently.

A desperate need to escape from poverty, coupled with the trappings of wealth, were what drove him to consider the girls he bought and sold as expendable. And while he might be out of the cycle, there are still plenty of young children living on the streets, potential fodder for the next generation of unscrupulous pimps. That's why my next port of call is to a homeless shelter for kids.

That story, along with a handful of others, was collected by ECPAT, translated into Nepali, and distributed among homeless children to warn them of the many dangers they face on the streets, as well as to tell them where to find support and shelter. The following extract is from an interview with one of the managers of a shelter, and a composite character from several different true stories. This was the cover image.

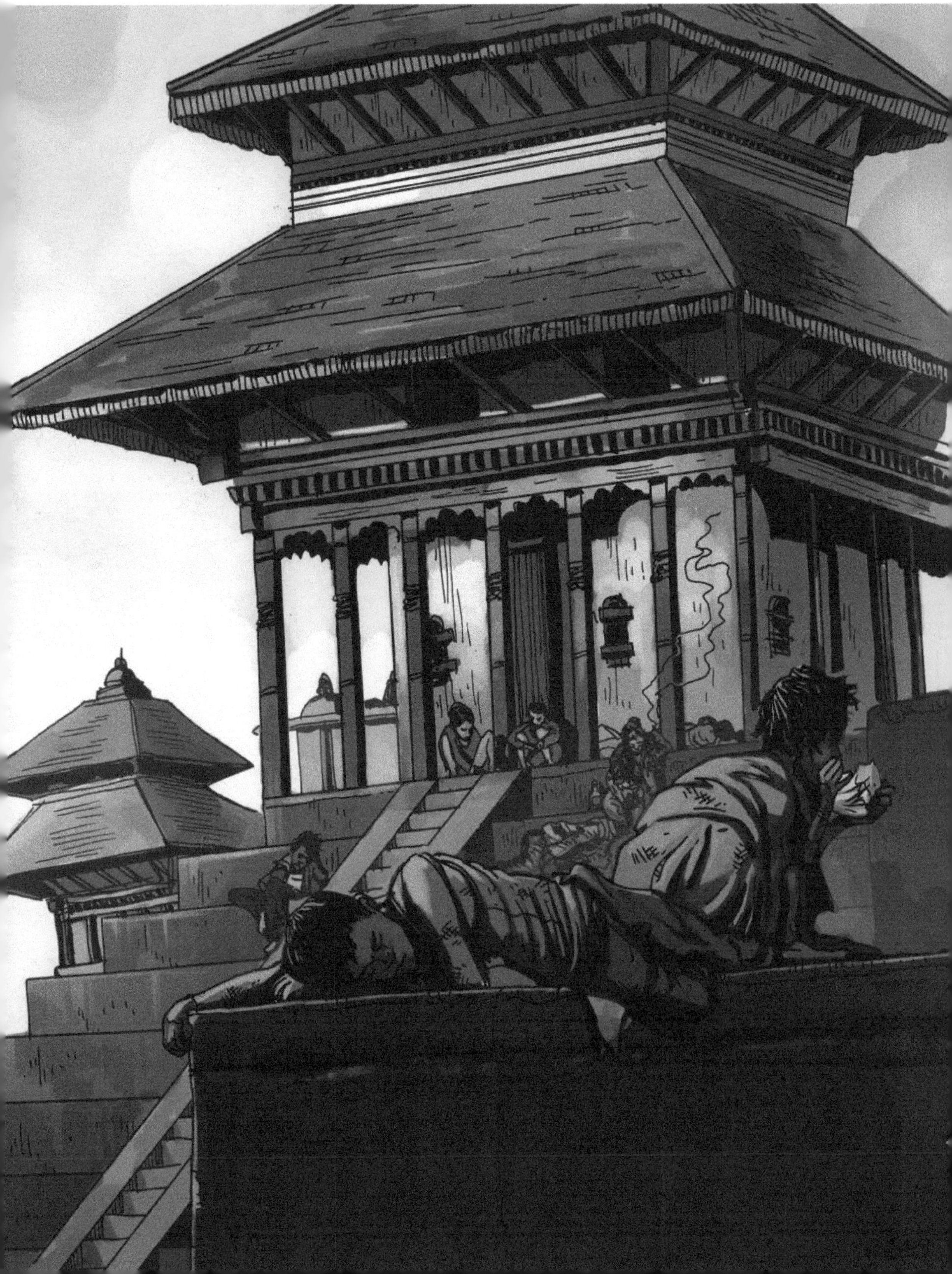

LIFE ON THE STREETS

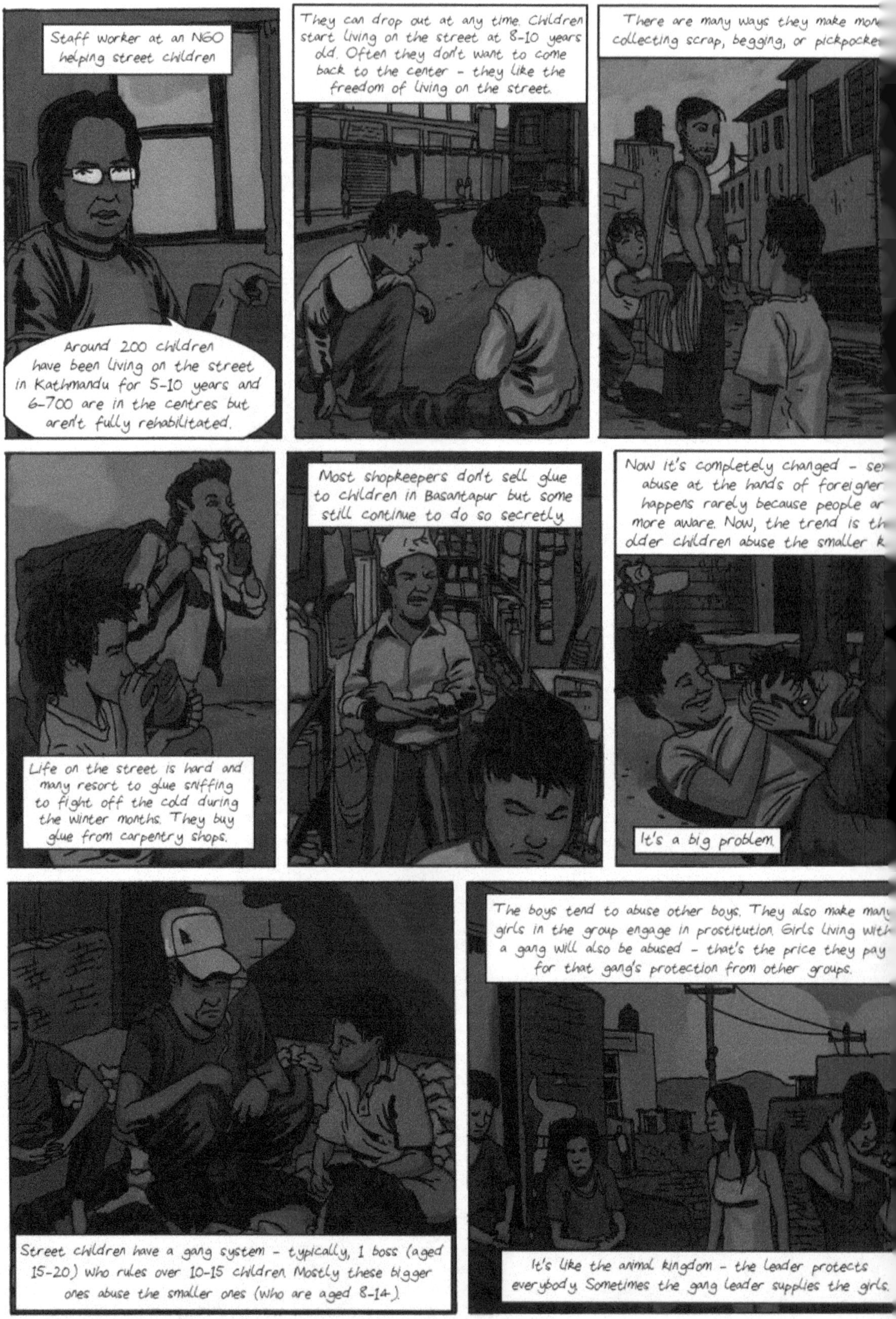
Staff worker at an NGO helping street children
Around 200 children have been living on the street in Kathmandu for 5-10 years and 6-700 are in the centres but aren't fully rehabilitated.
They can drop out at any time. Children start living on the street at 8-10 years old. Often they don't want to come back to the center - they like the freedom of living on the street.
There are many ways they make mon
collecting scrap, begging, or pickpocke
Life on the street is hard and many resort to glue sniffing to fight off the cold during the winter months. They buy glue from carpentry shops.
Most shopkeepers don't sell glue to children in Basantapur but some still continue to do so secretly.
Now it's completely changed - se
abuse at the hands of foreigne
happens rarely because people ar
more aware. Now, the trend is th
older children abuse the smaller k
It's a big problem.
Street children have a gang system - typically, 1 boss (aged 15-20) who rules over 10-15 children. Mostly these bigger ones abuse the smaller ones (who are aged 8-14).
The boys tend to abuse other boys. They also make many girls in the group engage in prostitution. Girls living with a gang will also be abused - that's the price they pay for that gang's protection from other groups.
It's like the animal kingdom - the leader protects everybody. Sometimes the gang leader supplies the girls.

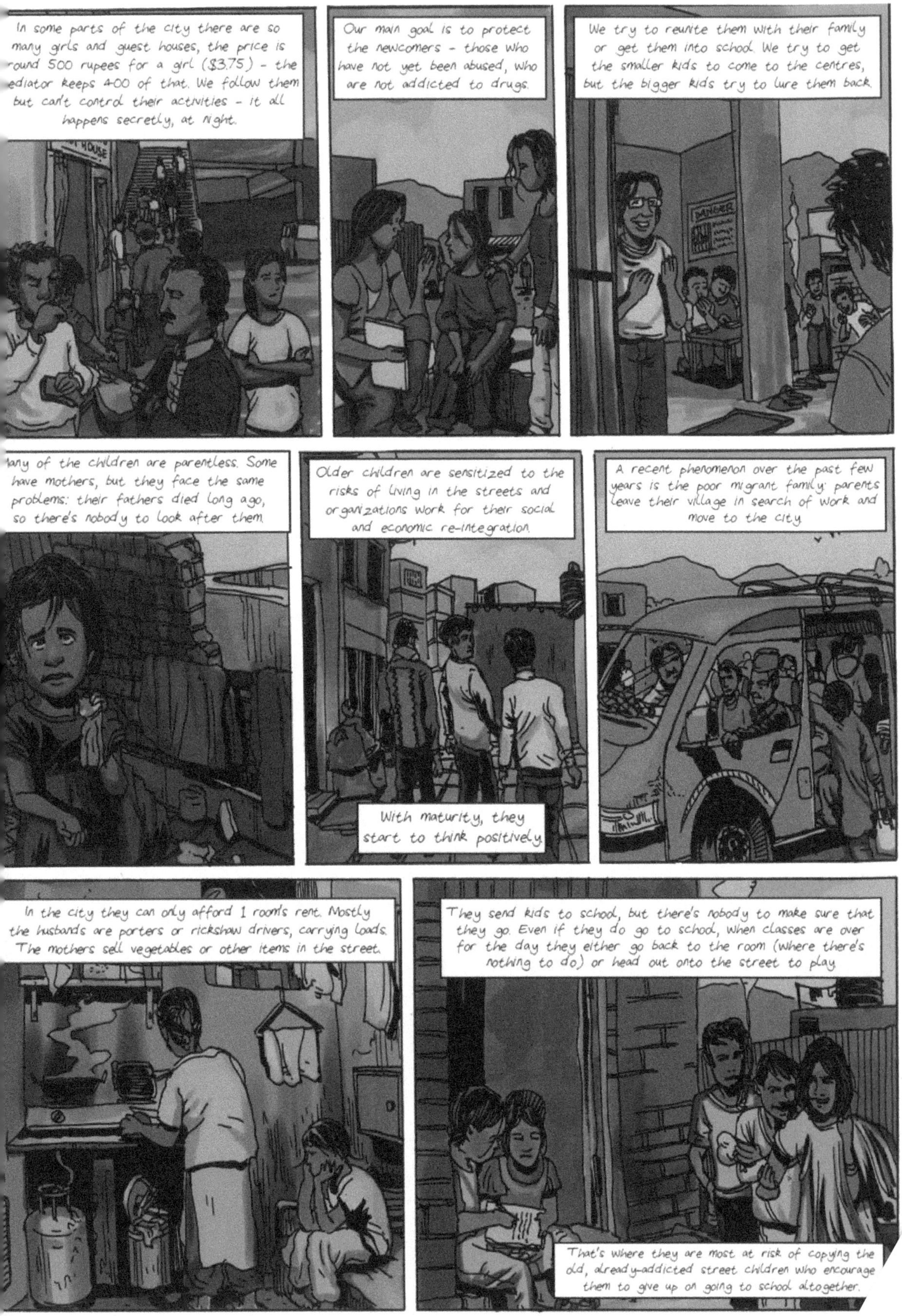

In some parts of the city there are so many girls and guest houses, the price is round 500 rupees for a girl ($3.75) - the ediator keeps 400 of that. We follow them but can't control their activities - it all happens secretly, at night.
Our main goal is to protect the newcomers - those who have not yet been abused, who are not addicted to drugs.
We try to reunite them with their family or get them into school. We try to get the smaller kids to come to the centres, but the bigger kids try to lure them back.
lany of the children are parentless. Some have mothers, but they face the same problems: their fathers died long ago, so there's nobody to look after them.
Older children are sensitized to the risks of living in the streets and organizations work for their social and economic re-integration.
With maturity, they start to think positively.
A recent phenomenon over the past few years is the poor migrant family: parents leave their village in search of work and move to the city.
In the city they can only afford 1 room's rent. Mostly the husbands are porters or rickshaw drivers, carrying loads. The mothers sell vegetables or other items in the street.
They send kids to school, but there's nobody to make sure that they go. Even if they do go to school, when classes are over for the day they either go back to the room (where there's nothing to do) or head out onto the street to play.
That's where they are most at risk of copying the old, already-addicted street children who encourage them to give up on going to school altogether.

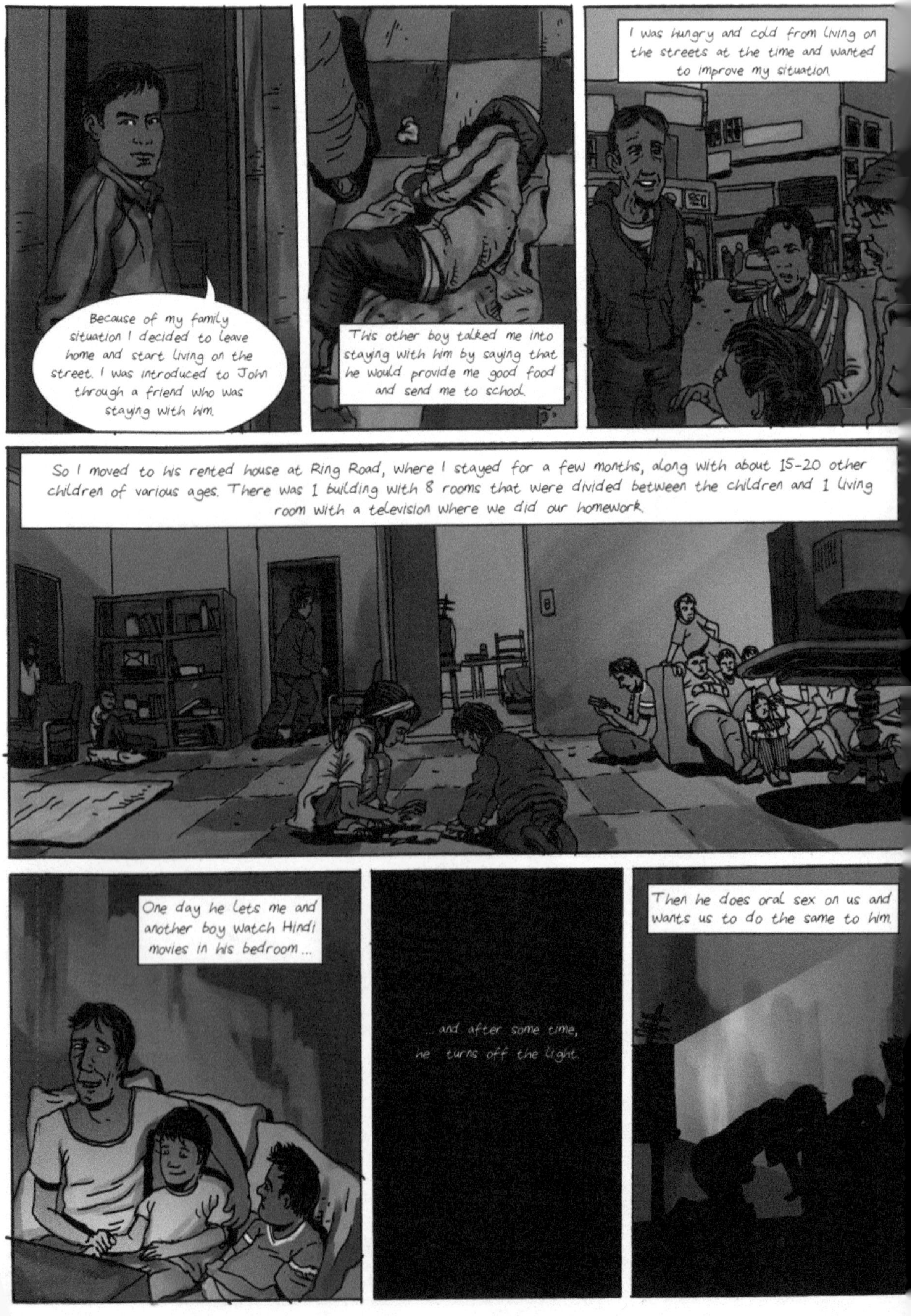
Because of my family situation I decided to leave home and start living on the street. I was introduced to John through a friend who was staying with him.
This other boy talked me into staying with him by saying that he would provide me good food and send me to school.
I was hungry and cold from living on the streets at the time and wanted to improve my situation.
So I moved to his rented house at Ring Road, where I stayed for a few months, along with about 15-20 other children of various ages. There was 1 building with 8 rooms that were divided between the children and 1 living room with a television where we did our homework.
One day he lets me and another boy watch Hindi movies in his bedroom ...
... and after some time, he turns off the light.
Then he does oral sex on us and wants us to do the same to him.

At first I refused but he said that he would give me 750 NRs ($5.63) if I did.

My friend did it and said that it was an easy way to make money

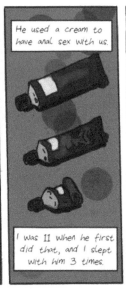

He used a cream to have anal sex with us.

I was 11 when he first did that, and I slept with him 3 times.

What he did to me hurt, but he said it was good for my growth so I had to do it.

Sometimes he took a small group of us boys out to dinner at a restaurant.

Once, when I went to the toilet, a foreign lady told me that John was behaving badly with us.

When I came back to the table, John took my face in his hands like we were a couple.

I am your family. But if you want to stay with me, you have to stop talking with other people.

Then he kissed me on the mouth

He used to say it was normal for men to hug and kiss children in Asian culture.

He hit the children ...

... and gave us money to get whisky for him while he was sexually abusing us.

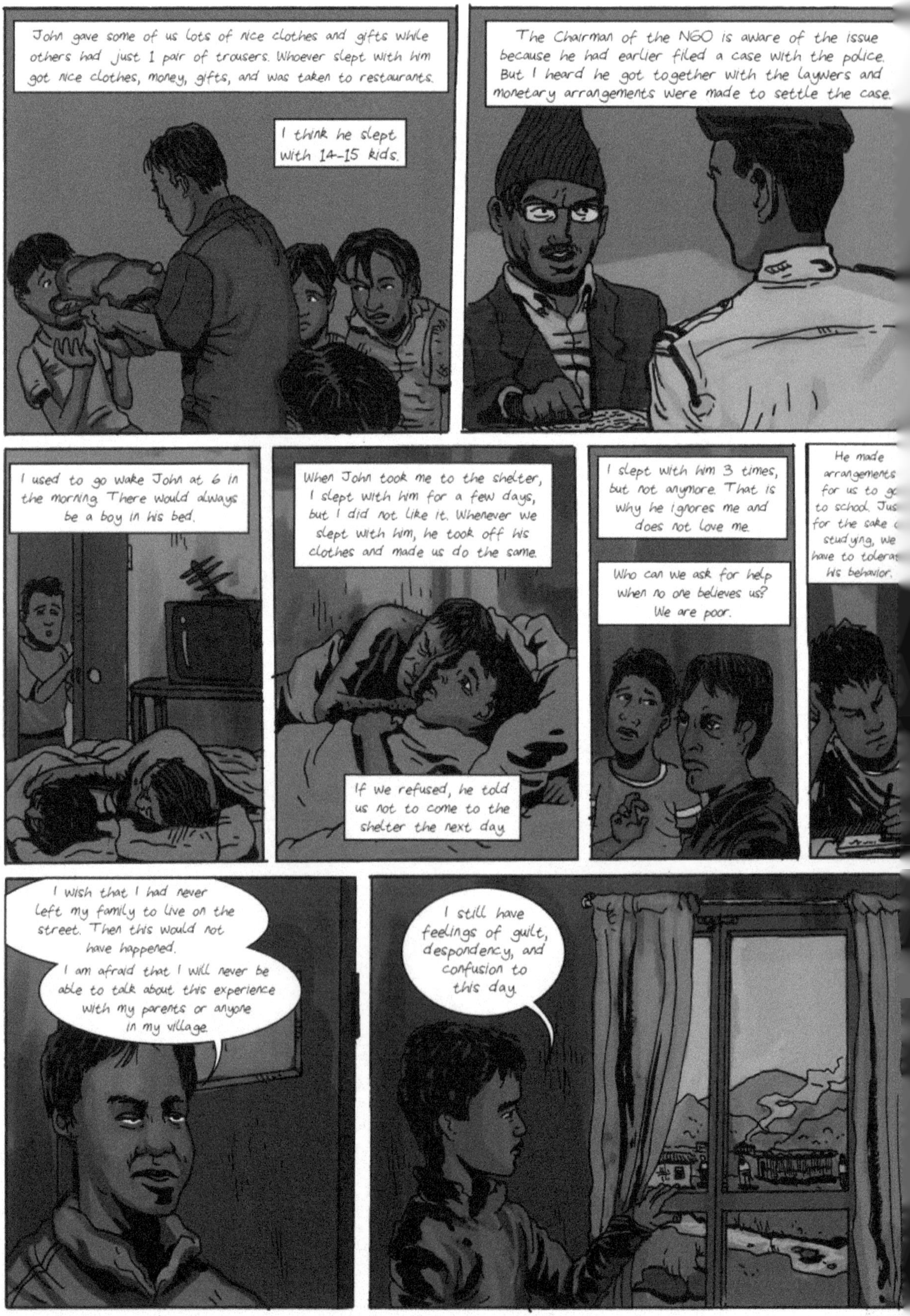
John gave some of us lots of nice clothes and gifts while others had just 1 pair of trousers. Whoever slept with him got nice clothes, money, gifts, and was taken to restaurants.
I think he slept with 14-15 kids.
The Chairman of the NGO is aware of the issue because he had earlier filed a case with the police. But I heard he got together with the laywers and monetary arrangements were made to settle the case.
I used to go wake John at 6 in the morning. There would always be a boy in his bed.
When John took me to the shelter, I slept with him for a few days, but I did not like it. Whenever we slept with him, he took off his clothes and made us do the same.
If we refused, he told us not to come to the shelter the next day.
I slept with him 3 times, but not anymore. That is why he ignores me and does not love me.
Who can we ask for help when no one believes us? We are poor.
He made arrangements for us to g to school. Jus for the sake studying, we have to tolera his behavior.
I wish that I had never left my family to live on the street. Then this would not have happened.
I am afraid that I will never be able to talk about this experience with my parents or anyone in my village.
I still have feelings of guilt, despondency, and confusion to this day.

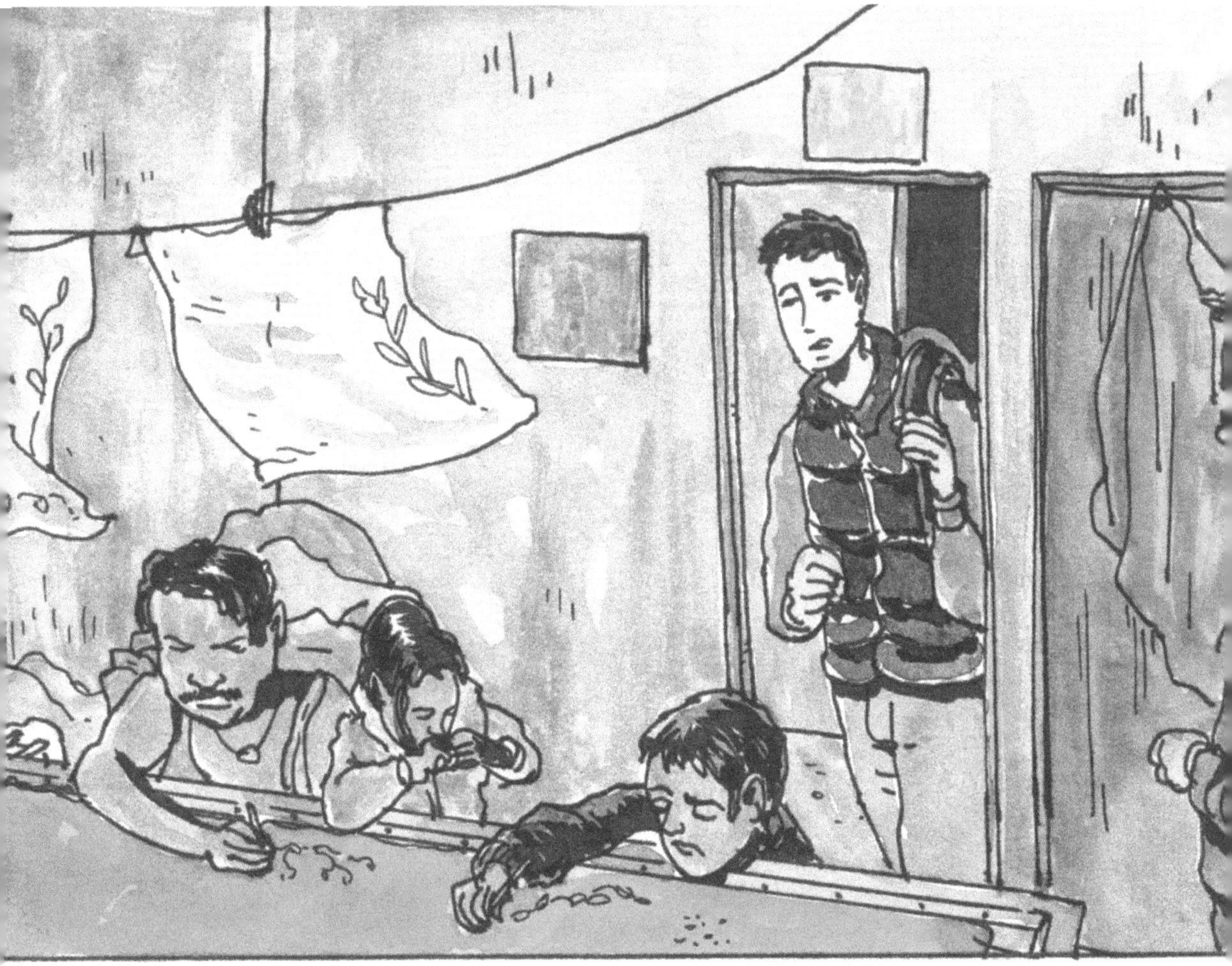

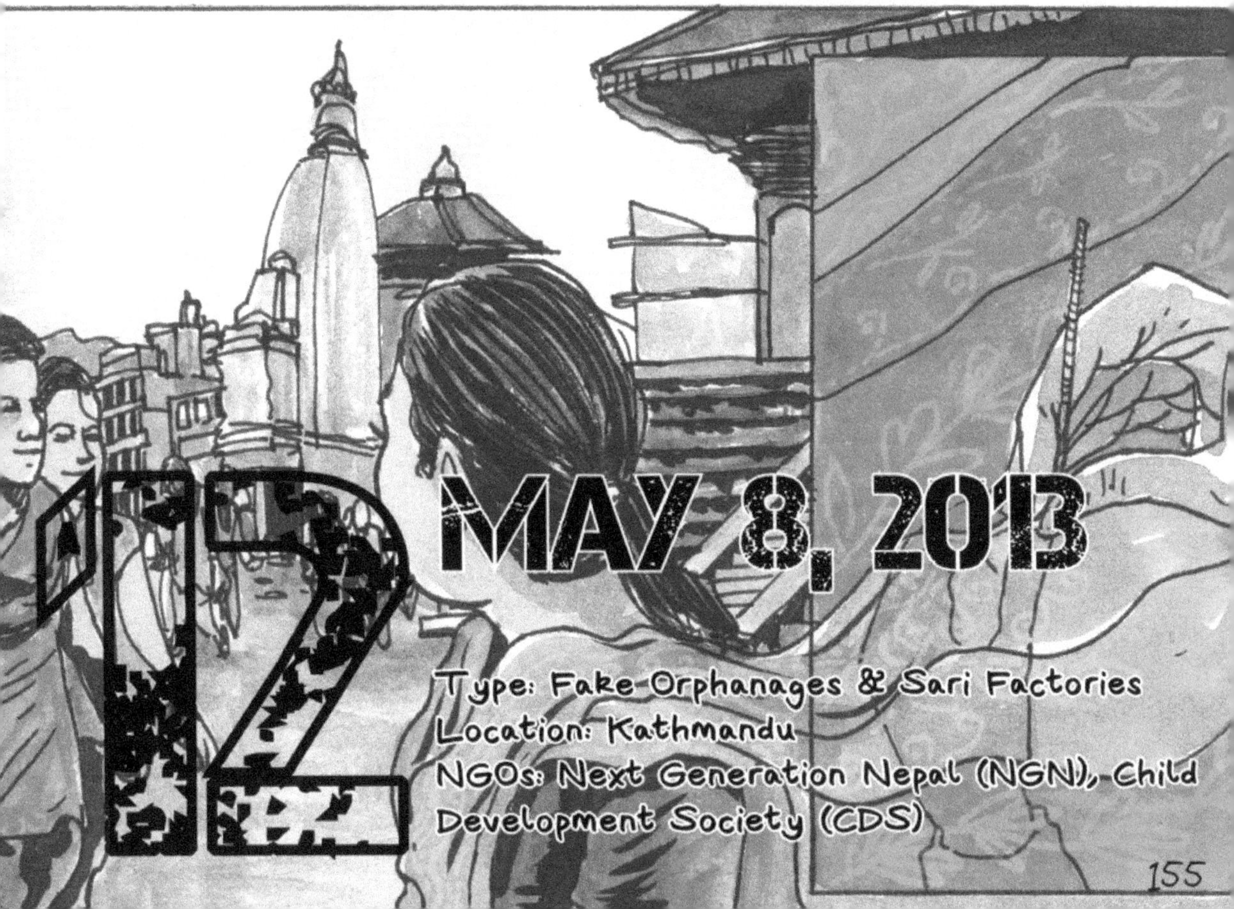

12 MAY 8, 2013

Type: Fake Orphanages & Sari Factories
Location: Kathmandu
NGOs: Next Generation Nepal (NGN), Child Development Society (CDS)

VOLUNTOURISM AND FAKE NGOS

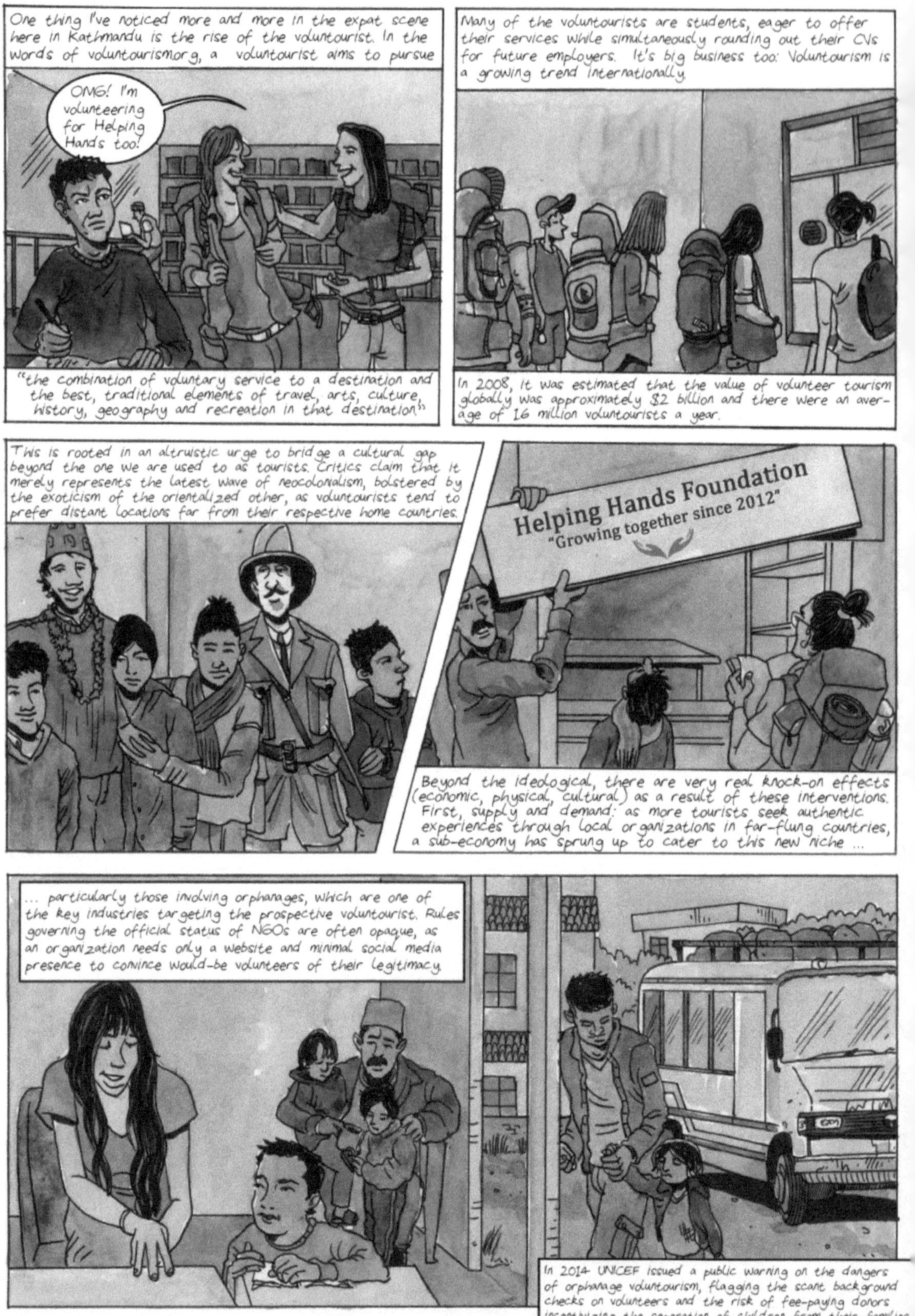

One thing I've noticed more and more in the expat scene here in Kathmandu is the rise of the voluntourist. In the words of voluntourism.org, a voluntourist aims to pursue
OMG! I'm volunteering for Helping Hands too!
"the combination of voluntary service to a destination and the best, traditional elements of travel, arts, culture, history, geography and recreation in that destination."
Many of the voluntourists are students, eager to offer their services while simultaneously rounding out their CVs for future employers. It's big business too: Voluntourism is a growing trend internationally.
In 2008, it was estimated that the value of volunteer tourism globally was approximately $2 billion and there were an average of 16 million voluntourists a year.
This is rooted in an altruistic urge to bridge a cultural gap beyond the one we are used to as tourists. Critics claim that it merely represents the latest wave of neocolonialism, bolstered by the exoticism of the orientalized other, as voluntourists tend to prefer distant locations far from their respective home countries.
Helping Hands Foundation
"Growing together since 2012"
Beyond the ideological, there are very real knock-on effects (economic, physical, cultural) as a result of these interventions. First, supply and demand: as more tourists seek authentic experiences through local organizations in far-flung countries, a sub-economy has sprung up to cater to this new niche ...
... particularly those involving orphanages, which are one of the key industries targeting the prospective voluntourist. Rules governing the official status of NGOs are often opaque, as an organization needs only a website and minimal social media presence to convince would-be volunteers of their legitimacy.
In 2014 UNICEF issued a public warning on the dangers of orphanage voluntourism, flagging the scant background checks on volunteers and the risk of fee-paying donors incentivizing the separation of children from their families.

About 30,000 foreigners are believed to volunteer in Nepal each year, regardless of the fact that the majority do so on tourist visas, which is technically illegal in the eyes of the government, although ignored for the most part. One of the many documented cases of abuse was at Mukti Nepal, a supposed orphanage established in Kathmandu by Goma Luitel.

In 2010, Luitel secured a Spanish donor who could cover all of the orphanage's running costs. She still continued to fundraise with volunteer help.

A girl at the orphanage was hit by a vehicle on her way home from school. She then became very ill ...

... so Luitel ordered the children to take her to the roof and beat her with metal rods and nettles.

Although the girl was taken to the hospital by relatives of Luitel's ...

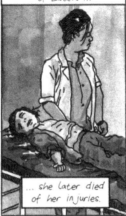

... she later died of her injuries.

A few months later, a former volunteer from Germany uncovered the truth during a visit to Mukti. She questioned the children about the case and reported it to Terre des Hommes.

Thanks to these efforts, the Central Child Welfare Board and police began a rescue operation with help from several NGOs, like NGN and THIS.

Twenty children were transferred to homes run by NGN and THIS. Over the next 2.5 years, 18 were reunited with their families.

A court convicted Luitel of abusing 16 children, sentenced her to 1 month in jail, and ordered her to pay a fine of 5,000 NRs (around $38).

Luitel was never arrested, and to this day she has neither served her sentence nor paid the fine.

There have been numerous other instances where children have not been subject to the same outward punishments, but have been denied access to their families and basic human rights ...

... despite being superficially well cared for (in terms of food and shelter).

The same truth remains: they have been trafficked for profit. Many are called "Paper Orphans" due to the illegal paperwork that was forged to declare the children orphans,* despite having 1 or both living parents.

Worse still are the stories of foreign pedophiles setting up fake NGOs in order to lure vulnerable children into their care, only to then force them into sex using bribes and coercion

*They are estimated to make up 85% of the over 16,000 children housed in Nepali orphanages.

A SARI STATE OF AFFAIRS

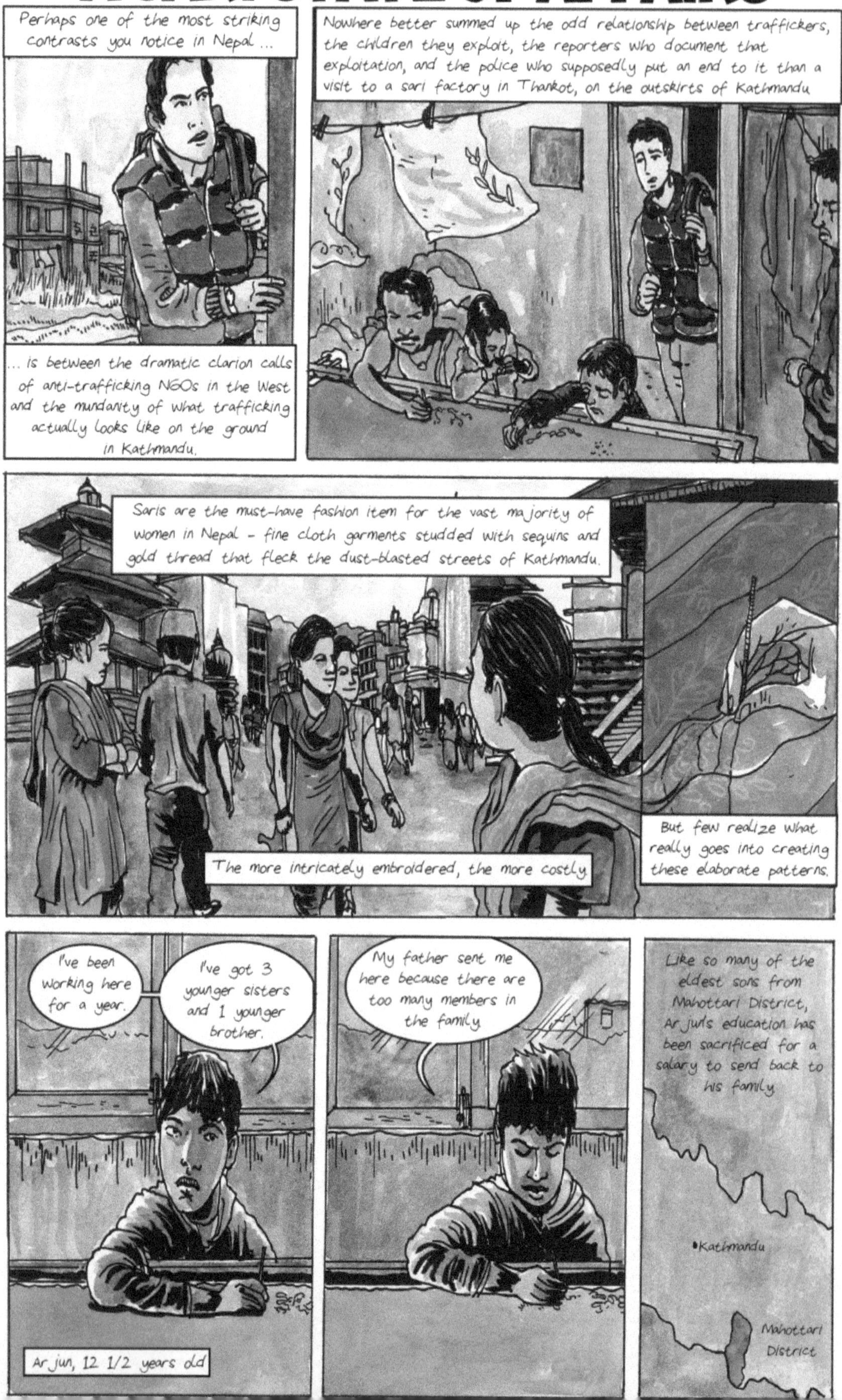
Perhaps one of the most striking contrasts you notice in Nepal ...
... is between the dramatic clarion calls of anti-trafficking NGOs in the West and the mundanity of what trafficking actually looks like on the ground in Kathmandu.
Nowhere better summed up the odd relationship between traffickers, the children they exploit, the reporters who document that exploitation, and the police who supposedly put an end to it than a visit to a sari factory in Thankot, on the outskirts of Kathmandu
Saris are the must-have fashion item for the vast majority of women in Nepal - fine cloth garments studded with sequins and gold thread that fleck the dust-blasted streets of Kathmandu.
The more intricately embroidered, the more costly.
But few realize what really goes into creating these elaborate patterns.
I've been working here for a year.
I've got 3 younger sisters and 1 younger brother.
Arjun, 12 1/2 years old
My father sent me here because there are too many members in the family.
Like so many of the eldest sons from Mahottari District, Arjun's education has been sacrificed for a salary to send back to his family.
Kathmandu
Mahottari District

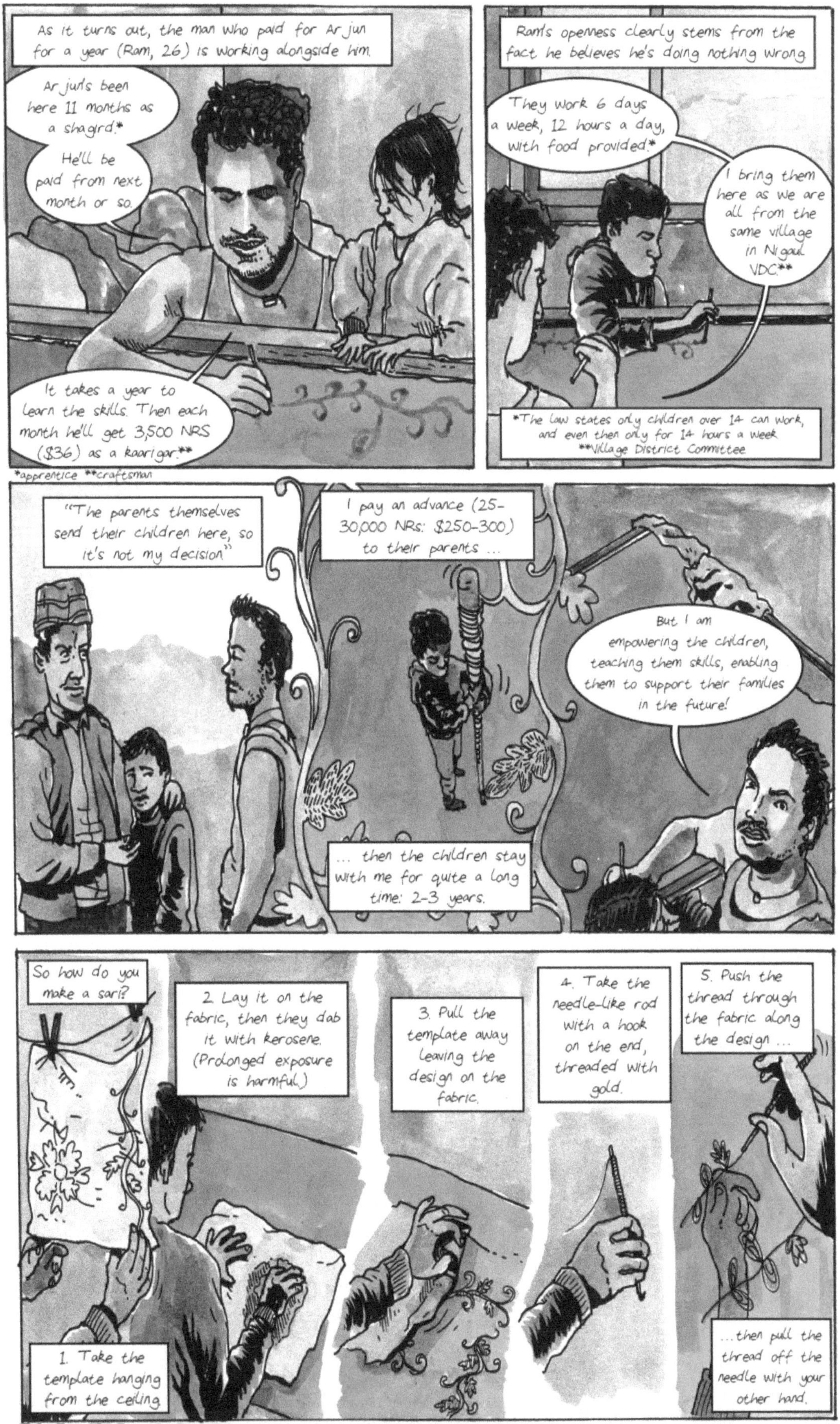

As it turns out, the man who paid for Arjun for a year (Ram, 26) is working alongside him.
Arjun's been here 11 months as a shagird.*
He'll be paid from next month or so.
It takes a year to learn the skills. Then each month he'll get 3,500 NRS ($36) as a kaarigar.**
*apprentice **craftsman
Ram's openness clearly stems from the fact he believes he's doing nothing wrong.
They work 6 days a week, 12 hours a day, with food provided.*
I bring them here as we are all from the same village in Nigaul VDC.**
*The law states only children over 14 can work, and even then only for 14 hours a week.
**Village District Committee
"The parents themselves send their children here, so it's not my decision"
I pay an advance (25-30,000 NRs: $250-300) to their parents ...
... then the children stay with me for quite a long time: 2-3 years.
But I am empowering the children, teaching them skills, enabling them to support their families in the future!
So how do you make a sari?
1. Take the template hanging from the ceiling.
2. Lay it on the fabric, then they dab it with kerosene. (Prolonged exposure is harmful.)
3. Pull the template away leaving the design on the fabric.
4. Take the needle-like rod with a hook on the end, threaded with gold.
5. Push the thread through the fabric along the design ...
...then pull the thread off the needle with your other hand.

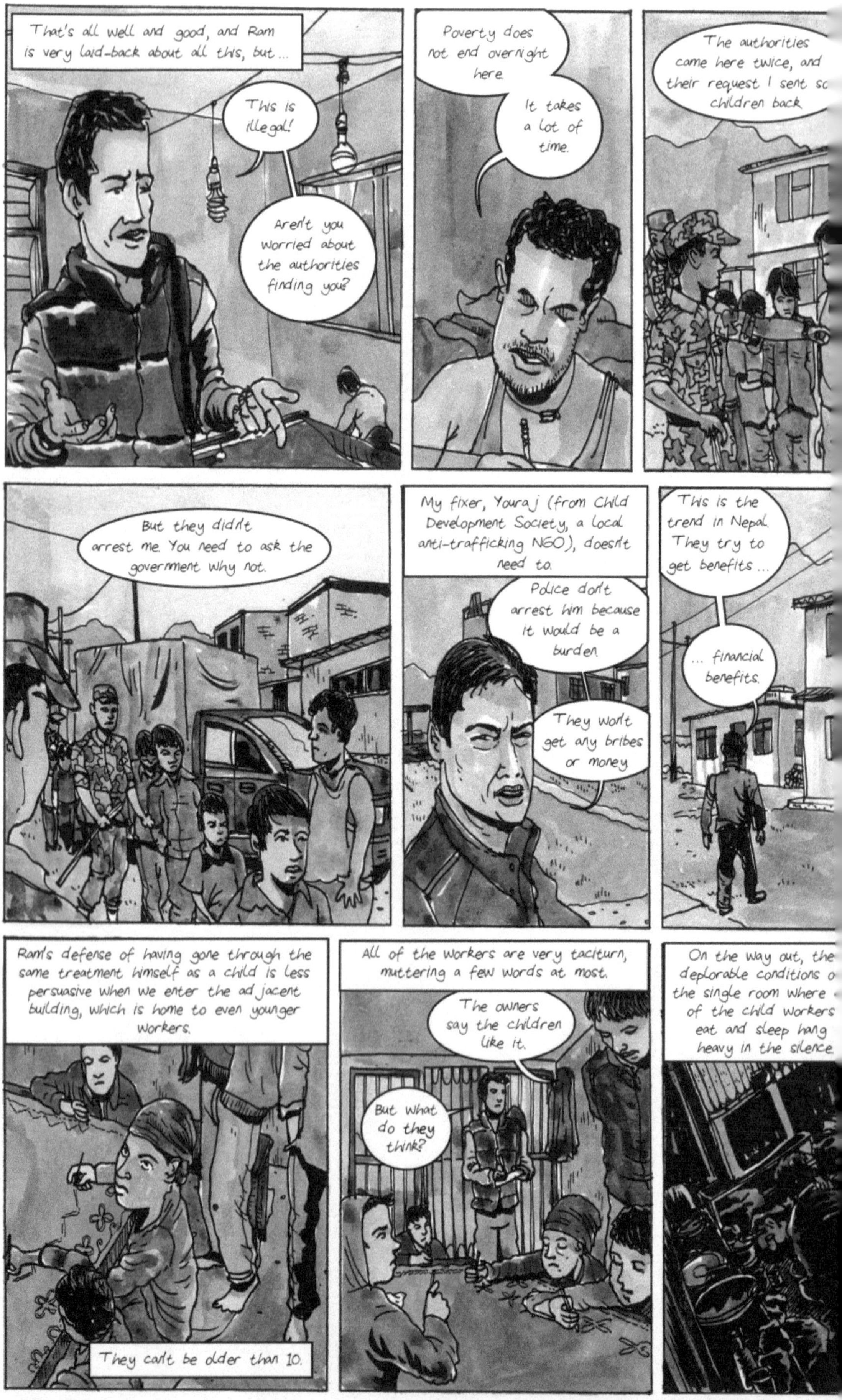
That's all well and good, and Ram is very laid-back about all this, but ...
This is illegal!
Aren't you worried about the authorities finding you?
Poverty does not end overnight here.
It takes a lot of time.
The authorities came here twice, and their request I sent sc children back
But they didn't arrest me. You need to ask the government why not.
My fixer, Youraj (from Child Development Society, a local anti-trafficking NGO), doesn't need to.
Police don't arrest him because it would be a burden.
They won't get any bribes or money.
This is the trend in Nepal. They try to get benefits ...
... financial benefits.
Ram's defense of having gone through the same treatment himself as a child is less persuasive when we enter the adjacent building, which is home to even younger workers.
They can't be older than 10.
All of the workers are very taciturn, muttering a few words at most.
The owners say the children like it.
But what do they think?
On the way out, the deplorable conditions o the single room where of the child workers eat and sleep hang heavy in the silence.

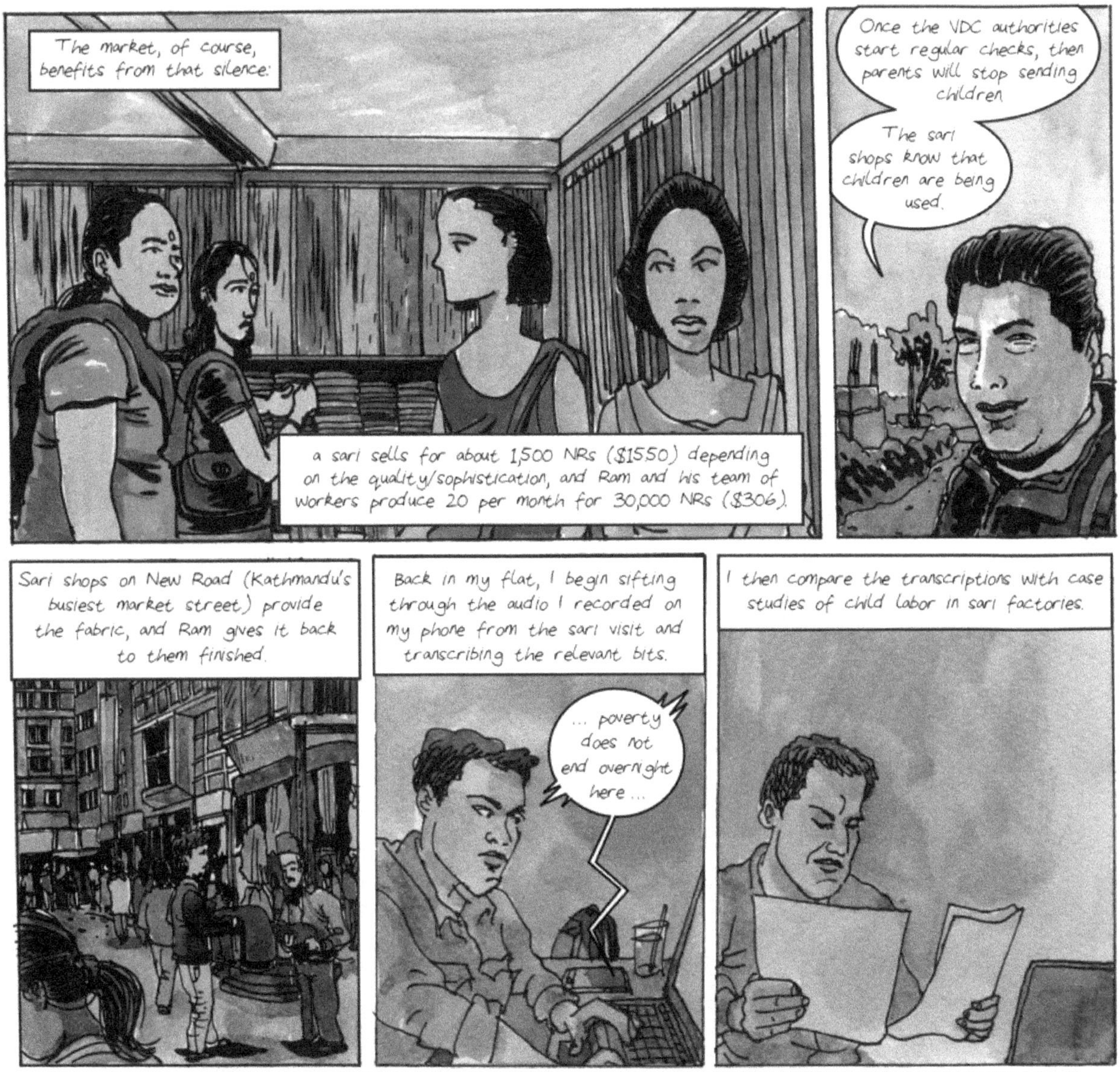

The market, of course, benefits from that silence.
a sari sells for about 1,500 NRs ($15.50) depending on the quality/sophistication, and Ram and his team of workers produce 20 per month for 30,000 NRs ($306).
Once the VDC authorities start regular checks, then parents will stop sending children.
The sari shops know that children are being used.
Sari shops on New Road (Kathmandu's busiest market street) provide the fabric, and Ram gives it back to them finished.
Back in my flat, I begin sifting through the audio I recorded on my phone from the sari visit and transcribing the relevant bits.
... poverty does not end overnight here ...
I then compare the transcriptions with case studies of child labor in sari factories.

The Human Trafficking Vulnerability Project is finally into production mode, meaning the current task is to put together a sample bunch of stories that each reflect the different realities of being trafficked.

#	ID	Trafficking Type	Sub-Categories & Themes	Sex	Name	Format (English)	Link	Updated Eng Script? (Y/N)	Art Done? (Y/N)	Nepali Translation? (Y/N)?	Treatment Type? (Danger, Empowerment)	Comments
1	A1	Sex Trafficking	- Foreign (Mumbai) - Drugged Food/Drink - HIV stigma	F	Laxmi	Script	#A1 Laxmi S	Y	Y	Y	E	
2	A2	Sex Trafficking	- Foreign (Raxaul) - Promised Good Job (Circus) - Bonded Labor	F	Monu Lama	Interview	#A2 Monu I	Y	N			
3	A3	Sex Trafficking	- Foreign (Mumbai)	F	Shanti Lama	Interview	#A3 Shanti I	Y	N			
4	A4	Sex Trafficking	- Foreign (New Delhi) - Promised Good Jobs - Traffic Victim Stigma	F	Rina	Interview	#A4 Rina I	Y	N			
5	A5	Sex Trafficking	- Foreign (Mumbai) - Fake Proposal - Drugged Food/Drink	F	Birmaya	Interview	#A5 Birmaya I	Y	N			
6	A6	Sex Trafficking	- Forced Marriage - Foreign (New Delhi) - Promised Good Jobs	F	Sita Shaha	Interview	#A6 Sita I	Y	2p			not ea lice
7	A6	Sex Trafficking	- Forced Marriage - Foreign (New Delhi) - Promised Good Jobs	F	Sita Shaha	Script	#A6 Sita S	Y	2p			not ea lice
8	A7	Sex Trafficking	- Domestic - Seeking Good Jobs	F	Meera	Script	#A7 Meera S		Y			
9	B1	Domestic Servitude	- Promise of Education	M	Kamal Rasi (Munal)	Script	#B1 Munal S		Y			
10	B2	Domestic Servitude	- Seeking Good Job - Kamlari	F	Sita Kumar	Script	#B2 Sita S					

Namely:

Sex trafficking
(Women and children, cabin restaurant/massage parlor)

Domestic servitude

Forced labor (sari factory)
Forced labor (brick kilns)
Forced labor (migrants)

Organ trafficking

The stories are based on the interviews that I've done with real survivors, and then adapted to suit our study.

As we prepare those stories, I simultaneously work with some of our NGO partners to produce posters and comics with a more positive message than the standard scaremongering.

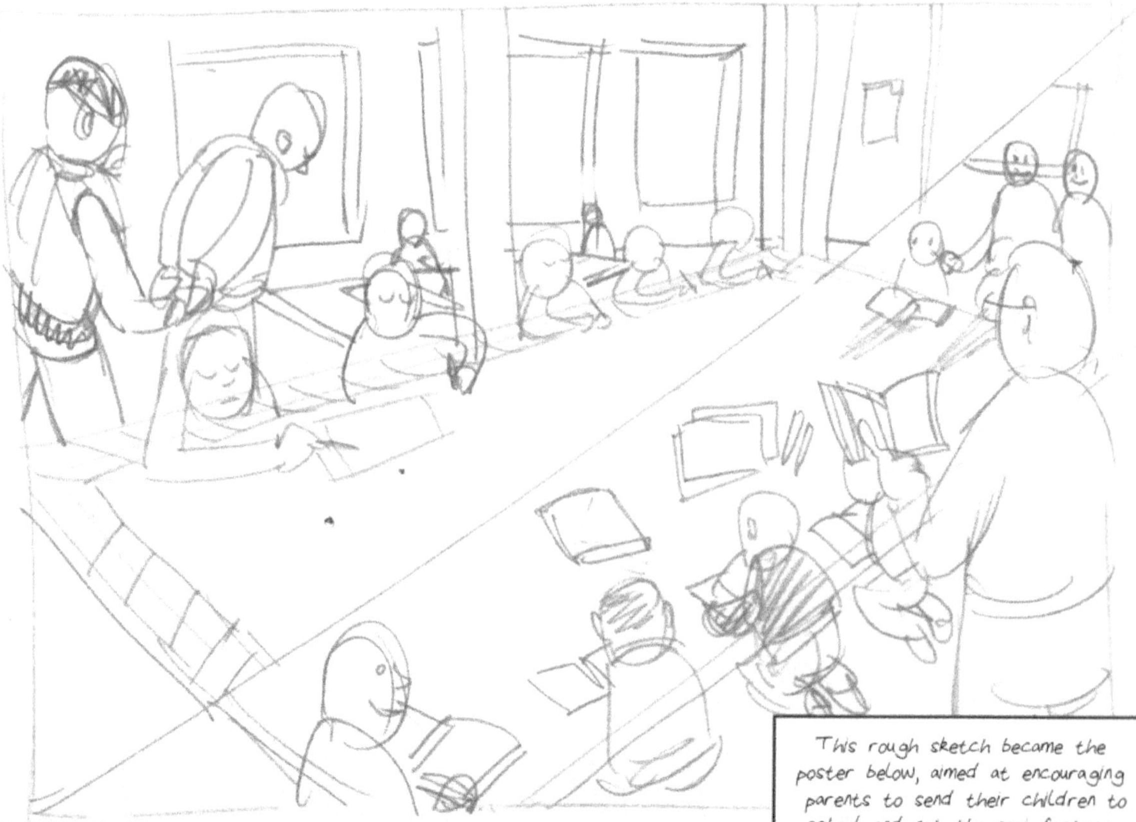

This rough sketch became the poster below, aimed at encouraging parents to send their children to school and not the sari factory.

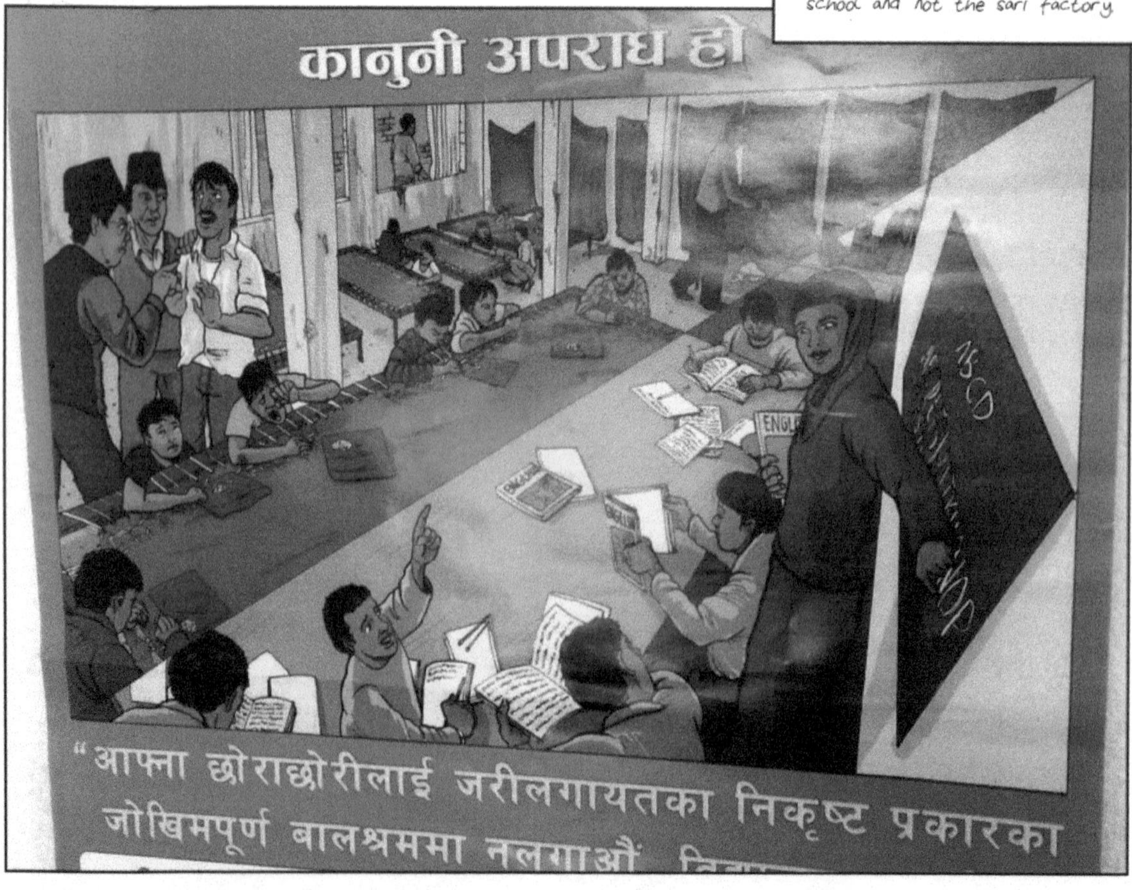
कानुनी अपराध हो
“आफ्ना छोराछोरीलाई जरीलगायतका निकृष्ट प्रकारका
जोखिमपूर्ण बालश्रममा नलगाऔं

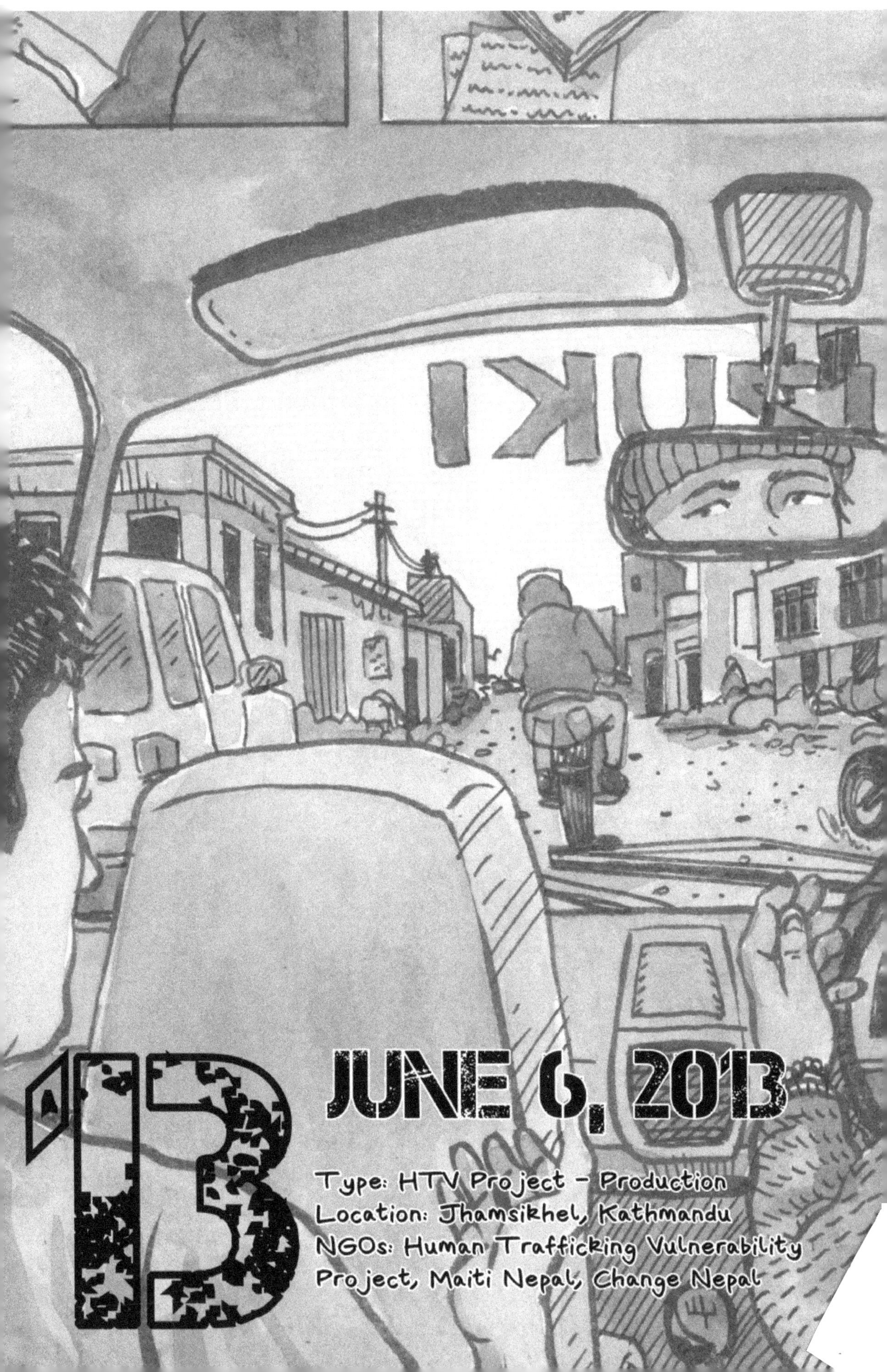

13

JUNE 6, 2013

Type: HTV Project – Production
Location: Jhamsikhel, Kathmandu
NGOs: Human Trafficking Vulnerability Project, Maiti Nepal, Change Nepal

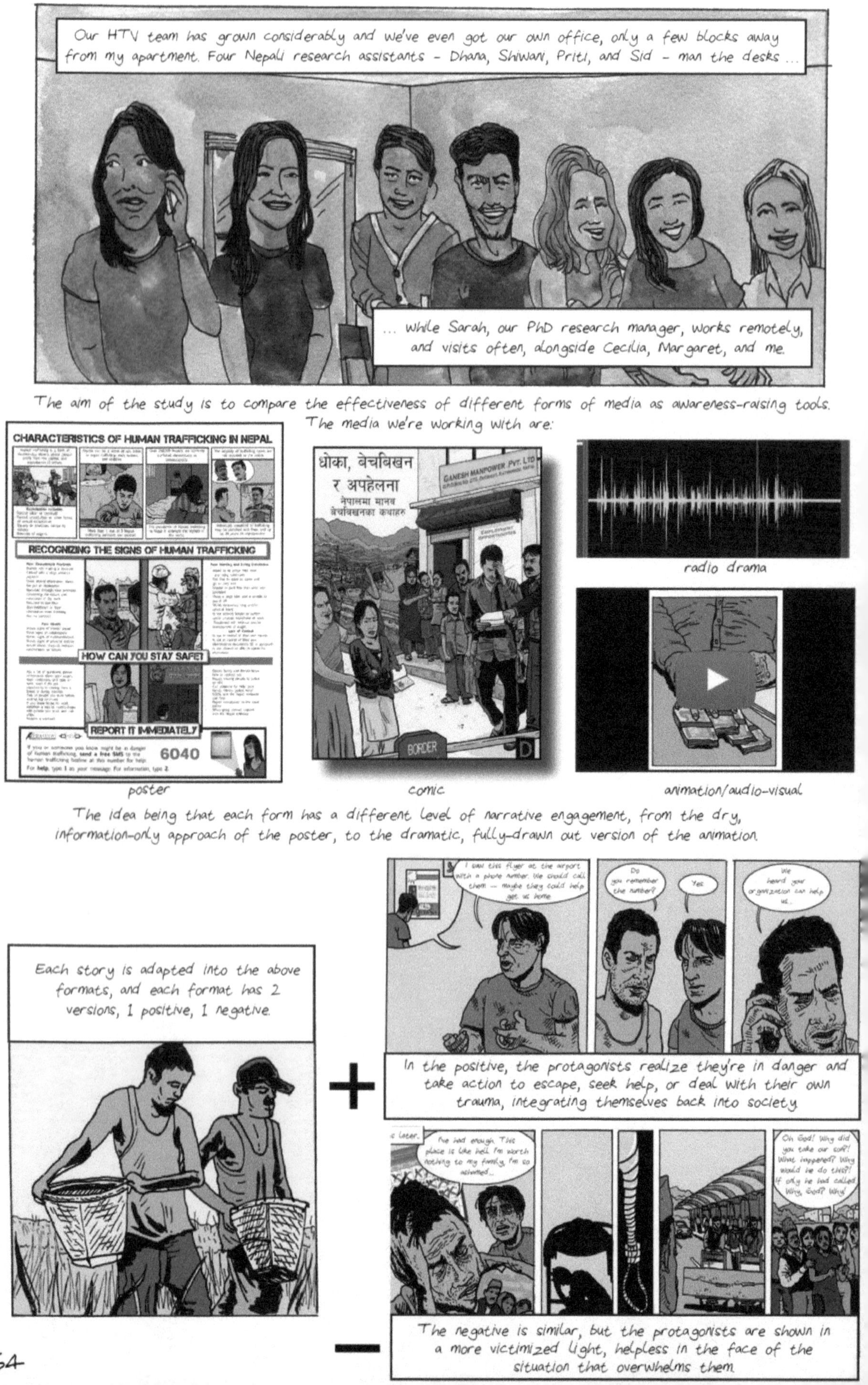

Our HTV team has grown considerably and we've even got our own office, only a few blocks away from my apartment. Four Nepali research assistants – Dhana, Shiwani, Priti, and Sid – man the desks ...
... while Sarah, our PhD research manager, works remotely, and visits often, alongside Cecilia, Margaret, and me.
The aim of the study is to compare the effectiveness of different forms of media as awareness-raising tools. The media we're working with are:
CHARACTERISTICS OF HUMAN TRAFFICKING IN NEPAL
RECOGNIZING THE SIGNS OF HUMAN TRAFFICKING
HOW CAN YOU STAY SAFE?
REPORT IT IMMEDIATELY
6040
poster
धोका, बेचबिखन र अपहेलना
नेपालमा मानव बेचबिखनका कथाहरु
GANESH MANPOWER PVT. LTD
BORDER
comic
radio drama
animation/audio-visual
The idea being that each form has a different level of narrative engagement, from the dry, information-only approach of the poster, to the dramatic, fully-drawn out version of the animation.
Each story is adapted into the above formats, and each format has 2 versions, 1 positive, 1 negative.
+
I saw this flyer at the airport with a phone number. We should call them – maybe they could help get us home.
Do you remember the number?
Yes
We heard your organization can help us...
In the positive, the protagonists realize they're in danger and take action to escape, seek help, or deal with their own trauma, integrating themselves back into society.
I've had enough. This place is like hell. I'm worth nothing to my family. I'm so ashamed...
Oh God! Why did you take our son? What happened? Why would he do this? If only he had called. Why, God? Why!
–
The negative is similar, but the protagonists are shown in a more victimized light, helpless in the face of the situation that overwhelms them.

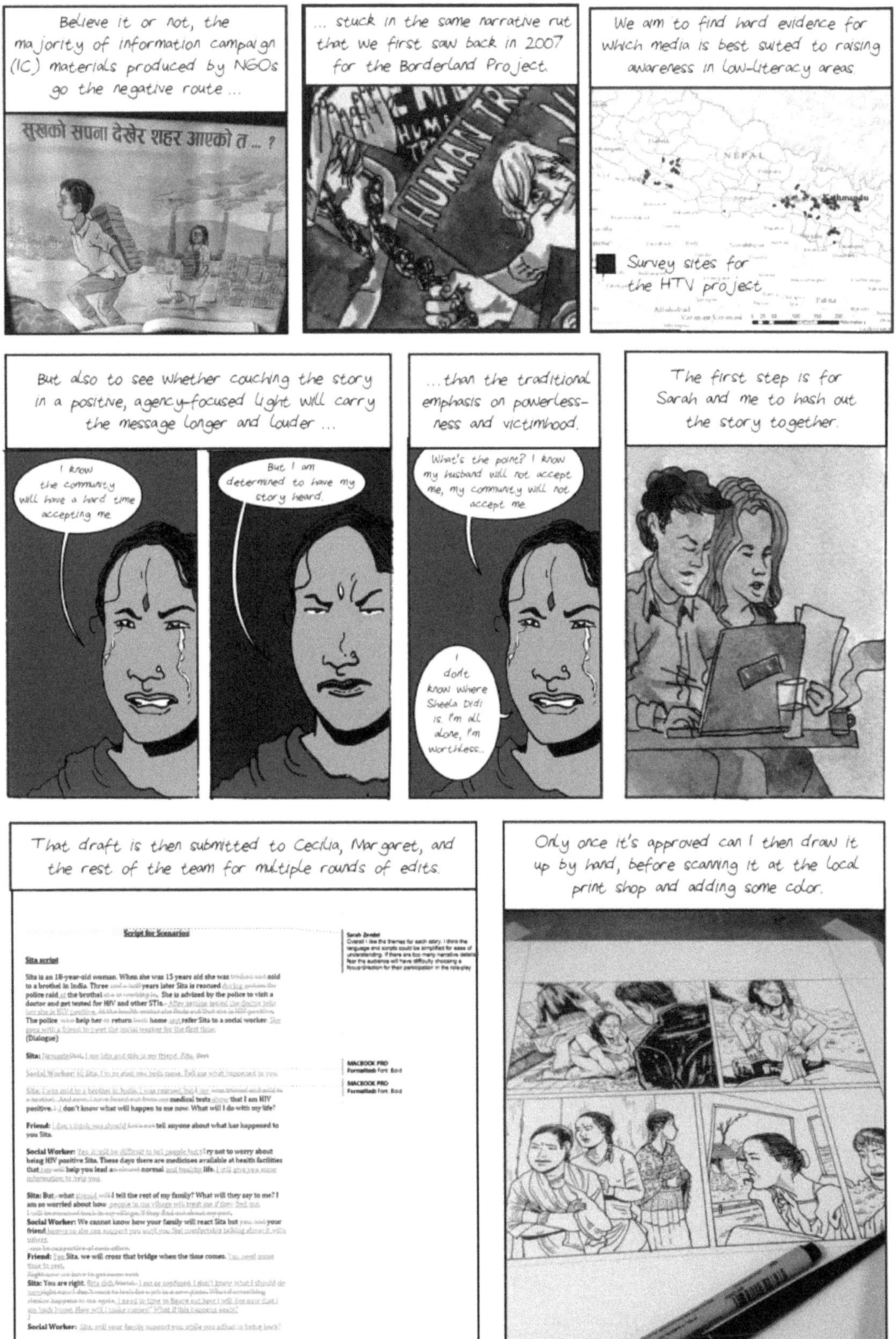

Believe it or not, the majority of information campaign (IC) materials produced by NGOs go the negative route ...
सुखको सपना देखेर शहर आएको त ... ?
... stuck in the same narrative rut that we first saw back in 2007 for the Borderland Project.
HUMAN TRA
We aim to find hard evidence for which media is best suited to raising awareness in low-literacy areas.
NEPAL
Kathmandu
Survey sites for the HTV project
Patna
But also to see whether couching the story in a positive, agency-focused light will carry the message longer and louder ...
I know the community will have a hard time accepting me.
But I am determined to have my story heard.
... than the traditional emphasis on powerlessness and victimhood.
What's the point? I know my husband will not accept me, my community will not accept me.
I don't know where Sheela Didi is. I'm all alone, I'm worthless...
The first step is for Sarah and me to hash out the story together.
That draft is then submitted to Cecilia, Margaret, and the rest of the team for multiple rounds of edits.
Script for Scenarios
Sita script
Sita is an 18-year-old woman. When she was 15 years old she was sold to a brothel in India. Three years later Sita is rescued police raid the brothel. She is advised by the police to visit a doctor and get tested for HIV and other STIs.
The police help her return home refer Sita to a social worker.
(Dialogue)
Sita:
Sarah Zendel
Overall I like the themes for each story. I think the language and scripts could be simplified for ease of understanding. If there are too many narrative details fear the audience will have difficulty choosing a focus/direction for their participation in the role-play
MACBOOK PRO
Formatted: Font: Bold
MACBOOK PRO
Formatted: Font: Bold
medical tests that I am HIV positive. don't know what will happen to me now. What will I do with my life?
Friend: tell anyone about what has happened to you Sita.
Social Worker: Try not to worry about being HIV positive Sita. These days there are medicines available at health facilities that help you lead a normal life.
Sita: But what I tell the rest of my family? What will they say to me? I am so worried about how
Social Worker: We cannot know how your family will react Sita but your friend
Friend: Sita, we will cross that bridge when the time comes.
Sita: You are right.
Social Worker:
Only once it's approved can I then draw it up by hand, before scanning it at the local print shop and adding some color.

But before I put pen to paper, I have to thumbnail out each page. This means taking the approved script and breaking each page down into a rough layout, which I then use as a blueprint for drawing up the final artwork.

Each number corresponds to a line of text from the script. The process of writing, thumbnailing, penciling, inking, and coloring a page takes around 2 days, working at a fair old clip.

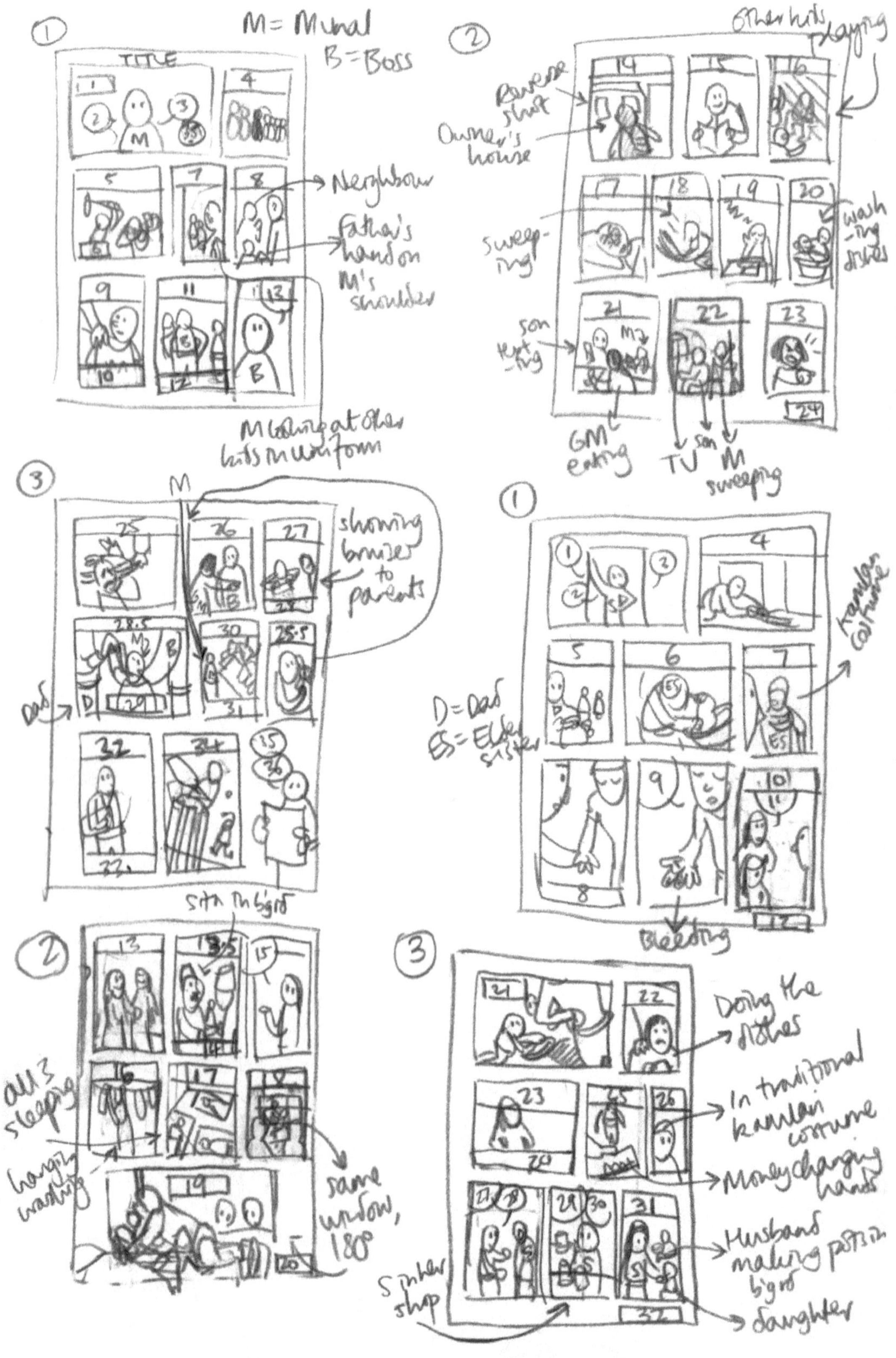

TITLE
B=Boss
Neighbour
Father's hand on M's shoulder
Other kids playing
Reverse shot
Owner's house
Sweeping
washing dishes
son texting
GM eating
TV
son
M sweeping
showing bruises to parents
Dad
D=Dad
ES=Elder sister
Bleeding
All 3 sleeping
hanging washing
same window, 180°
Doing the dishes
In traditional kamlari costume
Money changing hands
daughter

THE LINGO

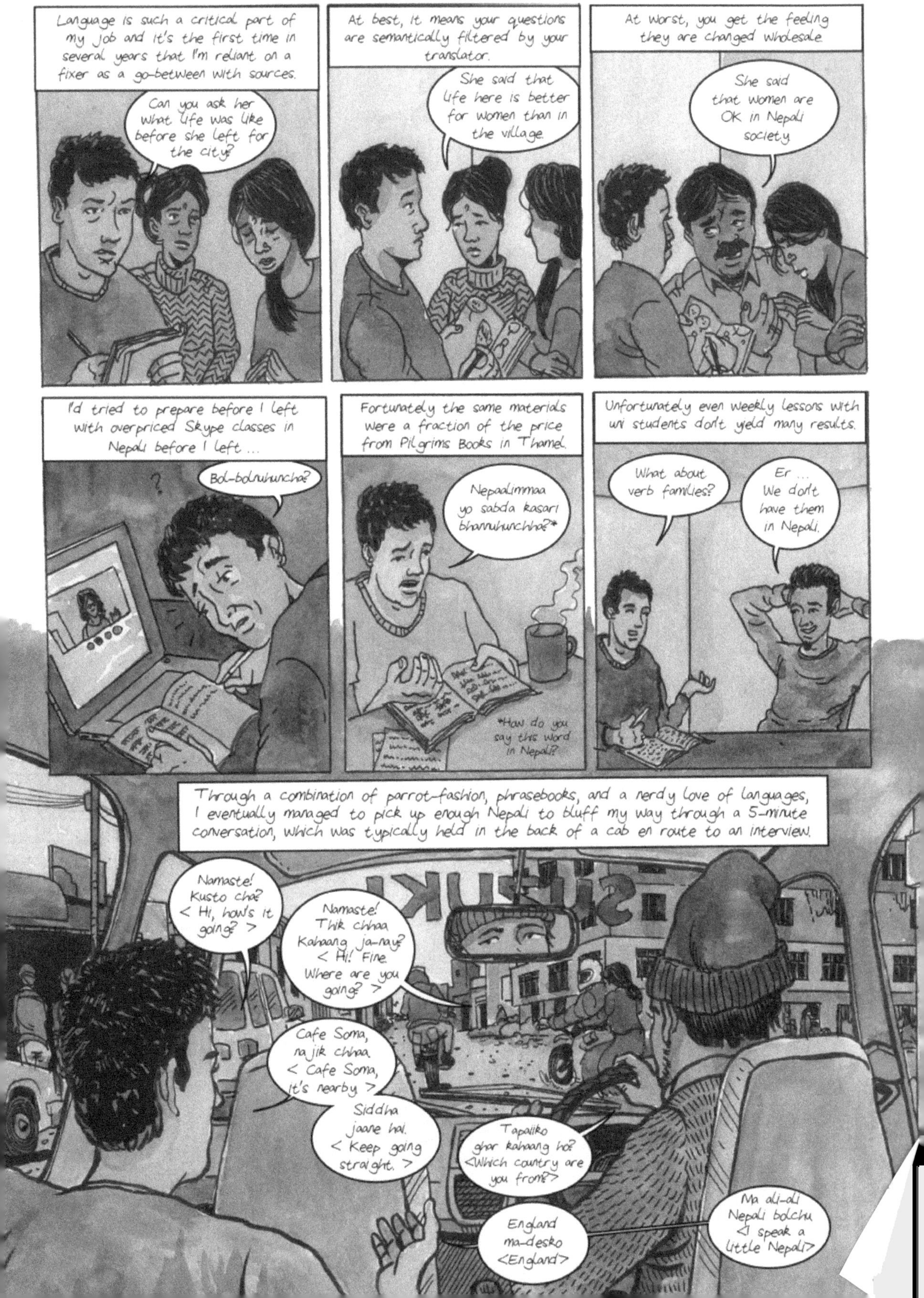

Language is such a critical part of my job and it's the first time in several years that I'm reliant on a fixer as a go-between with sources.
Can you ask her what life was like before she left for the city?
At best, it means your questions are semantically filtered by your translator.
She said that life here is better for women than in the village.
At worst, you get the feeling they are changed wholesale.
She said that women are OK in Nepali society.
I'd tried to prepare before I left with overpriced Skype classes in Nepali before I left ...
?
Bol-bolnuhuncha?
Fortunately the same materials were a fraction of the price from Pilgrims Books in Thamel.
Nepaalimmaa yo sabda kasari bhannuhunchha?*
*How do you say this word in Nepali?
Unfortunately even weekly lessons with uni students don't yield many results.
What about verb families?
Er ... We don't have them in Nepali.
Through a combination of parrot-fashion, phrasebooks, and a nerdy love of languages, I eventually managed to pick up enough Nepali to bluff my way through a 5-minute conversation, which was typically held in the back of a cab en route to an interview.
Namaste! Kusto cha? < Hi, how's it going? >
Namaste! Thik chhaa Kahaang ja-nay? < Hi! Fine Where are you going? >
Cafe Soma, najik chhaa. < Cafe Soma, it's nearby. >
Siddha jaane hai. < Keep going straight. >
Tapaiiko ghar kahaang ho? <Which country are you from?>
England ma-desko <England>
Ma ali-ali Nepali bolchu <I speak a little Nepali>

Another key road to self-expression was the one to my stomach

From October 2012 to May 2013 (and then 2 stints in 2014) my nightly ritual was to hit the old-school gym run by a former Mr. Nepal bodybuilder for a Muay Thai class, and then reward myself with dinner at the Mustang Thakali kitchen next door. Every night we'd follow the same routine:

Namaste!

Namaste sir!

Daal Bhaat Thali with all the trimmings.

<More sir?>

Dere dhanyabad!*

Gundruk: radish

Kaankro: cucumber

Palak: spinach

Bhaat: rice

Kaaulee: cauliflower

Gaajar: carrot

Daal: lentils

I have to confess: my record was 3 full refills of my veggie platter before I rolled home.

*Thank you very much

As delicious as it was, nothing came close to Jaya's home-cooked daal, or her amazing paneer.

Dere mito chhaa!*

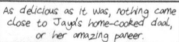

*Very delicious!

I like to think that I returned the linguistic favor by giving weekly English classes at Change Nepal to the girls there...

TODAY'S LESSON: INTRODUCTIONS

HELLO MY NAME IS...

I AM FROM...

... but I think they were probably just as mystified as I was.

PILOTING

Next is piloting: testing that the comics are legible, readable, and intelligible to a Nepali audience.

Here the reading culture is a little different, so the comics have been cut into strips as opposed to pages, to facilitate narrative flow.

To do that, we take test comics to Change Nepal to get feedback from some of the girls and women there.

Dhana gives the dozen or so assembled women an overview of the project and what we're looking for from them.

I draw some of the participants' reactions as they read and make sense of the stories.

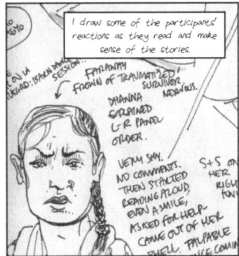

Of course, the levels of literacy vary wildly and I spot a few women surreptitiously asking their neighbors for reading help.

It takes longer than 10 minutes per page and by the end of it we have copious notes highlighting interesting contrasts in visual story-telling cues that didn't bridge the language gap.

Here's a sample comic from the piloting on migrant labor that also featured in the comic I produced for World Education that was printed locally and distributed in Nepal.

LURED TO LIBYA

My name is Sarmila.

I'm 21 years old.

And the eldest of 3 siblings.

I'm from Birse VDC, Sindupalchowk.

Before this happened I was in Grade 5 at school.

It all started with my cousins going to Lebanon for work about 5 years ago.

Everything's OK?

Yes, Auntie.

It was my idea to go.

The agent I went to is a neighbor from my village. I had seen him many times.

My father knew him and there was a family connection.

I didn't have a passport and they had to increase my age as I was underage (17).

The agent made the passport for me. It cost 5,000 NRs.

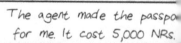

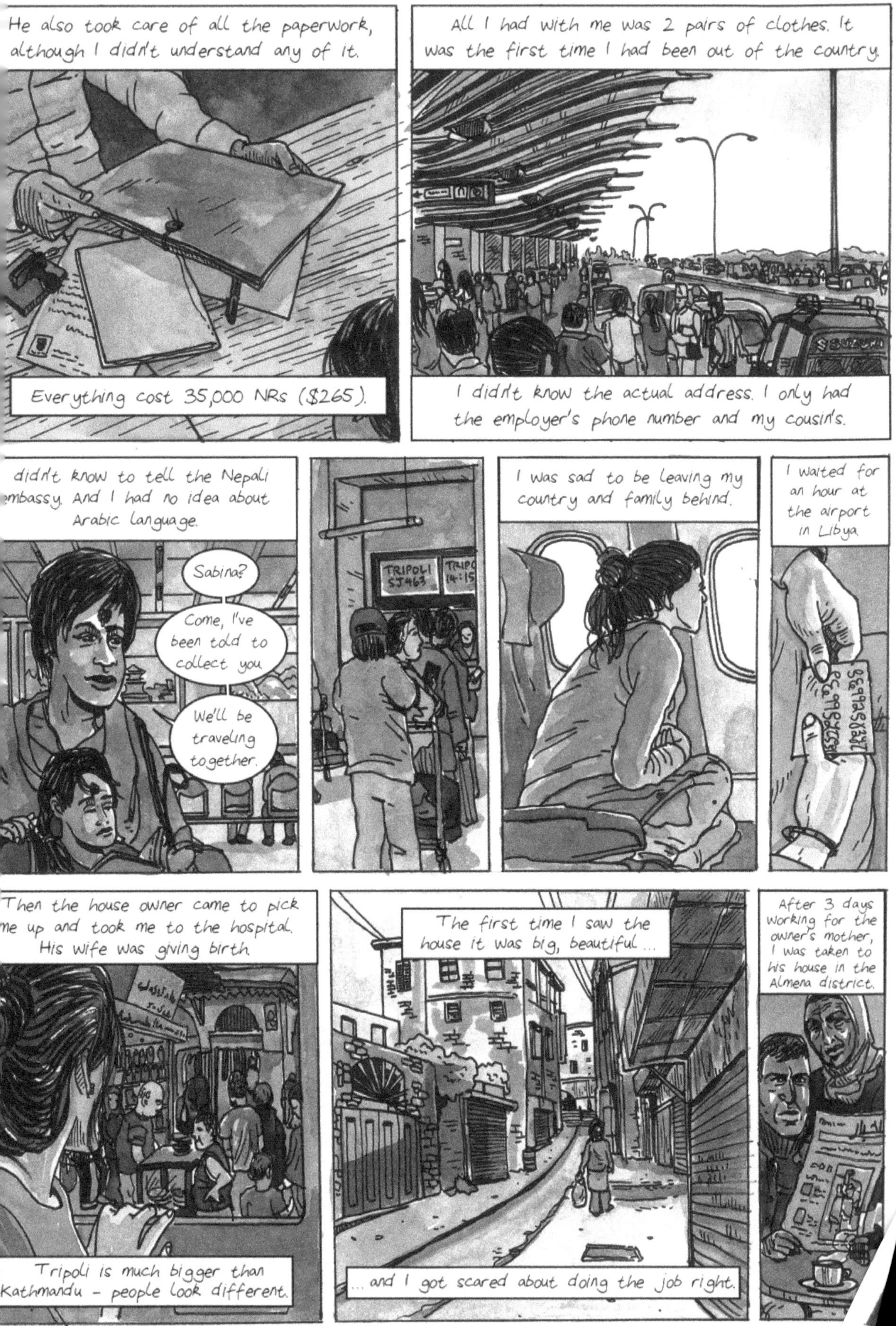
He also took care of all the paperwork, although I didn't understand any of it.
Everything cost 35,000 NRs ($265).
All I had with me was 2 pairs of clothes. It was the first time I had been out of the country.
I didn't know the actual address. I only had the employer's phone number and my cousin's.
didn't know to tell the Nepali embassy. And I had no idea about Arabic language.
Sabina?
Come, I've been told to collect you.
We'll be traveling together.
TRIPOLI SJ463
I was sad to be leaving my country and family behind.
I waited for an hour at the airport in Libya.
Then the house owner came to pick me up and took me to the hospital. His wife was giving birth.
Tripoli is much bigger than Kathmandu – people look different.
The first time I saw the house it was big, beautiful ...
... and I got scared about doing the job right.
After 3 days working for the owner's mother, I was taken to his house in the Almena district.

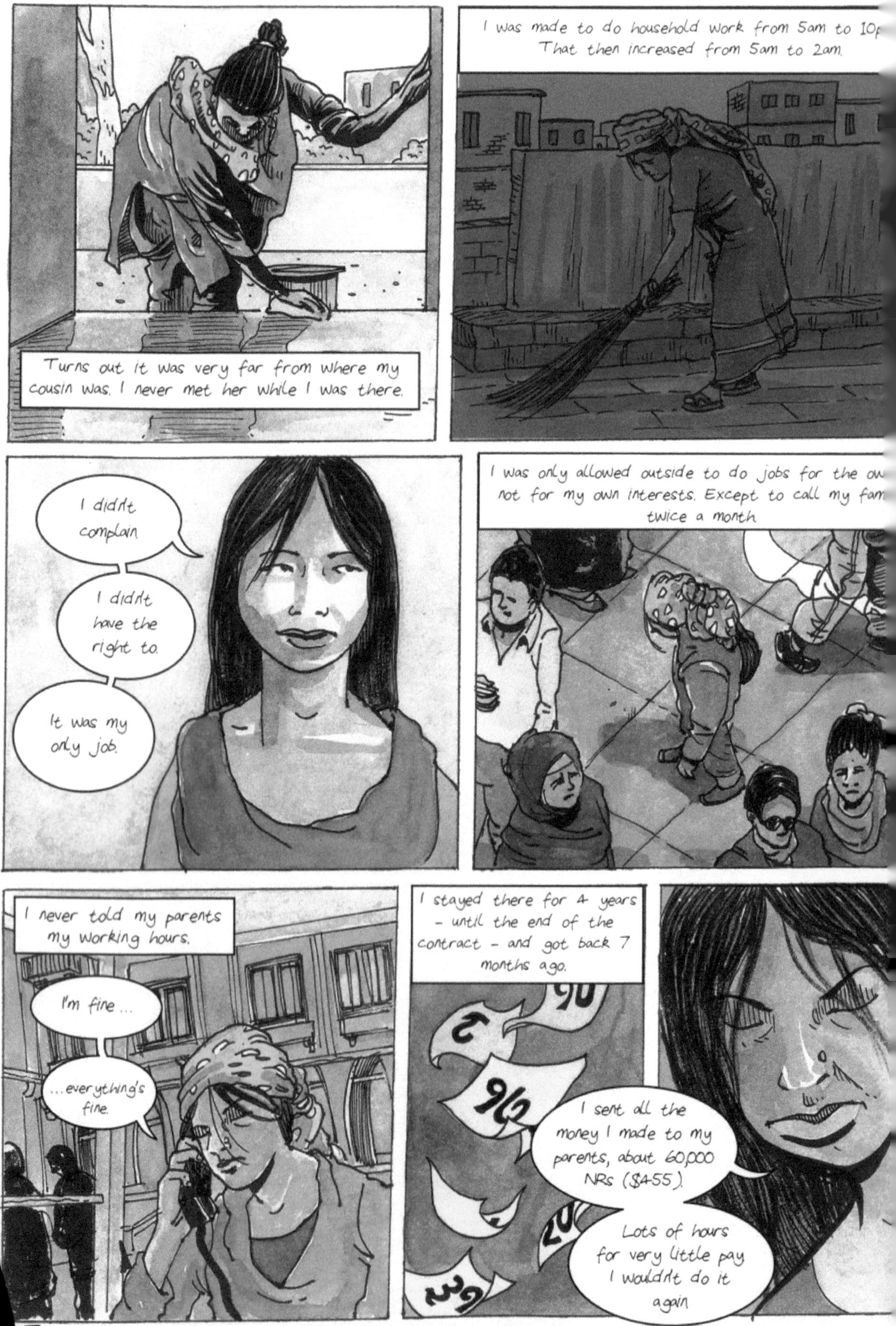
Turns out it was very far from where my cousin was. I never met her while I was there.
I was made to do household work from 5am to 10p
That then increased from 5am to 2am.
I didn't complain
I didn't have the right to.
It was my only job.
I was only allowed outside to do jobs for the ow
not for my own interests. Except to call my fam
twice a month
I never told my parents my working hours.
I'm fine ...
... everything's fine.
I stayed there for 4 years – until the end of the contract – and got back 7 months ago.
I sent all the money I made to my parents, about 60,000 NRs ($455).
Lots of hours for very little pay I wouldn't do it again

FEEDBACK

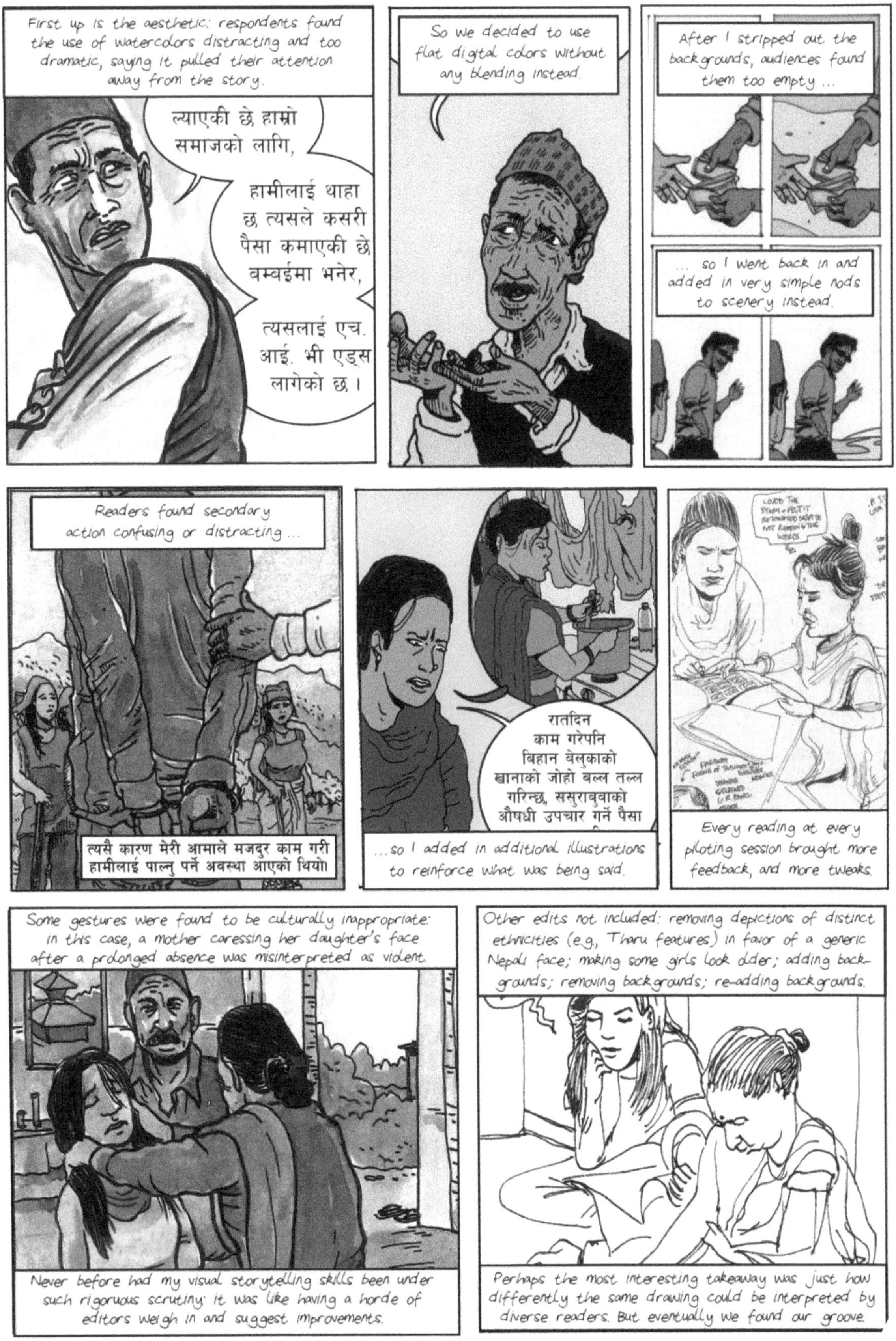

First up is the aesthetic: respondents found the use of watercolors distracting and too dramatic, saying it pulled their attention away from the story.
ल्याएकी छे हाम्रो समाजको लागि,
हामीलाई थाहा छ त्यसले कसरी पैसा कमाएकी छे बम्बईमा भनेर,
त्यसलाई एच. आई. भी एड्स लागेको छ ।
So we decided to use flat digital colors without any blending instead.
After I stripped out the backgrounds, audiences found them too empty ...
... so I went back in and added in very simple nods to scenery instead.
Readers found secondary action confusing or distracting ...
त्यसै कारण मेरी आमाले मजदुर काम गरी हामीलाई पाल्नु पर्ने अवस्था आएको थियो।
रातदिन काम गरेपनि बिहान बेलुकाको खानाको जोहो बल्ल तल्ल गरिन्छ, ससुराबुबाको औषधी उपचार गर्ने पैसा
...so I added in additional illustrations to reinforce what was being said.
Every reading at every piloting session brought more feedback, and more tweaks.
Some gestures were found to be culturally inappropriate: in this case, a mother caressing her daughter's face after a prolonged absence was misinterpreted as violent.
Never before had my visual storytelling skills been under such rigorous scrutiny: it was like having a horde of editors weigh in and suggest improvements.
Other edits not included: removing depictions of distinct ethnicities (e.g., Tharu features) in favor of a generic Nepali face; making some girls look older; adding backgrounds; removing backgrounds; re-adding backgrounds.
Perhaps the most interesting takeaway was just how differently the same drawing could be interpreted by diverse readers. But eventually we found our groove.

I originally thought that comics, given their emphasis on the visual and reduced amount of text, had a more global appeal than traditional prose stories, like SOLD. What I failed to recognize is that literacy isn't just a question o deciphering words, but also pictures. A visual style that tested well among Western audiences (watercolors, heightene realism, depth of field cues) was unappealing and even confusing to the Nepali audiences we held pilots with.

For example, here's the first pass artwork I did for Sabina's story.

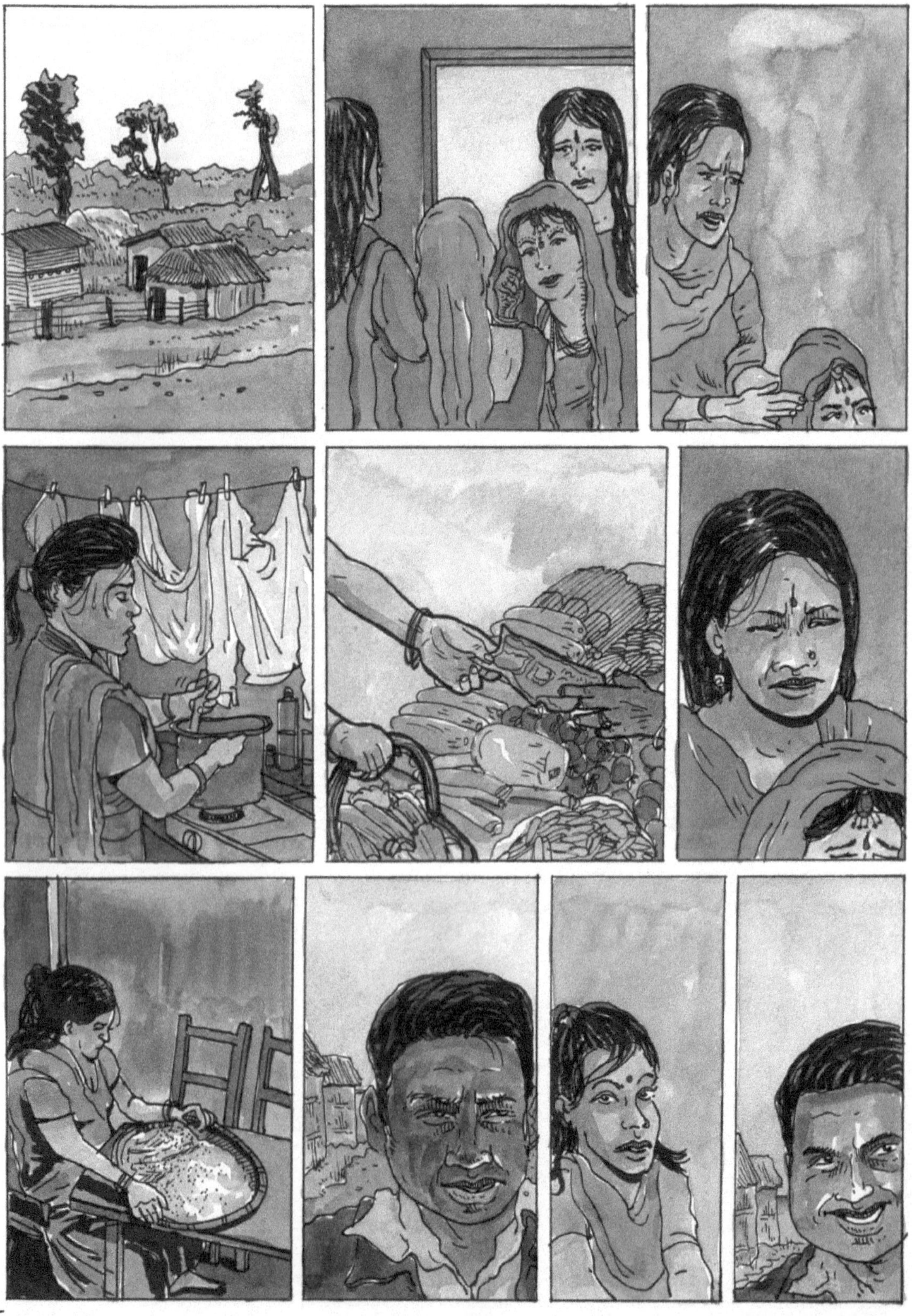

And here's the same page of that story after multiple iterations, incorporating feedback such as saturating and digitizing the colors, flattening the depth cues, and making the shots more consistent and medium range.

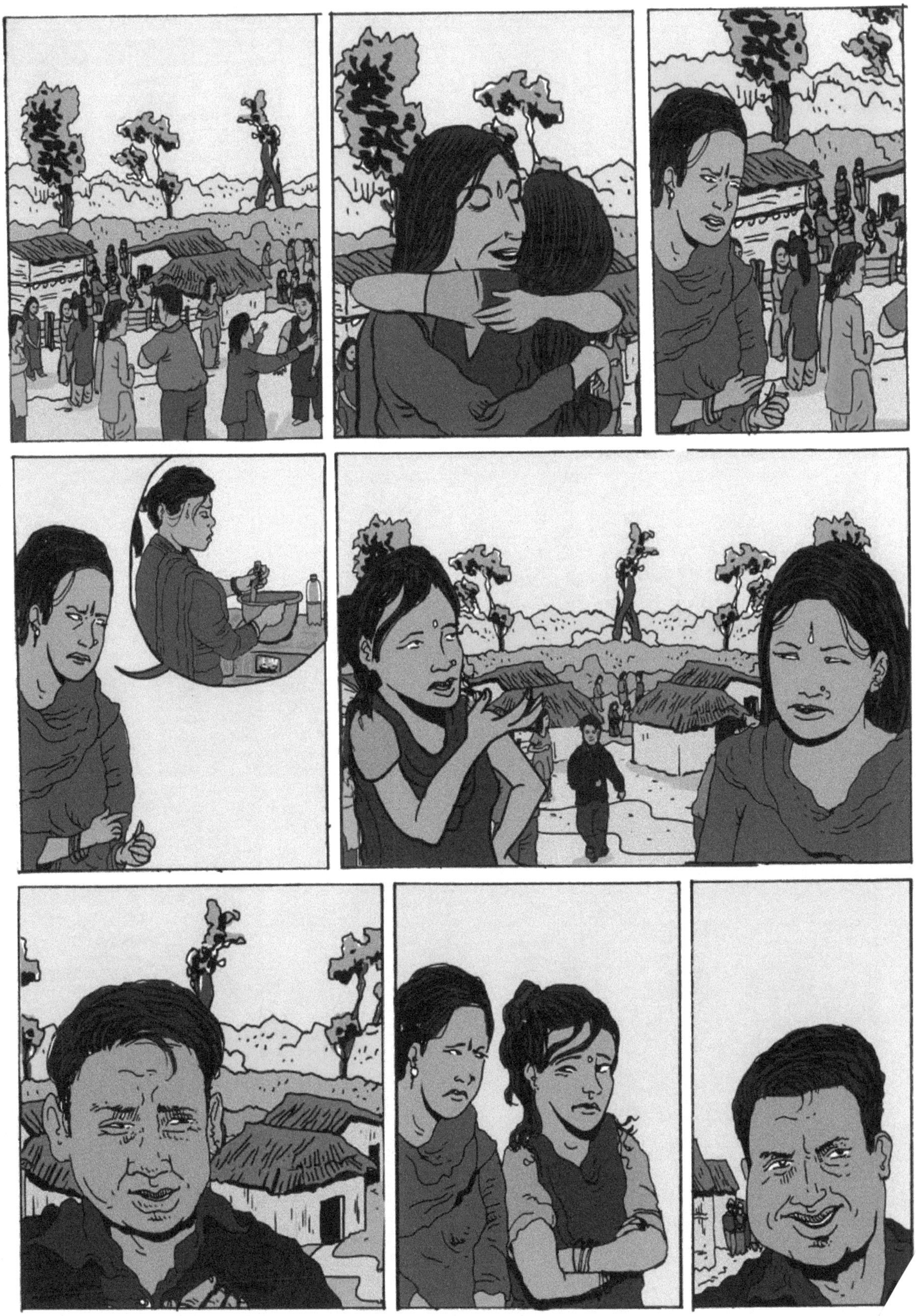

WE COULD BE HEROES

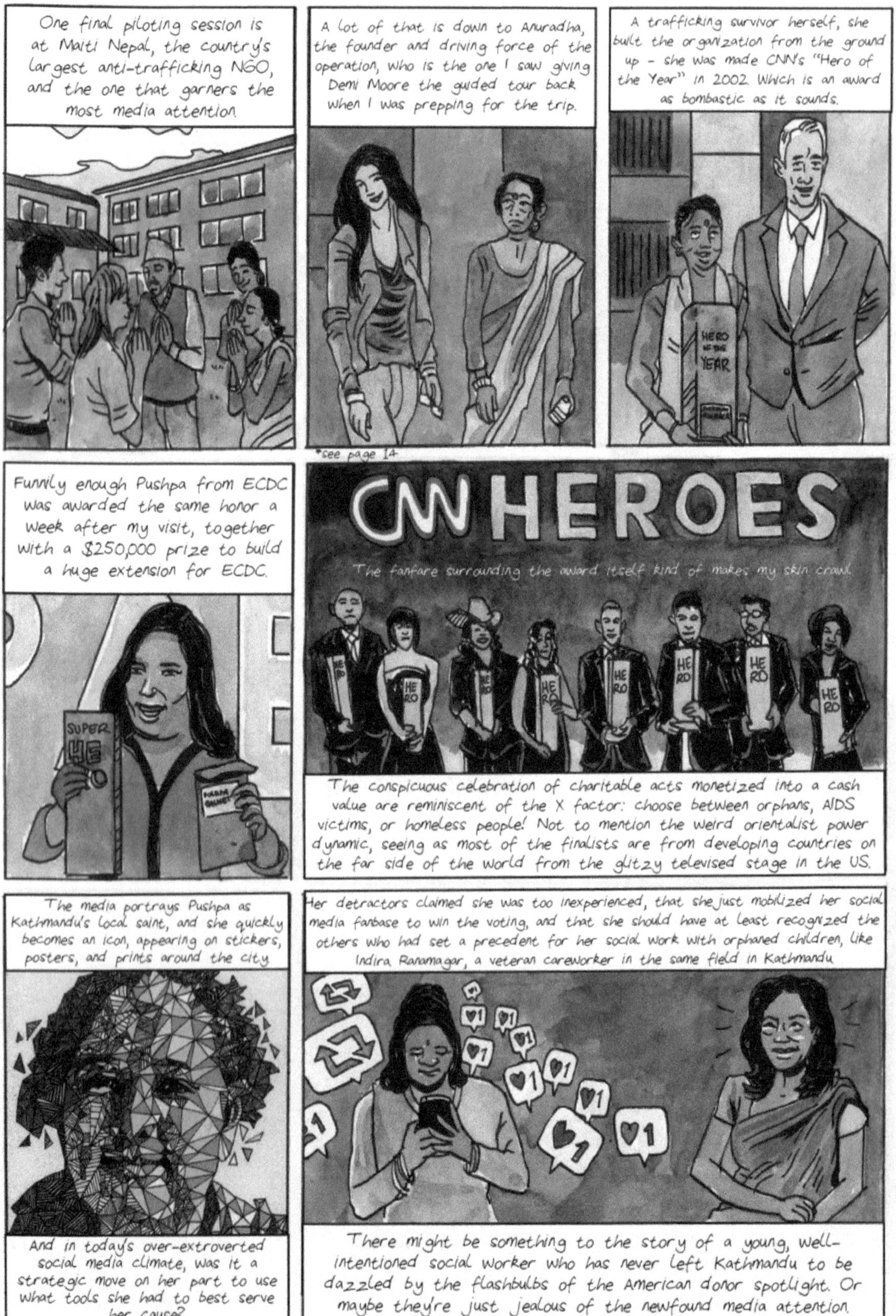

One final piloting session is at Maiti Nepal, the country's largest anti-trafficking NGO, and the one that garners the most media attention.
A lot of that is down to Anuradha, the founder and driving force of the operation, who is the one I saw giving Demi Moore the guided tour back when I was prepping for the trip.
A trafficking survivor herself, she built the organization from the ground up - she was made CNN's "Hero of the Year" in 2002. Which is an award as bombastic as it sounds.
HERO OF THE YEAR
*see page 14
Funnily enough Pushpa from ECDC was awarded the same honor a week after my visit, together with a $250,000 prize to build a huge extension for ECDC.
SUPER HE
CNN HEROES
The fanfare surrounding the award itself kind of makes my skin crawl.
HERO
The conspicuous celebration of charitable acts monetized into a cash value are reminiscent of the X factor: choose between orphans, AIDS victims, or homeless people! Not to mention the weird orientalist power dynamic, seeing as most of the finalists are from developing countries on the far side of the world from the glitzy televised stage in the US.
The media portrays Pushpa as Kathmandu's local saint, and she quickly becomes an icon, appearing on stickers, posters, and prints around the city.
And in today's over-extroverted social media climate, was it a strategic move on her part to use what tools she had to best serve her cause?
Her detractors claimed she was too inexperienced, that she just mobilized her social media fanbase to win the voting, and that she should have at least recognized the others who had set a precedent for her social work with orphaned children, like Indira Ranamagar, a veteran careworker in the same field in Kathmandu.
There might be something to the story of a young, well-intentioned social worker who has never left Kathmandu to be dazzled by the flashbulbs of the American donor spotlight. Or maybe they're just jealous of the newfound media attention.

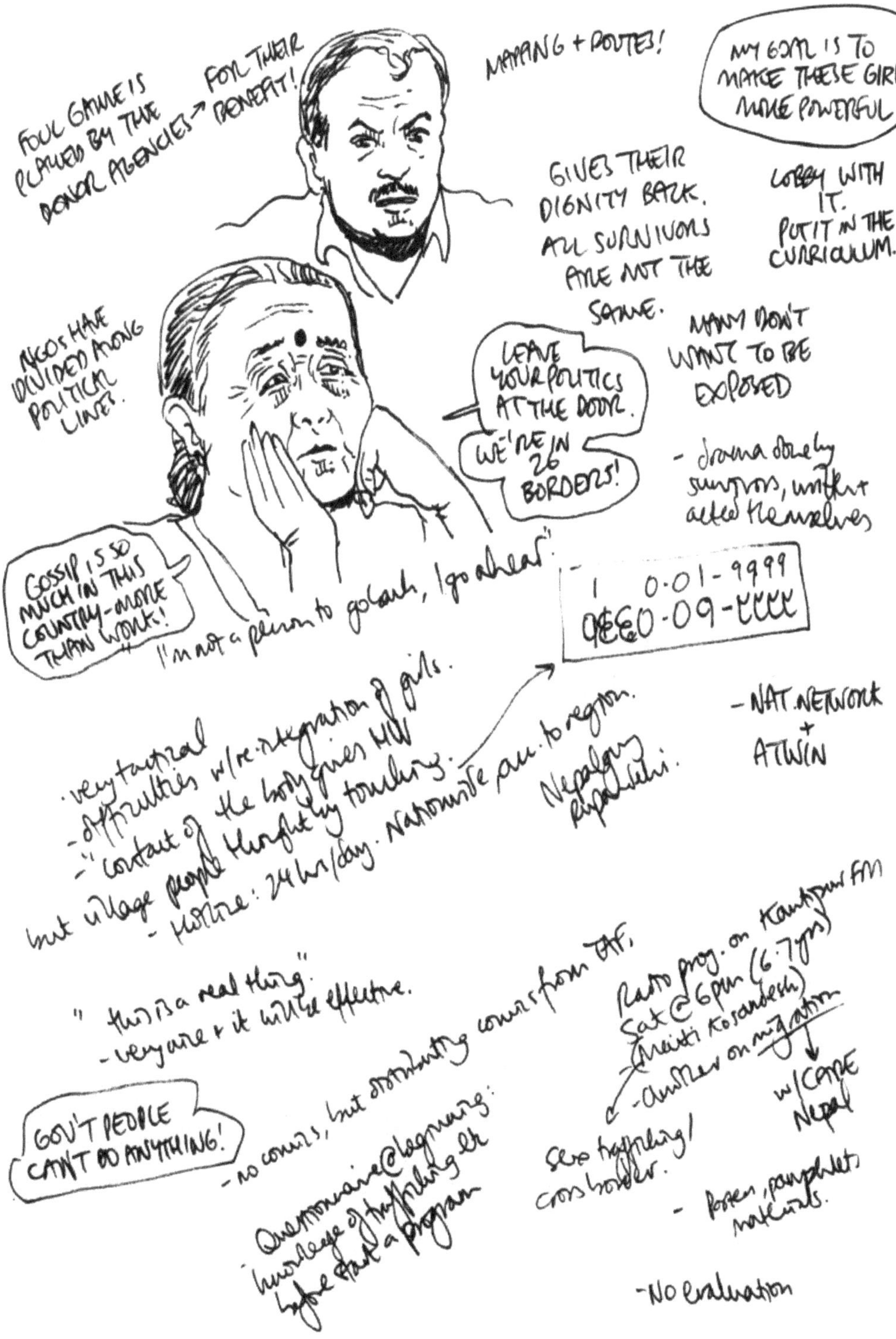
FOUL GAME IS PLAYED BY THE DONOR AGENCIES → FOR THEIR BENEFIT!
MAPPING + ROUTES!
MY GOAL IS TO MAKE THESE GIRLS MORE POWERFUL
GIVES THEIR DIGNITY BACK.
ALL SURVIVORS ARE NOT THE SAME.
LOBBY WITH IT. PUT IT IN THE CURRICULUM.
NGOs HAVE DIVIDED ALONG POLITICAL LINES.
LEAVE YOUR POLITICS AT THE DOOR.
WE'RE IN 26 BORDERS!
MANY DON'T WANT TO BE EXPOSED
- drama done by survivors, written + acted themselves
GOSSIP IS SO MUCH IN THIS COUNTRY—MORE THAN WORK!
"I'm not a person to go back, I go ahead"
1 0-01-9999
· very practical
- difficulties w/ re-integration of girls.
- "contact of the body gives HIV" but village people thought by touching.
- hotline: 24 hrs/day. Nationwide acc. to region.
Nepalganj Rupandehi.
- NAT. NETWORK + ATWIN
" this is a real thing"
- very aware + it will be effective.
- no courses, but orientating courses from TAF.
Radio prog. on Kantipur FM Sat @ 6pm (6-7 yrs) Maiti Kosandesh
- another on migration
w/ CARE Nepal
Sex trafficking! cross border.
GOV'T PEOPLE CAN'T DO ANYTHING!
- Questionnaire @ beginning: knowledge of trafficking etc before start a program
- Posters, pamphlets, materials.
- No evaluation

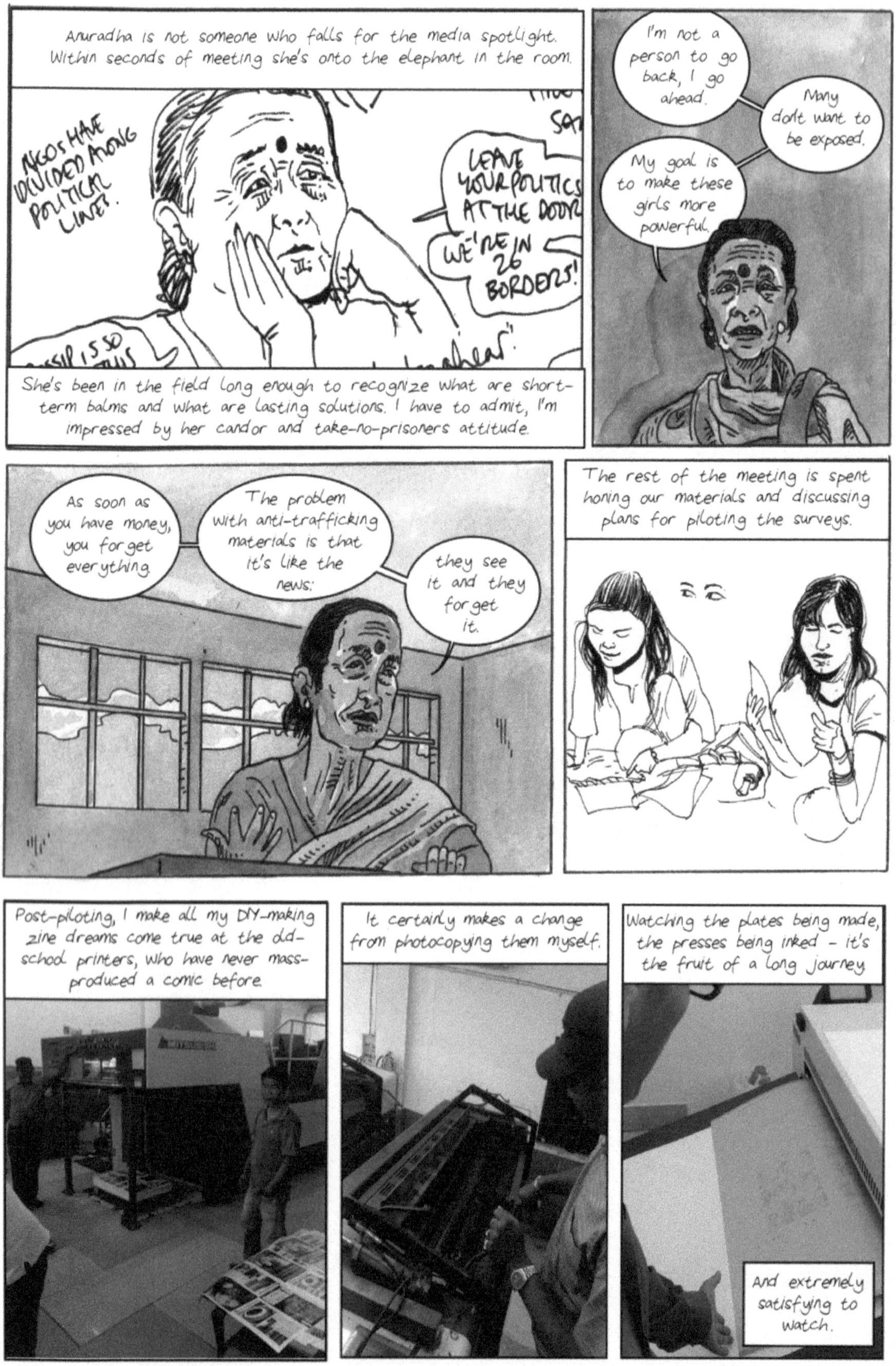
Anuradha is not someone who falls for the media spotlight. Within seconds of meeting she's onto the elephant in the room.
NGOs HAVE DIVIDED ALONG POLITICAL LINES.
LEAVE YOUR POLITICS AT THE DOOR!
WE'RE IN 26 BORDERS!
She's been in the field long enough to recognize what are short-term balms and what are lasting solutions. I have to admit, I'm impressed by her candor and take-no-prisoners attitude.
I'm not a person to go back, I go ahead.
Many don't want to be exposed.
My goal is to make these girls more powerful.
As soon as you have money, you forget everything.
The problem with anti-trafficking materials is that it's like the news:
they see it and they forget it.
The rest of the meeting is spent honing our materials and discussing plans for piloting the surveys.
Post-piloting, I make all my DIY-making zine dreams come true at the old-school printers, who have never mass-produced a comic before.
It certainly makes a change from photocopying them myself.
Watching the plates being made, the presses being inked – it's the fruit of a long journey.
And extremely satisfying to watch.

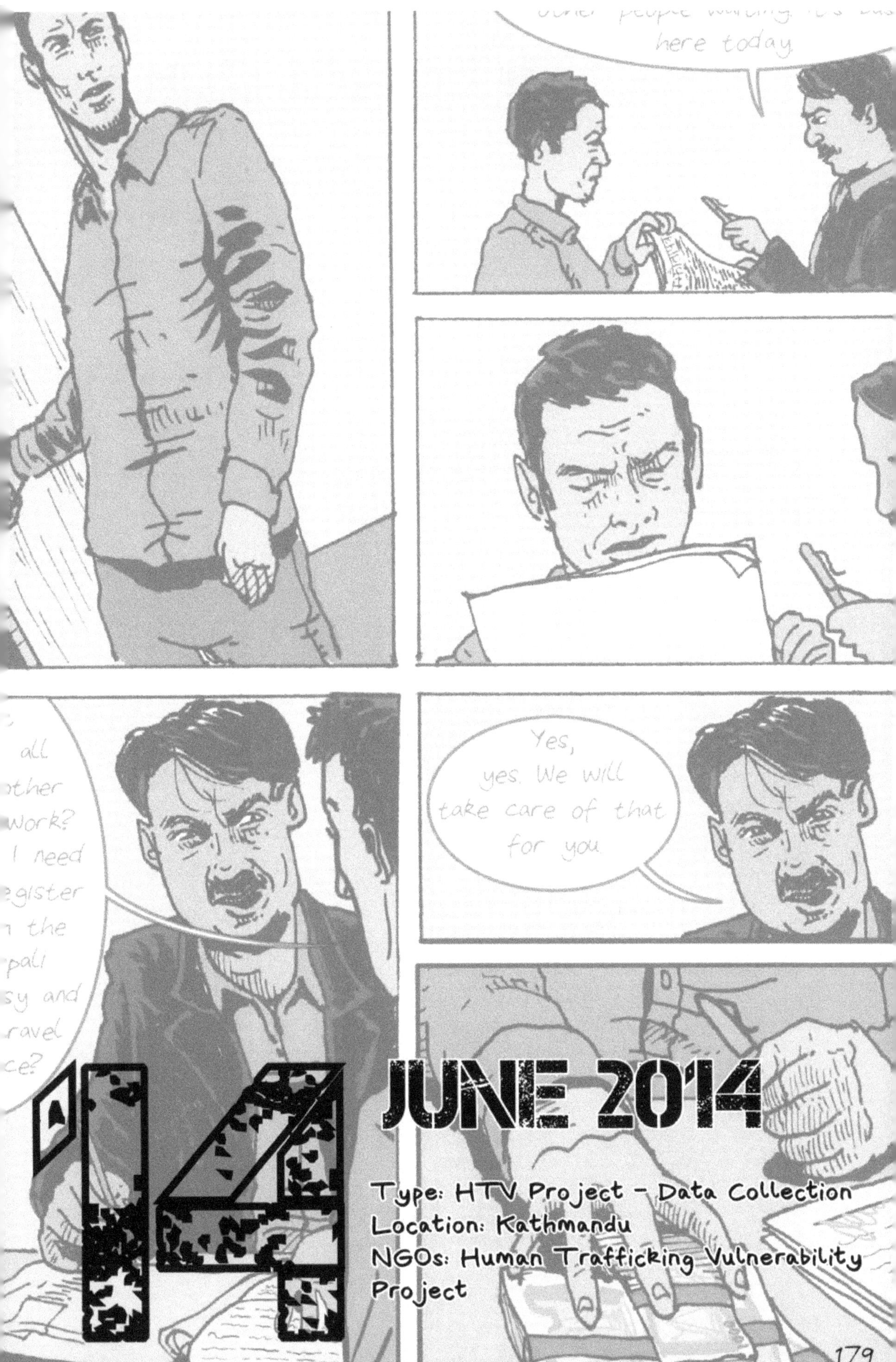

here today
Yes, yes. We will take care of that for you

14 JUNE 2014

Type: HTV Project – Data Collection
Location: Kathmandu
NGOs: Human Trafficking Vulnerability Project

DATA COLLECTION

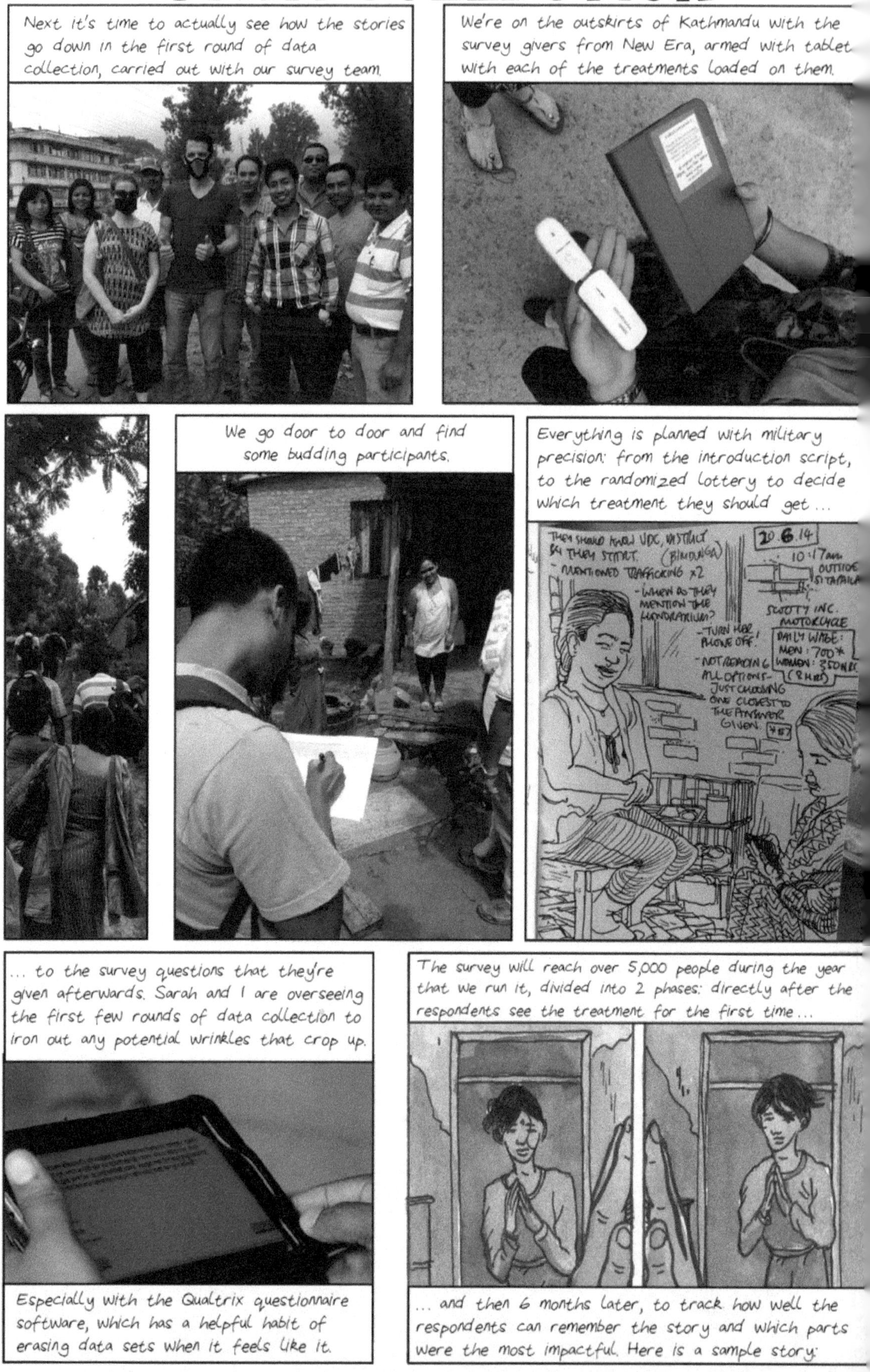
Next it's time to actually see how the stories go down in the first round of data collection, carried out with our survey team.
We're on the outskirts of Kathmandu with the survey givers from New Era, armed with tablets with each of the treatments loaded on them.
We go door to door and find some budding participants.
Everything is planned with military precision: from the introduction script, to the randomized lottery to decide which treatment they should get ...
20.6.14
10:17am
MENTIONED TRAFFICKING x2
TURN HER PHONE OFF!
DAILY WAGE:
MEN: 700*
(8 HRS)
JUST CHOOSING ONE CLOSEST TO THE ANSWER GIVEN.
... to the survey questions that they're given afterwards. Sarah and I are overseeing the first few rounds of data collection to iron out any potential wrinkles that crop up.
Especially with the Qualtrix questionnaire software, which has a helpful habit of erasing data sets when it feels like it.
The survey will reach over 5,000 people during the year that we run it, divided into 2 phases: directly after the respondents see the treatment for the first time ...
... and then 6 months later, to track how well the respondents can remember the story and which parts were the most impactful. Here is a sample story:

THE CHEATED MIGRANT: NEGATIVE VERSION

Suraj is a 24-year-old farmer. His family is struggling financially, and he decides to migrate to the Middle East to work as a manual laborer.

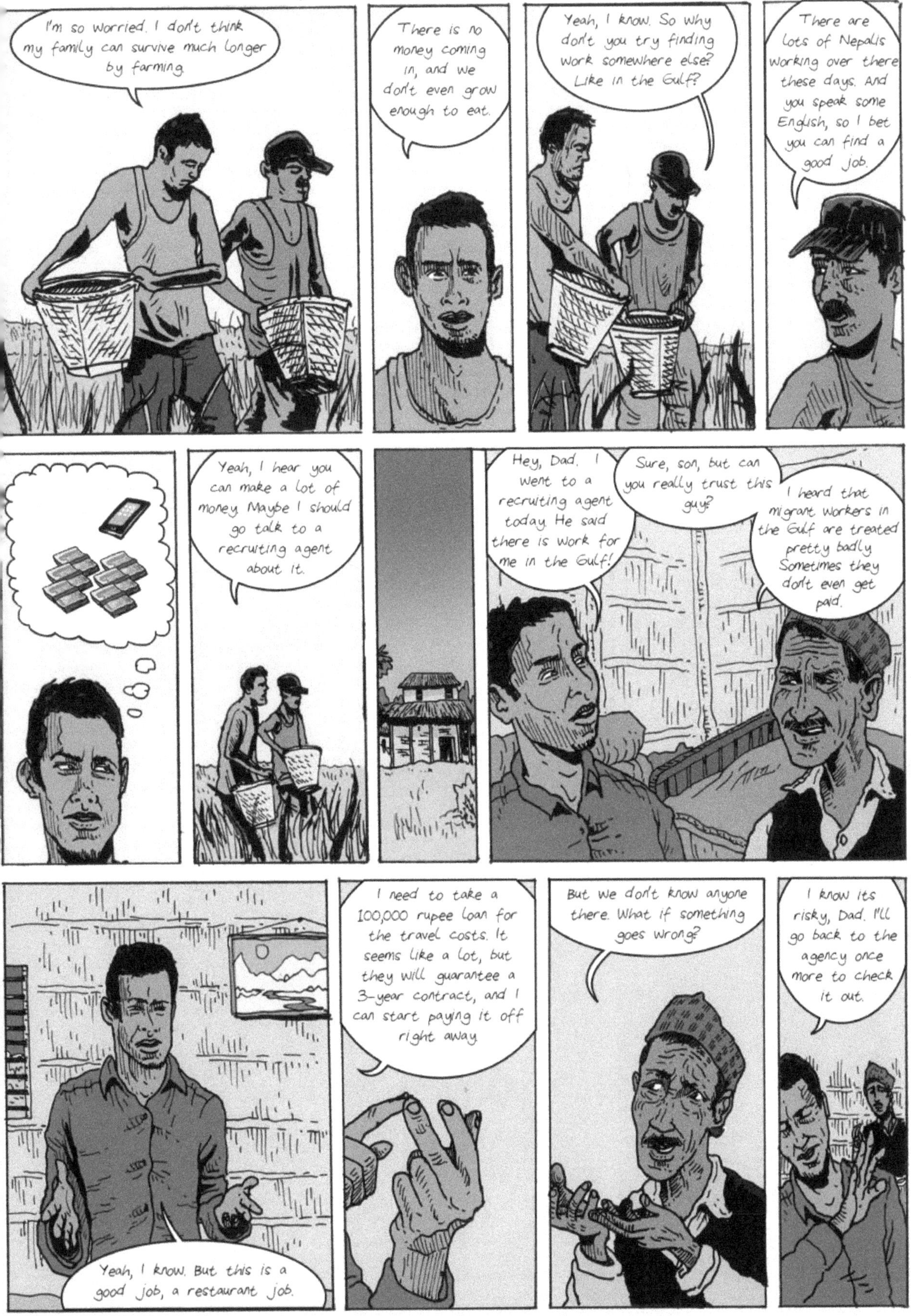

I'm so worried. I don't think my family can survive much longer by farming.
There is no money coming in, and we don't even grow enough to eat.
Yeah, I know. So why don't you try finding work somewhere else? Like in the Gulf?
There are lots of Nepalis working over there these days. And you speak some English, so I bet you can find a good job.
Yeah, I hear you can make a lot of money. Maybe I should go talk to a recruiting agent about it.
Hey, Dad. I went to a recruiting agent today. He said there is work for me in the Gulf!
Sure, son, but can you really trust this guy?
I heard that migrant workers in the Gulf are treated pretty badly. Sometimes they don't even get paid.
Yeah, I know. But this is a good job, a restaurant job.
I need to take a 100,000 rupee loan for the travel costs. It seems like a lot, but they will guarantee a 3-year contract, and I can start paying it off right away.
But we don't know anyone there. What if something goes wrong?
I know its risky, Dad. I'll go back to the agency once more to check it out.

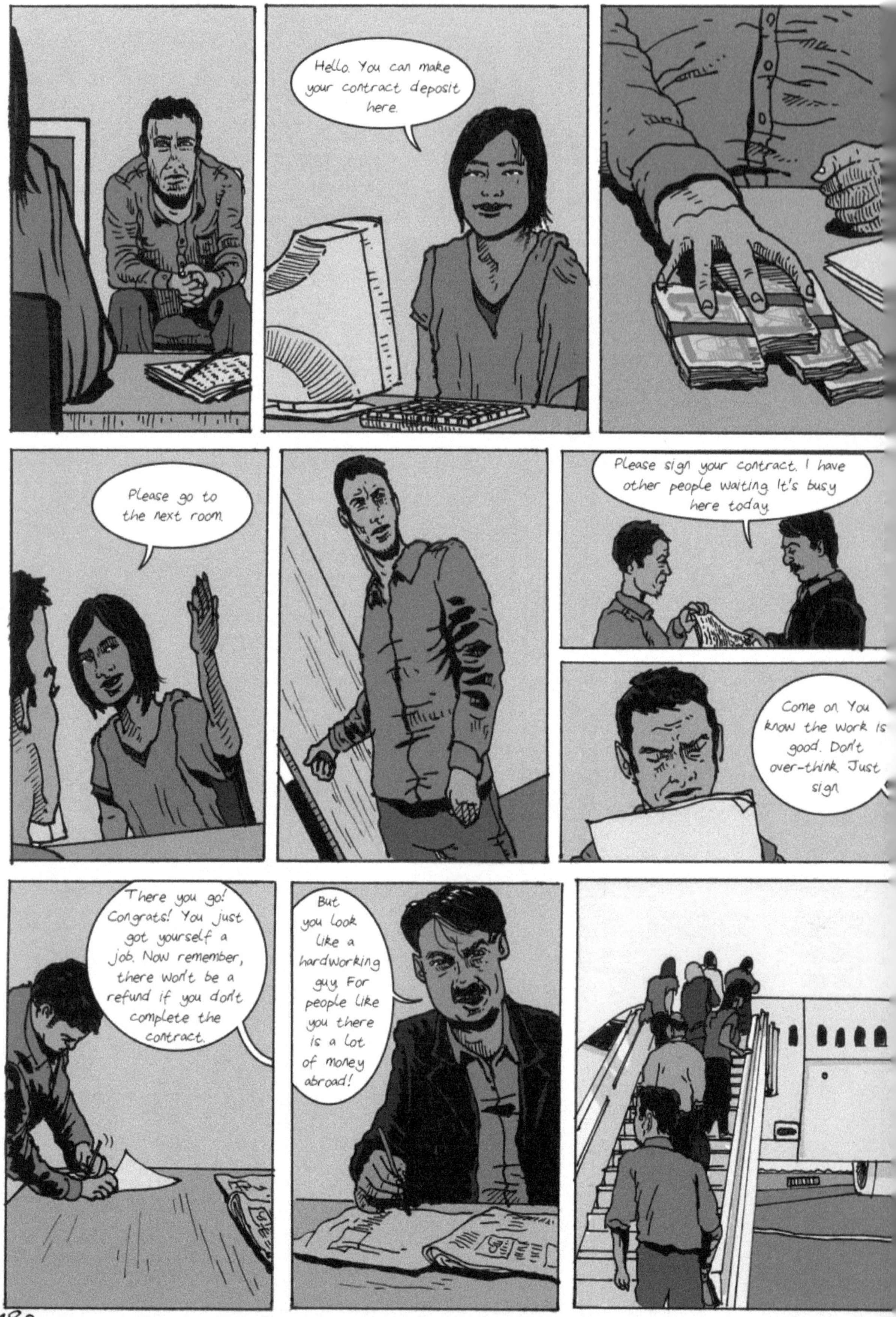
Hello. You can make your contract deposit here.
Please go to the next room.
Please sign your contract. I have other people waiting. It's busy here today.
Come on. You know the work is good. Don't over-think. Just sign.
There you go! Congrats! You just got yourself a job. Now remember, there won't be a refund if you don't complete the contract.
But you look like a hardworking guy. For people like you there is a lot of money abroad!

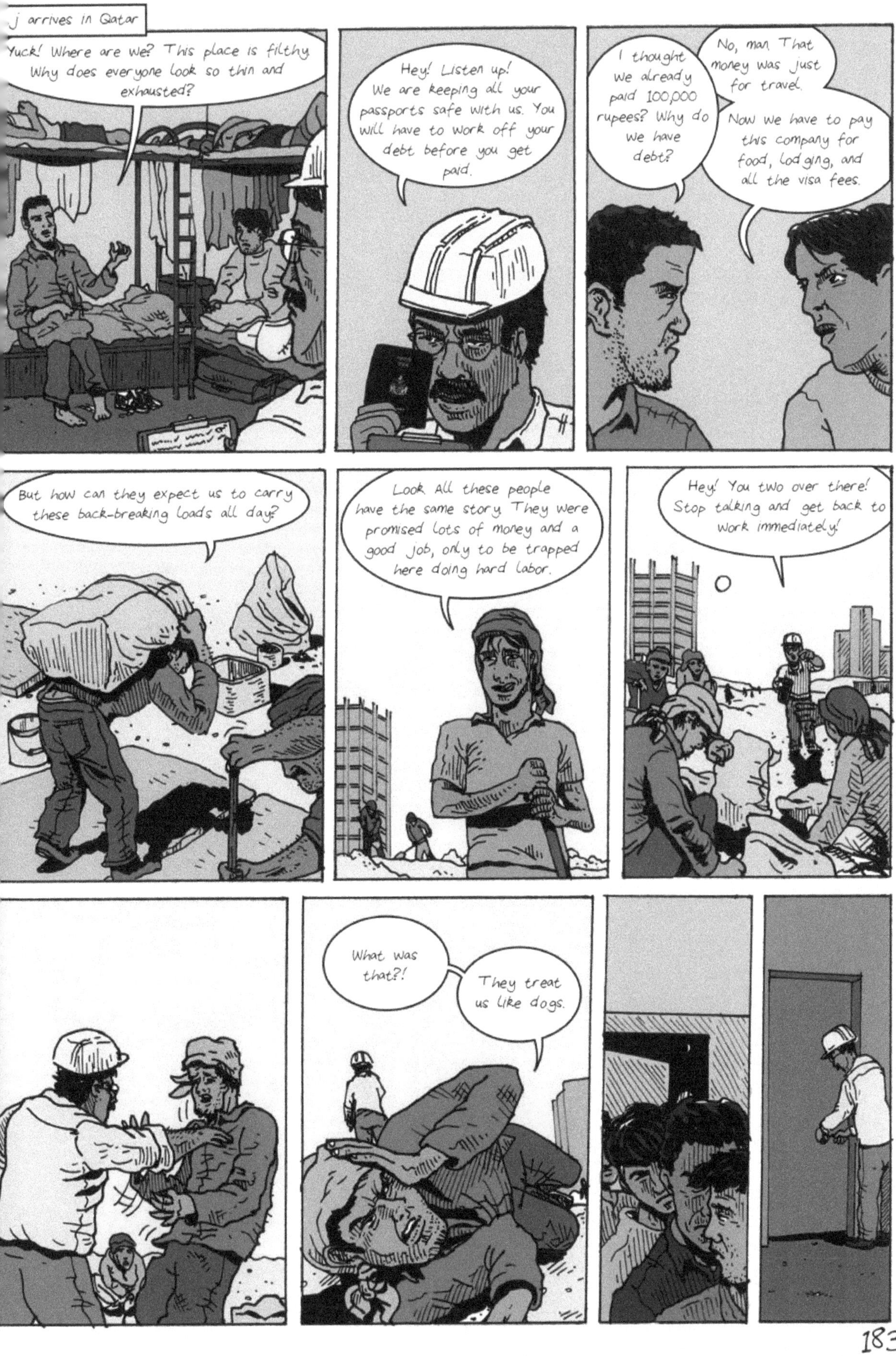
j arrives in Qatar
Yuck! Where are we? This place is filthy. Why does everyone look so thin and exhausted?
Hey! Listen up! We are keeping all your passports safe with us. You will have to work off your debt before you get paid.
I thought we already paid 100,000 rupees? Why do we have debt?
No, man. That money was just for travel.
Now we have to pay this company for food, lodging, and all the visa fees.
But how can they expect us to carry these back-breaking loads all day?
Look. All these people have the same story. They were promised lots of money and a good job, only to be trapped here doing hard labor.
Hey! You two over there! Stop talking and get back to work immediately!
What was that?!
They treat us like dogs.

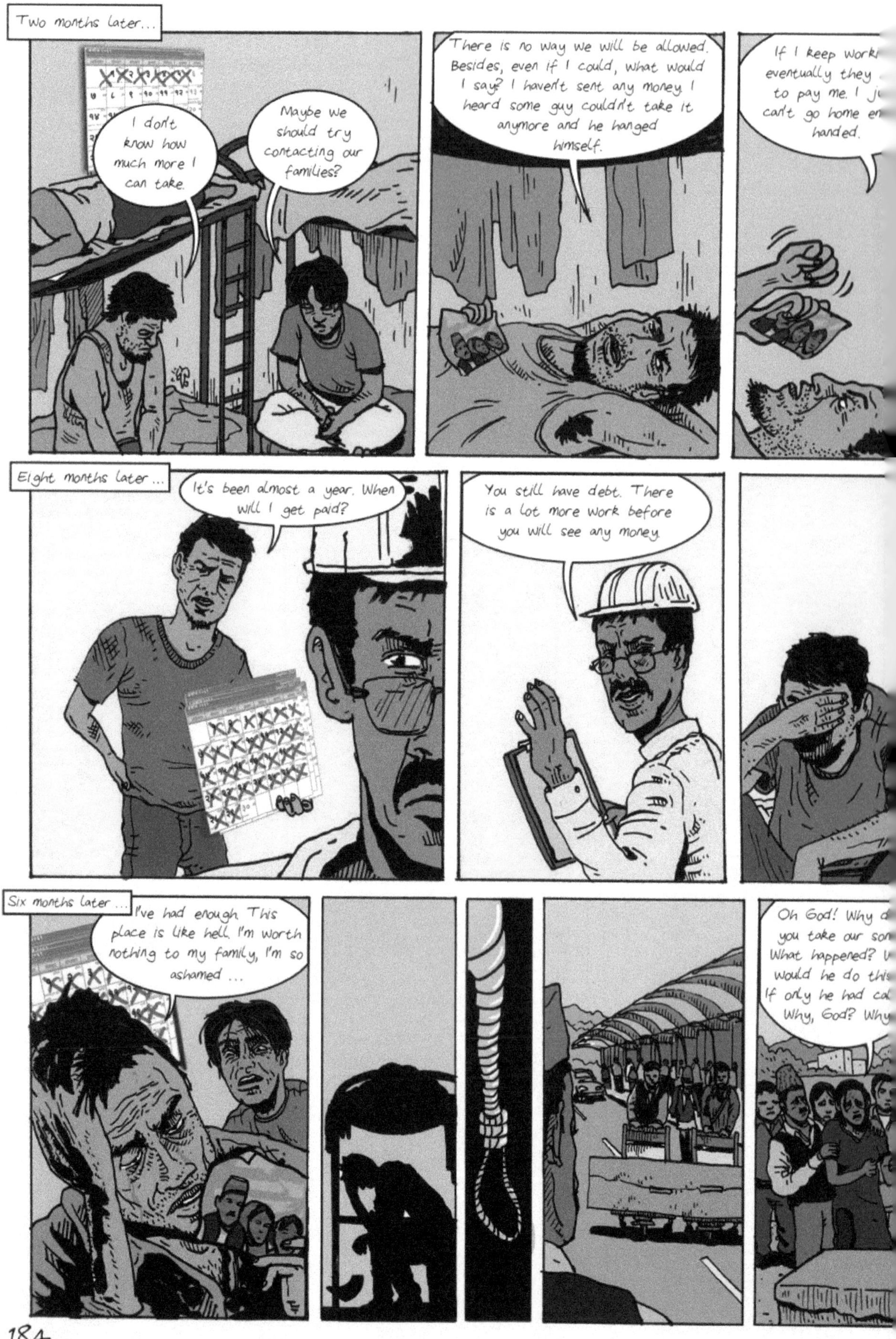

Two months later...
I don't know how much more I can take.
Maybe we should try contacting our families?
There is no way we will be allowed. Besides, even if I could, what would I say? I haven't sent any money. I heard some guy couldn't take it anymore and he hanged himself.
If I keep worki eventually they to pay me. I j can't go home en handed.
Eight months later...
It's been almost a year. When will I get paid?
You still have debt. There is a lot more work before you will see any money.
Six months later...
I've had enough. This place is like hell. I'm worth nothing to my family, I'm so ashamed ...
Oh God! Why d you take our son What happened? W would he do this If only he had ca Why, God? Why

THE CHEATED MIGRANT: POSITIVE VERSION

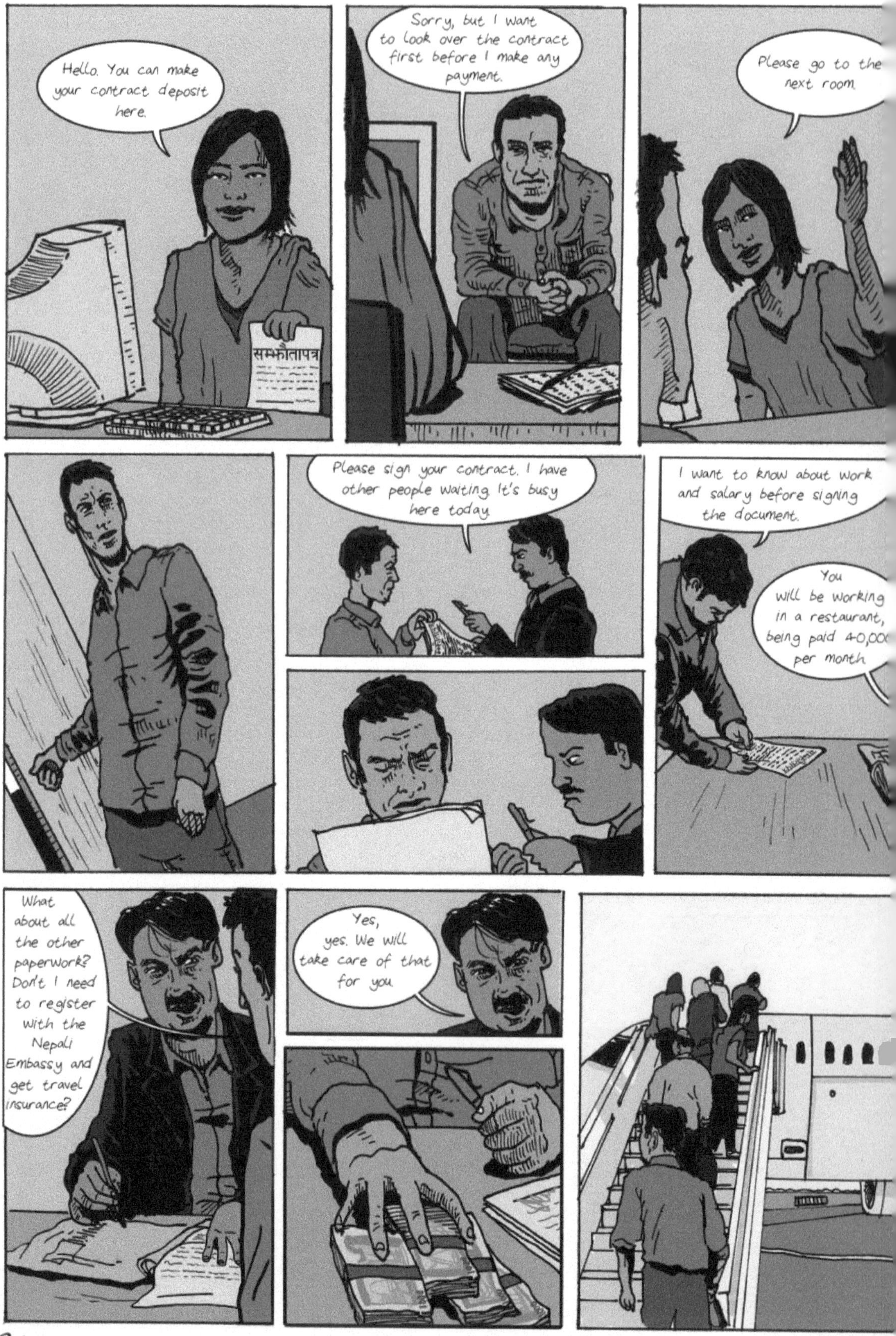
Hello. You can make your contract deposit here.
सम्झौतापत्र
Sorry, but I want to look over the contract first before I make any payment.
Please go to the next room.
Please sign your contract. I have other people waiting. It's busy here today.
I want to know about work and salary before signing the document.
You will be working in a restaurant, being paid 40,00
per month
What about all the other paperwork? Don't I need to register with the Nepali Embassy and get travel insurance?
Yes, yes. We will take care of that for you.

Yuck! Where are we? This place is filthy. Why does everyone look so thin and exhausted?

Hey! Listen up! We are keeping all your passports safe with us. You will have to work off your debt before you get paid.

I thought we already paid 100,000 rupees? Why do we have debt?

No, man. That money was just for travel.

Now we have to pay this company for food, lodging, and all the visa fees.

But how can they expect us to carry these back-breaking loads all day?

Look. All these people have the same story. They were promised lots of money and a good job only to be trapped here doing hard labor.

Hey! You two over there! Stop talking and get back to work immediately!

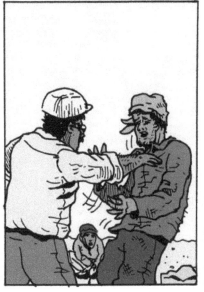

What was that?!

They treat us like dogs.

187

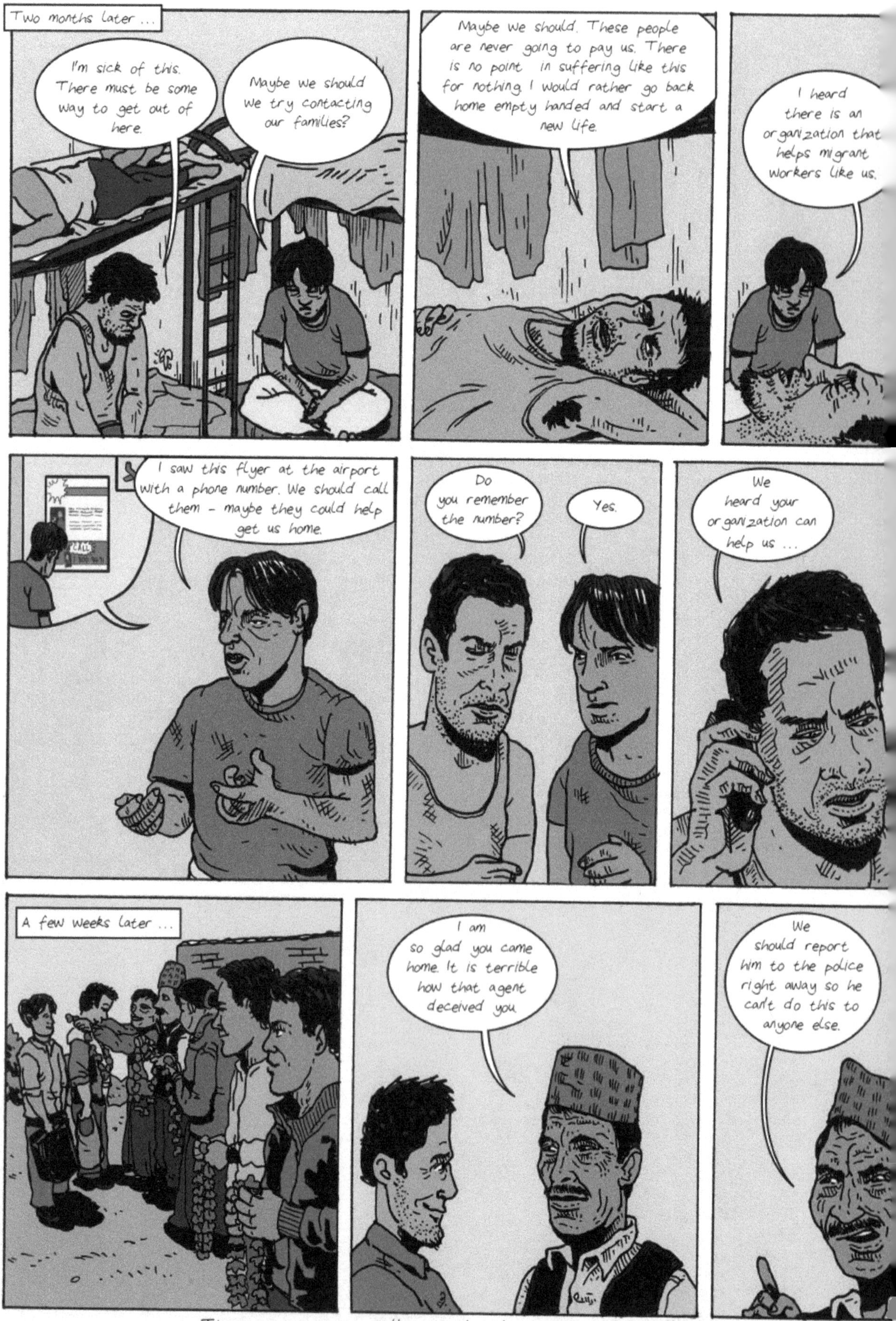
Two months later ...
I'm sick of this. There must be some way to get out of here.
Maybe we should we try contacting our families?
Maybe we should. These people are never going to pay us. There is no point in suffering like this for nothing. I would rather go back home empty handed and start a new life.
I heard there is an organization that helps migrant workers like us.
I saw this flyer at the airport with a phone number. We should call them - maybe they could help get us home.
Do you remember the number?
Yes.
We heard your organization can help us ...
A few weeks later ...
I am so glad you came home. It is terrible how that agent deceived you
We should report him to the police right away so he can't do this to anyone else.

The treatments were well-received, and phase 1 of data collection a success.
There was just one unforeseen factor we hadn't counted on ...

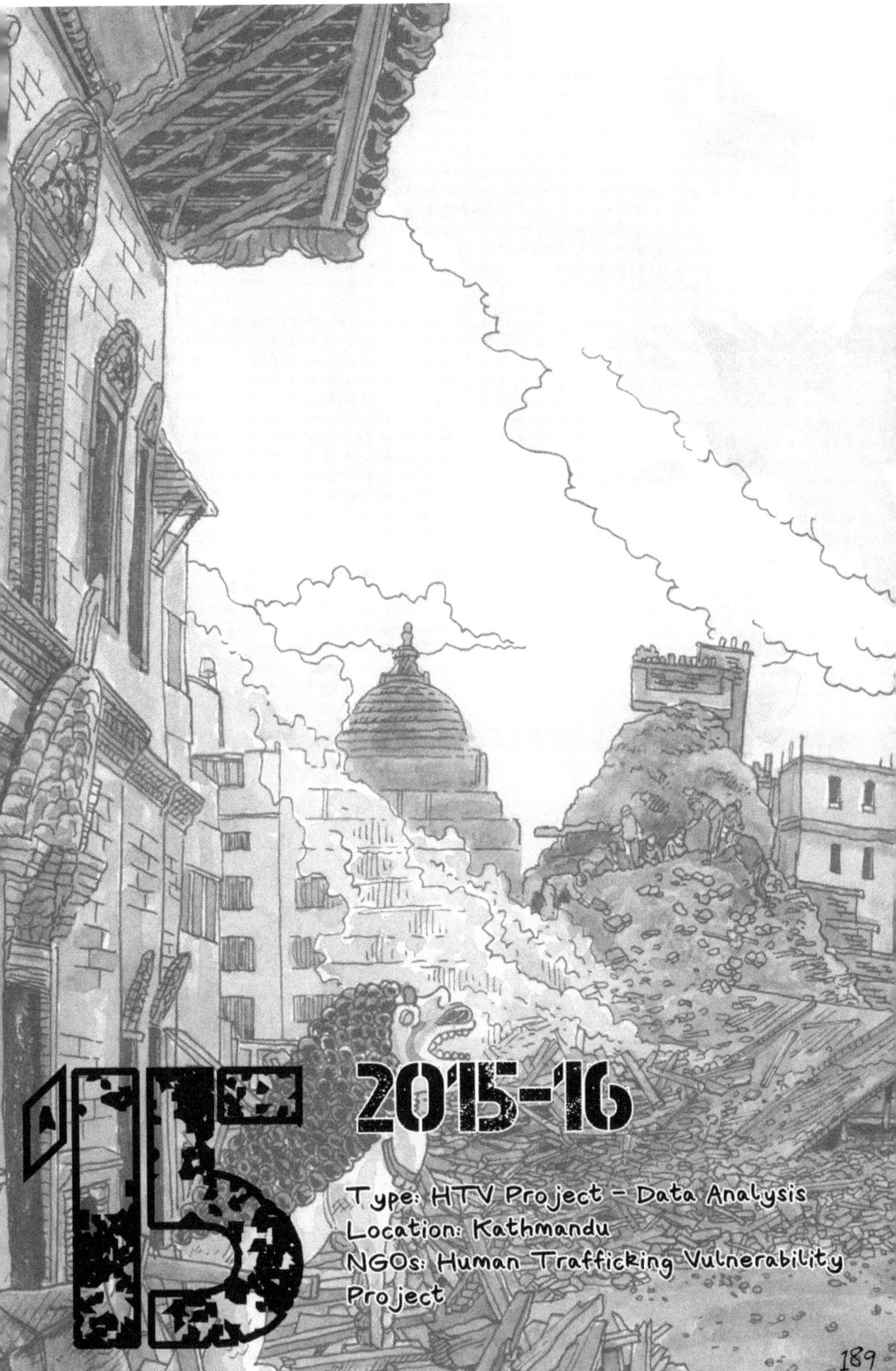

15

2015-16

Type: HTV Project – Data Analysis
Location: Kathmandu
NGOs: Human Trafficking Vulnerability Project

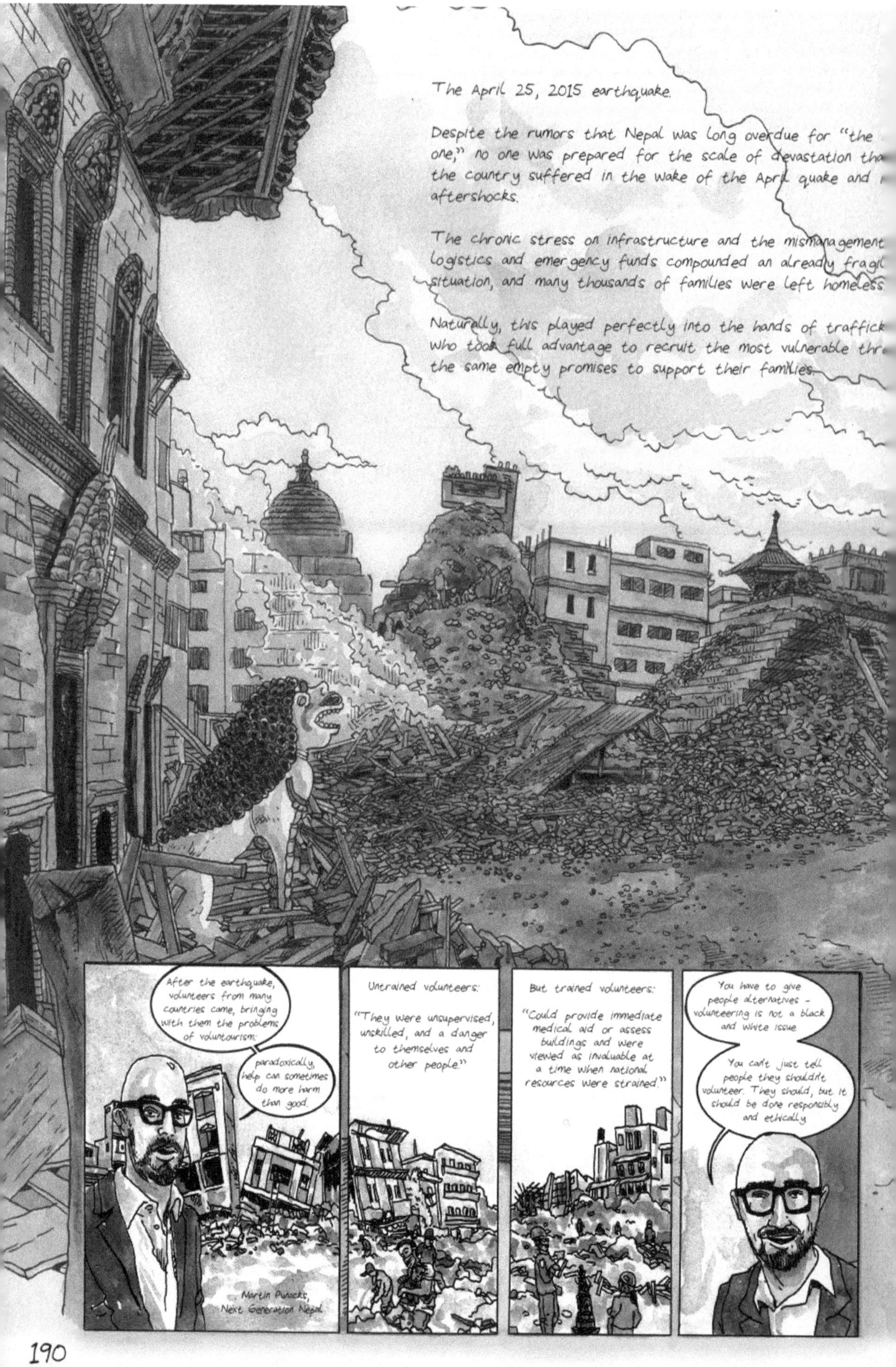
The April 25, 2015 earthquake.
Despite the rumors that Nepal was long overdue for "the one," no one was prepared for the scale of devastation tha the country suffered in the wake of the April quake and aftershocks.
The chronic stress on infrastructure and the mismanagement logistics and emergency funds compounded an already fragil situation, and many thousands of families were left homeless
Naturally, this played perfectly into the hands of traffick who took full advantage to recruit the most vulnerable thr the same empty promises to support their families.
After the earthquake, volunteers from many countries came, bringing with them the problems of voluntourism:
paradoxically, help can sometimes do more harm than good.
Martin Punaks, Next Generation Nepal
Untrained volunteers:
"They were unsupervised, unskilled, and a danger to themselves and other people."
But trained volunteers:
"Could provide immediate medical aid or assess buildings and were viewed as invaluable at a time when national resources were strained."
You have to give people alternatives - volunteering is not a black and white issue.
You can't just tell people they shouldn't volunteer. They should, but it should be done responsibly and ethically.

CONCLUSIONS

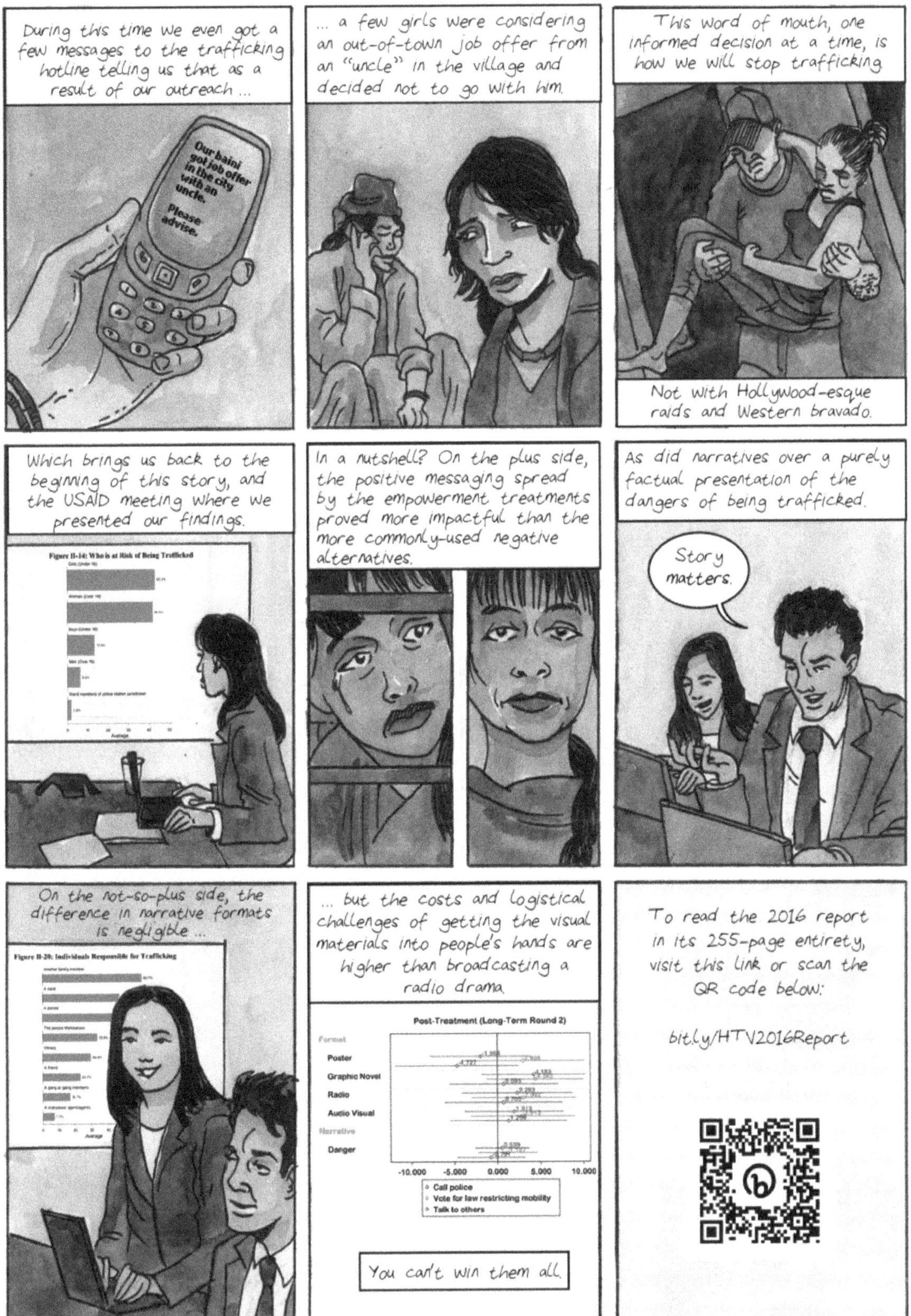

During this time we even got a few messages to the trafficking hotline telling us that as a result of our outreach ...
Our baini got job offer in the city with an uncle. Please advise.
... a few girls were considering an out-of-town job offer from an "uncle" in the village and decided not to go with him.
This word of mouth, one informed decision at a time, is how we will stop trafficking.
Not with Hollywood-esque raids and Western bravado.
Which brings us back to the beginning of this story, and the USAID meeting where we presented our findings.
Figure II-14: Who is at Risk of Being Trafficked
In a nutshell? On the plus side, the positive messaging spread by the empowerment treatments proved more impactful than the more commonly-used negative alternatives.
As did narratives over a purely factual presentation of the dangers of being trafficked.
Story matters.
On the not-so-plus side, the difference in narrative formats is negligible ...
Figure II-20: Individuals Responsible for Trafficking
... but the costs and logistical challenges of getting the visual materials into people's hands are higher than broadcasting a radio drama.
Post-Treatment (Long-Term Round 2)
Format
Poster
Graphic Novel
Radio
Audio Visual
Narrative
Danger
-10.000
-5.000
0.000
5.000
10.000
Call police
Vote for law restricting mobility
Talk to others
You can't win them all.
To read the 2016 report in its 255-page entirety, visit this link or scan the QR code below:
bit.ly/HTV2016Report

HOW YOU CAN HELP

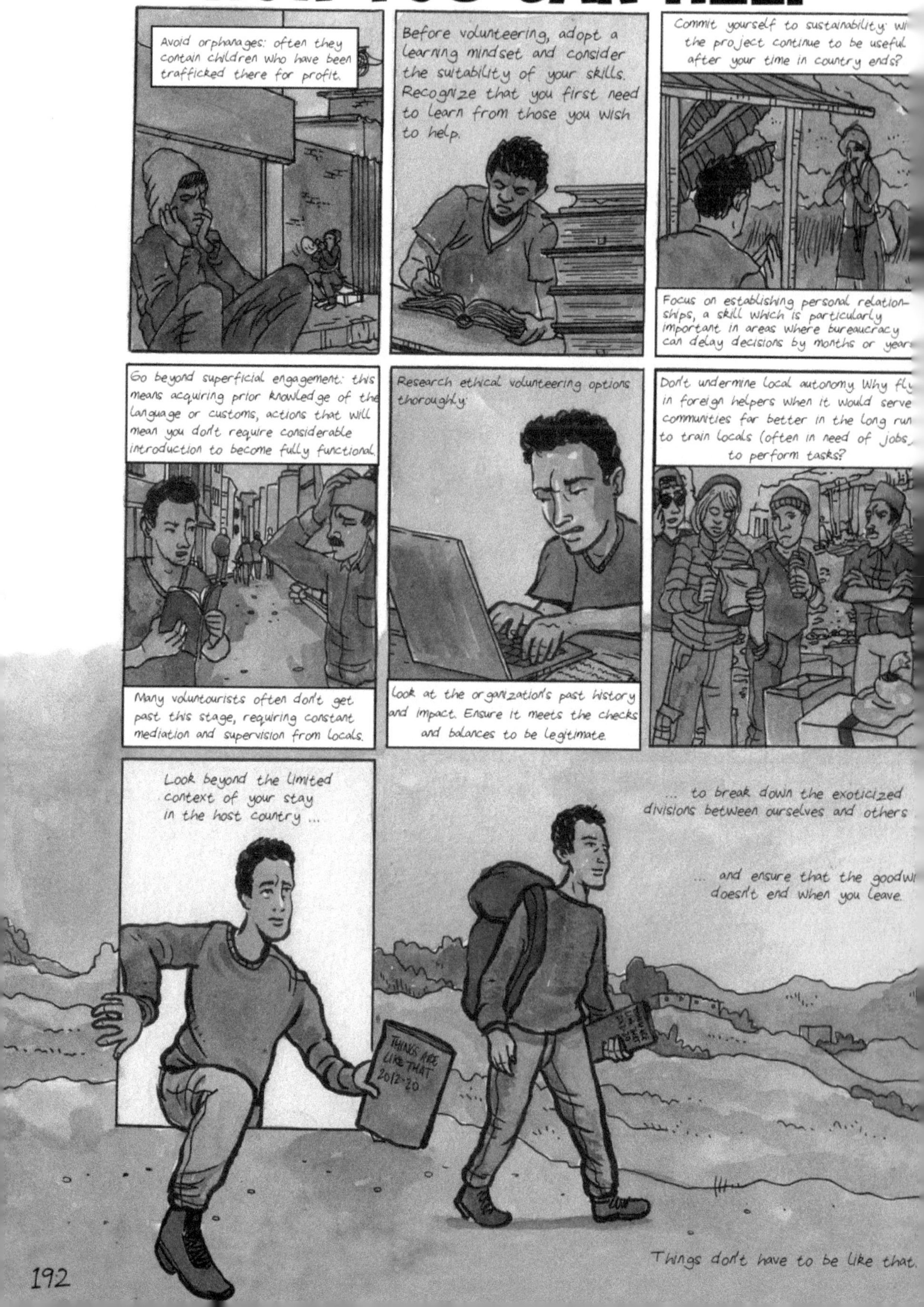

Avoid orphanages: often they contain children who have been trafficked there for profit.
Before volunteering, adopt a learning mindset and consider the suitability of your skills. Recognize that you first need to learn from those you wish to help.
Commit yourself to sustainability: wi the project continue to be useful after your time in country ends?
Focus on establishing personal relationships, a skill which is particularly important in areas where bureaucracy can delay decisions by months or years
Go beyond superficial engagement: this means acquiring prior knowledge of the language or customs, actions that will mean you don't require considerable introduction to become fully functional.
Many voluntourists often don't get past this stage, requiring constant mediation and supervision from locals.
Research ethical volunteering options thoroughly:
Look at the organization's past history and impact. Ensure it meets the checks and balances to be legitimate.
Don't undermine local autonomy. Why fly in foreign helpers when it would serve communities far better in the long run to train locals (often in need of jobs) to perform tasks?
Look beyond the limited context of your stay in the host country ...
THINGS ARE LIKE THAT 2012-20
... to break down the exoticized divisions between ourselves and others
... and ensure that the goodwi doesn't end when you leave.
Things don't have to be like that.

LIST OF NGOS ACTIVE IN NEPAL YOU CAN CONTRIBUTE TO:

Anti-Slavery International

Center for Awareness Promotion

Change Nepal

Child Development Society

Child Workers in Nepal

Circus Kathmandu

Early Childhood Development Center

ECPAT

Friends of Needy Children

Himalayan Human Rights Monitor

International Organization for Migration

Maiti Nepal

Nepal Youth Foundation

Next Generation Nepal

People's Forum for Human Rights/National Network for Safe Migration

Plan International

Planète des Enfants

Pourahki

Shakti Samuha

The Asia Foundation

The Didi Project

UN Women

Voice of Children

World Education

KEY CONTRIBUTORS FEATURED IN THIS BOOK

With such a vast scope, a project like this would have been impossible without the expertise and generosity of colleagues in the field. The list below is not exhaustive and some may no longer be affiliated with the organization.

Madhu Acharya,
Antenna Foundation — 1

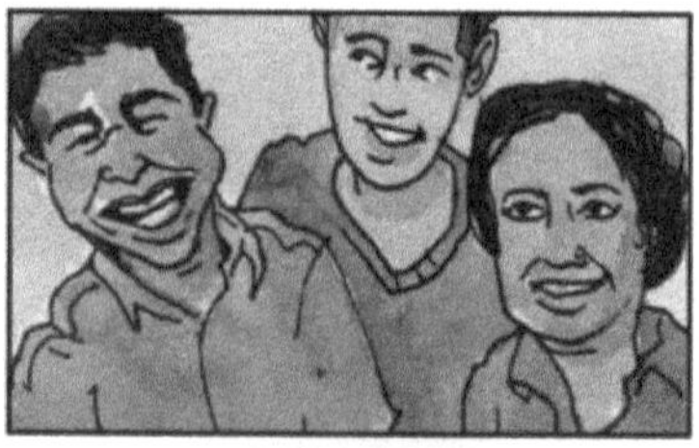

Jaya Luintel,
Storykitchen — 1

Pushpa Basnet,
ECDC — 1, 2, 13

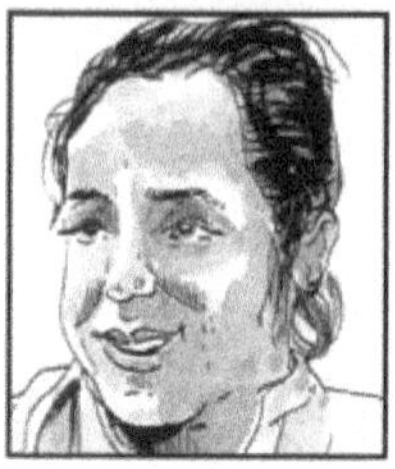

Helen Sherpa,
World Education — 1, 5

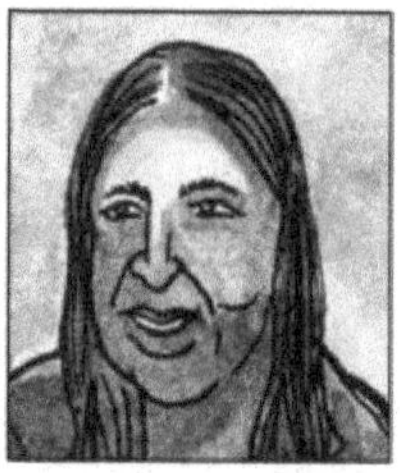

Dr Sunil Joshi — 5

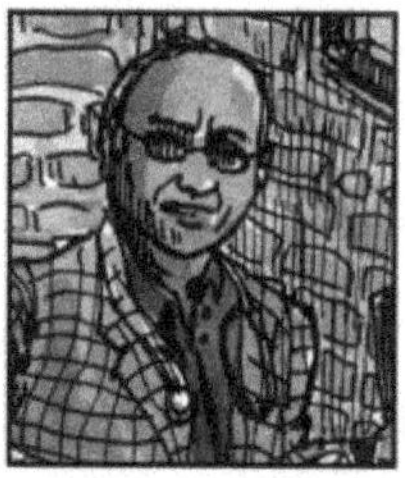

Pramesh Pradham and Sabina,
Change Nepal — 1, 10, 13

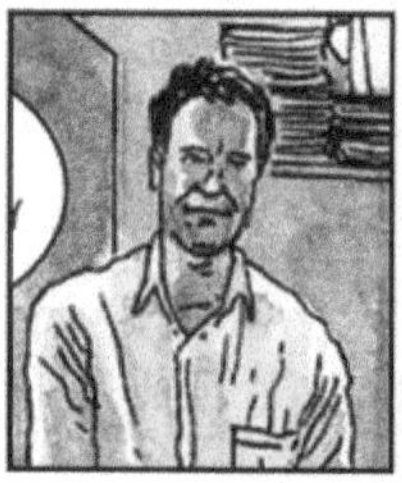

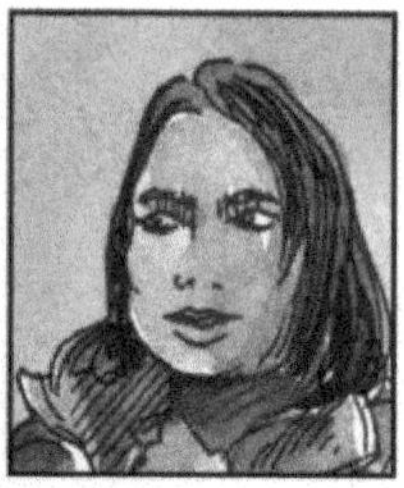

Youraj Roka,
Child Development Society — 1, 5, 12

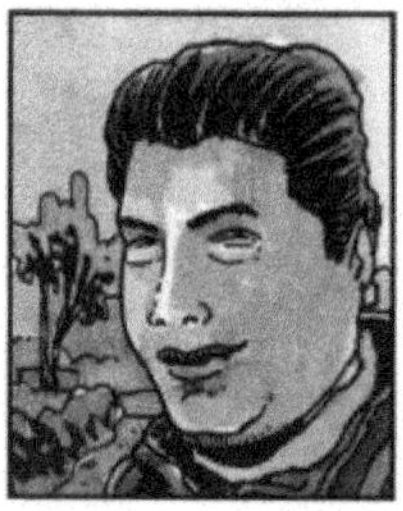

Charimaya Tamang,
Shakti Samuha

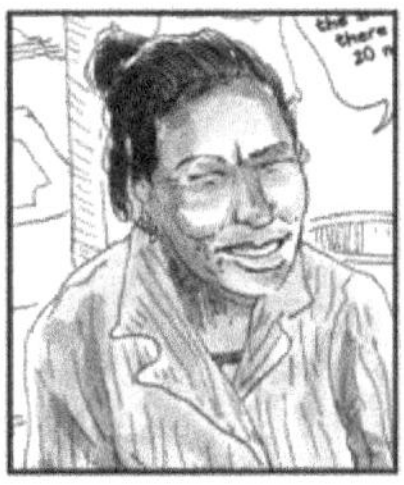

1

The Didis:
Joyce, Heidi, and Leslie

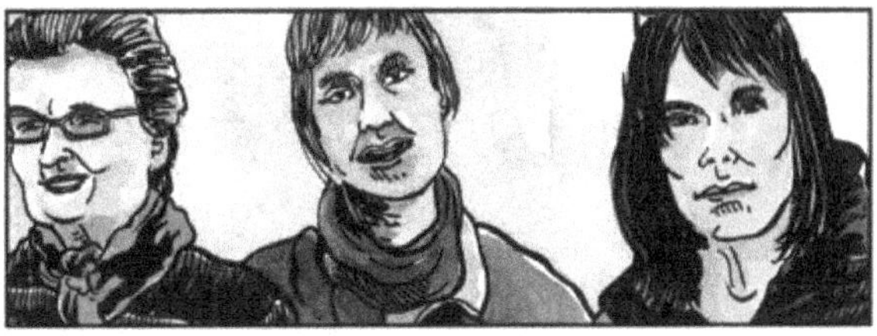

3, 4

Som Paneru,
Nepali Youth Foundation

6, 7

Man Bahadur Chettri,
Friends of Needy Children

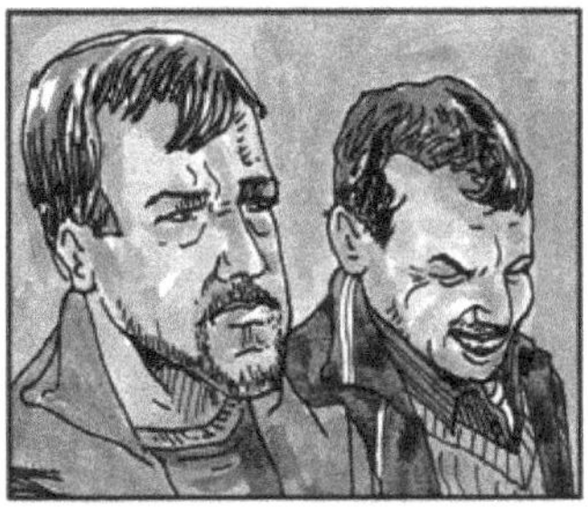

6, 7

Anuradha Koirala,
Mayasuri Bhatt,
Maiti Nepal

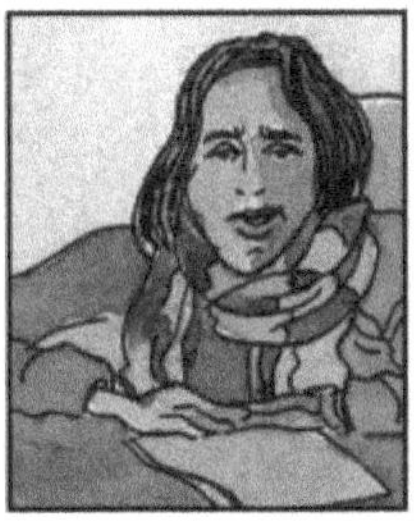

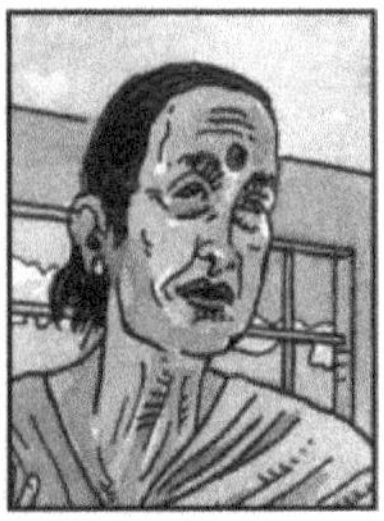

8, 13

Deepa Limbu Subba, ECPAT

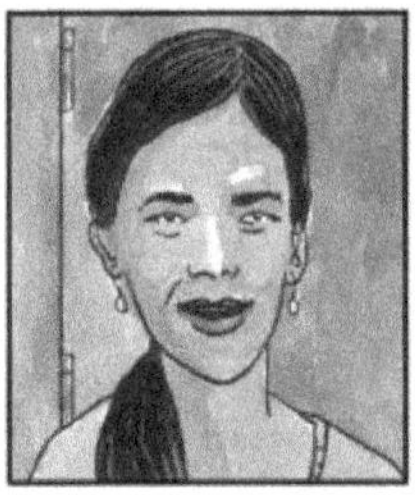

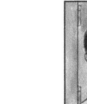

11

Martin Punaks, Next Generation Nepal

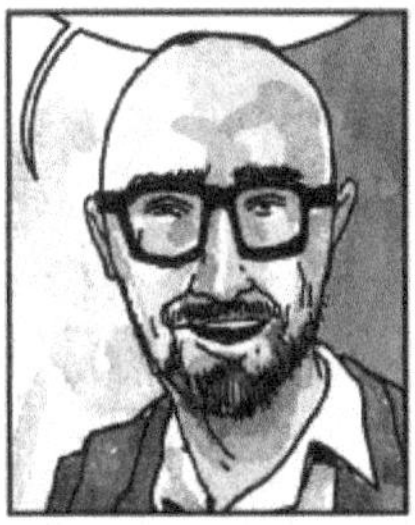

15

With special thanks to
Cecilia Mo,
Margaret Boittin,
Sarah Rich-Zendel,
HTV Team

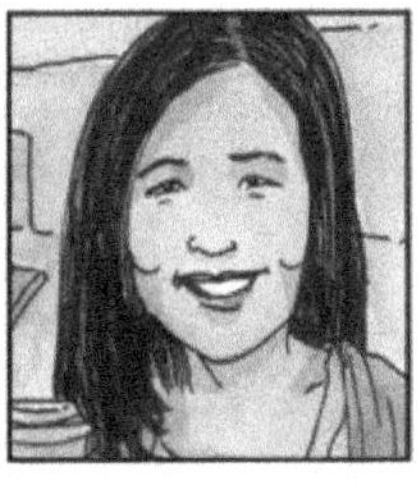

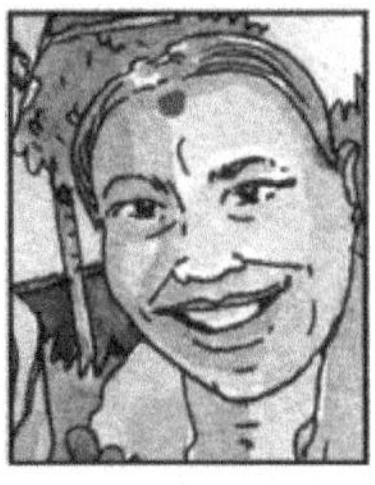

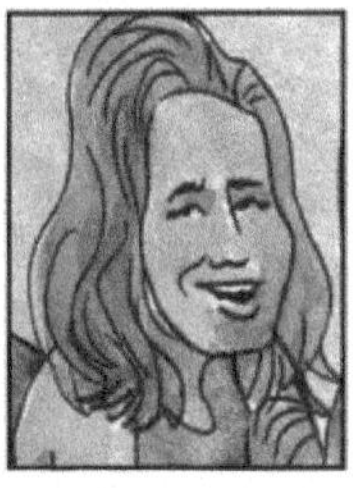

0, 9, 13, 14, 15

A long overdue THANK YOU to the original Kickstarters of this project. Witho
your help, I wouldn't have got this off the ground. Thank you for your patienc

Sarah Stein Greenberg
Dave Baxter
Craig Warner
Brett Schenker
Olga Trusova
John Melas-Kyriazi
Wilson Lievano
Dan Lehner
Adriana Garcia Martinez
Linda Decelle
Katie Smith
Jessi Hersey
Raman Singh
Carolyn Purvis
Spiros Polikandriotis
Nikil Saval
kamikazetruths
CJ Joughin
Stephen Bissette
Aaron Churchill
Matt Bors
Adriano Farano
John Bracken
Andrew Donohue
Susan Hanes
Anna Shields
Giles Wilson
Jill B
Elizabeth Kay de Keyser
Sebastian Esser
Sumoslap
Dushan Yovovich
Linda Tam
Joshua Lipay
Saffron Scott
Graham Archer

Jonathan Campbell
Francoise Frigola
Adam Nelson
Di Pinheiro
Erin Polgreen
Daniel Steinbock
Caroline Dijckmeester-Bins
Jeanette Haenseroth
Jessie Labov
Thomas Estler
Cindy Nakano
Fahd Butt
Nathan Edwards
pistik
Ricardo Cortes
Spencer Toyama
Borin Pin
Ryan Meyers
Nathan Glaesemann
Soham Dhakal
Patrick Davidson
JJ
Chris McLaren
Kyle
Asle Ysteb
Karen Green
Annie Sedwick
Michael V. Marcotte
Ruth
Gavin Anthony Simmons McCullum
Henry Barajas
Hillary Lauren
Jeff
Jorit Bookheim
Monica Sack
Caleb Anderson
Grace Griffin

Jodie Archer
Beth Duff-Brown
Michael & Susan Archer
Andrea
Simon Vivian
Antony Kaslatter
Mark Kaslatter
Dan Carino
Wendy Norris
Christine Kaslatter
Jigar Mehta
Emma and Alex Telford
Sarah Kovacs
Jane Reeder
Jose Medina
Alec Longstreth
Cindy Liou
Daniel Cooney
Melodie Wong
Olivia Adderley
Alison Lavery
Matthew Bahls
Leef Smith
Ronjan Sikdar
Paddy Hirsch
Simo Muinonen
James Leek
Chris Thinnes
Peter Walter
David Axe
David Liu
Michael Zimmerman
Claudia andersen
Clayton Tuttle
Brad LaBriola
Djurdja Padejski
Sara Zimmerman

Kristian Claus	Geri Migielicz	Steve, Marie & Emma Capps
Mikey McManus	Lila LaHood	My extremely patient patreons:
Sirn Lloyd-Wiggins	Hugo Rupert	Jason Das
Benjamin Wachtel	Jonah Willihnganz	Christopher Lin
Sterling Daniels	Sid Espinosa	Marek Bennett
Mark Smallwood	Margaret Lewisohn	Andrew Losowsky
Daniel Gintner	Chris Beck	
Hanna Sistek	Christine P. Wu	With special thanks to the
Sally Bowers	Lisa Melas-Kyriazi	University of Toronto Press team:
Stephen Zimmerman	David Tyler	
John Haugeland	Gus D	Carli Hansen for shepherding the
MaxPower 2U	Daniele Archambault	book into its final finished form,
Da Kof	horizonfactory	Sherine Hamdy for getting the
Carl Andrew Warren	Adam Johnson	ball rolling, and Perrin Lindelauf
Eric Damon Walters	Jeanne O'Connell	for his eye for detail ...

First and foremost, I am extremely grateful to everyone featured in this book: the human rights defenders, survivors, NGO founders, activists, translators, fixers, and frontline workers toiling away in the trenches every day to make a difference. Special thanks to my fellow Human Trafficking Vulnerability Project members, who spent countless hours/days/weeks over the years with me both in the field and on video calls: Cecilia Mo, Margaret Boittin, Sarah Rich-Zendel, and the rest of the HTV team: Dhana Hamal, Shivani Palikhe, Priti Shrestha, Siddharta Baral. The support of Catherine Chen at Humanity United and the dozens of staffers at USAID's Department of Labor was also critical to ensuring the HTV Project's success. Thank you to James Sturm, Jason Lutes, Michelle Ollie, and Steve Bissette at the Center for Cartoon Studies; Adam Johnson, Dawn Garcia, and Jim Bettinger at Stanford University; Matt Bors et al. at the Nib; Michael Stoll and Lila LaHood at SF Public Press; and Paul Buhle, Jodie Archer, Matt Bahls, Joe Sacco, and Paul Keyte for their encouragement early on. Cheers to fellow ink slingers/writers Nick Abadzis, Josh Neufeld, Christian Clark, and Stephen Whitehead for their read-throughs and encouraging feedback. To Mum, Dad, Sophie, Mark, Stuart, Jo, and Stephen – here's hoping this clarifies what I've been working on all this time! Much love to all the Archer, Carvalho, Koehler, and Zimmerman clans too.

The HTV Project has since been adapted to Hong Kong, where we've been using animations to monitor awareness of the precarious (and often exploitative) labor conditions facing domestic migrant workers. I will be forever grateful to HTV for leading me to Raquel, a fearless human rights journalist whose love, patience, and support has meant the world to me as I wrapped up this epic project.

For more updates, check out @archcomix on IG/X, or visit www.archcomix.com.
In solidarity,
Dan Archer
May 2024.

WHAT IS GRAPHIC JOURNALISM?

Let's start with the basics: Comics or graphic journalism is an umbrella term that covers any approach to reporting that combines words and images in sequential panels, as opposed to the conventional model – text with separate illustrations (usually photos). The following pages present an introduction to comics journalism – in the form of comics journalism – from over a decade ago that still holds true today.

The main difference between comics journalism and conventional, text-based journalism is that stories are filed as a few pages of artwork with text inside speech balloons or captions. They are not comic strips – three or four panels with a punch line at the end, such as *Garfield* or *Doonesbury*. They are not single-panel editorial cartoons, such as those syndicated in opinion pages, which use symbolic or reductive imagery to provoke debate or elicit a response. They are not intrinsically "comic" or funny.

Within graphic journalism and the larger umbrella of graphic nonfiction there are different offshoots, such as (and this is not an exhaustive list):

- **Illustrated reportage:** sketches done in the field at an event or during an interview (often where the use of a camera is intrusive or inappropriate) that are directly scanned and filed to cover a faster breaking story or provide more of an immediate feel for a situation on the ground.
- **Investigative:** long-form feature articles comprising several pages or entire graphic novels that introduce a topic and include interviews, on-the-ground reporting, and some degree of comment or opinion.
- **Explainers:** illustrated guides to complex topics, such as the financial crisis or the conflict in Syria. These essentially condense a large amount of information into only a few pages – and often are written from a third-person perspective with multiple talking heads.
- **Graphic memoir:** nonfiction (often autobiographical) comics that explore a particular subject matter from the protagonist's point of view, often focusing on a particular historical period or event.
- **Graphic histories:** similar to extended explainers, these book-length works try to explain complex historical events from a third-person perspective, like a drawn documentary.
- **Graphic ethnographies:** comics based on the field research of anthropologists, sociologists, and other social scientists, often created in collaboration with one or more members of the community where the research took place.

Some stories certainly lend themselves better to the medium than others. I personally try to avoid "talking heads," which are essentially direct dialogue with superfluous illustrations. In those cases, bringing in the visual doesn't add much to the reader's experience. But I believe that even a few hand-drawn sketches of an event can capture a situation in a more immediate, impactful way than photos can. I also tend to shy away from the "explainer" type of comics journalism these days for the simple reason that I think too often comics are associated with the requisite process of simplification – plus I prefer to work in the field. I often see comics as a way of being an indie filmmaker on a shoestring budget, since I'm the self-appointed cameraman, director, set designer, and editor. Using illustrated (and, occasionally, animated) visuals, I can enter into storytelling territory that

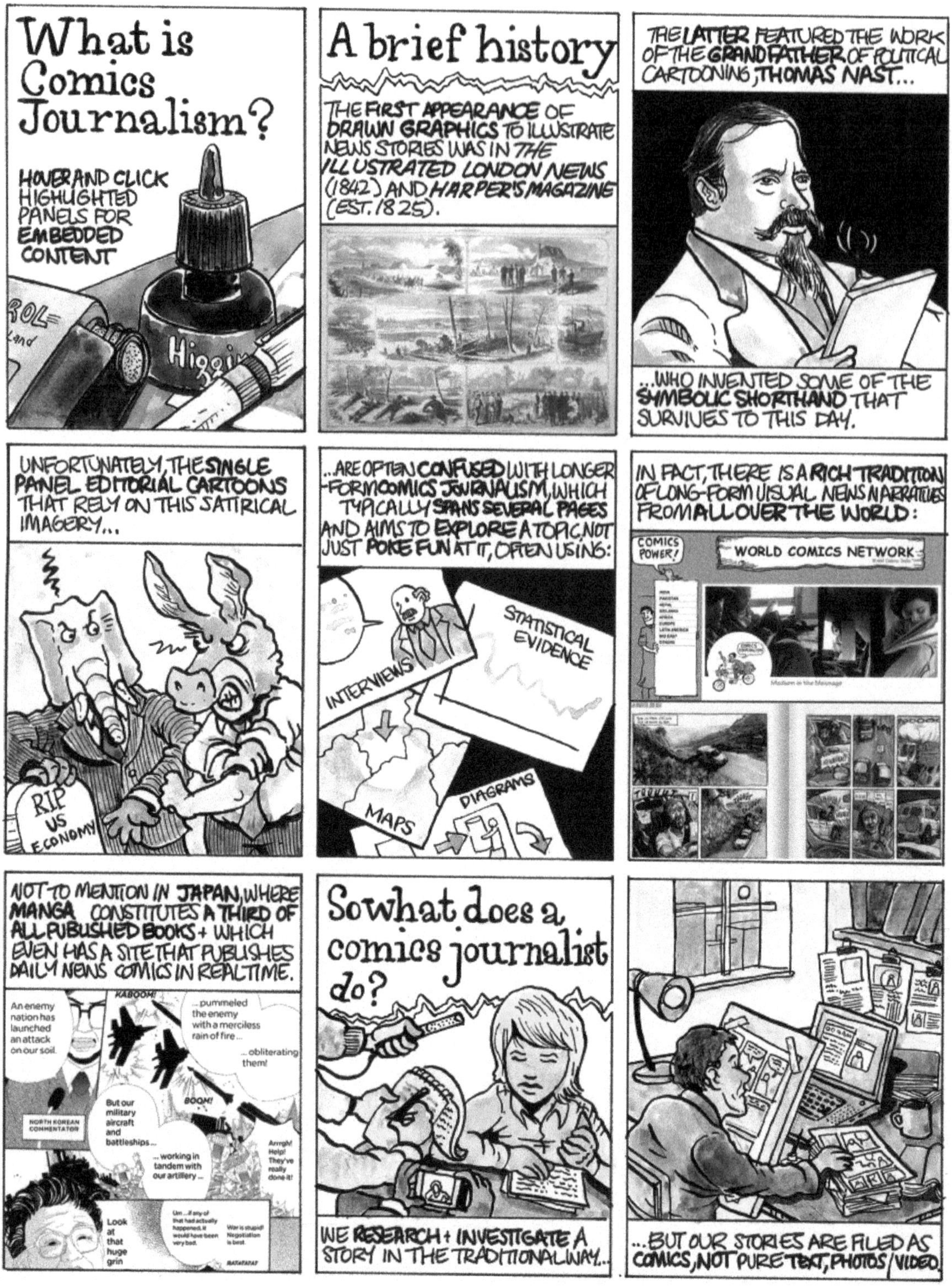
What is Comics Journalism?
HOVER AND CLICK HIGHLIGHTED PANELS FOR EMBEDDED CONTENT
Higgins
A brief history
THE FIRST APPEARANCE OF DRAWN GRAPHICS TO ILLUSTRATE NEWS STORIES WAS IN THE ILLUSTRATED LONDON NEWS (1842) AND HARPER'S MAGAZINE (EST. 1825).
THE LATTER FEATURED THE WORK OF THE GRANDFATHER OF POLITICAL CARTOONING, THOMAS NAST...
...WHO INVENTED SOME OF THE SYMBOLIC SHORTHAND THAT SURVIVES TO THIS DAY.
UNFORTUNATELY, THE SINGLE PANEL EDITORIAL CARTOONS THAT RELY ON THIS SATIRICAL IMAGERY...
RIP US ECONOMY
...ARE OFTEN CONFUSED WITH LONGER-FORM COMICS JOURNALISM, WHICH TYPICALLY SPANS SEVERAL PAGES AND AIMS TO EXPLORE A TOPIC, NOT JUST POKE FUN AT IT, OFTEN USING:
INTERVIEWS
STATISTICAL EVIDENCE
MAPS
DIAGRAMS
IN FACT, THERE IS A RICH TRADITION OF LONG-FORM VISUAL NEWS NARRATIVES FROM ALL OVER THE WORLD:
COMICS POWER!
WORLD COMICS NETWORK
NOT TO MENTION IN JAPAN, WHERE MANGA CONSTITUTES A THIRD OF ALL PUBLISHED BOOKS + WHICH EVEN HAS A SITE THAT PUBLISHES DAILY NEWS COMICS IN REALTIME.
An enemy nation has launched an attack on our soil.
NORTH KOREAN COMMENTATOR
KABOOM!
...pummeled the enemy with a merciless rain of fire...
... obliterating them!
BOOM!
But our military aircraft and battleships...
... working in tandem with our artillery...
Arrrgh! Help! They've really done it!
Look at that huge grin
Um ... if any of that had actually happened, it would have been very bad.
War is stupid! Negotiation is best.
RATATATAT
So what does a comics journalist do?
WE RESEARCH + INVESTIGATE A STORY IN THE TRADITIONAL WAY...
...BUT OUR STORIES ARE FILED AS COMICS, NOT PURE TEXT, PHOTOS / VIDEO.

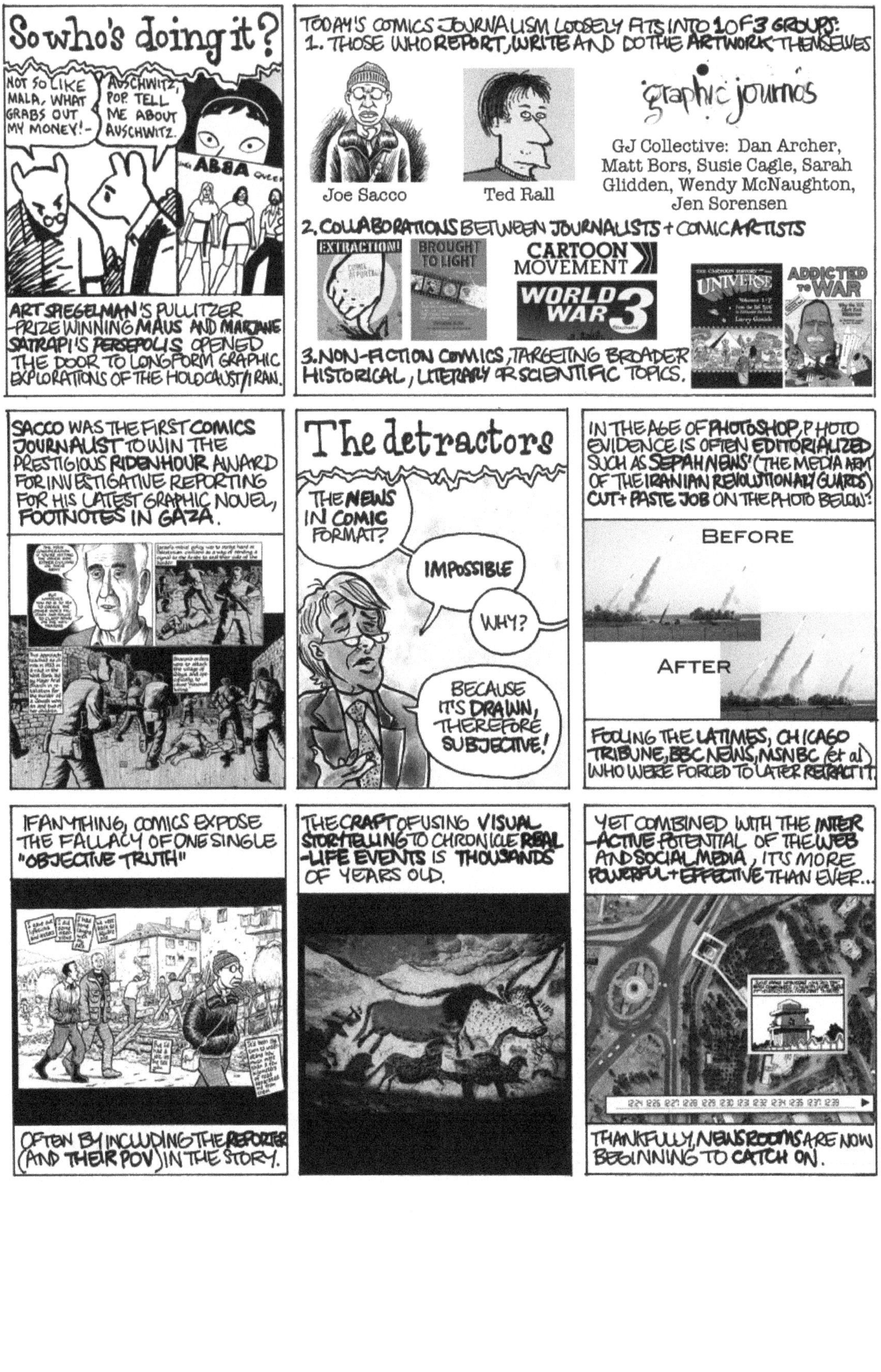
So who's doing it?
NOT SO LIKE MALA, WHAT GRABS OUT MY MONEY!-
AUSCHWITZ, POP. TELL ME ABOUT AUSCHWITZ.
ABBA
ART SPIEGELMAN'S PULLITZER-PRIZE WINNING MAUS AND MARJANE SATRAPI'S PERSEPOLIS OPENED THE DOOR TO LONGFORM GRAPHIC EXPLORATIONS OF THE HOLOCAUST/IRAN.
TODAY'S COMICS JOURNALISM LOOSELY FITS INTO 1 OF 3 GROUPS:
1. THOSE WHO REPORT, WRITE AND DO THE ARTWORK THEMSELVES
Joe Sacco
Ted Rall
graphic journos
GJ Collective: Dan Archer, Matt Bors, Susie Cagle, Sarah Glidden, Wendy McNaughton, Jen Sorensen
2. COLLABORATIONS BETWEEN JOURNALISTS + COMIC ARTISTS
EXTRACTION!
BROUGHT TO LIGHT
CARTOON MOVEMENT
WORLD WAR 3
3. NON-FICTION COMICS, TARGETING BROADER HISTORICAL, LITERARY OR SCIENTIFIC TOPICS.
UNIVERSE
ADDICTED TO WAR
SACCO WAS THE FIRST COMICS JOURNALIST TO WIN THE PRESTIGIOUS RIDENHOUR AWARD FOR INVESTIGATIVE REPORTING FOR HIS LATEST GRAPHIC NOVEL, FOOTNOTES IN GAZA.
The detractors
THE NEWS IN COMIC FORMAT?
IMPOSSIBLE
WHY?
BECAUSE IT'S DRAWN, THEREFORE SUBJECTIVE!
IN THE AGE OF PHOTOSHOP, PHOTO EVIDENCE IS OFTEN EDITORIALIZED SUCH AS SEPAH NEWS' (THE MEDIA ARM OF THE IRANIAN REVOLUTIONARY GUARDS) CUT + PASTE JOB ON THE PHOTO BELOW:
BEFORE
AFTER
FOOLING THE LA TIMES, CHICAGO TRIBUNE, BBC NEWS, MSNBC (et al) WHO WERE FORCED TO LATER RETRACT IT.
IF ANYTHING, COMICS EXPOSE THE FALLACY OF ONE SINGLE "OBJECTIVE TRUTH"
OFTEN BY INCLUDING THE REPORTER (AND THEIR POV) IN THE STORY.
THE CRAFT OF USING VISUAL STORYTELLING TO CHRONICLE REAL-LIFE EVENTS IS THOUSANDS OF YEARS OLD.
YET COMBINED WITH THE INTER-ACTIVE POTENTIAL OF THE WEB AND SOCIAL MEDIA, IT'S MORE POWERFUL + EFFECTIVE THAN EVER...
THANKFULLY, NEWSROOMS ARE NOW BEGINNING TO CATCH ON.

otherwise might be deemed unpalatable or unsuitable, or broach subjects that might prove too much for audiences in a photo or video format.

The main challenge is tying a journalistically rigorous story to a visual narrative thread that combines a compelling narrative with a pleasing aesthetic. At the end of the day, the goal is to give the reader a unique reading experience while simultaneously moving, informing, and engaging them in equal share. Through my work I hope to draw readers to subjects that they might overlook if the same stories were presented in text alone. The same goes for the devices and techniques of visual storytelling: as opposed to video or photojournalism, comics journalists can give the reader a first-person perspective by putting them in their shoes at the events that they are reporting on, similar to the recent trend of "found footage films," but, importantly, unmediated by a camera. To use the words of Joe Sacco (arguably the preeminent graphic journalist), "prose writers can be very evocative … but I find there is nothing like thrusting someone right there. And that's what I think a cartoonist can do."[1]

This is especially important in the context of human trafficking, where all too often the survivors are shown as the third-person "other" – typically young girls from Asia or Eastern Europe with their eyes blacked out by superimposed rectangles or shown through grainy night vision photography. I wanted to present their experience while respecting their dignity and not resorting to any of those same visual clichés. Danish development expert Jorgen Lessner referred to this nefarious practice in the context of charity drives by NGOs working in Africa over forty years ago:

> The starving child image is seen as unethical, firstly because it comes dangerously close to being pornographic. In my definition, pornography is the exhibition of the human body and soul in all its nakedness, without any respect and piety for the person involved. The public display of an African child with a bloated kwashiorkor-ridden stomach in advertisements is pornographic because it exposes something in human life that is as delicate and deeply personal as sexuality, that is, suffering. It puts people's bodies, their misery, their grief and their fear on display with all the details and all the indiscretion that a telescopic lens will allow.
>
> It is very telling that this type of social pornography is so prevalent in fundraising campaigns for the benefit of other races in far-away places but virtually non-existent when it comes to domestic concerns. I can recall few examples of pornographic advertisements and posters designed to raise money for disadvantaged people in Western countries.[2]

Although the context is clearly different, the critique is identical: it is paramount that we protect and respect those whose stories we are helping to share, without exploiting their vulnerability or removing their sense of agency. These repeated victimizing visual motifs will only serve to ingrain a reductive, disempowered perception of the very people we're trying to help, regardless of our best intentions.

What follows is an overview of my production process, from live sketch in the field to finished printed comics page. I'll cover the reasons I use live sketching as my starting point, the advantages and disadvantages, as well as how I integrate it into the end comic.

---

1 Adam Rosenblatt and Andrea A. Lunsford, "Critique, Caricature, and Compulsion in Joe Sacco's Comics Journalism," in *The Rise of the American Comics Journalist*, ed. Paul Williams and James Lyons (Jackson: University Press of Mississippi, 2010), 68–88.

2 Jorgen Lissner, "Merchants of Misery," *New Internationalist*, June 1, 1981, https://newint.org/features /1981/06/01/merchants-of-misery.

The Theory

First and foremost, the act of illustrated reportage is centered around building trust with someone whom, in most cases, you're meeting face-to-face for the first time. In what is usually an awkward moment when you're sizing each other up, I show my interviewees how they'll be represented, often beginning with leafing through my current sketchbook and showing them examples. It's a way of breaking the ice and establishing trust, as they can see how they'll be represented when I flip my sketchbook around and show them directly. In group situations, which can be even more sensitive, and in which suspicion easily spreads, I can approach a group of people with my sketchbook and overcome the barriers of language and skin color by tapping into the universal visual language of comics. Often this has a domino effect: once one person sees it, the rest want their likeness drawn too.

In terms of how the power of live sketching does this, I think there are many different mechanisms at work. From my perspective, I agree with the illustrated reportage practitioners Embury and Minichiello about drawing being both a "thinking and a physical process." This allows the artist to be selective, whereas the "point and shoot" nature of the camera captures everything and has to be edited at a later stage. By contrast, the artist selects what to draw as they draw. This has the effect of steering the viewer's attention to the crux of the story.[3]

The shape of the story coalesces organically as I pull significant quotes out during the interview, and the conversation crystallizes into a constellation of speech balloons around the visual fulcrum of the interviewee's portrait, which often sits in the middle of the page. It's sort of like analog atomic thinking, whereby different comments and thoughts can be linked or bridged to other related comments. This helps me to organize my thoughts on the fly, giving me a working overview of the story as it comes together in real-time, allowing me to change my line of questioning accordingly. I'll use bold for emphasis or add jagged edges to a balloon for emotional effect or a heightened sense of tone. This state of parsing all the available information in real-time (visual, audio, verbal, gestural) is similar to what Lunsford and Rosenblatt describe in Joe Sacco's work as a new paradigm for listening as part of the reporting process that is inherent to comics journalism,[4] a paradigm that "uses the unique properties of the comics medium, to fashion a model of listening that suits [Sacco's] ethos as a reporter, storyteller and humanist."

In my experience, people in a journalistic context rarely want to be on camera from the outset and require some convincing to pose for a photograph. A camera can break the fragile bond you establish with a stranger, as can any form of recording equipment – interrupting the sense of trust you might have established that put someone at ease – and immediately puts people on guard, a conspicuous reminder that their words have a permanency that will outlive the current conversation. Visually, this broken trust was embodied by the black rectangles or blurred faces stamped over the eyes of photo subjects – a graphic othering. It's also the difference between the smiling posed photo face that people instinctively make when facing a camera and the more natural way they react to you during a conversation.

---

3 Gary Embury and Mario Minichiello, *Reportage Illustration: Visual Journalism* (London: Bloomsbury, 2018).

4 Andrea A. Lunsford and Adam Rosenblatt, "'Down a Road and into an Awful Silence': Graphic Listening in Joe Sacco's Comics Journalism," in *Silence and Listening as Rhetorical Arts*, ed. Cheryl Glenn and Krista Ratcliffe (Carbondale: Southern Illinois University Press, 2011), 130–46.

People recognize photographic equipment (or smartphones) these days. As a graphic journalist, you pose less of a threat: you can pass under the radar with just a sketchbook, as typically people in positions of power discount drawing as a reporting tool. This was true when I was a court sketcher in London's Old Bailey and also a press visitor to the demilitarized zone between North and South Korea, both contexts where photography is prohibited.

In the age of the machine, the hand-drawn image still holds some currency – but only because people routinely underestimate it. By breaking from the "truth" of photographic representation, we can actually access a point of view that is more subjective but also more honest and transparent. My perspective on reality is obviously filtered by a drawing ability that is unmistakably mine – but that's what makes it stand out above the noise of cell phones and citizen journalism. The veracity of the photographic image is going through a crisis right now, having first braved the choppy waters of Photoshop and manual manipulation as in the case of the polemic surrounding Paul Hansen's photo, which won the World Press Photo of the Year Award[5] a decade ago but was found to have been manipulated for better lighting and composition, or other instances when footage from protests or armed conflicts has been misattributed to the wrong region. Now, the greater danger is that entire photos can be generated and refined from scratch, thanks to Artificial Intelligence (AI) technology and Large Language Model–based algorithms that create photorealistic imagery from written prompts using software such as Midjourney or DALL-E. Seeing is no longer believing, but images still carry more weight than words. Audiences now not only need to be on their guard against manipulated imagery but also against their innate bias toward believing fake news when it is accompanied by a (seemingly) innocuous photograph.[6] In this post-truth (Oxford Dictionary's 2016 word of the year) hinterland of AI images, Photoshop, miscaptioned imagery, and deep fakes, at least a live-sketched drawing holds itself up and admits it has literally been manipulated (albeit offline).

Employing a similar technique to Joe Sacco's self-portraits in his early work as a cartoonish figure of fun, or what Kate Evans describes as "making myself the butt of the joke, because … the bumbling white Western do-gooder deserves to be laughed at,"[7] the sketchbook works as a mirror of sorts: to those who don't take the time to look closely, they see only an adult sketching or taking notes in a notebook, an incongruous hobbyist. But to those who take the time to flip through the pages – though very few people ever do – the purpose and information contained in a single "sketch" is self-evident. The same was true in the brick kilns I visited with Youraj: in the context of a kiln, a camera would have been yet another signifier of my otherness, both racially, as another snap-happy *bideshi* (foreigner), and economically (as the device itself would have meant literally decades of work for the kiln workers). The tools of pen and paper are more accessible and democratic. You can also be more discrete, not attracting attention when recording events, people, or images in a way that a camera would immediately flag your intentions to external observers.

5 Ian Steadman, "'Fake' World Press Photo Isn't Fake, Is Lesson in Need for Forensic Restraint," *Wired*, May 16, 2013, https://www.wired.co.uk/article/photo-faking-controversy.

6 https://www.abc.net.au/news/2018-11-22/fake-news-image-information-believe-anu/10517346.

7 Dominic Davies, "Comics Activism: An Interview with Comics Artist and Activist Kate Evans," *Journal of Comics Scholarship* 7, no. 1 (2017): 18. https://openaccess.city.ac.uk/id/eprint/20305/1/114-1254-1-PB.pdf.

The Practice

Enough with the theory – let's talk about practice. I usually start with the eyes of my subject and build out from the face to the body, working directly in ink as underdrawing in pencil would take too much time, and I'm constantly moving from drawing to quote-writing when natural breaks in the conversation occur. As I flesh out the torso, I'll decide on the most dominant gesture, trying to capture the paralinguistic personality of my subject. Are they withdrawn, shy, or more garrulous and dominant? I'll work from multiple angles if possible as this will give me more flexibility and better references to work from when I create a full-color comic. I'll be always thinking about pulling out the key quotes and organizing them spatially by topic around the page. I'll also zoom in on specific details, such as hand gestures, jewelry, or particular features of their clothing. I include inset blueprint sketches of locations they describe – how many rooms there were, how large the space was, what they could see – that will serve me later if I need to do any visual reconstructions. See below for an example sketch I made on the fly while interviewing a cabin restaurant worker. I'll ask them to think about what they were wearing at the time, as well as any other sensory information – the weather, the smell, the light – that can help to trigger additional memories. The same goes for other people they mention – I'll ask for a brief description to build a quick facial composite on the fly, though in my experience, these tend to always skew toward "the average": average build, average height, average weight, etc. As I work, I'll try to capture mannerisms, tics, gestures, and expressions, not dissimilar to animated keyframes.

Thumbnailing

Once I have the sketched image, like the scanned page of Mohan in the prologue, I'll break down the content of what the subject said into a chronological order, sorting by place names, and iron out any details in the story. I'll look for thematic links between sections, as well as find any holes that might need filling in with the help of follow-up questions. Then, the next key factor to consider before moving onto thumbnails is how many pages I have to tell the story. As I mention in the commentary related to the format constraints for the BBC piece, the size of the panels and the page format will dictate how much creative freedom I have when it comes to decisions like splash panels, inset panels, and breaking up the formal structure of the tier-by-tier format. You can see this directly in Laxmi's story in chapter 3 – and how I gave the non-BBC panels more space to breathe after the first half of her story, when the page assignment wasn't an issue.

For example, I made more creative choices with the composition on p. 49 and in my adaptation of a passage from Patricia McCormick's *SOLD*, which you can see the corresponding thumbnail of on p. 18. The act of thumbnailing is similar to putting a puzzle together: you have all the different pieces, with the key captions and images, and you just have to find a way to fit them together that accentuates the narrative beats that you want. This approach was drilled into me at the Center for Cartoon Studies (CCS) when I was assigned David Mamet's *On Directing Film* in my first year, which heavily emphasized the reductive scale of a taut feature narrative: "The unit with which the director most wants to concern himself is the scene … make the beats serve the scene, and the scene will be done; make the scenes, in the same way, the building blocks of film, and the film will be done." Similar to the much-abused mantra "show, don't tell" that warns off script writers from relying too heavily on verbal exposition (something that Mamet rails against), the key in comics is the push and pull between words and pictures, so that the combination of the two produces an end effect that is more than the sum of its parts. This is neither prose writing nor illustration.

Thumbnailing for external editorial scrutiny and approval is very different to thumbnailing pages that only I will see. The examples I show on p. 166 correspond to the comics pages on pp. 127–9 and pp. 94–6 respectively – you can see the layout, as well as the numeric captions, which accompany the chunks of text that will fit into each panel. Often I will combine a photo of the thumbnail and the accompanying text in a collaborative Google doc so that the editor and I can make any necessary changes in real-time, although as you can see on the script screenshot on p. 165, sometimes team members prefer to use the track changes feature in Word. I'll make notes to myself on the thumbnailed pages (as you can see on the last page on p. 166) when the size of the panel doesn't allow enough room for showing specific details like emotions or clothing. You can also make out the changes I've made to the pages on the middle tier, altering the panel order, as well as redrawing the final panel in the second thumbnailed page. The whole point of the thumbnails being rough and basic is precisely so you don't grow too attached to them and can confidently rework the order or layout to best suit the story if the flow is off, something that would be much harder to do if you had already invested hours in penciling the layout.

DRAWING AND INKING

Speaking of which, while I may have begun this book by starting every page with a penciled underdrawing, I soon moved to drawing my pages directly in ink in order to speed up the production time. I think this indirectly helped my ability to live-sketch on the fly since I was much more prepared to work with mistakes and try to fix them in real-time, instead of laboring over erasing and redrawing the perfect line until I got it just right. Personally I think this also gives the pages – and my line – a bit more dynamism and personality. For the first handful of years as a cartoonist I was wed to the ritualized approach of penciled underdrawings, then India ink with long sable brushes and crow quill nibs (the Hunt 102 and 106 being my favorites, as I never really got the hang of the much-lauded G-nib that cartoonists like Gabby Schulz[8] expertly use) before finishing off final details with micron pens (0.2–0.3), but on assignments with tight turnarounds I found this process too laborious. My mentor at CCS, Jason Lutes,[9] used the Rotring pens for a very clean, uniform *ligne clair* style, and I used the Extra Fine nib for a short while, before finding that it was prone to clogging and didn't offer very much flexibility when it came to line width. Instead, I settled on the Carbon pen, which had the flexibility and portability of a fountain pen, but a fine enough nib that it responded nicely to pressure to give the line a bit of variety (you can make out its signature tail in the last panel of p. 165, along with a micron pen). Its designers cunningly included a ball bearing inside each cartridge to ensure the ink doesn't dry out and clog up the pen. I usually then reinforced the thickest lines with the long-standing cartoonist brush pen of choice, the Pentel pocket brush pen.

[WATER] COLORING

The challenge with inking directly was doubled when it came to applying watercolors, which I chose to incorporate to fit better with the watercolors I use on my live sketches (time willing). One major hurdle I soon discovered was that watercoloring directly on top of my inked pages meant that I couldn't use any white out or manual corrections on the page, since the watercolor wash wouldn't take on those treated areas. Unbelievably, I thought that water coloring would be the fastest way of applying color, since I usually used a water-reservoir pen filled with water and a portable artist's palette to throw down a base layer, then build up highlights and shadows. In my defense, I wanted to cut down on my screen time as much as possible, not only since applying color in Photoshop (as seen on pp. 145–54, with thanks to Anton Magdalin for his amazing digital coloring touch-up skills) can leave you lost in the black hole of never-ending layer effects and undo buttons, but also because the power supply in Nepal was not always consistent and load shedding (when different parts of the power grid were shut down to put less strain on the system) occurred daily.

I recognize that in terms of production value, separating my blacks and lightboxing my water-colors on a different page would have been preferable, but I chose to keep things all on the same page for convenience: first and foremost, I only brought so many blank pages with me to Nepal, so doubling up meant I used half the amount; second, it helped me to see (and display, like at the gallery showing at Image Ark on p. 144) the pages in their entirety and gave me a more tangible sense of where I was in terms of completion; and last, it made the process of scanning my pages far easier. Since I was obviously unable to bring a scanner with me, I struck up a friendship with the printing/passport photo/office supply shops on the Yala Saldak Road in Jhamsikhel and would visit on a weekly basis with my armful of pages to scan to a USB stick. Page 174 is a direct scan of what those watercolor pages looked like.

---

8 Author of *Monsters*, *Sick*, and *Welcome to the Dahl House* among others – largely works of graphic memoir.
9 Author of the incredible, prize-winning *Berlin* graphic novel series.

Post-Production and Lettering

The last part, once I had high-res TIFF scans of my watercolor pages, was to adjust the image settings and complete any touch-ups in Photoshop before adding text in InDesign. The beauty of lettering – and adding the speech balloons – digitally was the far greater freedom when it came to adding translated versions and edits later on down the line. Earlier on in my career I did everything by hand, using an Ames lettering tool and hand lettering on my drawing board with a T-square, but it was infinitely faster to create a couple of hand lettered digital fonts to mimic my handwriting throughout and apply the text in InDesign. The same was true of the speech balloons themselves: it was extremely useful to be able to move the caption boxes and speech balloons around the page, along with their accompanying text, instead of being forced to occupy their empty space, as would have been the case if they had been inked by hand. The final step was to then export print-ready, high-res (300dpi) PDF files for the printers to use, be they my smaller-scale friends on the Yala Saldak Road or the industrial-sized machines you see on p. 178.

Graphic Journalism and Human Trafficking Awareness

I can remember when I first started my research on human trafficking that the same shocking statistics used to circulate at anti-trafficking events. When asked about the scale of the problem, the response would always be, "There are more slaves now than at any other point in history," along with a number that hovered around the 25 million mark. The International Labour Organization (ILO) estimates that the number has since risen to "**49.6 million** people living in modern slavery in 2021, of which **27.6 million** were in forced labor and **22 million** in forced marriage."[10] According to the accompanying press release, "10 million more people were in modern slavery in 2021 compared to 2016 global estimates. Women and children remain disproportionately vulnerable."[11]

Historically, the first reference to trafficking as a "modern form of slavery" was used in 1993 in an Asia Watch report.[12] However, in the words of David Feingold, "The identification of 'trafficking' with chattel slavery – in particular, the transatlantic slave trade (which was all most people knew about) – was tenuous at best,"[13] not only because slavery was rooted in very specific geographic and historical contexts but also because "while some trafficking victims are kidnapped … for most, trafficking is migration gone terribly wrong."

Most trafficking is a real cause of outrage at the combination of the worst criminal acts: violence, bodily harm, coercion, rape, kidnapping. But too often the shock tactics of NGOs/self-proclaimed

---

10 "Forced Labour, Modern Slavery and Human Trafficking," International Labour Organization, https://www.ilo.org/global/topics/forced-labour/lang--en/index.htm.

11 "50 Million People Worldwide in Modern Slavery," International Labour Organization, https://www.ilo.org/global/about-the-ilo/newsroom/news/WCMS_855019/lang--en/index.htm.

12 Asia Watch, *A Modern Form of Slavery: Trafficking Burmese Women and Girls into Brothels in Thailand* (New York: Asia Watch, 1993).

13 David A. Feingold, "Trafficking in Numbers: The Social Construction of Human Trafficking Data," in *Sex, Drugs, and Body Counts: The Politics of Numbers in Global Crime and Conflict*, ed. Peter Andreas and Kelly M. Greenhill (Ithaca: Cornell University Press, 2010), 46–74.

abolitionists weaponize this moral outrage to garner media attention or investment. This in turn perpetuates a cycle of predictably conspicuous suffering, where the horror of different survivor stories is hoisted high on the media masthead, following the grisly tabloid adage "if it bleeds, it leads." These stories often feature a formulaic cast: victim, antagonist, protagonist (often not the victim). These characters may vary in their specific characteristics, but ultimately fall into one of the three categories of "heroes (and allies), villains (and enemies), and victims."[14] Trafficking narratives often construct victims as passive. They may transition to the role of survivor, but that transition is rarely caused by their own actions.[15]

This distinction is made all the more conspicuous in mass media portrayals and Hollywood has mined trafficking as a rich seam of inspiration for many of its latter-day heroes to pit themselves against: *Sound of Freedom*, *Taken*, *Sold*, *Eastern Promises*, *The Equalizer*, *Hyena*, even *Trafficked: A Parent's Worst Nightmare*. Troublingly, aside from the crass reduction of the act of trafficking and casual depiction of what is typically sexualized violence against young women, another common aspect is the "othering" of the malevolent traffickers themselves – Albanians, Arabs, or Russians from the list of titles I mentioned above. Rarely are they white Anglophone males. Fortunately, there are rare exceptions, in the case of *The Whistleblower* and *You Were Never Really Here* – both tellingly directed by women, and both the only to present wealthy Western Caucasian males as the perpetrators, or to situate the trafficking on the West's doorstep (the former, inside a UN camp, the latter, New York City's upper echelons of power). Yet as a smash hit, earning almost a billion dollars worldwide across the franchise, *Taken*'s impact cannot be underestimated. As a result, as Erin O'Brien mentioned, "the impact of the film goes far beyond entertainment value, telling hundreds of thousands of moviegoers their first human trafficking story." Clearly, there are a number of things that are problematic here, not least the fact that the story is designed "to thrill, rather than to educate." Seldom is much screen time dedicated to the inner life of the survivors. The main focus is typically on the heroic (often white) savior who kicks down doors à la Liam Neeson to rescue the helpless victim.

Part of the appeal of using comics journalism to cover human trafficking stories is precisely to move away from these reductive tropes and performative violence. Even with a benevolent eye behind the shutter, I found many NGO anti-trafficking campaigns to only further objectify and distance trafficking survivors from audiences, with visuals that tend to focus on two types of girls: the first, abstracted into silhouettes or cropped into alluring body parts, with faces obscured or blurred; or the second, helpless young girls with their hands bound in chains, their mouths covered, or imprisoned behind bars, as I point out in the prologue on p. 11. A Google image search for "human trafficking" only proves the point. In fact, a Google Ngram search (charting the prevalence of search terms across books, documents, and other printed sources) of the same term shows how exponential the level of interest in the term has become in the last twenty years. I appreciate that in today's crowded market for audience attention, NGOs need every weapon in their arsenal, and shocking imagery is guaranteed to generate outrage or at least attract more eyeballs or likes. This is the compounding effect of social media: from the slacktivists who like, follow, and share but lack the inclination to engage at a deeper level in the long term, to the unwitting White Saviors who spend time on the ground but whose selfies conspicuously reveal the ongoing power dynamics of

---

14 Michael B. Jones and Mark K. McBeth, "A Narrative Policy Framework: Clear Enough to Be Wrong," *Policy Studies Journal* 38, no. 2 (2010): 329–53.

15 Erin O'Brien, *Challenging the Human Trafficking Narrative: Victims, Villains, and Heroes* (London: Routledge, 2018).

a Westerner coming to the rescue of non-white locals (who will rarely know where those photos will end up). Dwindling attention spans mean a window of only a few seconds before users doom-scroll past the next story or reel. And celebrity/influencers championing the next cause. Instead, what we need is prolonged, informed engagement – in the words of Ugandan social worker Alaso Olivia, founder of No White Saviors, "We are trying to give our children a better education. We are developing our countries. We need aid but it must not come with strings attached. We are saying that if you want to help, first listen to us and provide what we need – not what you think we need."[16]

Research has shown that we often struggle to empathize with humanitarian crises where the sheer scale of the population involved becomes too much to bear. Paul Slovic introduced the term "psychic numbing" to describe this sense of indifference in the face of an insurmountable challenge, a phenomenon he witnessed the opposite of in 2015, at the peak of the Syrian refugee crisis. Instead, it was the tragic photo of a single three-year-old Syrian boy, Aylan Kurdi, lying face down on a Turkish beach, that triggered an outpouring of international aid for refugees.

Aylan's terrible fate brought the Syrian plight into sharp focus, humanizing a struggle into a form that was far closer to home: rather than a nebulously vast population of millions, his tiny body could have belonged to the little brother, son, or grandson in any of our families. It's the opposite of the incomprehensible statistics on trafficking (that so often frame discussions on trafficking) that add up to the tens of millions. One goal of this book is to emphasize that every voice comes from a very human perspective at ground level, showing the circumstances that led my interviewees to make the choices they did, and how they dealt with the consequences. I wanted to ensure that their voices resonated louder, as did their stories of resilience and empowerment in overcoming their previous situations. They are adamantly *survivors*, not victims, and choose not to define themselves by what has happened to them but by what actions they are taking *now* as they move forward. I also didn't want to be reductive or formulaic in approaching a topic (or a country) that can encompass so many different variables. As Kate Beaton said about her nonfiction comics memoir *Ducks: Two Years in the Oil Sands*: "People constantly try and make the oil sands about one thing. To refine it down to one issue. *Ducks* shows why that's impossible. Life isn't that way."[17] That is why the danger versus empowerment comparison was so integral to our study: to try and reshape the way we as human rights advocates and journalists respond to – and raise awareness of – a topic that is as multi-faceted and complex as the umbrella term of "human trafficking."

The Future of Graphic Journalism

I began this appendix with an introduction to comics journalism, so I wanted to bookend it with a glance at what the future might hold. For me, the total freedom of the blank page means you can explore the time and space of a story without needing a Hollywood budget – the real beauty is that the reader is always the one who provides the agency, intuitively building bridges between the sequential images to create the narrative. Unlike the passive reel of the moving image, the reader dictates the speed and flow of the comics page, which comics creators can deliberately play with, misdirect, or confuse.

---

16 Dipo Faloyin, *Africa Is Not a Country* (New York: Random House, 2022), 108.

17 Kate Beaton, "Kate Beaton's New Graphic Memoir Is about the Dark Type of Job You Take for Money," interview by Andrew Limbong, NPR, October 7, 2022, https://www.npr.org/2022/10/07/1126934628 /book-ducks-kate-beaton-hark-vagrant.

I've always been interested in harnessing the power of that agency and combining the mechanics of digital interactive storytelling with the rigor of graphic journalism, experimenting in both two and three dimensions. Pieces such as *The Nisour Square Shooting* (published as an interactive Flash mini-site in 2011) and *Ferguson Firsthand* (see below for a visual), a virtual reality reconstruction of the fatal shooting of Michael Brown by police officer Darren Wilson in Missouri in 2014, both incorporated comics into an interactive framework that relied on reader/user input, which led comics scholar Laura Schlichting to describe the process as "story exploring" as opposed to storytelling.[18]

The Nisour Square Shooting was an attempt to explode the narrative of a tragic shooting in real-time, juxtaposing the eyewitness accounts of Iraqi civilians with the Blackwater military contractors who were later found guilty of murder. Scrubbing through a timeline allowed the user to move back and forth in time, hovering over different color-coded protagonists in the story to replay the incident from their perspective. Clicking on the inset panels themselves brought up a pop-up window hyperlinked to the original source material, be it an embassy cable or news agency wire.

I played with a similar conceit in another webcomic format that explored the use of directional scrolling to dictate the level of depth that the reader was presented with in a comic on the International Criminal Court for *Cartoon Movement*, but unfortunately the piece (like so many online experiments) has since been taken offline.

Ryan Davies also deconstructed some of the narrative multiplicities and layers of agency, evidence, and interactivity in his essay *Between the Real and the Virtual: Dan Archer's Ferguson Firsthand*, as part of the *Art of the News: Comics Journalism* symposium held at the University

18 Laura Schlichting, "Interactive Graphic Journalism," *VIEW: Journal of European Television History and Culture* 5, no. 10 (2016): 22–39.

of Oregon in November 2021.[19] There is a growing willingness of editors to integrate more ambitious visuals into their publications, which has given rise to a growing wave of comics journalists across a range of media outlets, perhaps most noticeably in the *Nib*'s[20] trajectory. First launched by disruptive news startup First Look Media (FLM) in 2013, it then relaunched as an independent outlet in 2019 after cutting ties with FLM, and tragically issued notice of its definitive closure[21] in August 2023 after a decade of publications and host of industry awards. Perhaps one of the *Nib*'s greatest accomplishments was bringing together such a diverse, international community of nonfiction cartoonists under one umbrella, planting the seed for countless offshoots that will continue to flourish long after its shuttering.

Despite the obvious financial challenges to running comics-only publications, alternative and interactive models of nonfiction storytelling are becoming increasingly accepted, such as the Pulitzer Prizes for Mark Fiore's animated news cartoons in 2010 (satirical but rooted in a tragic political reality) and, more recently, Mona Chalabi's data comics in 2023.

I remain engaged with using graphic journalism to cover human trafficking, and I am currently involved in two separate investigations. The first, which began under the title of *Lost in Europe*, focuses on telling the stories of the estimated ten thousand missing migrant minors who are lost in the system after arriving in Europe from Africa and the Middle East. You can read some of the interactive interviews from *Lost in Europe* here: https://lostineurope.eu/team/dan-archer. These interviews were designed to feel like an online chat that brought each of the individuals' stories to life. It has since evolved into a wider examination of refugees of all ages (adults and minors) seeking asylum in Europe over the past several years. I am currently experimenting with ways to depict these stories in collaboration with photographer Ahmet Polat, combining my mixed media graphic journalism and his photos. The second, in partnership with investigative reporter Raquel Carvalho and backed by the European Journalism Fund, centers around the recent influx of migrant laborers to Eastern Europe and the unregulated employment agencies who profit from them.

I am confident we are approaching a point where editors and readers alike can get past the *form* of comics, breaking free of the anachronistic genre association they have as a result of the golden and silver ages of US superhero comics prior to the advent of television. The next generation of graphic journalists can and will combine these truly novel visual approaches to unearth new perspectives on the capabilities of nonfiction storytelling – and, most importantly, the impact it can have on raising awareness of the human rights stories that matter the most.

---

19 Ryan Davies, "Between the Real and the Virtual: Dan Archer's *Ferguson Firsthand*," in *Art of the News: Comics Journalism*, ed. Katherine Kelp-Stebbins and Ben Saunders (Eugene: Jordan Schnitzer Museum of Art, 2021), 320–3, https://issuu.com/jsmauo/docs/art_of_the_news_catalog-digital-v2.
20 https://thenib.com/.
21 https://thenib.com/the-future-of-the-nib/.

USAID REPORT

The following text was taken from the 2016 USAID report *Reducing Vulnerability to Human Trafficking: An Experimental Intervention Using Anti-Trafficking Campaigns to Change Knowledge, Attitudes, Beliefs and Practices in Nepal* that I was a co-Principal Investigator on, along with my fellow co-PIs, Cecilia Hyunjung Mo (Berkeley University) and Margaret Boittin (York University).

You can read the full report here: https://www.iie.org/publications/dfg-vanderbilt-publication/.

Visual Storytelling as a Tool for Advocacy

The use of illustrated sequential narratives in presenting advocacy campaigns has risen dramatically across a wide range of formats in recent years, from journalism to publishing, and from print to digital. It is worth highlighting some of the milestones that have contributed to increasing the supposed legitimacy of graphic novels as an appropriate format for addressing sensitive nonfiction issues, such as human trafficking or human rights abuses. However, first and foremost it is worth defining the term "graphic novel" and what separates it from a traditional "comic book."

Defining the Graphic Novel

In his seminal work, *Understanding Comics*, Scott McCloud (1993) defines comics as "juxtaposed pictorial and other images in deliberate sequence, intended to convey information and/or to produce an aesthetic response in the viewer." The principal characteristics of comics are as follows: serialized, typically on a monthly basis; mass-produced by a team comprised of several individuals – a writer, penciler, inker, letterer, editor, and colorist; a uniform length (approximately thirty pages); and continue ongoing storylines and character arcs from previous issues.

The term "graphic novel" was first coined during the latter half of the twentieth century and is historically associated with Will Eisner,[22] an American artist and writer from New York, who appropriated the visual language, syntax, and format of comics to tell stories that are more emotionally complex and deal with mature themes that might be unsuitable for younger readers.

In print, awards and attention lauded on graphic novelists such as Art Spiegelman (*Maus*, Pulitzer Prize winner in 1992), Marjane Satrapi (*Persepolis*, a commercial success both on paper and as an animation), and Joe Sacco (*Palestine, Footnotes in Gaza*, Ridenhour Investigative Journalism Prize winner) have established graphic novels in the mainstream, receiving dedicated coverage in publications ranging from the *New Yorker* to the *Guardian* newspaper. Recent years have also seen animation, a hitherto stigmatized medium best known for "cartoons" aimed at children, also target a more adult audience. *Waltz with Bashir*, for example, a 2012 animation by Israeli writer and director Ari Folman, chronicled his journey through the traumatic memories rooted in his service in the war in Lebanon during the 1980s and was a critical and commercial success.

---

22 Naturally, there is considerable debate stemming from the fact that visual narratives have been produced worldwide in centuries prior, but Eisner's contribution heralded a new wave of publishing in the West.

Visualizing the Advocate's Voice

Visual storytelling through graphic novels is ideally suited to the explanation of complex situations and characters that advocacy and awareness campaigns require. The form offers a number of advantages for advocacy throughout the production pipeline: during the reporting phase, the production phase, and the delivery mechanism.

The Reporting Phase

Many non-governmental organizations (NGOs) in the anti-trafficking space face significant challenges in demonstrating the impact of their work to donors and the general public. Trafficking survivors often do not wish to be identified for fear of stigmatization and the risk of being marginalized by their local community. By rendering a trafficking survivor through a drawn likeness or by recording their audio testimony instead of using live action video or photography, organizations can preserve their anonymity while ensuring their testimony is shared. Direct quotes and audio can be used in conjunction with the drawn images for an added degree of verisimilitude and impact. By presenting the stories of survivors in appealing formats such as a radio drama or comic, organizations can foster interest in and engagement of a younger demographic with stories that might not be so widely read were they to be presented in a purely textual format.

A live sketch drawn during the interview process with the respondent also serves as living proof of the dialogic nature of the interaction and in most cases prompts an exchange between sketcher and interviewee. This in turn fosters a rapport grounded in understanding and mutual trust. Admittedly, the same amount of dialogue is crucial to the recording process of video and audio, though the interviewee's means for listening or watching what has been recorded are more limited than their ability to simply look over at the reporter's sketchbook. For the similarities of the different forms in their final, finished format, see the section below on phase 6, production workflow.

The Production Phase

Drawn reconstructions of oral testimonies are a powerful technique for allowing readers to directly empathize with survivors from a firsthand perspective. The visual environment can be drawn based on images from reference material and descriptions from survivors, and direct quotes are included in caption boxes and speech balloons to bring the survivor's voice to the foreground. The same immediacy is true of hearing the emotion in an audio recording, or the combination of both audio and video in an animation.

Long-form narratives, be they visual or audio, can tackle multiple aspects of the trafficking experience in a nuanced, complex manner. The characters featured can reveal more of their personalities and interiority, which greatly assists with reader-based empathy. While admittedly graphic novels contain more text than a purely illustrative poster or cartoon, the visual nature of the form ensures it can be consumed faster and promulgated more readily than a purely textual story.

Delivery Mechanism

Many organizations have used comics to visually explain the roots of extended, multi-faceted conflicts, combining statistical and historical data with maps, annotations, photography, and illustrations to improve accessibility and attract greater attention. Many organizations have also used graphic novels, radio dramas, posters, and booklets to chronicle their work and objectives at both a national and international level.[23] These include the United Nations, World Education, and Save the Children, to name only a few. Each of the different media platforms has its own concomitant advantages and disadvantages. In print, organizations can produce their own materials that can be permanently left in target areas, do not require electricity to operate, are always available to read, and are not bound to a specific broadcast schedule, unlike radio or television programming. Furthermore, one issue can be consumed and shared between multiple readers multiple times. However, up-front print and shipping costs can prove steep and logistically challenging in terms of distribution. Television or radio are dependent on signal reception and electricity but are easily disseminated and unaffected by literacy levels. Posters can prove attention grabbing and contain a call to action but are inherently limited to a shorter, less narrative approach.

Treatment Development Pipeline: From Concept to Implementation

This research was conducted in Nepal, a country with particularly high levels of vulnerability to human trafficking. Human trafficking impacts hundreds of thousands of Nepali citizens. According to the Gallup World Poll, 229,000 Nepalis were subject to some form of trafficking in 2014 alone. Before deciding to implement our own materials, we needed to conduct a thorough benchmarking study of the existing approaches to gauge their relative merits and shortcomings.

Phase 1. Developing an Understanding of Past/ Present Awareness Campaign Models

An understanding of the existing information campaign (IC) ecosystem was essential before embarking on our study in order to appreciate our target audience's familiarity with visual awareness-raising media.[24] Our team members (hereafter referred to as the Human Trafficking Vulnerability – HTV – Team), led by me, interviewed several directors of communication at influential NGOs based in Kathmandu (both international and domestic) to ascertain their long- and short-term strategies, gain insight into prevalent trends in awareness-raising campaigns, and consider new approaches from their gathered research and materials. What follows is by no means an exhaustive account of the work in this sector but instead includes some examples that convey various public service messages in Nepal.

---

23 In 2014, I worked with Save the Children UK to depict their fulfillment of the UN Millennium Development Goals as part of their "Every One" campaign: https://issuu.com/gcampaign/docs/millennium_kid__english__hires.

24 Theatrical dramatizations known as "street dramas" were also highlighted by several NGOs as an effective way of fostering interest at a local level in myriad issues, although they are financially and logistically difficult to implement.

United Nations Children's Fund [UNICEF]

In 1998, UNICEF launched the Meena Communication Initiative (MCI). UNICEF developed Meena, a cartoon character who is a spirited young girl from South Asia, to increase awareness in narrative form about important social issues in the region, such as education, health, gender equity, and abuse (UNICEF 2015). The MCI focused on a national television campaign with supplementary radio programming that was co-produced by the BBC.

Meena focused on gender inclusion by making the protagonist of the campaign an empowered young girl. However, the sheer size and heterogeneity of the South Asian target area necessitated omitting key local details at both the narrative and textual level. The visual style is also at a slight remove from a fully sequential comic book approach: illustrations span an entire page and are followed by paragraphs of text. This significantly limits the story's ability to include details or information beyond a broad introduction to the topics addressed.

World Education

World Education has published several graphic novels focusing on types of trafficking specific to Nepal, often with a regional focus and a willingness to engage with issues that some would consider taboo in visual format, such as the commercial sexual exploitation of young boys by men – a topic that receives little attention in trafficking vulnerability reports, where the focus has historically been more on young girls.

Child Development Society [CDS]

CDS has focused on single-image posters for maximum impact (see p. 164 for a sample poster). These are chiefly placed in communal target areas such as brick kilns or schools to disseminate information about the risks of bonded and child labor.

Himalayan Human Rights Monitors [HimRights]

Graphic novels were produced as part of workshops by those directly involved in the stories. By involving victims so directly, HimRights was able to utilize a powerful, affordable means of production that was also potentially therapeutic for those who contributed firsthand. However, this production style often came with a disadvantage in that the narrative and concomitant illustrations were not always coherent.

Change Nepal

Much like CDS, Change Nepal has traditionally focused on illustrated posters with a relatively small amount of text, predominantly focused on brick kilns. The impetus is distinctly danger-oriented and depicts those already trafficked from a third-person perspective, not showing interiority or character backstory. (See panel 1 on p. 167 for an example.)

Discernible Trends of Previous Awareness Campaigns

The degree of fiction incorporated into these earlier comics varied significantly, as did the different forms of trafficking featured. However, the tone of the messaging was often consistent, with a significant focus on the negative and preventive depictions of personal injury to the characters involved, and less positive depictions of trafficking survivors who had overcome their trauma to move on with their lives.

Phase 2. Story Gathering through Source Interviews

As part of our examination of existing methods of developing anti-trafficking materials, we made a list identifying different forms of trafficking and the respective NGOs that specialized in combating those distinct branches: forced labor (CWIN), sex trafficking (Change Nepal), bonded labor in brick kilns (CDS), migrant labor (ILO), and kidney trafficking (Asia Foundation). Naturally there is a degree of overlap between the work that these different organizations carry out.

In the case of bonded labor at brick kilns, members of the survey team went with a CDS representative to several kilns and interviewed/sketched workers while they worked. These were predominantly in the Bhaktapur area.

The full list of agencies consulted included Change Nepal, Children and Social Welfare, Child Workers in Nepal (CWIN), The Didi Project, Esther Benjamin Trust Nepal, Himalayan Human Rights Monitors (HimRights), Maiti Nepal, Ministry of Women, National Human Pourakhi Nepal, Sano Paila, Shakti Samuha, Terre des Hommes, The Asia Foundation, UNWomen, Women Rehabilitation Center (WOREC), and World Education.

Upon reaching out to each of these organizations, we asked them for assistance sharing information about cases of human trafficking that they had worked on. This included assistance in identifying trafficking survivors willing to share their experiences with us. Individuals who had more recent experiences with trafficking were generally less willing to discuss their stories than those who had been trafficked years ago.

Phase 3. Production of Story Outlines and Scripts from Source Interviews

Such sensitive material demanded an equally sensitive approach to conducting interviews. The typical process was as follows: contact the NGO and outline the project; send follow-up questions for the interviewee and NGO worker's approval; and meet with the interviewee at a "safe space" (often the NGO's office) with a psycho-social counselor in attendance. The counselor or NGO representative would translate the interview from Nepali to English.

Many agreed to their likeness being drawn directly as a reference for a future drawing in the comic; however, this was completely voluntary. When subjects were quizzical about the process, it was helpful to show examples of other interviewees sketched previously to show them that future identification would be impossible.

Sketches of floor plans of areas included in the stories were completed during interviews to ensure fidelity with the subjects' descriptions. Sketches of general facial profiles of the main characters were also completed during the interview. Often subjects were not forthcoming with the high level of detail required for a graphic depiction and required additional, gentle questioning. With regards to depictions of the trafficker, we asked questions such as "Was he old? Did he have facial hair? Did he wear jewelry? Was he fat/thin?" During this phase, we often received a lot of "average size, average age" responses, which we largely attributed to an understandable reluctance on the interviewee's part to cast their memory back to the experience. The coherence of the story also presented challenges during the interview process. The nature of the trafficking experience meant that some interviews were very fragmented and lacked a complete structure on the initial retelling. In such cases, follow-up questions, sometimes during a secondary interview, helped provide clarification. As ever, the priority was on preserving the mental health of those who had the courage to come forward and share their stories, so there was no pressure in response to any silence on their part. Safeguards, such as the preemptive screening of questions and the presence of a psycho-social counselor, were critical to ensuring that the subjects' well-being was paramount at all times.

The answers to the questions posed during the interview were then collated into single narratives and categorized according to which aspects of trafficking they featured. The HTV team then read through these notes and used them as a guideline for writing new scripts on which the IC materials were based. The scriptwriting process also incorporated news articles, documentaries, and other research on trafficking into the storylines.

Given the expense of full-color printing costs and the desired length of the awareness campaign graphic novel (each of the danger and empowerment treatment conditions were approximately thirty pages in total), each story had to be limited to approximately four pages, with each page comprising approximately nine panels on a three-by-three grid. Ideally a panel should not contain more than two sentences to avoid overcrowding the artwork (a particular consideration for readers toward the lower end of the literacy spectrum). Scripts were therefore broken down into rough page breaks, and from there, divided by panel.

Initial feedback from first drafts of the script was that some panels needed "unpacking" – too much action or text was happening in too small a panel, resulting in illegibility. This required maintaining a clear and consistent storyline with less text and also extending some stories from four to (at their longest) seven pages. Such changes allowed for the reader to maintain engagement with the stories, while also limiting their length.

Applying the Danger versus Empowerment Framework

The application of the danger versus empowerment framework was straightforward to implement. It typically involved finding a crux event within the narrative at which point the protagonist's behavior could bifurcate. The main challenge here was to preserve enough of the skeleton framework of the story to ensure that the two arcs remained comparable. Too great a deviation from the same core narrative would have separated the protagonist in the parallel treatments too much.

In all cases, the danger treatment was shorter, as the path to a negative outcome required fewer pages of script. Empowerment was predicated on the same negative situation as danger, with the additional inclusion of a section that showed the protagonist subsequently taking steps to overcome adversity. As a result, the two stories were often similar to a certain point before the positive version extended to show the character's path to future stability.

This last page of the empowerment version of Meera's story illustrates the positive ending added to the negative conclusion of the danger version. One challenge the empowerment stories presented was the creation of positive endings that did not remove agency from the protagonist. In the sample case shown below, Meera's mother rescues her, arguably limiting her own agency, though Meera does have the courage to ask for help.

Danger/Negative ending:

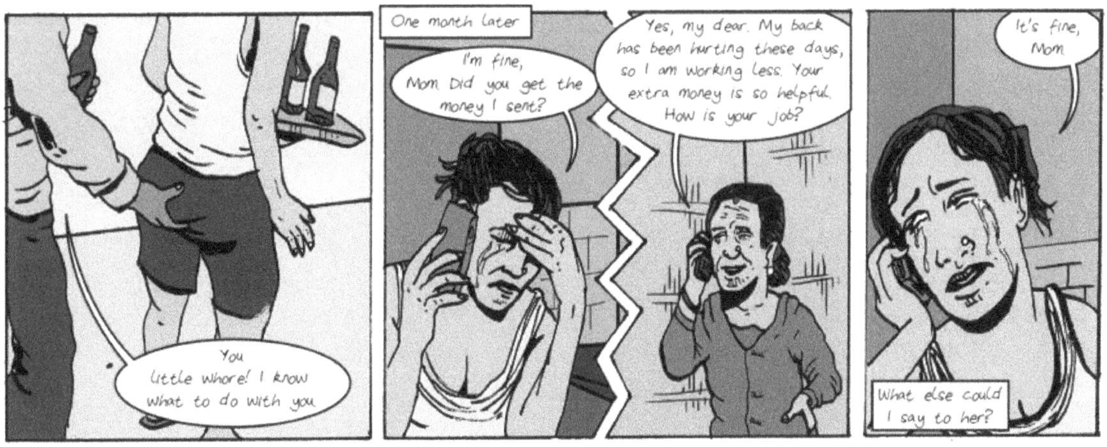
You little whore! I know what to do with you
One month later
I'm fine, Mom. Did you get the money I sent?
Yes, my dear. My back has been hurting these days, so I am working less. Your extra money is so helpful. How is your job?
It's fine, Mom
What else could I say to her?

Empowerment/Positive ending:

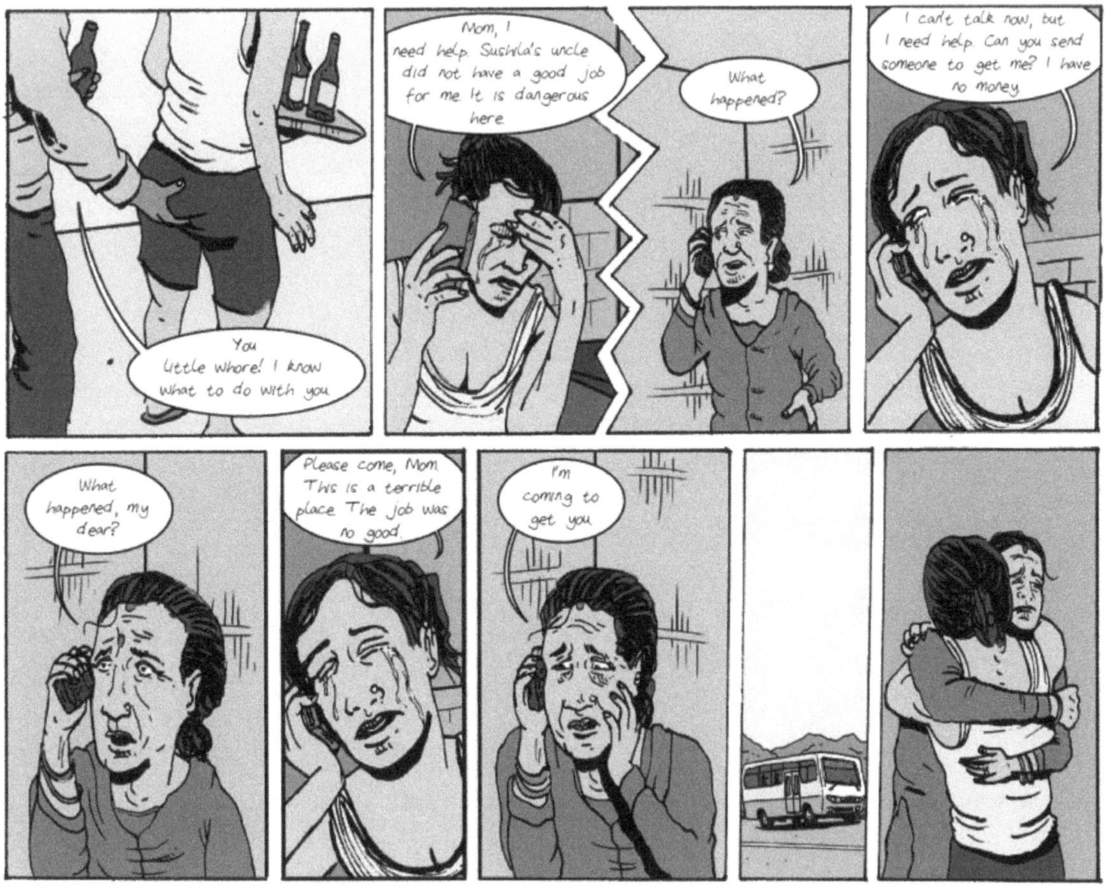
You little whore! I know what to do with you
Mom, I need help. Sushila's uncle did not have a good job for me. It is dangerous here.
What happened?
I can't talk now, but I need help. Can you send someone to get me? I have no money.
What happened, my dear?
Please come, Mom. This is a terrible place. The job was no good.
I'm coming to get you.

Phase 4. Artwork Production

Archer's background as a graphic journalist heavily influenced the artistic style toward representational (lifelike) drawing, often with the use of watercolors to suggest shade, light balance, and contrast. That was the technique followed in piloting – using pen and ink, colored with watercolors, then scanned and text overlaid digitally in desktop publishing software produced with both Adobe Photoshop and InDesign.

Phase 5. Piloting the Stories in the Field

Step 1: Establishing a Supportive Audience Network

To create high-quality and realistic awareness campaign materials, a rigorous piloting process was conducted at each stage of production (see pp. 169–75). At first, the HTV team printed and distributed (in a closed environment) a small sample of graphic novel stories to beneficiaries and staff members at NGO partner organizations. The readers attending the sessions then provided their feedback in a structured manner through guided questions. Participants were given ten minutes to read each individual graphic novel story on their own before returning to discuss them as a group.

The wide variety of different NGOs was critical to incorporating the polyphony of different voices into the feedback loop, which heavily influenced the final look and feel of the design. These included many organizations that had previously not participated in the preproduction of other IC materials (such as Dalit and women's rights groups). All comments and feedback were weighed and considered before being omitted or included in future revisions.

Throughout the piloting process, it was critical to have participants read the graphic novels in isolation, rather than in groups. Many readers struggling with literacy issues were observed asking their neighbors to decode or explain the story to them. Yet when directly questioned, those involved professed no need for help or explanation from moderators, possibly as a matter of pride. Correctly understanding comprehension issues was critical to reworking the stories in ways that would be accessible to individuals with lower literacy levels. To address this literacy issue, we experimented with wordless versions of the graphic novel. While these versions dramatically accelerated the media consumption time, they also led to much greater levels of ambiguity around story comprehension, particularly in highlighting differences between danger and empowerment versions of the narratives.

Step 2: Feedback Gathered from Piloting

Visual Style and Secondary Action

Participants in the pilot expressed that secondary action (panel 4, p. 173) was too confusing or complicated for readers with less visual literacy to follow. It was noted that depth of field was an issue, and foreshortening (such as the close focus on the handcuffed man) caused confusion and distracted readers. A more illustrative approach, often reinforcing the thread of the written narrative, proved more effective.

Participants found that the watercolor washes and textures were too distracting from the main narrative in the same way. As a result, multiple variations were produced, overlaying the black and white artwork and a digitally colored, more saturated color scheme, which tested more effectively (compare p. 174 and p. 175).

Illustration of what the characters were saying was said to dramatically improve understanding and retention of information. The dual speech balloon (middle panel, second tier, p. 173), with one balloon showing the action and the other describing it in text, was used in some graphic novel sections to facilitate understanding of the dialogue.

Ensuring that body language and intimacy were represented in culturally appropriate ways in the graphic novels was also a key learning point – the penultimate panel on p. 173 had to be redrawn to show the daughter touching her mother's feet, as opposed to the mother caressing her daughter after her safe return, as that action conveyed affection and respect more clearly. Initially, participants mistook the image as the mother striking, instead of embracing, her child.

Earlier versions of several treatments were deemed too sparse and simplified. To address this concern, additional levels of background treatment and clarifying, illustrative details were added. Panel order was also altered in some cases.

Localized Detail

We originally intended to specify characters' respective ethnicities to appeal to specific groups more effectively, and in consideration of historical marginalization that ethnic groups face in terms of representation in the Nepali mass media. Yet, given the broad geographic area covered in the survey sample, and the negligible increased impact attributed to samples with characters of specific ethnicities during piloting, we agreed on a more generic facial type.

Text

Colloquial phrasing, exclamations, and greetings received a positive response from respondents and were deemed important for determining register and relationships between characters. As already asserted above, participants preferred a more realistic (as opposed to fictitious) treatment. In particular, specific scenarios featuring nonfiction storylines and comments taken directly from interviews produced a heightened level of detail and brought local distinguishing features in the narrative to the surface. More generic stories were deemed too "foreign," predictable, and therefore not as relevant to our respondents, which in turn lessened their engagement and, as a result, the stories' impact.

Phase 6. Production Workflow for the Graphic Novel

Text and Visualization

Once piloting was complete and scripts were developed that combined sufficient details from interviews with the requisite amount of danger and empowerment variables, Archer began by converting the scripts into a storyboarded format. These pages were first thumbnailed in pencil to establish a rough layout and text placement. Once submitted and approved by the team, final art was then hand-drawn on 9 × 12-inch Bristol board paper, which was then scanned and saved as 300 dots per inch (dpi) print-resolution TIFF files. The files were then imported into Adobe InDesign, a graphic design program where the pages were laid out as a paginated (divisible by four for printing) graphic novel. After several rounds of editing the script in a Word document, the text was laid over the artwork on a separate layer, along with digitally created word balloons. It was essential to create the word balloons digitally in order to allow for variations in the amount of text between the Nepali and English translations.

Several problems arose during the process of digitally laying out the Nepali text in InDesign given that lettering text and vowel placements were affected by software (e.g., copying and pasting emailed Nepali text often produced very mixed results). Special care was taken to address all distortions.

Summary of Stories Included in the Graphic Novel

A summary of each of the six stories that were ultimately used in the study is provided here.

- Bijay, an eleven-year-old boy, is sent away by his father to a job in the city to raise money for the family, thinking he will also receive an education outside of work. When the father raises objections with the man who organized the supposed "job," he is given more money and told everything is fine. The reality is that Bijay is forced to work against his will in a sari factory and kept in squalor. In the empowerment version, the father does not believe the broker, seeks out Bijay himself, and reports the broker to the police.

- Meera is a fifteen-year-old girl who is promised a job at a canteen in the city. When she arrives, she discovers the job is actually working as a waitress in a cabin restaurant, where girls are expected to perform sexual services for clients. She is too ashamed and scared to return to her village so resigns herself to life in sexual slavery. In the empowerment version, she calls her mother, who comes to the city to rescue her.

- Rajiv is a twelve-year-old boy whose alcoholic mother forces him to work at a brick kiln. When a friend of his tells him about an easier way to make money in the city, he agrees to go with him. He is shocked to find that this easier "job" involves performing sexual services to a wealthy Western man in exchange for food, money, and shelter at his house. In the empowerment version, Rajiv refuses to acquiesce to the older man's demands, runs away, and calls a local NGO for help.

- Shobha is a twenty-eight-year-old widow who is forced into taking a job as a domestic servant in the Gulf in order to support her young family. When she arrives at the residence, the husband confiscates her passport and the wife subjects her to verbal and physical abuse. After one such confrontation she sustains a head injury and is considered so worthless by her employers that they bury her body in the desert instead of finding her medical care. In the empowerment version, she alerts an NGO to her predicament and a police officer is dispatched to arrest the homeowners and repatriate her to Nepal.

- Sita is a fifteen-year-old girl who was forced into an underage marriage. She accepts a job in Delhi alongside her sister only to find upon arrival that she has been trafficked into a brothel. She is drugged and forced into sexual slavery for three years. She is eventually freed in a police raid but is unable to find her sister and is diagnosed as HIV positive. In the empowerment version, she is determined to not accept her fate as a victim and manages to escape and notify the police. When the others are freed in the raid and she is diagnosed with HIV, she resolves to share her story so that others will not make the same mistake she did.

- Suraj, a farmer, hears from a friend about a lucrative restaurant job in the Gulf. He signs up with a manpower agency at considerable personal expense with no contract and is shocked to find the job is actually in construction under slave-like conditions. Left with no legal recourse after surrendering his passport, and depressed by the thought of bringing shame on his family, he hangs himself. In the empowerment version, Suraj demands a contract and is more aware of his rights. Having seen an anti-trafficking hotline number advertised at the airport, he is able to call for assistance and return safely to his family.

Other Treatments

Next, let's contrast the different approaches across different formats. A descriptive analysis of baseline data finds that the most accessible and frequently used forms of media in Nepal were TV and radio, both of which are leveraged as media formats in the study treatments. In addition, over 76 percent of respondents had been exposed to graphic novels prior to participating in the study.

The Radio Treatment

The graphic novel scripts proved to be a significant advantage for accelerating the production of the radio treatments, since they clearly laid out the scope, length, and characters for each story. However, there were some key changes that needed to be made to adapt the previously visual-based narrative into a purely auditory experience.

Graphic novel and radio narratives were almost identical. In several instances, additional effects had to be incorporated into the audio treatment to portray information that was represented visually in the graphic novel, such as the background environment or the demographics and characters featured in the stories.

Similarly, the insertion of introductory verbal synopses that prefaced the main story were important for setting the scene, providing contextual information, and letting listeners know what they were about to hear.

The subdivision of the script into a series of short scenes was also important for cutting the long pieces of audio into smaller, more discrete parts. This was especially helpful for participants with shorter attention spans, or in the event of distractions during user testing in large groups. Those who had lost the thread of the narrative were able to pick up the story from the next scene thanks to the recurring audio cue. The use of these musical intervals also served as an audio cue to open and close each section.

The Audiovisual Treatment

To a certain degree, the audiovisual treatment was the most straightforward of the treatments to produce since it involved combining the existing graphic novel and radio treatments. Its production involved editing the audio into smaller sections and matching them to their corresponding panels in the graphic novel artwork, which were displayed in a slideshow format.

One hurdle at this stage was that the dimensions of the artwork had not been designed to fit the landscape format of a video, which called for a degree of experimentation in deciding how large panels should be displayed. Zooming and panning effects were also originally considered, but discarded based on the decision that their inclusion would prove distracting for audiences. Single panels (separated from their accompanying speech balloons and captions) were therefore cut and pasted out of the full-color artwork in Photoshop and combined with the audio track using iMovie software. The end result was a video file that could then be easily uploaded onto tablets or projected for an audience.

CHARACTERISTICS OF HUMAN TRAFFICKING IN NEPAL

Human trafficking is a form of modern-day slavery where people profit from the control and exploitation of others.

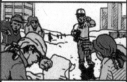

Exploitation includes:
- Forced labor or servitude
- Forced prostitution or other forms of sexual exploitation
- Slavery or practices similar to slavery
- Removal of organs

Anyone can be a victim of sex, labor, or organ trafficking: men, women, and children.

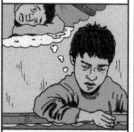

More than 1 out of 3 Nepali trafficking survivors are children.

Over 250,000 Nepalis are currently trafficked domestically or internationally.

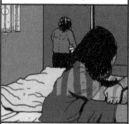

The prevalence of human trafficking in Nepal is amongst the highest in the world.

The majority of trafficking cases are not reported to the police.

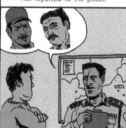

Individuals convicted of trafficking may be punished with fines and up to 20 years of imprisonment.

RECOGNIZING THE SIGNS OF HUMAN TRAFFICKING

Poor Recruitment Practices
- Rushed into making a decision
- Enticed with a large advance payment
- Given limited information about the job or destination
- Recruited through false promises concerning the nature and conditions of the work
- Required to use fake documentation or false information when traveling
- Has no contract

Poor Health
- Shows signs of mental abuse
- Show signs of helplessness
- Shows signs of malnourishment
- Shows signs of physical and/or sexual abuse, physical restraint, confinement, or torture

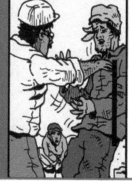

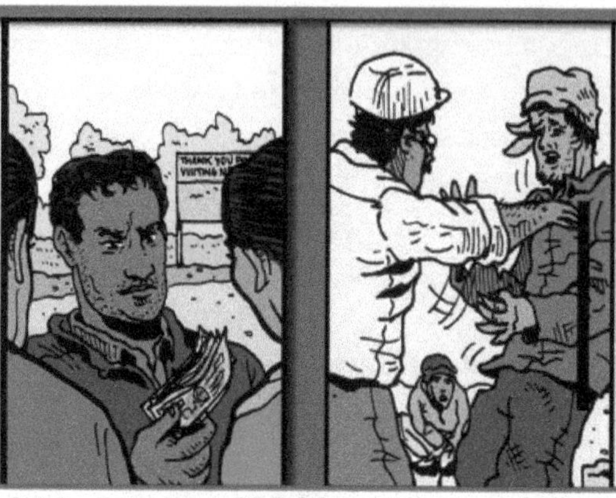

Poor Working and Living Conditions
- Asked to lie about their work and living conditions
- Not free to leave or come and go as they wish
- Unpaid or paid less than what was promised
- Owes a large debt and is unable to pay it off
- Works excessively long and/or unusual hours
- Is not allowed breaks or suffers under unusual restrictions at work
- Threatened with violence and/or non-payment of wages

Lack of Control
- Is not in control of their own money
- Is not in control of their own identification documents (ID or passport)
- Is not allowed or able to speak for themselves

HOW CAN YOU STAY SAFE?

- Ask a lot of questions: gather information about your wages, work conditions, and type of work, even if the job opportunity is coming from a friend or family member
- Talk to people you trust before making big decisions
- If you leave home for work, establish a way to communicate with people you trust, and call often
- Require a contract

सम्झौतापत्र
काठमाण्डौ
प्रहरी चौकी

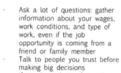

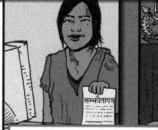

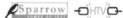

- Ensure family and friends know how to contact you
- Report missing people to police or VDC
- Call someone for help: your family, friends, police, local NGOs, and the Nepali embassy can help
- Report exploitation to the local police
- When going abroad, register with the Nepali embassy

REPORT IT IMMEDIATELY

Sparrow HTV

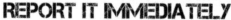

If you or someone you know might be in danger of human trafficking, **send a free SMS** to the human trafficking hotline at this number for help: **6040**

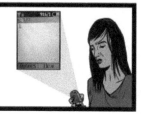

For **help**, type **1** as your message. For information, type **2**.

The Poster Treatment

The poster was the last of all treatments completed. The main challenge in this case was the inclusion of all the requisite information points while retaining a clear message. We wanted to ensure coherence in the design so that readers would not be put off by the large amount of text (the poster is presented on the previous page). To that end, balancing the amount of text with images was critical.

The poster size was increased to 19 × 23-inch size rather than a standard 8.5 × 11-inch (US letter) format in order to not overwhelm the viewer, and the same production pipeline as the graphic novels was used to produce the final printed product (Adobe Photoshop and InDesign). Images taken from the graphic novel were used to retain consistency, although depriving the panels of their context made the selection of particular images that functioned autonomously somewhat difficult.

We incorporated different sections into the poster to underscore the different aspects of information: introductory, preventive, and a call to action. The use of the red dividing lines in the middle section, "Recognizing the Signs of Human Trafficking," separates the before and after aspects of being trafficked.

Survey Results

Note: this section has been heavily abridged to include significant results. A detailed discussion of methodology and additional results can be found in the full report cited above.

Treatment-Based Results

The treatments were analyzed based on two outcomes: the first, their impact on awareness-raising and ability to affect participants' opinions on trafficking; the second, their impact on participants' desire to actually take action.

Danger versus Empowerment across All Treatments

For a more in-depth breakdown of the difference between the danger (negative) and empowerment (positive) versions of each story treatment, see Phase 3 of the Treatment Development Pipeline above.

Perception of Trafficking as a Local versus a National Problem

In the short term, each format is equally effective at increasing a person's perception that human trafficking is a big problem nationally, compared to the receipt of no information. Additionally, in the short term, the empowerment narrative is more effective than the danger narrative at increasing perceptions about the magnitude of the human trafficking problem in Nepal. However, there are no observable short-term or long-term differences by awareness campaign format or message type on the effect of awareness campaigns on a person's perception that human trafficking is a big problem locally.

Respondents' Attitudes toward Trafficking Victims

Compared to the empowerment narrative, the danger narrative reduced respondent willingness to talk and eat with victims of sex trafficking (by 3.7 percentage points and 2.9 percentage points, respectively). The effect on willingness to share a meal with a sex trafficking victim fell just short of statistical significance, but the effect on willingness to converse with a sex trafficking victim is significant.

Level of Empowerment, Personal Responsibility, and Police Helpfulness

The danger narrative decreased respondent agreement with the idea that victims are empowered by nearly 30 percentage points compared to the empowerment version. Such a strong negative effect provides clear evidence of how successfully the danger signs narratives actually conveyed a sense of fear to respondents. Compared to the empowerment narrative, the danger signs narrative also significantly decreased respondents' sense of police ability to help victims of trafficking, by 11 percentage points, and had a negligible effect on an individual's sense that victims are responsible for finding themselves in a situation of trafficking (less than 1 percentage point).

Sub-categories of Awareness-Raising in Individuals

Given the number of different categories that were included in the survey, I have only included findings that were statistically significant, which are below.

i. Concern about Human Trafficking and Prioritization of Anti-trafficking Policies and Programs

Exposure to awareness campaigns, regardless of the format, increases concern for human trafficking and the belief that the government should prioritize anti-trafficking action in the short term. Graphic novels have an especially great impact on eliciting concern, producing the largest change in levels of concern relative to each of the other IC formats. Additionally, the empowerment narrative is more effective than the danger narrative in triggering concern for human trafficking. However, all of these effects are short-lived. The positive effects of each awareness campaign, even the graphic novel, dissipated with time.

ii. Awareness of Different Types of Human Trafficking

In the short term, radio is a more effective medium than others at increasing perceptions that various forms of human trafficking occur in Nepal. The radio campaign is more effective than the poster and the audiovisual treatment in increasing perceptions that women are frequently sold into forced marriages. Additionally, radio campaigns have the strongest effect on perceptions that people in Nepal are frequently being forced to engage in prostitution. However, these effects are not enduring. Only the short-term effect on perceptions that people are frequently being forced to work for little or no pay is significant.

iii. Girls [under 16] and Women [over 16] are at Higher Risk of Being Trafficked

Relative to receiving no information, the graphic novel, radio, and audiovisual treatments similarly increase the likelihood of viewing women as being at high risk of trafficking (3.1 to 3.6 percentage points) in the short term only. All four message formats increase perceptions of the vulnerability of girls to human trafficking (3.0 to 4.9 percentage points). Graphic novels generated the largest increase in probability of seeing adult women as at risk of human trafficking (3.6 percentage points), while the audiovisual treatment generated the largest increase in seeing girls as at risk of being trafficked (4.9 percentage points). Compared to the danger narrative, those exposed to the empowerment narrative are more likely to view girls as being at high risk of trafficking. However, none of these effects is enduring.

iv. Boys [under 16] and Men [over 16] are at Higher Risk of Being Trafficked

As with what we saw when evaluating whether women and girls are viewed as vulnerable to human trafficking, relative to receiving no information, the graphic novel, radio, and audiovisual treatments similarly increase the likelihood of viewing men and boys as being high-risk populations for being trafficked (5.0–5.7 percentage points for men and 5.3–7.0 percentage points for boys) in the short term only. Posters are the notably weaker format in eliciting the perspective that boys are vulnerable to being trafficked in both the long term and short term. When looking at perspectives on the vulnerability of adult males, the poster is the weakest in the short term only, and there are no observable differences by format in the long term. Those exposed to the empowerment narrative are nearly 2 percentage points more likely to view both men and boys as being at high risk of human trafficking than those exposed to the danger narrative. However, this statistically significant effect is not enduring.

v. Members of the Ward Are at High Risk

Each of the information campaign formats corresponds to negligible effects on a person's belief that members of their own community are vulnerable to human trafficking; however, long-term effects are strong and negative. In other words, in the long term, awareness campaign materials lead to a perspective that human trafficking is not an issue at the local level. Danger and empowerment narratives have no distinguishable differences in either the short or long term.

vi. Human Trafficking Requires Movement across State or National Borders

Each of the information campaign formats corresponds to greater knowledge that transnational movement is not required for human trafficking, and the narrative awareness campaigns (the graphic novel, radio, and audiovisual treatments) are more effective than the fact-based poster treatment. In the short term, graphic novels were the most effective at correcting this misconception (10.6 percentage points), followed by the audiovisual presentation (9.6 percentage points), radio (8.3 percentage points), and finally the poster treatment (3.7 percentage points). Moreover, the graphic novel and audiovisual campaigns are statistically more effective than the poster treatment at increasing knowledge that transnational movement is not a criterion for human trafficking. However, these effects are short-lived. Danger and empowerment narratives have no differential impact in either the short or long term.

vii. Men Can Be Trafficked

In the short term, each of the story-based information campaign formats corresponds to about an 8.7 percentage point impact on knowledge that men can in fact be trafficked, while the poster treatment resulted in a 4.5 percentage point increase. Effects are not enduring, however. Danger and empowerment narrative effects do not differ in either the short or long term.

viii. Level of Empowerment, Personal Responsibility, and Police Helpfulness

As a whole, awareness campaigns elicit an increase in perceptions that victims are empowered, police can help victims, and that victims should not be held responsible for what happened to them. Narrative-based treatments are particularly effective at moving the needle on perceptions of empowerment and police helpfulness. Graphic novels had a particularly great impact on reducing perceptions that victims should be held responsible. Compared to the control condition, each of the three story-based treatment conditions – the graphic novel, radio, and audiovisual treatments – increased respondent support for the statements about a victim's level of empowerment to change his or her situation (values range from 25.1 to 30.7 percentage points) and the ability of police to provide victims with assistance (values range from 23.4 to 25.5 percentage points for empowerment). The empowerment narrative, as expected, elicits a greater belief that victims are empowered to change their situation and that the police can be helpful than the danger narrative. There is no difference between the two message types with respect to their effects on the extent to which victims should be held responsible for their situation. The graphic novel elicited the greatest reduction in perceptions that victims should be held responsible, and, when we conducted pairwise comparisons, the graphic novel had stronger negative effects than the radio and audio treatment campaigns.

ix. Provide Stricter Punishment for Traffickers and Prevent Government Corruption

Our awareness campaigns do not increase support for more police training, stricter punishment for traffickers, or prevention of government corruption in the short term. However, in the long term, the graphic novel triggers greater support for stricter punishments of traffickers. There are no differential effects by message type for any of these three measures, in either the short or long term.

Actions to Combat Human Trafficking

Would Call the Police, Vote for Legislation, and Talk to Family or Friends about Trafficking

Overall, narrative-based awareness campaigns are more effective than fact-based awareness campaigns (i.e., the poster treatment) in triggering a desire to take action to call the police, vote for a restrictive migration law, or talk to family and friends about human trafficking. In the short term, narrative-based awareness campaigns are more powerful than fact-based poster campaigns in triggering support for a restrictive migration law and a commitment to call the police to report human trafficking cases. In the long term, the graphic novel is much more effective than the poster in eliciting greater willingness to call the police, and the audiovisual treatment is more effective than the poster in increasing a person's long-term willingness to talk to others about human trafficking. The danger narratives engender less willingness to report human trafficking to the police and have conversations about human trafficking than empowerment narratives. However, this is a short-lived effect.

Would Volunteer Time and Donate Money to an Anti-trafficking Organization

Narrative-based awareness campaigns are more effective than fact-based poster campaigns at triggering a greater commitment to donate time and money to anti-trafficking organizations, at least in the short term. The danger narrative engenders less willingness to volunteer time than the empowerment narrative does; however, the danger narrative is just as effective as the empowerment narrative at eliciting a willingness to donate money.

Would Sign an Anti-trafficking Petition

Awareness campaigns, especially the graphic novel campaign, elicit a small increase in the likelihood of a person participating in a petition campaign. The graphic novel is more effective than the radio and audiovisual formats. There is no difference in petition participation by message narrative type. Compared to the control condition of receiving no information, the graphic novel treatment format was the most effective at increasing willingness to sign a petition (by 1.3 percentage points), which is a statistically meaningful effect. This particular format is statistically more effective than the radio format and the audiovisual format. Interestingly, the radio treatment resulted in a negative effect (–0.5 percentage points) and was statistically less effective than each of the other formats. Further research is necessary to determine if radio is particularly ineffective at eliciting this type of action, or if this is a statistical anomaly.

Individual versus Group Exposure to Anti-trafficking Media Campaigns

Respondents were also exposed to mass media campaign materials in two different ways: individually (see results above) and in groups. When respondents were treated individually, a surveyor would first administer a pre-treatment survey questionnaire. The respondent would then be presented with one of eight possible individual treatment combinations (audiovisual, graphic novel, radio, poster – danger or empowerment versions). Following exposure to the treatment, the respondent would then answer a series of post-treatment questions.

When respondents were treated in groups, a surveyor would first administer a pre-treatment survey questionnaire to each participant. The next day, respondents were exposed to the treatment (which was always the audiovisual treatment), in groups of twelve people, with the groups divided by gender. Following exposure to the narrative, participants were then asked to engage in a series of group activities, including a surveyor-led discussion about the materials they had just viewed, and a role-play activity around a hypothetical human trafficking scenario. Individuals exposed to the awareness campaigns in groups were provided an opportunity to hear other perspectives, and, hence, converge on norms and beliefs that could differ from what they would have thought if they had viewed the awareness campaign separately. Following these activities, respondents answered the same post-treatment questionnaire as those receiving the individual-level treatment. As with the individual treatments, both the pre-treatment and the post-treatment questionnaires were administered one-on-one for group treatment participants.

Conclusion: Viewing awareness campaigns with other members of your community and having opportunities to have conversations about the content of the awareness campaigns increases respondent awareness of the experiences of human trafficking of friends and family, at least in the short term. This does not persist over the long run, however.

FURTHER READING

The following books and articles stand as a good entry point into graphic journalism in all of its different forms, and I've tried to split them into their respective categories per my introduction at the beginning of this text.

Books

Investigative

Evans, Kate. *Threads: From the Refugee Crisis*. New York: Verso, 2017.

Glidden, Sarah. *How to Understand Israel in 60 Days or Less*. New York: Vertigo, 2010.

–. *Rolling Blackouts: Dispatches from Turkey, Syria, and Iraq*. Montreal: Drawn & Quarterly, 2016.

Guibert, Emmanuel, Didier Lefèvre, and Frédéric Lemercier. *The Photographer: Into War-Torn Afghanistan with Doctors without Borders*. Translated by Alexis Siegel. New York: First Second, 2009.

Neufeld, Josh. *A.D.: New Orleans after the Deluge*. New York: Pantheon, 2009.

Sacco, Joe. *The Fixer: A Story from Sarajevo*. Seattle: Fantagraphics, 2003.

–. *Footnotes in Gaza*. New York: Metropolitan Books, 2009.

–. *Journalism*. London: Jonathan Cape, 2012.

–. *Palestine*. Seattle: Fantagraphics, 2001.

–. *Paying the Land*. New York: Metropolitan Books, 2020.

–. *Safe Area Gorazde: The War in Eastern Bosnia 1992–1995*. Seattle: Fantagraphics, 2000.

Illustrated Reportage

Butler, G. *Drawn across Borders: True Stories of Migration*. London: Walker Books, 2021.

Kugler, O. *Escaping Wars and Waves: Encounters with Syrian Refugees*. Brighton: Myriad Editions, 2018.

Graphic Memoir

Beaton, Kate. *Ducks: Two Years in the Oil Sands*. Montreal: Drawn & Quarterly, 2022.

Bechdel, Alison. *Fun Home: A Family Tragicomic*. Boston: Houghton Mifflin, 2006.

Cruse, Howard. *Stuck Rubber Baby*. New York: Paradox Press, 1995.

Duin, Steve, and Shannon Wheeler. *Oil and Water*. Seattle: Fantagraphics, 2011.

Lewis, John, Andrew Aydin, and Nate Powell. *March: Book One*. Marietta, GA: Top Shelf Productions, 2013.

Lockpez, Inverna, and Dean Haspiel. *Cuba: My Revolution*. New York: Vertigo, 2010.

Passmore, Ben. *Your Black Friend and Other Strangers*. San Francisco: Silver Sprockct, 2018.

Satrapi, Marjane. *Persepolis*. New York: Pantheon, 2004.

Spiegelman, Art. *Maus: A Survivor's Tale*. New York: Pantheon, 1986.
Yannow, Sophie. *War of Streets and Houses*. Minneapolis: Uncivilised Books, 2023.

Travel Journals

Abel, Jessica. *La Perdida*. New York: Pantheon, 2006.
Bennett, Marek. *Nicaragua Comics Travel Journal*. Comics Workshop, 2009.
Delisle, Guy. *Pyongyang: A Journey in North Korea*. Montreal: Drawn & Quarterly, 2005.
Thompson, C. *Carnet de Voyage*. Montreal: Drawn & Quarterly, 2018.

Graphic Histories

Anderson, Ho Che. *King: A Comics Biography of Martin Luther King, Jr.* Seattle: Fantagraphics, 2005.
Buhle, Paul, and Nicole Schulman, eds. *Wobblies! A Graphic History of the Industrial Workers of the World*. New York: Verso, 2005.
Darnall, Steve, and Alex Ross. *Uncle Sam*. New York: Vertigo, 2009.
Dix, Benjamin, and Lindsay Pollock. *Vanni: A Family's Struggle through the Sri Lankan Conflict*. University Park, PA: Penn State University Press, 2019.
Mirk, Sarah, ed. *Guantanamo Voices: True Accounts from the World's Most Infamous Prison*. New York: Abrams ComicArts, 2020.
Moore, Alan, and Bill Sienkiewicz. *Brought to Light: 33 Years of Drug Smuggling, Arms Deals and Covert Action*. New York: Warner Books, 1988.
Ojeda, Diana, Pablo Guerra, Camilo Aguirre, and Henry Diaz. *Caminos Condenados (Condemned Roads)*. Bogota: Laguna Libros, 2020.
Pekar, Harvey, and Gary Dumm. *Students for a Democratic Society: A Graphic History*. New York: Hill & Wang, 2008.
Rodriguez, Spain. *Che: A Graphic Biography*. New York: Verso, 2008.
Tobocman, Seth. *Disaster and Resistance: Comics and Landscapes for the Twenty First Century*. Oakland: AK Press, 2008.
Walker, David F. *The Black Panther Party: A Graphic Novel History*. New York: Ten Speed Graphic, 2021.
Zinn, Howard, Mike Konopacki, and Paul Buhle. *A People's History of American Empire: A Graphic Adaptation*. New York: Metropolitan Books, 2008.

Anthologies

Baldry, Edd. *Excessive Force: A Comix Anthology against the Police*. London: Last Hours, 2011.
Kuper, Peter, and Seth Tobocman, eds. *World War 3 Illustrated: 1979–2014*. Oakland: PM Press, 2014.

Graphic Journalism Commentary

Duncan, Randy, Michael Ray Taylor, and David Stoddard. *Creating Comics and Journalism, Memoir and Nonfiction*. London: Routledge, 2016.

Embury, Gary, and Mario Minichiello. *Reportage Illustration: Visual Journalism*. London: Bloomsbury, 2018.

Mirk, Sarah, and Eleri Harris. *Drawn from the Margins: The Power of Graphic Journalism*. New York: Abrams ComicArts, 2024.

Human Trafficking

Kenway, Emily. *The Truth about Modern Slavery*. London: Pluto Press, 2021.

May, Meredith. *From Busan to San Francisco*. Stanford: Stanford Graphic Novel Project, 2012.

McCormick, Patricia. *SOLD*. New York: Hyperion, 2006.

Skinner, E. Benjamin. *A Crime So Monstrous: Face-to-Face with Modern-Day Slavery*. New York: Simon & Schuster, 2008.

Trusova, Olga, and Dan Archer. *Borderland: Seven Stories of Trafficking from Ukraine*. Borderland Comics, 2007.

US Department of State. "Trafficking in Persons Reports." Last updated June 15, 2023. https://www.state.gov/trafficking-in-persons-report/.

Articles

Bake, Julika, and Michaela Zöhrer. "Telling the Stories of Others: Claims of Authenticity in Human Rights Reporting and Comics Journalism." *Journal of Intervention and Statebuilding* 11, no. 1 (2017): 81–97. https://doi.org/10.1080/17502977.2016.1272903.

Gilbert, Jérémie, and David Keane. "Graphic Reporting: Human Rights Violations through the Lens of Graphic Novels." In *Graphic Justice: Intersections of Comics and Law*, edited by Thomas Giddens, 236–54. Abingdon: Routledge, 2015.

Kozol, Wendy. "Complicities of Witnessing in Joe Sacco's *Palestine*." In *Theoretical Perspectives on Human Rights and Literature*, edited by Elizabeth Goldberg and Alexandra S. Moore, 165–79. New York: Routledge, 2011.

O'Brien, Erin. *Challenging the Human Trafficking Narrative: Victims, Villains, and Heroes*. London: Routledge, 2018.

Orbán, Katalin. "Mediating Distant Violence: Reports on Non-photographic Reporting in *The Fixer* and *The Photographer*." *Journal of Graphic Novels and Comics* 6, no. 2 (2015): 122–37. https://doi.org/10.1080/21504857.2015.1027943.

Scherr, Rebecca. "Framing Human Rights: Comics Form and the Politics of Recognition in Joe Sacco's *Footnotes in Gaza*." *Textual Practice* 29, no. 1 (2015): 111–31. https://doi.org/10.1080/0950236X.2014.952771.

Weber, Wibke, and Hans-Martin Rall. "Authenticity in Comics Journalism: Visual Strategies for Reporting Facts." *Journal of Graphic Novels and Comics* 8, no. 4 (2017): 376–97. https://doi.org/10.1080/21504857.2017.1299020.

Woo, Benjamin. "Reconsidering Comics Journalism: Information and Experience in Joe Sacco's *Palestine*." In *The Rise and Reason of Comics and Graphic Literature: Critical Essays on the Form*, edited by Joyce Goggin and Dan Hassler-Forest, 166–77. Jefferson, NC: McFarland, 2010. https://bookcandy.typepad.com/files/woo_sacco.pdf.

Online

http://www.graphicjournalism.com – Swiss graphic journalist/cartoonist Patrick Chappatte's website.

https://drawingthetimes.com – A graphic journalism platform based in the Netherlands.

https://thenib.com – A treasure trove of graphic journalism that remains online, despite closing its doors to new work in September 2022. The core team – Matt Bors, Eleri Harris, Andy Warner, and Mattie Lubchansky – are all veteran cartoonists.

https://thenib.com/authors/ – An encyclopedic resource of contributors to the magazine over the years.

https://appliedcartooning.org/ – The Center for Cartoon Studies' Applied Cartooning Lab, using comics to create unique educational resources and public education campaigns.

https://www.worldcomicsindia.com – The brainchild of Sharad Sharma, a prolific grassroots cartoonist and educator focusing on empowering workshop participants around the world by giving them the tool to create their own one (and more) pagers.

http://www.larevuedessinee.fr – France's historic home of nonfiction reportage comics in print and online.

http://www.graphicvoices.org – Inspired by the above, a collection of comics from participants all over the world at workshops that I've given.

https://entrevinetas.cl – A Colombian comics collective based in Medellin.

https://positivenegatives.org – Stories drawn from ethnographic research on social, humanitarian, and environmental issues.

https://www.susiecagle.com – Susie is a master of long-form digital graphic journalism covering climate change and inequality in California. Her graphic novel, *The End of the West*, is due out from Random House in 2025.

https://www.archcomix.com – My own website!

ethno GRAPHIC

Editors: Sherine Hamdy (University of California, Irvine) and Marc Parenteau (cartoonist)

This groundbreaking series realizes ethnographic research in graphic novel form. The series speaks to a growing interest in comics as a powerful narrative medium and to the desire for a more creative and collaborative anthropology that engages the public with contemporary issues. Books in the series are informed by scholarship and combine text and image in ways that are accessible, open-ended, aesthetically rich, and that foster greater cross-cultural understanding.

Books in the Series

Toxic: A Tour of the Ecuadorian Amazon, written by Amelia Fiske, illustrated by Jonas Fischer (2024)

Forecasts: A Story of Weather and Finance at the Edge of Disaster, written by Caroline E. Schuster, illustrated by Enrique Bernardou and David Bueno (2023)

Messages from Ukraine, written by Gregg Bucken-Knapp, illustrated by Joonas Sildre (2022)

The King of Bangkok, written by Claudio Sopranzetti, illustrated by Sara Fabbri, adapted by Chiara Natalucci (2021)

Light in Dark Times: The Human Search for Meaning, written by Alisse Waterston, illustrated by Charlotte Corden (2020)

Gringo Love: Stories of Sex Tourism in Brazil, written by Marie-Eve Carrier-Moisan, adapted by William Flynn, illustrated by Débora Santos (2020)

Things That Art: A Graphic Menagerie of Enchanting Curiosity, written and illustrated by Lochlann Jain (2019)

Lissa: A Story about Medical Promise, Friendship, and Revolution, written by Sherine Hamdy and Coleman Nye, illustrated by Sarula Bao and Caroline Brewer, lettering by Marc Parenteau (2017)